DOUBLE AWARD

FOUNDATION SCIENCE *for* GCSE

GRAHAM HILL
DAVID ROWLANDS
GEORGE SNAPE

Hodder & Stoughton

A MEMBER OF THE HODDER HEADLINE GROUP

Preface

Foundation Science for GCSE: Double Award will help students as they study key stage 4 of the National Curriculum and prepare for examinations at the Foundation Tier of Double Award Science.

In a single volume, we have thoroughly covered the recently revised specifications of all the awarding bodies, whilst maintaining a concise, informative and easily understood presentation, page by page.

Each of the chapters covers a major theme and ends with a page of GCSE examination questions taken from Foundation Tier papers and chosen to match the new specifications.

Highlighted boxes emphasise the key facts and ideas and there is a summary at the end of each chapter. Carefully chosen in-text questions maintain interest and enhance the understanding of the topics studied. A glossary at the end of the book provides definitions of all important words and terms.

Our own names may appear on the cover of the book, but we must thank two other colleagues who have contributed very considerably and creatively to its success – Ruth Hughes, the desk editor from Hodder and Stoughton Educational and Elizabeth Hill. Without their co-ordination, liaison and efficiency, the book would not have been possible.

Graham Hill
David Rowlands
George Snape

January 2001

Orders: please contact Bookpoint Ltd, 130 Milton Park, Abingdon, Oxon OX14 4SB.
Telephone: (44) 01235 827720, Fax: (44) 01235 400454. Lines are open from 9.00 - 6.00, Monday to Saturday, with a 24 hour message answering service.

A catalogue record for this title is available from The British Library

ISBN 0 340 77535 1

First published 2001
Impression number 10 9 8 7 6 5 4 3 2
Year   2006 2005 2004 2003 2002

Cover photo from Science Photo Library
Typeset by Wyvern 21, Bristol.
Printed in Italy for Hodder & Stoughton Educational, a division of Hodder Headline Plc, 338 Euston Road, London NW1 3BH.

Contents

This red-eyed tree frog resting on a palm leaf sits waiting for his next meal. Diet and digestion are discussed in Chapter 2 and food chains are described in Chapter 9. The whole of this section is about Biology – the study of life processes and living things.

Life processes and living things

Cells and life

1.1 The variety of life

Walk in your garden or in a park. Look and see how many different animals and plants there are – birds, mammals, insects, grasses, flowers and trees. All these different animals and plants are part of the variety of life.

The place where an animal or plant lives is called its **habitat**.

A garden and a park are two examples of the different habitats where living things can be found. Habitats can be very large, like a city or a forest. Habitats can be much smaller, like a garden, or even tiny, like a puddle or a stone.

Look at the variety of life (animals and plants) in the photos below. Notice their different habitats. Some living things have special features to help them in their habitat.

A hummingbird collecting pollen from a flower

Wildebeest and zebra in the Serengeti National Park, Africa

Feeding geese in the park

They are **adapted** to their habitat. Some adaptations are very obvious, like fish to rivers and birds to trees. Other adaptations are less obvious.

★ How are camels adapted to living in the desert?

★ How are polar bears adapted to living in the frozen Arctic?

| 1.2 | **Life processes in animals and plants** |

Usually, it is easy to tell whether something is living or not. It is obvious that blackbirds and daisies are living and that stones and water are not living.

Living things, like blackbirds, daisies, spiders, goldfish and oak trees, are called **organisms**. All organisms carry out seven important processes to stay alive. These are sometimes called **life processes**.

1 Movement

Living things can move. Most animals can move quite quickly from one place to another. Plants can also move but much more slowly. For example, plants move as they grow. They grow towards sunlight.

2 Reproduction

Animals and plants can reproduce. Animals give birth to young (offspring). Plants produce seeds from which new, young plants grow. **Sexual reproduction** involves male and female parents. **Asexual reproduction** involves only one parent. It occurs when an organism grows parts which separate and become a new organism. For example, a strawberry plant produces runners from which new plants take root and grow.

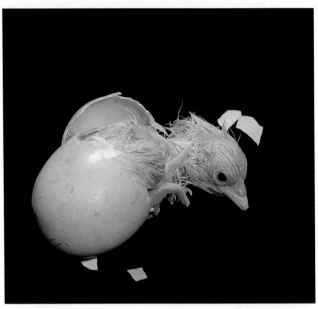

This chick, hatching out of its egg, follows the mating of a hen and a cock

Wildebeest on the move

3 Sensitivity

Animals and plants are sensitive to changes around them. The changes cause animals and plants to respond (react). For example, if the telephone rings, you answer it. The sound acts as a **stimulus** to which you respond.

Animals respond to movement, sound, light, touch, heat and chemicals. Plants are usually less sensitive and respond more slowly than animals.

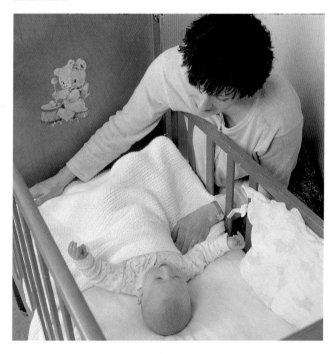

This baby is responding to his mother's voice and smile

4 Growth

Animals and plants grow. Young animals grow into adults. Seedlings grow into larger plants.

Buds and then flowers emerge as this honeysuckle grows

5 Respiration

Animals and plants need energy to grow and move. They get this energy by breaking down food in a process called **respiration**. In respiration, food and oxygen react in our cells to release energy.

Respiration gives Paula Radcliffe enough energy to run the 1500 metres

6 Nutrition

Animals and plants must feed in order to live. This process of taking in food and water is called **nutrition**.

Plants and animals feed in different ways. Animals take in their food by **eating** other animals and plants. They break down the food to get energy and are able to grow.

A monkey eating an orange

Green plants can make their own food. They do this by taking in carbon dioxide and water which they turn into carbohydrates. To do this, the plants need energy which comes from the Sun. This process of making food in plants is called **photosynthesis**.

7 Excretion

When animals and plants feed and respire, they produce waste products. These waste products must be removed. The process of removing waste products is called **excretion**. For example, animals get rid of extra water and nitrogen compounds by urinating.

An elephant urinating

1　How many life processes are there?

2　Name **three** things animals respond to.

3　How do plants feed?

4　Is a paper clip alive? Explain your answer.

1.3	**Animal cells and plant cells**

All living things are made of **cells**. Cells are the basic units of life. They are the building blocks for organisms in the same way that bricks are the building blocks for houses.

Your body contains one hundred million cells. Each cell is about one thousandth of a centimetre wide ($\frac{1}{1000}$ cm). You cannot see them, but they can be seen with a microscope.

Figure 1 shows a typical animal cell side by side with a typical plant cell.

All animal and plant cells have a **nucleus**, **cytoplasm** and a **cell membrane**.

★ The **nucleus** controls how the cell works, how it grows and how it divides.

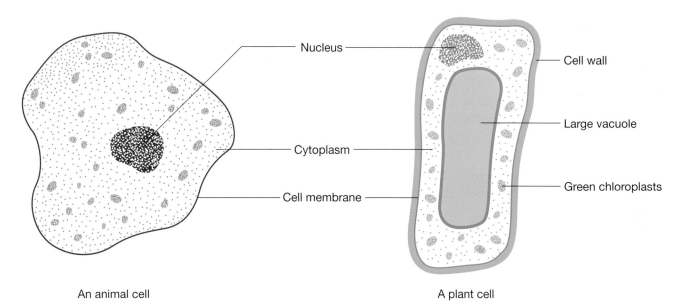

An animal cell

A plant cell

Nucleus

Cytoplasm

Cell membrane

Cell wall

Large vacuole

Green chloroplasts

Figure 1 A typical animal cell and a typical plant cell

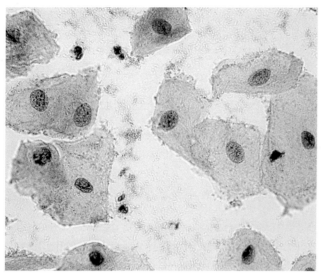

Human cheek cells magnified 1000 times

★ The **cytoplasm** is a watery jelly which fills most of the cell. Most of the chemical reactions of living things take place in the cytoplasm. These reactions provide the cell with energy and help it to grow.

★ The **cell membrane** is a thin skin which holds the cell together. The cell membrane also controls the movement of substances into and out of the cell. Usually, small molecules from foods pass into the cell while waste products pass out.

In addition to a nucleus, cytoplasm and a cell membrane, plant cells have some extra parts. These are a **cell wall**, **chloroplasts** and a **vacuole**.

★ The **cell wall** is on the outside of the cell membrane. The cell wall is made of a tough material called **cellulose**. The cell wall is much thicker than the cell membrane. It is very porous and allows water and small molecules to pass through it easily. The job of the cell wall is to support and protect the cell.

★ **Chloroplasts** are small organelles in the cytoplasm. Photosynthesis takes place in the chloroplasts which contain a green pigment called **chlorophyll**. Chlorophyll is needed for photosynthesis.

★ The **vacuole** is in the centre of the cell. It contains a watery liquid called **cell sap**. The vacuole fills most of the cell and is separated from the cytoplasm by a thin membrane. The vacuole has two jobs. First, it acts as a storage place for dissolved plant foods such as sugars and salts. Secondly, it creates a pressure on the cell wall and keeps the cell wall rigid.

5 What is a cell?

6 How many cells are there in the human body?

7 What is cytoplasm?

8 What is the job of the chloroplasts?

1.4 From cells to organisms

The different parts of living things (like muscles, nerves and roots) have different jobs to do in the body. Because of this there are different kinds of cells. The different cells are adapted to their different jobs.

Muscle cells, for example, need to contract and then relax (Figure 2a). This is why they are long and thin.

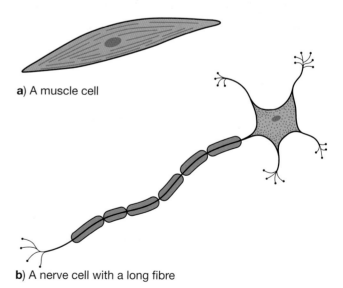

a) A muscle cell

b) A nerve cell with a long fibre

Figure 2 Muscle cells and nerve cells are specially adapted to the jobs they do in our bodies

6

Nerve cells are smaller and rounder with long thin fibres leading from them (Figure 2b). This is because they have to carry messages from one part of the body to another.

When lots of the same cells are grouped together, they form a **tissue**. For example, in our bodies we have muscle tissue, skin tissue and nerve tissue (Figure 3).

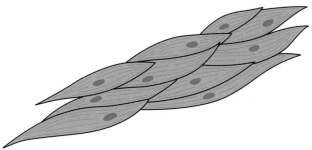

Figure 3 Muscle cells group together to form muscle tissue

In our bodies, different tissues can work together to form **organs**. Organs are complex parts of living organisms which have a particular job, such as our eyes. Sometimes, several organs work together to make up an **organ system**. So, the heart, arteries, veins and capillaries make up the circulatory system (section 4.1). The brain, spinal cord and the nerves make up the nervous system (section 7.2). Organ systems work together to form an **organism**.

Figure 4 shows a flow diagram of the way in which cells form tissues, tissues form organs, organs form organ systems and organ systems make up organisms such as a human being.

Organ systems, like cells, are specially **adapted** for the jobs they do in our bodies. For example, the digestive system is made of a long muscular tube (the gut). Food is moved along the gut by muscles. As the food moves through the gut, it is broken down (digested) and absorbed into the bloodstream. The waste which cannot be broken down is excreted. The length of the tube gives time for the food to be digested and its muscles keep the food moving.

| 1.5 | **Movement of substances into and out of cells** |

All animal and plant cells contain a lot of water. Most of the cytoplasm is water. In plants, most of the cell sap is water. This water contains dissolved substances. Water and other substances can enter and leave cells through the cell membrane. The cell membrane *controls* which particles pass into and out of the cell.

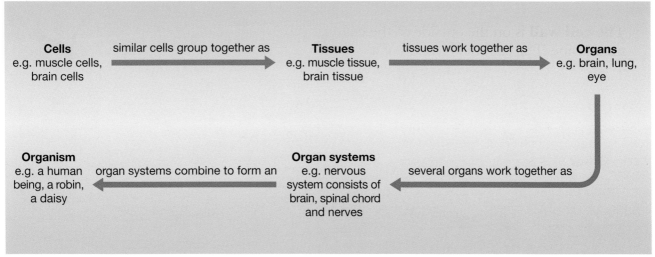

Figure 4 From cells to organisms

The cell membrane lets certain particles pass through, but it will block the passage of others. We say it is **partially permeable**.

Water molecules and dissolved particles roll round and bounce off each other in the cell liquid. They move about randomly. Because of this movement, the dissolved particles and water molecules spread out in the cell liquid.

This spreading of a substance is called **diffusion**.

As diffusion occurs in living things, water molecules and other small particles sometimes pass through partially permeable cell membranes.

Examples of diffusion in living things include:

★ small molecules from digested food diffusing from the gut into blood capillaries

★ oxygen diffusing from the air sacs in the lungs into blood capillaries

★ carbon dioxide diffusing from blood capillaries into the air sacs in the lungs.

Substances with small molecules, such as oxygen, carbon dioxide and water, will usually diffuse easily through a cell membrane.

Substances with larger particles, such as sugar molecules, diffuse much more slowly through cell membranes.

9 Which part of the cell controls what goes in and out?

10 What does *partially permeable* mean?

11 Name **three** small molecules which can easily get into a cell.

12 Give **two** examples of diffusion and where they happen in the human body.

Biologists have a special name for the diffusion of water through a partially permeable membrane. The special name is **osmosis**.

Look at the experiment shown in Figure 5. Visking tubing is a very thin membrane. It has tiny, invisible holes which allow water particles to pass through, but not larger sugar particles. The visking tubing is a partially permeable membrane, like a cell membrane.

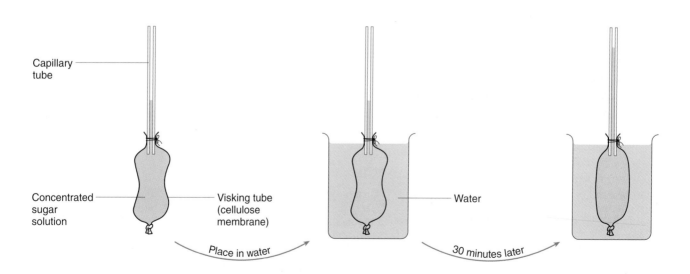

Capillary tube

Concentrated sugar solution

Visking tube (cellulose membrane)

Place in water

Water

30 minutes later

Figure 5 Osmosis in action

The visking tubing containing sugar solution is placed in water. Water passes into the bag and the liquid rises in the capillary tube.

Osmosis has occurred. Water molecules have diffused from a region of high water concentration through the partially permeable membrane (visking tube) to a region of lower water concentration.

Osmosis can be explained using the kinetic theory (section 14.3). Molecules of sugar and water are moving and bombarding the partially permeable membrane (Figure 6). Sometimes, a water molecule passes through one of the tiny holes.

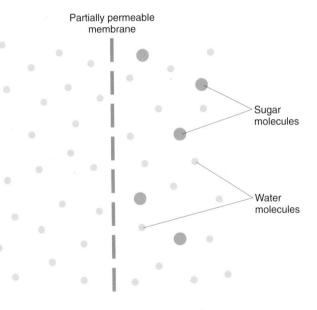

Partially permeable membrane

Sugar molecules

Water molecules

Figure 6 How does osmosis occur?

If we had pure water on both sides of the membrane, equal numbers of water molecules would flow in both directions. There would be no overall change.

In the sugar solution, large sugar molecules hinder the movement of water molecules. Sometimes this prevents water passing through the holes. So, more water molecules flow from the pure water to the sugar solution than the other way. Overall, water flows through the membrane and into the sugar solution.

Osmosis in living things

Osmosis is very important in living organisms because the membranes of cells are partially permeable.

Suppose some red blood cells are placed in salt solutions of different concentrations (Figure 7). Cell cytoplasm contains a solution of various substances (salts, sugars, proteins, etc.) in water. When the red blood cells are placed in water or very dilute salt solution, water flows through the cell membrane and into the cell. The cell swells and may even burst (Figure 7a). The opposite happens in concentrated salt solution (Figure 7b) and the cell shrinks.

From this you can see how important it is to have the right concentration of solutes in the liquid around cells.

In animals, a number of processes keep body fluids at the right concentration. The kidneys play an important part in this process which is called **osmo-regulation**. A solution containing 0.6% salt in water (usually called **saline**) is just the right concentration to prevent osmosis in humans. Saline is used widely in hospital, especially after major operations.

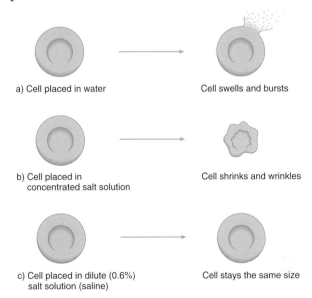

a) Cell placed in water   Cell swells and bursts

b) Cell placed in concentrated salt solution   Cell shrinks and wrinkles

c) Cell placed in dilute (0.6%) salt solution (saline)   Cell stays the same size

Figure 7 The effect of different concentrations of salt solution on red blood cells

Summary

1 There are many different animals and plants on Earth. The places where living things can be found are called their **habitats**.

2 Living things are often adapted to their habitat. For example, fish are adapted to life in the sea. This is called **adaptation**.

3 Living things are called **organisms**. There are seven important processes which allow them to live. An easy way to remember these seven processes is **MRS NERG**.

Movement   **N**utrition
Reproduction   **E**xcretion
Sensitivity   **R**espiration
                   Growth

4 Organisms are made up of many **cells** which can only be seen under a microscope.

5 Animal and plant cells have three important structures:

   ★ a **nucleus** which controls how the cell works, grows and divides

   ★ the **cytoplasm** where chemical reactions take place

   ★ the **cell membrane** which acts like a skin to keep the cell together. It controls the movement of substances into and out of the cell.

6 Plant cells have three other structures:

   ★ a thick **cell wall** on the outside which supports and protects the cell

   ★ **chloroplasts** in the cytoplasm which contain the green pigment **chlorophyll**. This can absorb sunlight in order for the plant to make its own food

   ★ a **vacuole** in the centre of the plant cell which contains cell sap. The watery sap stores dissolved plant foods and keeps the cell rigid.

7 There are different kinds of cells in our bodies, doing different jobs. For example, muscle cells can contract and relax, causing movement.

8 Specialised cells group together and form a **tissue**. For example, lots of muscle cells form muscle tissue in the leg.

9 Different tissues can work together to form an **organ**. For example, the eye contains nerve tissue, muscle tissue and skin tissue.

10 Sometimes, several organs are grouped into an **organ system**. For example, the nervous system is made up of the brain, spinal cord and the nerves.

11 Water and dissolved particles are constantly moving into and out of cells through the cell membranes. Cell membranes allow some dissolved particles in the water to pass through and others are blocked. Cell membranes are **partially permeable**.

12 Water molecules and dissolved particles move about in a random way causing them to spread out. This spreading out is called **diffusion**.

13 Substances with small molecules, like oxygen, carbon dioxide and water, diffuse easily through the cell membrane. Substances like sugar have much larger molecules. These larger molecules diffuse more slowly.

1 The table is about the life processes of a tiger. Copy out the table and use words from the list to fill in your table.

excretion   growth   nutrition   reproduction
respiration   sensitivity

Life process	Activity of tiger
	increasing in size by using food
	getting rid of waste
	releasing energy from its food
	reacting to its surroundings

(4)

[AQA (NEAB) 1999]

2 The diagram shows an animal cell.

a) Copy out the diagram and add labels to your diagram. Choose words from this list.

cell membrane   nucleus   cell wall   vacuole
cytoplasm   (3)

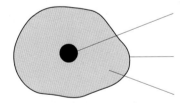

b) Each part of a cell does a job. Write down each part of a cell with its job. Each part of a cell must be linked to a different job. (2)

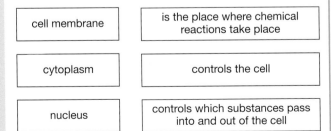

part of a cell | job

| cell membrane | is the place where chemical reactions take place |

| cytoplasm | controls the cell |

| nucleus | controls which substances pass into and out of the cell |

c) Cells are organised to form whole organisms. What is the missing word in the box? (1)

cells → tissues → ☐ → organism

[OCR (MEG) 1998]

3 The drawing shows part of a root hair cell.

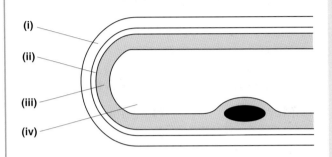

(i)
(ii)
(iii)
(iv)

a) Use words from the list to label parts **(i)** to **(iv)** of the root hair cell.

cell membrane   cell wall   cytoplasm
nucleus   vacuole   (4)

b) The diagram shows four ways in which molecules may move into and out of a cell. The dots show the concentration of molecules.

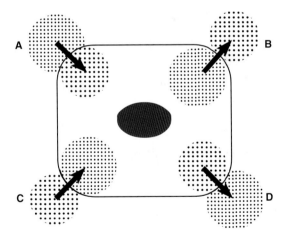

A

B

C

D

The cell is respiring aerobically.

Which arrow **A**, **B**, **C** or **D** represents:

(i) movement of oxygen molecules;

(ii) movement of carbon dioxide molecules? (2)

c) Name the process by which these gases move into and out of the cell. (1)

[AQA (NEAB) 1999]

2

Diet and digestion

2.1 Our diet

2.2 Digestion

2.3 The human digestive system

2.1   Our diet

Our diet is the food that we eat. We must eat to live and survive.

Eating food to stay alive is called **nutrition**. To be healthy we need to eat a **balanced diet**.

A balanced diet must have seven important and different foods.

I Carbohydrates

Carbohydrates provide about half of the **energy** which we need. The main carbohydrates in our diet are sugar and starch. Sugar is present in biscuits, cakes, jam and sweets. Starch is present in bread, potatoes, pasta and rice.

Some important carbohydrate-rich foods

Our bodies can change the carbohydrates which we don't use into layers of fat under our skin. This fat can be changed back into carbohydrate to give us energy.

2 Fats

Fats provide some of the energy we need. They also act as a store of energy and as insulators to keep us warm. Fats are present in milk, cream, cheese, butter, cooking oil and red meat.

Some foods containing fats

3 Proteins

Proteins provide the chemicals which we need for growth and for replacing dead cells. They are sometimes called body-building foods. Proteins are present in meat, chicken, fish, eggs, milk, peas and beans.

Some important protein-rich foods

In addition to these three important energy and body-building foods we also need:

4 Vitamins

For example, vitamin C which is found in oranges.

5 Minerals

For example, calcium in milk and iron in green vegetables. Calcium is needed for strong teeth and bones. Iron is needed to make red blood cells.

Vitamins and minerals are sometimes described as maintenance foods. They are needed in small amounts to keep our bodies running smoothly and to keep us healthy.

6 Water

Water is needed to keep the concentrations of substances in cells at a steady level. We can survive for weeks without food, but only a few days without water. We take in most water by drinking. Some solid foods such as fruits and vegetables contain plenty of water. You should drink at least one litre (about two pints) of water every day.

7 Fibre

Fibre is needed in our diet as **roughage**. You don't digest fibre, but it helps other foods to move through your gut more easily. This prevents constipation. Fibre is in fruit, vegetables, brown bread and cereals.

Some important foods containing fibre

1 List the **seven** food types needed in a balanced diet.

2 List **four** foods rich in protein.

3 Which vitamin is found in oranges?

4 What is calcium used for in our bodies?

5 Travellers in desert areas always carry lots of water with them. Why?

2.2 Digestion

Food is needed by every part of your body. But, how does the food we eat reach the different parts of our bodies? The experiment shown in Figure 1 will help you answer this question.

The visking tubing is a partially permeable membrane. It is filled with a solution containing starch and glucose (a simple sugar). The filled tubing is put in pure, warm water for one hour.

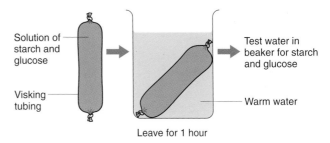

Solution of starch and glucose

Visking tubing

Test water in beaker for starch and glucose

Warm water

Leave for 1 hour

Figure 1 An experiment to explain digestion

13

Will the starch or glucose pass through the membrane and into the water? To check this, the water in the beaker is tested for starch with iodine and for glucose with Benedict's solution. We find that the water contains glucose, but no starch. How can this be explained?

Starch has very large molecules. It is formed when hundreds of smaller glucose molecules join together. The large starch molecules cannot pass through the tiny holes in the visking tubing. The small glucose molecules can. So, all the starch stays inside the visking tubing but glucose passes through the tubing into the warm water.

The digestive system in our bodies is like a long visking tube from the mouth to the anus. It is called the **gut** or the **alimentary canal** (Figure 2).

When we digest our food, we break down the large molecules of carbohydrates, proteins and fats into smaller particles. These smaller particles (like glucose) dissolve in water. They pass through the walls of the gut and into the bloodstream. This is just like the glucose molecules, passing through the visking tubing in the experiment. Once in the bloodstream, these smaller molecules are carried to all parts of our bodies. Undigested food, which cannot be broken down, passes all the way through the gut and out through the anus as faeces.

Digestive enzymes

The main processes in digestion are chemical reactions. In these reactions carbohydrates, proteins and fats, which have large, insoluble molecules, are broken down into smaller, soluble molecules. This breakdown of large molecules into smaller molecules is speeded up (catalysed) by **digestive enzymes**. These enzymes are made by glands which open into the gut.

> **Enzymes** are biological catalysts. A **catalyst** speeds up a chemical reaction. Biological catalysts speed up the reactions that happen in our bodies.

Every chemical reaction in our bodies is catalysed by an enzyme. All our cells contain lots of enzymes to catalyse the reactions that are going on.

The substance on which an enzyme works is called its **substrate**.

Enzymes are usually named by adding the ending **-ase** to the name of their substrate. So, **carbohydrases** are enzymes which catalyse the breakdown of carbohydrates.

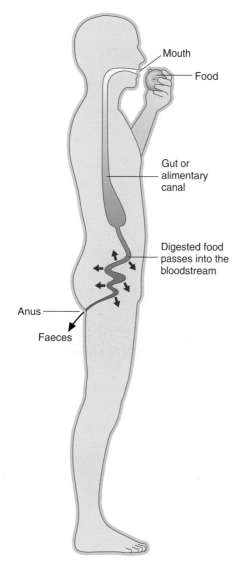

Mouth

Food

Gut or alimentary canal

Digested food passes into the bloodstream

Anus

Faeces

Figure 2 A diagram of the human digestive system

The most common carbohydrase in saliva is **amylase**. Amylase in saliva starts to break down the starch which is in the food we eat. Starch is a long chain of glucose molecules. Starch is chopped up by amylase into smaller molecules of glucose.

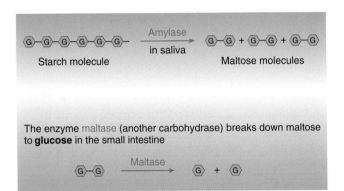

Starch molecule → Maltose molecules (Amylase in saliva)

The enzyme maltase (another carbohydrase) breaks down maltose to **glucose** in the small intestine

G—G → G + G (Maltase)

Proteins are broken down by **proteases** into amino acids. **Pepsin**, a protease in stomach juices, starts the breakdown of proteins.

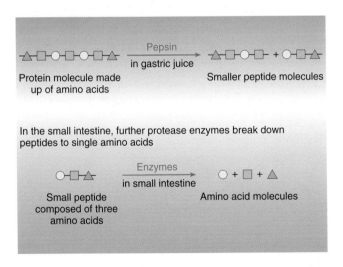

Protein molecule made up of amino acids → Smaller peptide molecules (Pepsin in gastric juice)

In the small intestine, further protease enzymes break down peptides to single amino acids

Small peptide composed of three amino acids → Amino acid molecules (Enzymes in small intestine)

6 Which is the smaller molecule, starch or glucose?

7 What does *partially permeable* mean?

8 What is an enzyme?

9 What do proteases do?

2.3 The human digestive system

Although the gut can be described as a long tube, it is made up of very different parts. Each of these parts has its own important job in digesting our food. Figure 3 shows how the human digestive system is arranged.

Notice that there are some organs which are not part of the long tube of the gut, but they are linked to it. These are the **salivary glands**, the **liver** and the **pancreas**. They are labelled on the right hand side of the diagram.

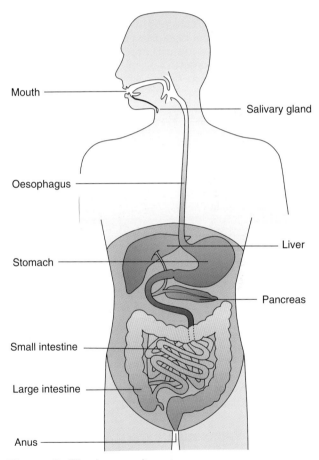

Figure 3 The human digestive system

What happens when we digest our food?

Figure 4 (on the next page) shows the gut from the mouth to the anus. At the side there is a description of what happens in each part.

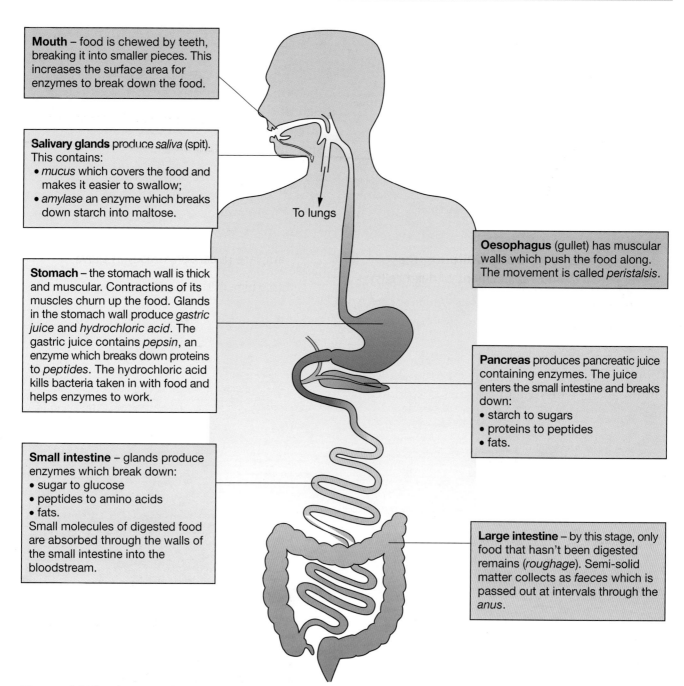

Mouth – food is chewed by teeth, breaking it into smaller pieces. This increases the surface area for enzymes to break down the food.

Salivary glands produce *saliva* (spit). This contains:
- *mucus* which covers the food and makes it easier to swallow;
- *amylase* an enzyme which breaks down starch into maltose.

To lungs

Stomach – the stomach wall is thick and muscular. Contractions of its muscles churn up the food. Glands in the stomach wall produce *gastric juice* and *hydrochloric acid*. The gastric juice contains *pepsin*, an enzyme which breaks down proteins to *peptides*. The hydrochloric acid kills bacteria taken in with food and helps enzymes to work.

Small intestine – glands produce enzymes which break down:
- sugar to glucose
- peptides to amino acids
- fats.
Small molecules of digested food are absorbed through the walls of the small intestine into the bloodstream.

Oesophagus (gullet) has muscular walls which push the food along. The movement is called *peristalsis*.

Pancreas produces pancreatic juice containing enzymes. The juice enters the small intestine and breaks down:
- starch to sugars
- proteins to peptides
- fats.

Large intestine – by this stage, only food that hasn't been digested remains (*roughage*). Semi-solid matter collects as *faeces* which is passed out at intervals through the *anus*.

Figure 4 What happens during digestion

The walls of the gut are thick and muscular. The muscles contract behind the food, and push it along. This is called **peristalsis**. When you swallow some water and then stand on your head, the water doesn't flow back because it is already being squeezed down to the stomach by peristalsis.

10 What process squeezes food down the gut?

11 Put these in the correct order for digestion:

large intestine   mouth   stomach   small intestine

12 What happens to all the food which is digested in the gut?

Summary

1 We need to eat to live. This is called **nutrition**.

2 We need to eat a balanced diet. This includes:

   ★ **carbohydrates** for **energy**

   ★ **fats** for **energy**, which can be stored in the body. Fat stores insulate us against the cold

   ★ **proteins** for **body building** (the growth and replacement of dead cells)

   ★ **vitamins** and **minerals** to keep us healthy

   ★ **fibre** as roughage to help food move through the gut.

3 **Digestion** occurs when large food molecules are broken down to smaller molecules. These smaller molecules can then be absorbed into the bloodstream and carried to other parts of the body.

4 **Enzymes** are made by glands opening into the gut. They speed up the breakdown of food molecules.

5 The gut is like a long tube in which digestion takes place. Food is broken down by:

   ★ chewing in the mouth

   ★ amylase (a carbohydrase) in saliva

   ★ churning in the stomach

   ★ pepsin (a protease) in the stomach

   ★ other enzymes in the small intestine.

6 Any undigested material passes into the large intestine and collects in the rectum. At regular intervals, it is egested through the anus.

Exam questions for Chapter 2

1 The table below shows the amounts of carbohydrate, protein and fat in **30g** of each of the foods.

Food	Carbohydrate(g)	Protein(g)	Fat(g)
Beef	0	4.2	7.9
Cabbage	1.5	0.5	0
Bread	15.0	2.5	0.5
Butter	0	0.1	23.5
Egg	0.5	3.5	3.5
Cheese	0	7.0	10.0
Potatoes	5.9	0.5	0

a) Using the information in the table answer the following questions:

(i) Which food contains the most carbohydrate?

(ii) Which food contains the least fat? *(1)*

(iii) Calculate how much protein is contained in a snack consisting of 30g beef 60g potatoes and 15g cabbage. *(3)*

(iv) Which of the foods in the table would you recommend to someone who was overweight? *(1)*

(v) Why would you recommend the food in (iv)? *(1)*

b) Name **two other** types of food substance which are needed for a balanced diet. *(2)*

[WJEC 1998]

2 The drawing shows some of the organs in the human abdomen. Copy the diagram.

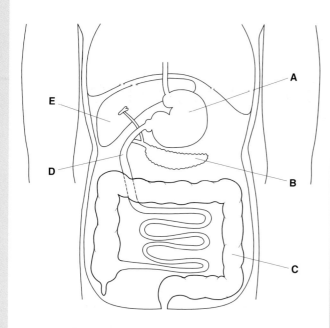

a) Use words from the list to label organs **A**, **B**, **C**, **D** and **E** on the diagram.

gullet   large intestine   kidney   liver
small intestine   pancreas   stomach   *(5)*

b) List **A** gives the names of five organs shown in the diagram. List **B** gives the jobs of these organs in a different order.

List A	List B
Gullet	Breaks down excess amino acids
Large intestine	Transports food to the stomach
Liver	Completes the digestion of food into soluble compounds
Pancreas	Absorbs much of the water into the bloodstream
Small intestine	Produces insulin

Copy out list **A** and then link it to its job in list **B**. One has been done for you. *(4)*

[AQA (NEAB) 1998]

3 The diagram shows the human digestive system. Copy the diagram.

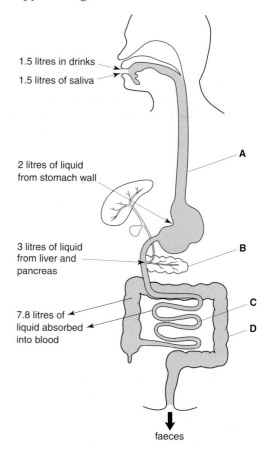

a) Write the names of the parts labelled **A**, **B**, **C** and **D**. Choose the names from this list.

large intestine   pancreas   liver
small intestine   oesophagus   stomach   *(4)*

b) The figures on the left side of the diagram show the amounts of liquid entering and leaving the various parts of the digestive system in an average day.

(i) Calculate the total amount of liquid (in litres) **entering** the digestive system in an average day. Show how you work out your answer. *(2)*

(ii) Calculate how much liquid (in litres) **leaves** the digestive system in the faeces in an average day. Show how you work out your answer. *(2)*

c) The liquid from the stomach wall contains water and other substances.

(i) Write down the name of **one** of these substances. *(1)*

(ii) What does this substance do? *(2)*

[OCR (MEG) 1998]

Breathing and respiration

3.1 Breathing first, respiration second

Breathing and respiration are very important processes. They are different processes.

★ **Breathing** is the movement of air into and out of our lungs. Breathing puts oxygen from the air into our blood. This oxygen is used in respiration.

★ **Respiration** occurs when chemical reactions take place in the cells of our bodies. These reactions use up oxygen and food to give us energy.

Remember that all living things need to respire. Respiration enables them to get the energy they need. In plants, oxygen is taken in and carbon dioxide is lost through the stomata in the leaves. This chapter looks at respiration in animals.

1 Explain what is meant by *breathing*.

2 What is used up during respiration?

3 What is made during respiration?

3.2 What happens when we breathe?

All animals breathe in and out, whether they are awake or asleep. We must breathe in order to take in (inhale) oxygen from the air and breathe out (exhale) carbon dioxide. If breathing stops, we die.

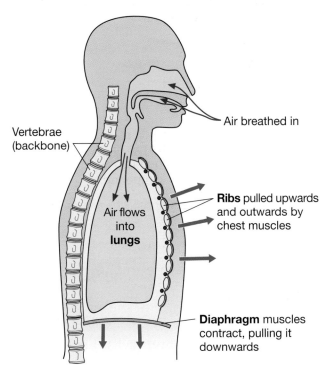

Vertebrae (backbone)

Air breathed in

Air flows into **lungs**

Ribs pulled upwards and outwards by chest muscles

Diaphragm muscles contract, pulling it downwards

Figure 1 The movement of the ribs and diaphragm when we breathe in

Breathing in – inhalation

As you breathe in, your ribs are pulled upwards and outwards by your chest muscles. At the same time, muscles pull your diaphragm downwards.

Both these changes increase the volume (size) of your chest and air flows into your lungs (Figure 1).

Breathing out – exhalation

When you breathe out, the muscles in your chest and diaphragm relax. Your chest moves in and your diaphragm rises into a dome shape. These changes squeeze the air out of your lungs (Figure 2).

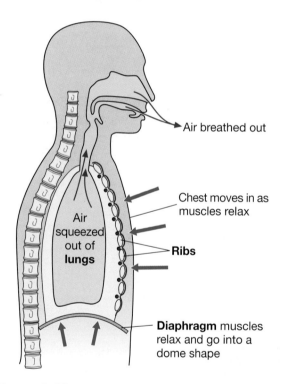

Figure 2 The movement of the ribs and diaphragm when we breathe out

3.3 Gas exchange in the lungs

Oxygen is only one fifth of the air but it is essential for respiration. The oxygen reacts with digested foods in our cells. These chemical processes in respiration produce the energy which we need to stay alive. At the same time, carbon dioxide is produced.

When we run up the stairs or play games, we need more energy. We must take in more oxygen and we will produce more carbon dioxide. Our bodies respond by breathing more quickly and deeply. A part of the brain contains cells that are very sensitive to the concentration of carbon dioxide in the blood. High concentrations of carbon dioxide in the blood set off (trigger) these cells. This makes us breathe faster.

These runners are in the Borrowdale Fells Race. They are breathing faster than normal. This allows extra oxygen, combined with digested food to give them extra energy for the climb.

Breathing allows oxygen to reach the body cells so that respiration can take place (section 3.5).

Inside the cells of animals, oxygen combines with digested food, such as glucose, to produce carbon dioxide, water and energy.

$$\text{glucose} + \text{oxygen} \rightarrow \text{carbon dioxide} + \text{water} + \text{energy}$$

Table 1 shows the temperature and composition of gases in dry inhaled air and in exhaled air.

	Dry, inhaled air	Exhaled air
% oxygen	21	14
% carbon dioxide	0	5
% water vapour	0	2
temperature (°C)	20	25

Table 1 The temperature and composition of gases in dry, inhaled air and in exhaled air. How does the percentage (%) of oxygen, carbon dioxide and water vapour change during respiration? Why do these changes happen? Why is the temperature of exhaled air higher than that of inhaled air?

Figure 3 shows the human breathing system in more detail.

When we inhale, air is taken in through the nose or the mouth. The **nasal cavity** contains membranes with a large surface area which produce **mucus**. This mucus is warm and moist. It filters dust and germs from the air before they can reach the lungs. The nasal membranes also have tiny hairs, called **cilia**. These sweep the mucus towards the throat to be swallowed.

The air then passes down the **trachea** (windpipe). It goes to the two **bronchi** (singular, **bronchus**) and then down to the **lungs**. In the lungs there is a branched system of elastic air passages called **bronchioles**. These branch into smaller and smaller bronchioles. They lead to thousands of tiny air sacs, called **alveoli**. Alveoli are collapsible. They inflate and deflate as we breathe in and out.

A network of **blood capillaries** covers the alveoli. On the surface of the alveoli two things happen.

1 *Oxygen* diffuses *out of the alveoli* and through the thin capillary walls into the blood. This oxygen is picked up by the pigment **haemoglobin**, which is found in **red blood cells**. It can then be carried to other parts of the body in the bloodstream.

2 *Carbon dioxide* diffuses *out of the capillaries* and *into the alveoli*. As the alveoli deflate, the carbon dioxide is exhaled.

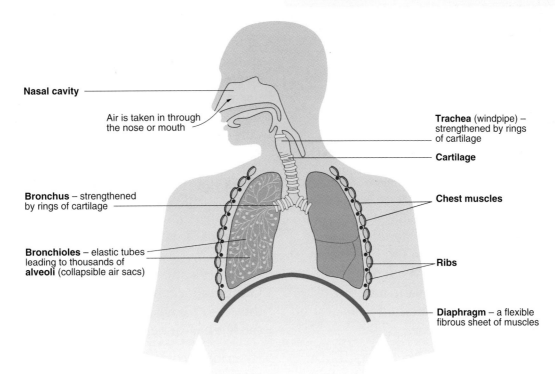

Nasal cavity

Air is taken in through the nose or mouth

Trachea (windpipe) – strengthened by rings of cartilage

Cartilage

Bronchus – strengthened by rings of cartilage

Chest muscles

Bronchioles – elastic tubes leading to thousands of **alveoli** (collapsible air sacs)

Ribs

Diaphragm – a flexible fibrous sheet of muscles

Figure 3 The structure of the human breathing system

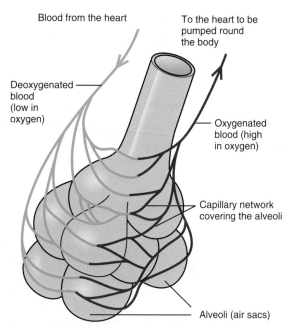

Figure 4 The blood supply to the alveoli

4 What is the word equation for respiration?

5 What are the tiny hairs lining the nasal cavity called? What is their job?

6 What happens to oxygen in the alveoli?

7 What happens to carbon dioxide in the alveoli?

3.4 Smoking and health

Most people now realise that smoking is a dangerous habit. Smoking damages your health. Every cigarette packet and advert must carry a health warning.

Tobacco smoke contains carbon monoxide, nicotine, tar and other poisons. The carbon monoxide diffuses into the capillaries and reacts with haemoglobin in red blood cells. It forms a stronger bond with haemoglobin than oxygen. This reduces the amount of oxygen carried by the red blood cells around the body.

The smoker's general health suffers. Their energy is reduced. Doctors strongly advise women not to smoke when they are pregnant.

A smoker is not a healthy person

Smoking may be the cause of a baby being born frail and underweight.

Nicotine in tobacco is **addictive**. It is a **carcinogen**. A carcinogen is a substance which can be the cause of cancer. Carcinogens cause normal cells to divide and grow abnormally. The abnormal cells can spread to other parts of the body and eventually lead to death.

The tar in cigarette smoke damages the cilia in the nasal cavity. This means that harmful bacteria and viruses which cause infections are not removed. So, even a common cold can be much more serious. Tar also contains carcinogens.

Over the years, smoking badly affects the heart and arteries. Carbon monoxide in smoke results in deposits of fat in the lining of the arteries. This is called **arteriosclerosis**. These fatty deposits reduce the blood circulation. Poor circulation in the legs and feet can lead to gangrene. Gangrene is when cells begin to die because they don't have enough oxygen. Sometimes, the leg has to be amputated (cut off).

Arteriosclerosis may lead to a blockage of the arteries which supply blood to the heart muscles. If this happens, the person has a heart attack.

3.5 Respiration

Respiration involves chemical reactions in the cells of our bodies. These reactions release energy from foods.

We need a supply of energy every minute of our lives. This energy comes from respiration. Our main sources of energy are carbohydrates and fats in our food.

Our food is first broken down by enzymes in the gut. This produces small molecules such as glucose. During respiration, glucose reacts with oxygen to form carbon dioxide, water and energy.

The process is called **aerobic respiration** because it uses oxygen.

The energy released during respiration is used by our bodies in four important ways.

1 We all need energy to run, skip and jump. Even the slightest muscular action, like the blinking of an eye, needs **mechanical energy**.

2 Most muscles are under the control of nerve impulses. These impulses are like tiny electric currents. So, nerve cells need **electrical energy**.

3 Some of the energy from food must be released as heat. This is called **thermal energy**. It is needed to keep us warm and maintain our body temperature.

4 As animals grow or repair damaged tissues, **chemical energy** is needed to make new tissues.

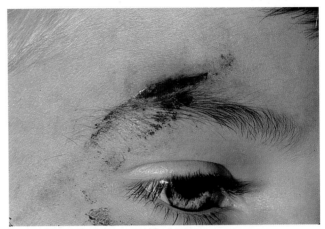

Damaged tissues, like this cut above the eyebrow, are repaired using chemical energy. Chemical energy is produced during respiration.

During respiration, we use up foods and oxygen. This produces carbon dioxide and water and gives us energy. This is like when fuels burn. Foods and fuels react with oxygen. These reactions are called **oxidation reactions**. The foods and fuels are **oxidised**.

$$\text{food or fuel} + \text{oxygen} \rightarrow \text{carbon dioxide} + \text{water} + \text{energy}$$

Foods are sometimes called **body fuels** or **biological fuels**.

Although aerobic respiration and burning are similar, they are different. The similarities and differences are shown in Table 2.

Similarities	Differences
• reactants contain carbon and hydrogen • reactants combine with oxygen • carbon dioxide is produced • water is produced • energy is released	• respiration is relatively slow but burning is usually rapid • respiration involves a large number of separate enzyme-catalysed reactions but burning is a direct process without enzymes

Table 2 Similarities and differences between aerobic respiration and burning

3.6 Anaerobic respiration

Respiration normally occurs in the presence of air (oxygen) and this is called aerobic respiration.

Respiration can also occur in the absence of oxygen. This is called **anaerobic respiration** (respiration without oxygen).

Anaerobic respiration in fermentation and bread making

Fermentation is used to make beer and wines. During the process, yeast uses sugar or glucose as its food.

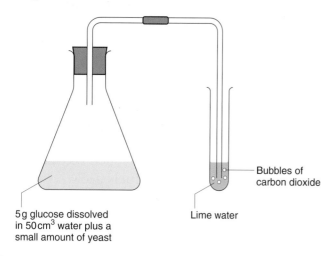

5g glucose dissolved in 50cm³ water plus a small amount of yeast

Lime water

Bubbles of carbon dioxide

Figure 5 In a closed container, yeast respires aerobically to start with. When all the oxygen is used up, it can respire anaerobically.

Yeast contains single-celled organisms. When yeast is mixed with a sugar or glucose solution, it soon starts to respire (Figure 5). The yeast uses sugar and oxygen dissolved in the water. It produces carbon dioxide, water and energy by aerobic respiration.

$$\text{glucose} + \text{oxygen} \xrightarrow{\text{yeast}} \text{carbon dioxide} + \text{water} + \text{energy}$$

When all the oxygen has been used up, the yeast starts to respire anaerobically.

Under anaerobic conditions, the yeast produces carbon dioxide and ethanol (alcohol) rather than carbon dioxide and water.

$$\text{glucose} + \xrightarrow{\text{yeast}} \text{carbon dioxide} + \text{ethanol} + \text{energy}$$

Anaerobic respiration releases much less energy than aerobic respiration. In anaerobic conditions, most of the energy in the glucose remains 'locked in' the ethanol.

Brewing

In brewing beer, a sweetish liquid is made by dissolving the sugars from barley in warm water. This liquid is called wort. Yeast is added. Fermentation takes place as the yeast converts the sugars to alcohol and carbon dioxide. Different types of beer are made by varying:

★ the type of yeast

★ the length of the fermentation time

★ the substances added, such as hops.

Beer is produced by fermenting wort in large vats. Why is there froth (bubbles of gas) on the liquid?

Wine making

In this case, the juice from grapes is fermented using the natural yeasts that occur on the skin of grapes. Different varieties of grapes produce wines of differing flavours. The climate, the soil in which the vines grow and differences in the wine-making process result in hundreds of different wines.

Bread making

Yeast is used in bread making because it can produce carbon dioxide quickly. Bakers add yeast and sugar to warm water and then mix it with flour to make bread dough. The yeast respires using the sugar. This produces bubbles of carbon dioxide which are trapped in the dough. The bubbles cause the dough to 'rise'. The baker puts this risen dough into a very hot oven. The heat kills the yeast, preventing any further rising. Alcohol evaporates away and the bread is baked.

This baker is kneading his dough. The yeast respires producing carbon dioxide. This makes the bread light and nice to eat. When you eat your next slice of bread, look for all the air pockets in it.

8 What is respiration with oxygen called?

9 What is respiration without oxygen called?

10 Name **three** things needed to make beer.

11 Why do bakers use yeast?

Summary

1 When we breathe in, our ribs move up and out. The diaphragm becomes flat and air flows into the lungs. This is called **inhalation**.

2 When we breathe out, our ribs move down and in. The diaphragm goes into a dome shape and air is squeezed out of the lungs. This is called **exhalation**.

3 We breathe in air containing **oxygen**. In the alveoli in the lungs, oxygen diffuses into the blood capillaries where it is picked up by red blood cells. The bloodstream supplies all our body cells with oxygen.

4 A chemical reaction takes place in the cells between digested food and oxygen.

The reaction produces carbon dioxide, water and **energy**. We need energy to stay alive. This reaction is called **respiration**.

5 Carbon dioxide is carried by the blood and diffuses into the alveoli. It is then breathed out.

6 Smoking can make you ill. Smoking can cause lung cancer. It can also lead to serious diseases of the heart and arteries.

7 **Aerobic respiration** occurs in the presence of air (oxygen).

Anaerobic respiration occurs without oxygen. Anaerobic respiration takes place in the fermentation of beer and wine.

1 The diagram shows part of the breathing system in a human. Copy the diagram.

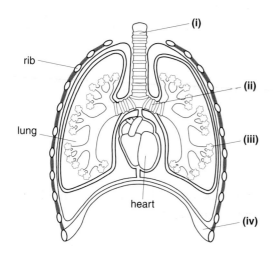

a) Use words from the list to label parts (i) to (iv) on the drawing.

> alveoli bronchiole bronchus diaphragm
> trachea (windpipe) *(4)*

b) Where in the lungs does oxygen enter the blood? *(1)*

c) Which process in cells produces carbon dioxide? *(1)* **[AQA (NEAB) 1999]**

2 a) The diagram shows someone breathing in.

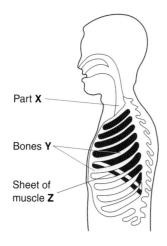

Copy the table below. Then use names from the box to complete the **four** spaces in your table. You may use each word once or not at all.

> backbone biceps diaphragm intercostal
>
> intestine pelvis ribs windpipe

Description	Name
Part **X**	
Bones **Y**	
Muscles between bones **Y**	
Sheet of muscle **Z**	

(4)

b) (i) Copy and complete the word equation for the process of aerobic respiration.

glucose +_____ → carbon dioxide + water *(1)*

(ii) Which organ removes carbon dioxide from your body? *(1)*

c) Copy the passage below and use names from the box to complete the **two** spaces in your passage.

> carbon dioxide   lactic acid   nitrogen
> oxygen   water

Anaerobic respiration can occur when an athlete does vigorous exercise. This is because there is not enough _____ in the body. The product of anaerobic respiration is _____ . *(2)*

d) Respiration is an exothermic reaction. What is an exothermic reaction? *(2)*

e) Yeast carries out another sort of anaerobic respiration. The process is called fermentation. The diagram shows a fermentation jar.

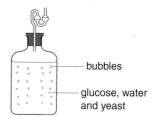

bubbles

glucose, water and yeast

What are the products of fermentation? *(2)*

[AQA (SEG) 1999]

3 a) The list shows some common human disorders. Which **three** of these often result from tobacco smoking?

> diabetes   kidney failure   emphysema
> liver disease   heart disease   lung cancer *(3)*

b) Explain why many people find it difficult to give up smoking. *(2)*

[AQA (NEAB) 1998]

Blood and circulation

4.1 What does blood contain?

Blood is a mixture of four things – **plasma**, **red cells**, **white cells** and **platelets**.

Red cells and white cells are shown in Figure 1. The drawings are magnified about 3000 times. These cells and platelets float in the plasma which is pumped around the body by the heart. This movement of blood around the body is called the **circulation** of the blood.

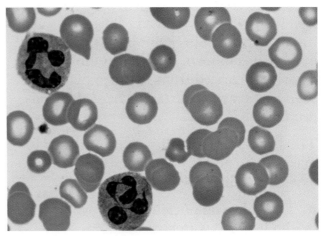

This photo of a blood smear shows red cells and two white cells stained dark purple.

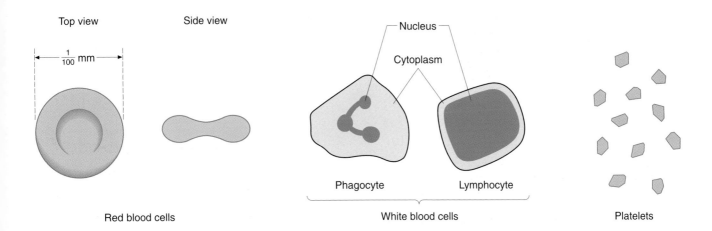

Top view   Side view

Nucleus

Cytoplasm

$\frac{1}{100}$ mm

Phagocyte   Lymphocyte

Red blood cells   White blood cells   Platelets

Figure 1 Blood cells and platelets

Plasma

Plasma is a pale yellow solution. It contains substances dissolved in water. As the blood circulates, the plasma carries:

★ **digested foods** (**nutrients**), such as glucose, amino acids and minerals from the small intestine to all other cells

★ **carbon dioxide** from all our cells to the lungs where it is breathed out

★ **hormones** from glands in our body to target organs (chapter 8).

Red blood cells

Red blood cells carry oxygen to our cells for respiration. There are millions of red cells in every cubic centimetre of blood.

Red blood cells contain a red pigment called **haemoglobin**. This combines with oxygen in the lungs to form **oxyhaemoglobin**. The oxygen is released from oxyhaemoglobin as soon as it reaches the cells where oxygen is needed.

The structure of red blood cells (Figure 1) makes them good at carrying (transporting) oxygen to other cells.

★ They have no nucleus, so the whole cell can be filled with haemoglobin.

★ Their cell membrane is very thin, so they absorb oxygen easily.

White blood cells

White blood cells protect us against disease. Notice in Figure 1 that there are two kinds of white cells. They are called **phagocytes** and **lymphocytes**. Lymphocytes produce chemicals called antibodies. These antibodies kill harmful germs and neutralise poisonous chemicals. Phagocytes engulf (eat) harmful germs.

Platelets

Platelets help the blood to clot when we have a cut. Platelets are bits of blood cells without a nucleus.

The platelets make a mesh of fibres where the skin is cut. The mesh traps red blood cells and a clot forms. As the clot dries, it leaves a **scab**. The scab prevents further bleeding and stops germs from getting in.

Paul Ince, England's captain, was cut badly on the head when his team drew with Italy in the World Cup qualifier in October 1997. Platelets helped to clot his blood.

1 List the **four** things which make up blood.

2 Which part of the blood carries oxygen around the body?

3 Which part of the blood protects us from disease?

4 What do platelets do?

<table>
<tr><td>4.2</td><td>**Why is blood important?**</td></tr>
</table>

Our blood has three important jobs (functions).

★ **Transporting** (carrying) digested food, oxygen and waste products.

★ **Protecting** us against germs and poisonous chemicals.

★ **Controlling** our **body temperature**.

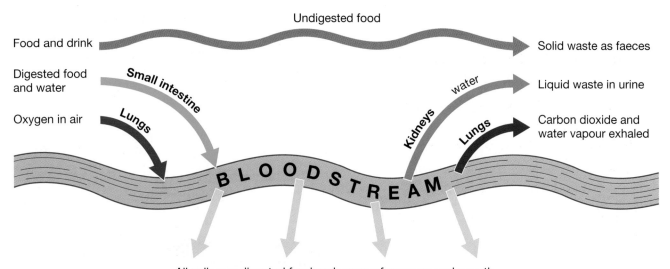

Food and drink

Undigested food

Solid waste as faeces

Digested food and water

Small intestine

water

Liquid waste in urine

Oxygen in air

Lungs

Kidneys

Lungs

Carbon dioxide and water vapour exhaled

B L O O D S T R E A M

All cells use digested food and oxygen for energy and growth

Figure 2 The blood transports substances to and from cells

Transport

Figure 2 shows the role of blood in transporting substances. Digested foods (nutrients), waste products and hormones are dissolved in the plasma and carried around our bodies. Oxygen is transported as oxyhaemoglobin in the red blood cells.

Digested food and water pass into the blood through the lining of the small intestine. Oxygen diffuses into blood capillaries which surround the alveoli in our lungs. As the blood circulates around our bodies, all cells use the digested food and oxygen for energy and growth.

When the blood passes through the kidneys, excess water and waste substances are removed and excreted as urine.

Carbon dioxide is made when cells respire to obtain energy. Carbon dioxide is carried away from cells by our blood and excreted when we breathe out.

Protection

White blood cells produce antibodies to protect us from harmful germs and poisonous chemicals. Platelets help the blood to clot and form a scab. The cut can then heal without it becoming infected.

Control of body temperature

The blood helps us to keep our body temperature constant. In cold weather, blood vessels and capillaries near the surface of the skin contract. So, less blood flows through them. We stay warm because less heat is lost. In warm weather and during exercise, surface blood vessels and capillaries expand. So, more blood flows through them and we lose more heat from our bodies.

4.3 Our circulatory system

The heart pumps blood around the body. The blood passes to other organs through tubes called **blood vessels**.

There are three types of blood vessel – **arteries**, **veins** and **capillaries**.

Arteries

Arteries carry blood *away* from the heart. They have thick, muscular walls because they carry blood at a high pressure.

Veins

Veins carry blood *back* to the heart. Veins have thinner, less muscular walls because they carry blood at a low pressure. They contain valves to prevent backflow.

Capillaries

Capillaries are very narrow tubes with walls that are only one cell thick. Capillaries branch off from arteries and then rejoin to form veins.

The heart, the blood and blood vessels make up our circulatory system. The blood carries oxygen and digested food to all parts of the body. It also carries away waste products.

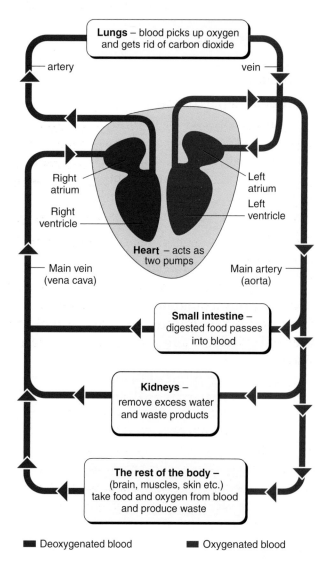

Figure 3 The human circulatory system

The main organs through which the blood circulates are shown in Figure 3. We can see a number of features of the circulatory system.

★ The **heart** pumps blood around the body.

★ In the **lungs**, the blood picks up oxygen and gets rid of carbon dioxide.

★ In the **small intestine**, the blood absorbs digested food (nutrients).

★ In the **kidneys**, waste products and excess water are removed from the blood.

★ The rest of the body (brain, muscles, skin, etc.) takes food and oxygen from the blood. Their waste products are carried away by the blood.

We can also see from Figure 3 that the heart acts as two pumps. There are two separate circuits from the heart. One circuit goes to the lungs and back to the heart. The second circuit goes to all the other organs and then back to the heart. So, we call it a **double circulatory system**. The blood passes through the heart twice for a full circulation through the body.

The blood leaving the lungs and returning to the heart is rich in oxygen. It is called **oxygenated blood**. This oxygenated blood is pumped from the heart along the main artery (**aorta**). It branches to the small intestine, the kidneys and the rest of the body. The oxygen is used by the various organs for energy and growth. The blood becomes **deoxygenated** and returns to the heart along the main vein (**vena cava**).

5 Which blood vessel is:
   a) a high pressure pipe
   b) a low pressure pipe
   c) a narrow tube with a wall one cell thick?

6 What is the main artery called?

7 What is the main vein called?

8 What is oxygenated blood?

4.4 The structure of the heart

Figure 4 shows the structure of the heart. The heart is a pump which sends blood around our bodies every minute of the day and night.

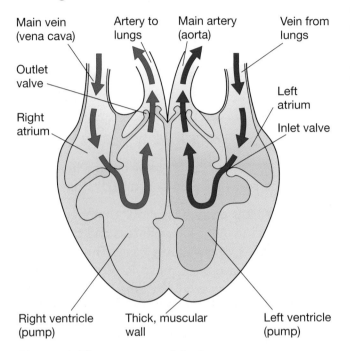

Main vein (vena cava)
Artery to lungs
Main artery (aorta)
Vein from lungs
Outlet valve
Right atrium
Left atrium
Inlet valve
Right ventricle (pump)
Thick, muscular wall
Left ventricle (pump)

Figure 4 The structure of the heart

Notice that each side in the heart has two chambers. There are two chambers where blood flows in. They are called the **left atrium** and the **right atrium**. There are two chambers where blood is pumped out. They are called the **left ventricle** and the **right ventricle**. Between an atrium and a ventricle is a **valve** to stop the blood flowing the wrong way.

The muscular walls of the ventricles contract and relax continuously. Every time the muscles contract, blood is pushed out through the outlet valves and into the arteries. The surge of blood causes your **heartbeat**. You can feel this surge of blood as a **pulse** in the artery at your wrist.

The ventricles have very thick walls made of strong muscle fibres. They need to be strong because they pump about 70 times every minute. This adds up to about 37 000 000 beats in just one year.

4.5 How does exercise, diet and smoking affect the heart?

The pumping action of the heart continues for the whole of our lives. To keep going, the heart needs a good supply of nutrients and oxygen. These are provided through the **coronary arteries** to thousands of capillaries spread over the walls of the heart.

Like other muscles in our bodies, regular exercise improves the heart muscles so that they are stronger and larger. The heart can then pump more blood around with each beat.

There are three main factors which cause heart and circulatory health problems. They are:
★ high blood pressure
★ poor diet
★ smoking.

High blood pressure

If someone has high blood pressure, their heart has to work harder to pump blood around the body. As we get older, the walls of our arteries get thicker and harder. A layer of fat forms on the inside making them narrower. This makes the flow of blood more difficult and can lead to high blood pressure.

Poor diet

If we eat too many fatty foods, we start to put on weight. This puts a strain on the heart. The arteries become narrower because of the layer of fat lining them. This can cause high blood pressure.

Smoking

Tobacco smoke contains a number of poisonous substances. Carbon monoxide is one of them. Carbon monoxide takes the place of oxygen in the haemoglobin of the red blood cells. This means that a smoker's blood can't supply as much oxygen as it should to the body cells.

So, the heart must beat faster. This increases the blood pressure and puts more strain on the heart.

Summary

1 Blood is a mixture of:

   ★ **plasma**, which carries digested food, carbon dioxide and hormones round the body

   ★ **red blood cells** which contain haemoglobin to carry oxygen round the body

   ★ **white blood cells** which kill germs and neutralise harmful chemicals

   ★ **platelets** which help the blood clot when the skin is cut.

2 Blood is important in three ways:

   ★ it **transports** nutrients (digested food), oxygen and waste products.

   ★ it **protects** us from harmful bacteria, viruses and chemicals.

   ★ it **controls body temperature** by allowing the blood vessels (mainly the capillaries) near the surface of the skin to expand when we get hot and contract when we get cold.

3 The blood flows around the body in blood vessels.

   ★ **Arteries** carry blood, rich in oxygen, away from the heart. They have thick, muscular walls.

   ★ **Veins** carry blood, lacking in oxygen, back to the heart. They have valves to prevent backflow.

   ★ **Capillaries** branch off from the arteries and rejoin to form veins. They are very narrow tubes. They allow food and oxygen to diffuse from the blood to the cells in the body. They allow carbon dioxide and other waste products to diffuse from the cells back into the bloodstream.

4 The heart is a **pump**. There are **two circuits** for the blood.

   ★ One circuit goes from the heart to the lungs and back again.

   ★ The other circuit goes from the heart to the rest of the body and back again.

5 The heart is divided into four chambers – **two atria** where blood enters and **two ventricles** where blood leaves. The ventricles have thick, muscular walls. They contract and relax all the time. When we are at rest, the heart beats at about 70 times a minute.

6 There are three factors that cause heart problems.

   ★ **High blood pressure** occurs when the heart is put under strain because there is a narrowing of the blood vessels.

   ★ **A poor diet** leading to a person being overweight can overload the heart.

   ★ **Smoking** reduces the amount of oxygen being carried round the body. The heart has to beat faster than normal and this can lead to high blood pressure.

1 Blood is made of many parts.

a) Choose labels for **(i)** and **(ii)** in the diagram. Choose the **best** words from this list. One has been done for you.

plasma   platelet   red blood cell
white blood cell   *(2)*

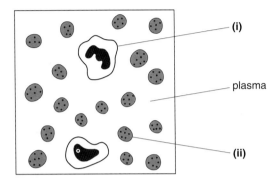

b) (i) Copy the table below then finish your table to show the job of each part of blood. The first one has been done for you.

Part of blood	Job
Plasma	Carries substances round the body
Platelet	
Red blood cell	

(2)

(ii) The plasma carries many substances round the body. Write down the name of **one** of them. *(1)*

[OCR 1999]

2 The diagram shows a human heart.

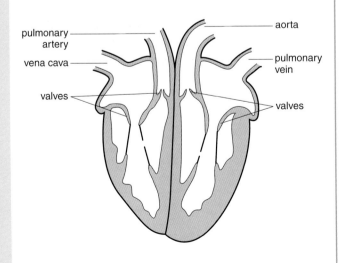

a) Copy and complete these sentences. Use the information in the diagram to help.

Blood from the body enters the right side of the heart through the blood vessel called the _____ .

The blood is pumped through the pulmonary _____ to the lungs.

The blood returns to the heart through the blood vessel called the _____ .

The blood is pumped to the body through the blood vessel call the _____ . *(4)*

b) What do valves do in the heart? *(1)*

c) Describe the differences between arteries and veins. *(4)*

d) Copy and complete this sentence.

In the lungs the blood loses _____ gas and picks up _____ gas. *(2)*

[AQA (SEG) 1999]

3 An athlete's blood can be tested to detect the use of a drug which increases the number of red blood cells. The maximum number of red blood cells allowed is 6.4 million/mm^3.

The bar chart shows the number of red blood cells in samples from a group of athletes.

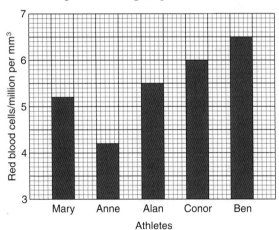

Use the bar chart and your knowledge to help answer the following questions.

a) How does the number of red blood cells in females differ from males? *(1)*

b) Who will fail this drug test? *(1)*

c) Suggest why an increase in the number of red blood cells may improve an athlete's performance. *(2)*

[NICCEA 1998]

5

Photosynthesis

5.1 Reactants and products in photosynthesis

5.2 A summary of photosynthesis

5.3 Leaves and photosynthesis

5.4 Factors affecting photosynthesis

5.5 How do plants use glucose?

5.1 Reactants and products in photosynthesis

Plants do not feed like animals. Plants can make their own food. Animals can't do this.

The process which plants use to make their own food is called **photosynthesis**.

Conditions needed for photosynthesis

Light for photosynthesis

Most plants can't grow well in dark, shady places where there is little light. Farmers and gardeners know how important light is for plants.

Crops need plenty of sunshine because they need light to photosynthesise.

We can do an experiment to show that plants need light in order to photosynthesise. The food they make is starch. To do the test, keep two similar geranium plants in the dark for several days. This uses up all the starch in their leaves. Then place one plant in the light and leave the other in the dark. After several days test a leaf from each plant for starch (Figure 1). Starch turns dark blue with iodine. The leaf which has been in the light turns dark blue with iodine. This shows that starch is in the leaf.

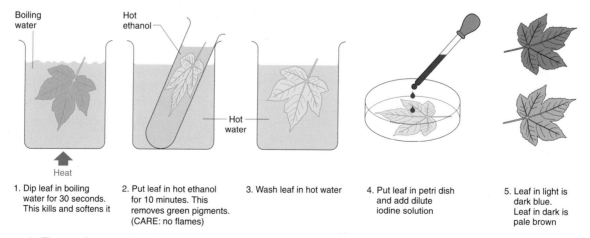

1. Dip leaf in boiling water for 30 seconds. This kills and softens it

2. Put leaf in hot ethanol for 10 minutes. This removes green pigments. (CARE: no flames)

3. Wash leaf in hot water

4. Put leaf in petri dish and add dilute iodine solution

5. Leaf in light is dark blue. Leaf in dark is pale brown

Figure 1 Testing for starch in leaves

Starch is made by photosynthesis.

The leaf that was kept in the dark went brown. It did not turn dark blue. There is no starch in this leaf. This shows that:

Light is necessary for photosynthesis.

Where does photosynthesis occur in the plant?

Which parts of the plant make starch by photosynthesis?

Figure 2 shows what happens when we do a starch test on a variegated leaf (one with white and green patches). Only the green parts of the leaf turn dark blue with iodine. This shows that the green parts of the leaf make starch. The white parts do not make starch. So, now we know that:

The green colour in leaves is necessary for photosynthesis. This green colour or pigment is called **chlorophyll**.

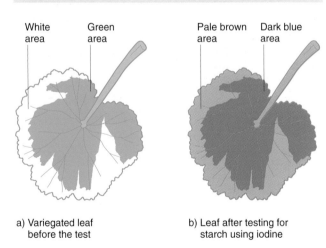

a) Variegated leaf before the test

b) Leaf after testing for starch using iodine

Figure 2 Testing a variegated leaf for starch using iodine

What are the products of photosynthesis?

We know from the experiment shown in Figure 1 that **starch** is one product of photosynthesis. The other product of photosynthesis is **oxygen**. We can show this with the apparatus in Figure 3.

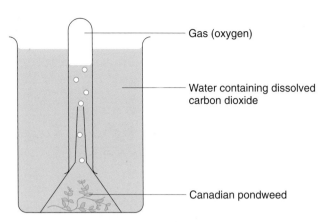

Figure 3 An experiment to show that oxygen is a product of photosynthesis

When we keep the apparatus in the light, bubbles of gas slowly collect in the test tube. After a few days, there is enough gas in the test tube to show that it is oxygen.

What chemicals (reactants) are used in photosynthesis?

We know from the experiments in Figures 1 and 2 that both **light** and **chlorophyll** are needed for photosynthesis. But, what are the reactants in photosynthesis?

Starch is a carbohydrate. It contains carbon, hydrogen and oxygen. Carbon dioxide and water are the most likely substances which plants use to make starch. Scientists have proved that plants make starch from carbon dioxide and water. Their experiments use radioactive carbon and oxygen.

Carbon dioxide and **water** are the reactants for photosynthesis.

1 Name the process by which plants make their food.

2 What chemical is used to test for starch?

3 What is the green colour in leaves called?

4 What are the products of photosynthesis?

5 What are the reactants of photosynthesis?

5.2   A summary of photosynthesis

The experiments described in section 5.1 tell us that:

★ carbon dioxide and water are the reactants for photosynthesis

★ light and chlorophyll are needed for photosynthesis to happen

★ starch and oxygen are the products of photosynthesis.

More about photosynthesis

Experiments show that the first product of photosynthesis is *not* starch, but glucose. The glucose molecules then link together forming starch.

The following word equation will help you understand photosynthesis.

$$\text{carbon dioxide} + \text{water} \xrightarrow[\text{chlorophyll}]{\text{light}} \text{glucose} + \text{oxygen}$$

Plants get their carbon dioxide for photosynthesis from:

★ the carbon dioxide which is made in plant cells during respiration and

★ the carbon dioxide in the air.

The water for photosynthesis is absorbed through the roots of plants and then moves to the leaves (section 6.2).

During photosynthesis, chlorophyll in plants absorbs light energy. The plant then uses this energy to turn carbon dioxide and water into glucose.

So, the overall result of photosynthesis is to turn light energy from the Sun into chemical energy in the molecules of glucose.

5.3   Leaves and photosynthesis

All plant cells which contain chlorophyll can photosynthesise. The chlorophyll is contained in small organelles called **chloroplasts** (section 1.3). Most of the cells with chloroplasts are in the leaves of plants.

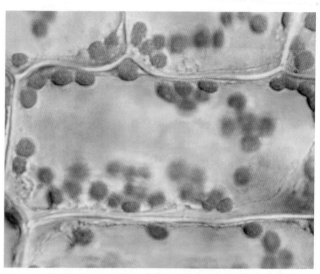

A magnified photo of leaf cells. The dark green blobs are chloroplasts containing chlorophyll

Leaves are usually flat and thin. They are well adapted for photosynthesis. Being flat gives them a large surface area. This allows them to absorb lots of light from the Sun. As the leaves are thin, carbon dioxide can easily reach all the cells once it has been absorbed.

Look at Figure 4. It shows how leaves are adapted for photosynthesis.

The carbon dioxide needed for photosynthesis enters through tiny holes called **stomata** (singular, stoma). Stomata are mainly on the underside of leaves.

The top side of a leaf often has a smooth, shiny appearance. This is due to a thin waxy layer called the **cuticle** which reduces evaporation (water loss).

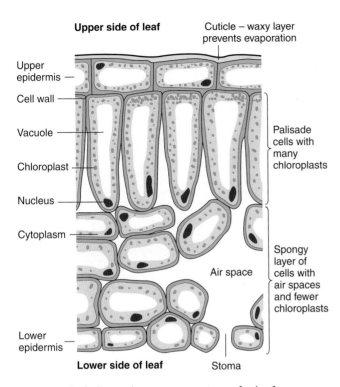

Upper side of leaf

Cuticle – waxy layer
prevents evaporation

Upper
epidermis

Cell wall

Vacuole

Chloroplast

Nucleus

Cytoplasm

Palisade
cells with
many
chloroplasts

Air space

Spongy
layer of
cells with
air spaces
and fewer
chloroplasts

Lower
epidermis

Lower side of leaf

Stoma

Figure 4 Cells in the cross section of a leaf

Below the cuticle and also on the underside of the leaf, there is a single layer of tightly fitting cells. This is called the **epidermis**. Leaves are usually a deeper green on their upper surface. This is because the cells near the upper surface contain more chlorophyll than those below. These cells are called **palisade cells**. They have lots of chloroplasts with dark green chlorophyll. The large number of chloroplasts allow maximim absorption of sunlight.

More rounded, **spongy cells** containing fewer chloroplasts are found below the palisade cells. There are air spaces between these cells. The air spaces allow gases to move easily in and out of the spongy layer. Carbon dioxide diffuses into the cells. Oxygen diffuses outwards into the air.

5.4 Factors affecting photosynthesis

The word equation for photosynthesis is:

$$\text{carbon dioxide} + \text{water} \xrightarrow[\text{chlorophyll}]{\text{light}} \text{glucose} + \text{oxygen}$$

We can measure how fast photosynthesis occurs by finding:

1 the rate at which carbon dioxide or water is used up, or

2 the rate at which glucose or oxygen are produced.

We usually measure how fast photosynthesis occurs by finding the rate of uptake of carbon dioxide. Figure 5 compares the rate of photosynthesis on a hot, sunny day with that on a cold, sunny day.

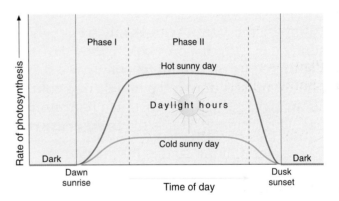

Figure 5 Comparing the rates of photosynthesis on a hot, sunny day and a cold, sunny day.

Plants need light in order to photosynthesise. If there is no light, then the process can't occur. You can see in Figure 5 that the rate of photosynthesis is zero before sunrise and after sunset. Look closely at the curve showing the rate of photosynthesis on a hot, sunny day. At dawn, the light appears and photosynthesis starts. As the light gets brighter during the morning, the rate of photosynthesis increases. This is shown as phase I on the graph.

After a while, probably about mid-morning, the rate of photosynthesis reaches a maximum and the graph becomes flat. Even though the light continues to get brighter until mid-day, the rate of photosynthesis does not change. The rate of photosynthesis stays constant (phase II) until late in the afternoon. As the afternoon light fades, the rate of photosynthesis falls.

During phase I, photosynthesis increases as the light intensity increases. This means that the rate of photosynthesis is being determined by or limited by the level of light intensity. In this case, light intensity is described as the **limiting factor** for the rate of photosynthesis.

In phase II, light intensity can't be limiting the rate of photosynthesis. Even though the light intensity increases towards mid-day and then starts to decrease, the rate of photosynthesis stays the same. Another factor must now be limiting the rate.

Compare the rate of photosynthesis on a hot, sunny day with that on a cold, sunny day in Figure 5. The maximum rate of photosynthesis during the middle of a cold, sunny day is lower than that on a hot, sunny day. The limiting factor is the **temperature**.

The major limiting factors for the rate of photosynthesis are:

★ poor light
★ low temperature
★ a shortage of carbon dioxide
★ shortage of water.

Commercial growers need to control the conditions in which flowers, fruit and vegetables grow. They manage the growing conditions in order to get good crops. In greenhouses, they can install extra lighting, heating and extra carbon dioxide can be added to the air. The plants are regularly watered.

Plants being grown in a commercial greenhouse

Roughly speaking, the rate of photosynthesis doubles if the temperature rises by 10°C. But, there is a limit to the temperature at which plants can survive. The rate of photosynthesis increases until the temperature reaches about 40°C. Above 40°C, photosynthesis slows down and stops. This is because the structures of **enzymes** are damaged. Enzymes are **catalysts** (sections 2.2 and 20.7). They control the reactions in all living things.

6 Look at Figure 5. Why does the rate of photosynthesis stay the same in the afternoon?

7 What happens to the rate of photosynthesis if the temperature is raised by 10°C?

8 Why do plants stop photosynthesising above 40°C?

5.5   **How do plants use glucose?**

The first products of photosynthesis are glucose and oxygen. Figure 6 summarises the three main uses of glucose in plants.

1 Glucose and oxygen can be used as raw materials for respiration

Respiration is a process in which glucose reacts with oxygen to form carbon dioxide and water.

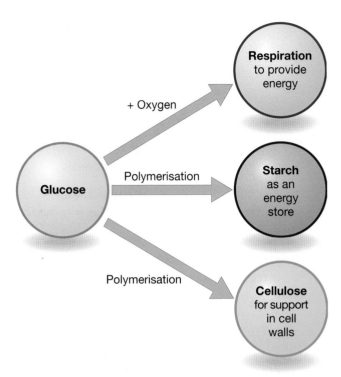

Figure 6 The main uses of glucose in plants

The equation for respiration is:

$$\text{glucose} + \text{oxygen} \rightarrow \text{carbon dioxide} + \text{water} + \text{energy}$$

The **energy** produced in respiration is used to drive other reactions in plants. These reactions include the synthesis of starch and cellulose from glucose as shown in Figure 6.

Notice that respiration is the reverse of photosynthesis.

2 Glucose can be changed to starch as an energy store

Sometimes a plant makes more glucose than it needs. In this case, the extra glucose molecules can join together to form much larger molecules such as starch. This process of joining together small molecules is called **polymerisation** (section 22.5). The larger molecules of starch provide a store of energy for later.

The leaves of plants contain starch. Root vegetables store starch in their roots as well. Potatoes store starch in root tubers. Carrots store it as a swollen tap root. Onions store starch as bulbs at the bottom of their long stems.

Starch is a carbohydrate like glucose. It is stored until the plant needs the energy for respiration, for growth or for the production of seeds.

We use this stored carbohydrate in plants for our food. For example, we eat bread made from wheat and chips made from potatoes.

3 Glucose can be changed to cellulose, which supports the plant as it grows

Plants can convert glucose to cellulose. They use the cellulose for support. Growth in plants takes place mainly at the tips of roots and shoots. It also occurs in storage organs such as potato tubers, swollen carrot roots and onion bulbs. To do this, glucose must reach these parts of the plant. Some of the glucose is converted into cellulose which builds cell walls and supports the plant. The glucose is transported up and down the stems and into and out of leaves and roots via the **phloem tissue** (**food tubes**).

9 What process makes energy from glucose and oxygen?

10 Why do plants change glucose into starch?

11 What is cellulose used for?

12 How is glucose moved around the plant?

Summary

1 **Photosynthesis** is a chemical process in which plants make their own food.

2 During photosynthesis, plants take in carbon dioxide from the air and water from the soil. Sunlight shines on the plant and is absorbed by chlorophyll in the leaves. The carbon dioxide and water react to form glucose and oxygen. Glucose is the food.

$$\text{carbon dioxide + water} \xrightarrow[\text{chlorophyll}]{\text{light}} \text{glucose + oxygen}$$

3 Leaves are flat and thin. Large surface area means that leaves can absorb lots of light from the Sun. Carbon dioxide is absorbed through the stomata on the underside of the leaves. Because leaves are thin, the carbon dioxide can diffuse through the leaf and easily reach all the cells.

4 Factors affecting the rate of photosynthesis are:

★ the brightness of light from the Sun

★ the temperature – as temperature rises, so does the rate of photosynthesis

★ the concentration of carbon dioxide – photosynthesis increases if there is more carbon dioxide

★ the supply of water – photosynthesis increases with a plentiful supply of water.

Exam questions for Chapter 5

1 The diagram shows part of a common plant that flowers in spring.

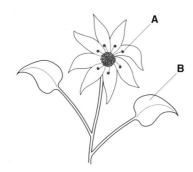

a) Name the parts labelled **A** and **B**. *(2)*

b) (i) What is the job of the leaves? *(1)*

(ii) Explain why the leaves are wide and flat. *(2)*

(iii) The leaves need water to keep their shape. Describe how the leaves obtain water. *(2)*

[AQA [NEAB] 1997]

2 The diagram shows a photosynthesis investigation.

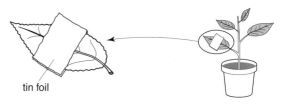

tin foil

The plant was left for 24 hours. The tin foil was removed and the leaf tested for starch.

(i) Which factor, affecting photosynthesis, is being investigated? *(1)*

(ii) Name the solution used to test for starch. *(1)*

(iii) On a copy of the diagram below, shade where you would expect to find starch. *(1)*

area which had been covered by tin foil

[NICCEA 1998]

3 Green plants make food in their leaves.

a) From where do the leaves get the energy that they need to make food? *(1)*

b) The graph shows the effect of temperature on the rate of photosynthesis. *(1)*

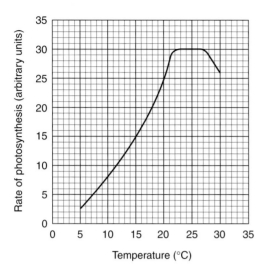

(i) Between which temperatures is the rate of photosynthesis fastest? *(1)*

(ii) Suggest why the rate of photosynthesis stays the same between these two temperatures. *(2)*

(iii) A greenhouse owner wants to grow lettuces as quickly and cheaply as possible in winter. At what temperature should he keep his greenhouse in order to grow the lettuces as quickly and cheaply as possible?

Explain your answer. *(3)*

[AQA (NEAB) 1998]

4 This question is about gaseous exchange in plants.

Jo did an experiment to find out about gaseous exchange in pond weed. She used an indicator solution. The indicator changes colour according to how much carbon dioxide is present. The table shows this.

Colour of indicator	Amount of carbon dioxide present
orange	**same** amount of carbon dioxide as in air
yellow	**more** carbon dioxide than in air
purple	**less** carbon dioxide than in air

Jo set up three tubes as shown below. She filled up each tube with orange indicator.

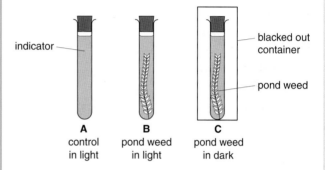

a) (i) Write down **two** things that Jo did to make sure that her experiment was a fair test. *(2)*

(ii) Explain why Jo set up a control (tube **A**). *(2)*

b) (i) What process is taking place in tube **B**, but **not** in tube **C**?

Choose the correct answer from:

excretion   photosynthesis   transpiration

(1)

After one hour Jo recorded the results in a table.

(ii) Copy and finish the table. There are **two** gaps.

Tube	Colour of indicator after one hour
A	orange
B	
C	

(2)

[OCR 1999]

Food and water for plants

6.1 Introduction

Plants need food and water to live and grow. This involves moving (transporting) food and water from one part of the plant to another.

Look at Figure 1 and you will see that:

★ **Water** must be transported from the soil into the roots and up to the leaves for photosynthesis.

★ **Glucose** which is produced during photosynthesis must be transported from the leaves to other parts of the plant. The glucose may be needed for the plant to grow. If there is more glucose than the plant needs, it can be changed into starch. This is stored in the leaves and roots.

★ **Minerals** containing nitrates, phosphates and magnesium must also be absorbed from the soil. Minerals are needed in all parts of the plant.

Glucose and minerals are solids. They move from one part of a plant to another dissolved in water as solutions.

These solutions move through the plant in a system of tubes connecting the roots, the stem and the leaves.

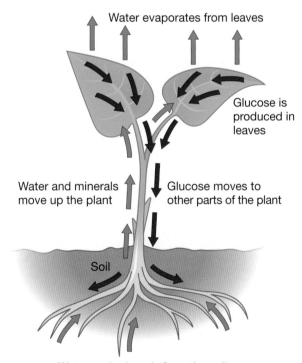

Water evaporates from leaves

Glucose is produced in leaves

Water and minerals move up the plant

Glucose moves to other parts of the plant

Soil

Water and minerals from the soil

Figure 1 The movement (transport) of water, glucose and minerals in a plant.

This transport system is called the plant's **vascular system**. It can be compared to the blood system in an animal.

If you cut a plant stem, liquid oozes out. This liquid, escaping from the cut vascular system, is called **sap**.

Time from start of experiment (days)	Volume of water in cylinder (cm³)
0	100
1	97
2	94
3	92
4	89

Table 1 The results of the experiment to find out the uptake of water by a plant

6.2 How much water do plants need?

Figure 2 shows an experiment to investigate water uptake by a small plant.

The volume of water in the cylinder was recorded at the start of the experiment. It was recorded again on each of the next four days. The results are shown in Table 1.

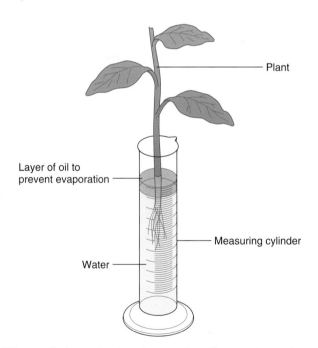

Figure 2 Investigating the uptake of water by a plant

The results in Table 1 show how much water was taken up by the plant.

Roots hold plants firmly in the ground. They allow plants to absorb water. Water enters the roots of a plant through specially adapted cells called **root hair cells** (Figure 3).

The outer wall of each root hair cell has a long projection into the soil. This increases the surface area. The bigger the surface area, the more water it can take up. The cell wall of this projection is also thinner, allowing water to pass through easily. Minerals dissolved in the water can also pass into the root hair cells easily.

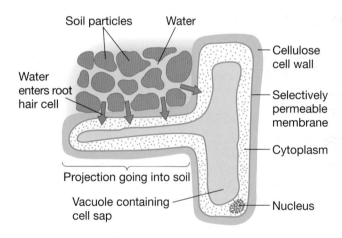

Figure 3 A root hair cell

Some of the water absorbed by a plant is used in photosynthesis. Most of the water evaporates from cells in the leaves and escapes through the stomata (see Figure 4 in Chapter 5). As water is lost from the leaves, it is replaced by more water from the roots.

The evaporation of water from the leaves of a plant is called **transpiration**. The continuous flow of water through the plant from roots to leaves is called the **transpiration stream**.

The rate of transpiration is determined by the weather and atmospheric conditions. These affect evaporation from the leaves.

Transpiration will increase:

★ on hot days when the temperature is high and more water evaporates from the leaves

★ on dry days when evaporation of water vapour into the atmosphere is easier

★ on windy days when moving air helps evaporation

★ on sunny days when the extra light keeps the stomata wide open. Stomata open in response to light. This allows more carbon dioxide to enter the leaves for photosynthesis.

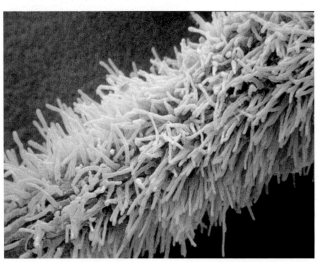

Hundreds of root hair cells allow this plant to absorb water from the soil

1 What is the job of root hair cells?

2 What gets into a plant dissolved in the water from the soil?

3 What is transpiration?

4 What weather conditions will make plants transpire quickly?

6.3 How does water help to support plants?

Plant cells differ from animal cells in having a strong, fairly rigid cell wall. Water and dissolved solutes can pass easily through the cell wall. The cell wall is completely **permeable** to water and solutes.

When cells in the leaves and stem of a plant have a good supply of water, they fill up and pack together tightly. Water moves up the plant and into the cells. The epidermis of the leaf or the stem holds the cells in place. The cells press against one another and make the leaf or stem firm, yet flexible (Figure 4a). The leaves and the stem are stiffened by filling the cells with water. This is like a bicycle tyre which is stiffened by filling the inner tube with air.

When plant cells are swollen in this way, we say they are **turgid**. The support which the swollen cells give to a plant is called **turgor**.

Turgor is very important in the support of non-woody plants, like dandelions, daffodils and grasses.

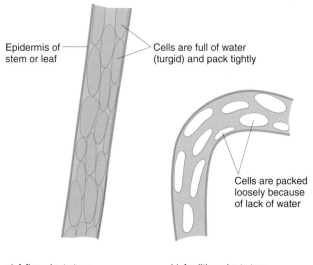

Epidermis of stem or leaf

Cells are full of water (turgid) and pack tightly

Cells are packed loosely because of lack of water

a) A firm plant stem   b) A wilting plant stem

Figure 4 The importance of water in the support of plant tissue

When the plants lose their water supply, their cells are no longer stiffened by turgor. The leaves droop and the stem wilts (Figure 4b).

This busy lizzie plant was wilting on a hot summer's day

The same plant has recovered after watering

Trees, shrubs and perennial flowering plants which continue to grow from year to year, produce hard, strong woody tissue. This makes their stems stiff and the plants do not rely on turgor for support.

6.4 How do plants transport food, water and minerals?

The photo in Figure 5 shows a section through the stem of a clematis plant. We can see the inside of the plant stem very clearly.

The stem structure is made up of four tissues:

★ epidermis
★ growing tissue
★ vascular system
★ packing tissue.

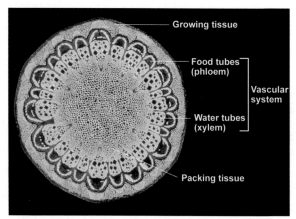

Figure 5 This is a section through the stem of a climbing plant called a clematis. Look for the epidermis, the growing tissue, the vascular system and the packing tissue. The magnification is 15 times.

1 The **epidermis** is an outer layer of living cells which acts like a skin. On the stem and on the top of the leaves there is a waxy layer called the **cuticle**.

2 **Growing tissue** lies between the epidermis and the vascular system. It contains living, growing cells.

3 The **vascular system** is made up of two kinds of tubes. They are called **phloem tubes** (pronounced 'flowum' tubes) and **xylem tubes** (pronounced 'zylem' tubes). The vascular system transports food and water around a plant.

4 **Packing tissue** fills the centre of the stem. This consists of rounded dead cells packed close together.

In the roots and stem, the vascular system is composed of lots of phloem and xylem tubes running side by side. These regions in the plant roots and stem are called **vascular bundles**. Look at Figure 6.

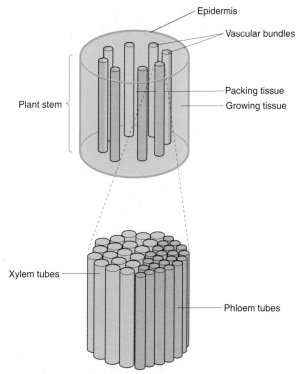

Figure 6 The vascular bundles of xylem and phloem tubes in a plant stem

The **phloem tubes** are often described as the **food tubes** of a plant. They carry glucose dissolved in water to the growth or storage areas.

The **xylem tubes** are often described as the **water tubes** of a plant. They carry water and dissolved minerals in the transpiration stream from the roots to the stem and leaves.

The phloem and xylem tubes run in vascular bundles through the length of a plant from roots to leaves. This means that:

★ water taken in through the roots can be transported up the stem and to the leaves

★ glucose which is produced by photosynthesis in the leaves can pass to the stem and roots.

In each vascular bundle, xylem tubes are nearer the inside of the plant. These are composed of long, thin, dead cells joined end to end like capillary tubes.

The walls of living plant cells are made up of **cellulose**. As the cell walls get older and die, the cellulose is changed to **lignin**. This is less permeable and much harder. Lignin is the material in the walls of xylem tubes. So, xylem tubes play an important part in supporting woody and perennial plants. In time, xylem tubes become part of the packing tissue.

The outer tissue in vascular bundles is phloem tubes. These are very long, thin living cells. The phloem cells are joined end to end and run from the roots, along the stem and into the leaves. Glucose is produced by photosynthesis in the leaves. It is then transported to the roots, the growing tips, the flowers and the fruit along the phloem tubes.

Table 2 summarises the differences between xylem and phloem tubes in a plant.

	Xylem	Phloem
Living or dead	dead	living
Material of cell wall	lignin	cellulose
Nature of cell wall	non-permeable	permeable
Materials transported	water and minerals	glucose
What provides support?	lignin (woody tissue) – firm, strong	turgor from water – flexible

Table 2 A summary of the differences between xylem and phloem tubes

In a tree trunk, the phloem tubes are in the soft, inner part of the bark. If a complete ring is cut from the bark, food cannot be transported to the roots and the tree will slowly die.

5 What are the main parts of the vascular system?

6 In which direction does water flow in a plant?

7 In older plants, what can cellulose change into?

8 What happens if someone cuts a complete ring around the bark of a tree?

6.5 Which elements do plants need?

Plants need certain elements to grow well, and produce good flowers and fruit. These elements are called the **essential elements**. The most important essential elements for plants are carbon, hydrogen and oxygen. They are obtained from water in the soil and from oxygen and carbon dioxide in the air.

In addition to carbon, hydrogen and oxygen, the most important elements for plants are nitrogen, phosphorus and potassium.

Nitrogen is used by plants to make proteins and nucleic acids. Plants get their nitrogen from ammonium salts (containing NH_4^+ ions) and nitrates (containing NO_3^- ions) in the soil.

Phosphorus is used by plants for reactions involving the transfer of energy in cells. Phosphorus is also needed to make nucleic acids. Plants get their phosphorus from phosphates (containing PO_4^{3-} ions) in the soil.

Potassium is needed by plants for cell membranes to work well. Plants get their potassium from mineral salts in the soil containing potassium ions (K^+).

Other elements, such as **magnesium** and **iron** are needed in smaller amounts. Magnesium is an essential part of chlorophyll. Iron is a part of the enzymes which make chlorophyll.

Poor supplies of these essential elements will result in weak plants. The fruit or vegetable crop from the plants will be poor.

Different plants require different amounts of essential elements. If one particular crop is grown year after year in the same soil, a deficiency in certain minerals may result. When the same crop is grown on a plot year after year we call it **monoculture**. Fertilisers must be used to provide the essential elements. Then we get a high crop yield.

A healthy tomato plant leaf

A tomato plant growing in soil with no magnesium. Magnesium ions are needed to form chlorophyll. If the plant does not have magnesium, it cannot make chlorophyll and the leaves turn yellow.

9 Copy and complete this table.

Mineral element	Use
Nitrogen	
Phosphorus	
Potassium	
Magnesium	

Summary

1 In order to grow, plants must take in water and minerals from the soil. They do this through their roots. The roots have many **root hair cells** which project into the soil. Water and minerals are taken up through the thin cell walls of root hair cells.

Water is needed for:

* photosynthesis
* support of the plant
* transport of solutions.

Water is taken up the stem of the plant and from there to the leaves where most of it evaporates. This is called **transpiration**. The continuous flow of water through the plant to the leaves is called the **transpiration stream**.

2 Plant cells differ from animal cells in having strong, rigid cell walls. When the plant has taken in plenty of water, the cells fill up and pack tightly.

When plant cells are swollen in this way, the plant is supported. This support is called **turgor**. If a plant like a dandelion has not had enough water, it will flop and may wither and die.

3 The stem of a plant is composed of:

* the **epidermis** – an outer layer which acts like a skin
* **growing tissue** just inside the epidermis
* **vascular bundles** of two kinds of tubes. These are called **phloem** and **xylem tubes**. Phloem or **food tubes** carry water with dissolved glucose to all parts of the plant. Xylem or **water tubes** carry water from the roots to the stem.
* **packing tissue** in the centre of the stem. This tissue contains lots of round cells all packed close together.

4 Plants need certain elements so that they can grow and be healthy. The most important elements, called **essential elements**, are **oxygen**, **hydrogen** and **carbon**. Plants get these elements from water in the soil and from oxygen and carbon dioxide in the air.

The next three important elements which plants need and take in from the soil are:

* **nitrogen** from nitrates and ammonium salts
* **phosphorus** from phosphates
* **potassium** from potassium salts.

1 a) Copy and complete the following sentences.

Green plants produce their own food by a process called photosynthesis. In this process the raw materials are _____ and carbon dioxide. Glucose and _____ are produced. _____ energy is absorbed by the green substance called _____ .*(4)*

b) Name **two** things that can happen in the plant to the glucose produced in photosynthesis. *(2)*

c) Plants need mineral salts.

(i) Through which part do mineral salts get into the plant? *(1)*

(ii) Explain why water is important in this process. *(2)*

Some students set up water cultures to find out how plants use nitrates. They had two sets of nutrient solutions. A full solution provided the plant with all the required nutrients.

The results table shows the average mass of the seedlings after 28 days of growth.

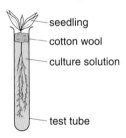

- seedling
- cotton wool
- culture solution
- test tube

Culture solution	Average mass of seedling in g
Distilled water	0.14
Full solution with no nitrates	0.29
Full solution	0.43

d) (i) Give a conclusion you could make from these results. *(1)*

(ii) Calculate the difference in average mass caused by the addition of nitrates to the culture solution. *(1)*

(iii) What are nitrates used for in the seedling? *(1)*

(iv) Some factors need to be controlled to keep this test fair. Name **two** of them. *(2)*

(v) Suggest **one** way you could improve the experiment. *(1)*

[AQA (SEG) 1999]

2 a) The table shows the uptake of water by the roots of a plant.

Water content of soil (%)	0	6	9	12	13	17	19
Volume of water absorbed/mm³ per hour	0	0	18	35	38	45	45

(i) Use the information in the table to draw a line graph. Plot volume of water absorbed along the vertical axis and water content of soil along the horizontal axis. Use the graph to answer the following questions. *(3)*

(ii) What happens to the water uptake when the water content of the soil falls below six per cent? *(1)*

(iii) Describe the changes in water uptake by the root when the water content of the soil rises above six per cent. *(2)*

b) Diagrams **A** and **B** represent two root hair cells. **A** is from a root in very dry soil and **B** is from the same root after water has been added to the soil.

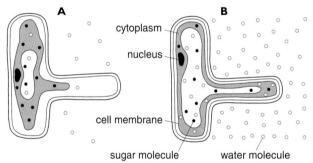

A   B

- cytoplasm
- nucleus
- cell membrane
- sugar molecule
- water molecule

(i) Give **two** ways cell **B** differs in structure from cell **A**. *(2)*

(ii) What has entered cell **B**? *(1)*

(iii) Name the process which has occurred in cell **B**. *(1)*

(iv) What cell structure limits this process? *(1)*

c) (i) Name the **two** types of cells which make up the transport system of a plant. *(2)*

(ii) Copy and complete the table below to show the function of mineral ions in plants.

Mineral ion	Function
Calcium	
Magnesium	

(2)

[NICCEA 1998]

Our senses and nerves

7.1 Senses and stimuli

We depend on our senses for survival. Our senses help us to avoid danger. They also enable us to find food, drink and light. If someone whistles in the street, you would probably look round. The sound of the whistle causes a change in your ears.

Changes like this which can be detected by our sense organs (ears, eyes, etc.) are called **stimuli** (singular, stimulus). Our reactions to stimuli are called **responses**.

So, the whistle is a stimulus and your response is to look round.

Figure 1 shows our various senses, sense organs and the stimuli detected.

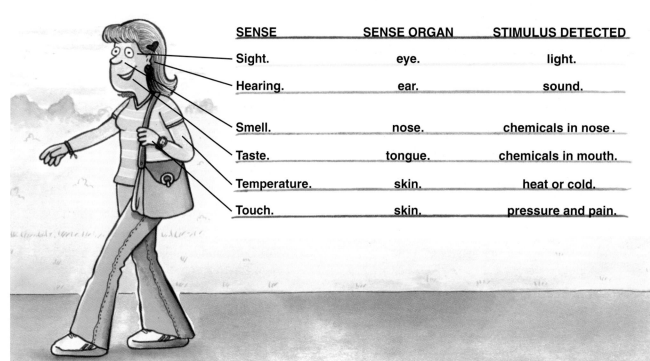

SENSE	SENSE ORGAN	STIMULUS DETECTED
Sight.	eye.	light.
Hearing.	ear.	sound.
Smell.	nose.	chemicals in nose.
Taste.	tongue.	chemicals in mouth.
Temperature.	skin.	heat or cold.
Touch.	skin.	pressure and pain.

Figure 1 Our various senses, sense organs and the stimuli they detect

Our sense organs help us to react to our surroundings. For example, when we see something, we may change what we are doing. Our sense organs are linked with the brain and our nervous system so that we can control our behaviour.

All our sense organs have specialised cells called **receptors**. Receptors are cells which detect stimuli like heat, pressure and chemicals.

We rely on our senses. Which senses are these students using to help them cross the road safely?

Receptors include:

★ cells in the retina at the back of our eyes which are sensitive to light (section 7.4)

★ cells in our ears which are sensitive to sound

★ cells in our nose and on the tongue which are sensitive to chemicals

★ cells in our skin which are sensitive to touch, pain and temperature.

After our receptors have detected a stimulus, they send a signal to the brain. The signal is a tiny electrical **impulse** which passes along nerve fibres.

This baby has made a smiling response to a tickling stimulus

1 Why do we have senses?

2 What is a stimulus?

3 Name **three** stimuli which our receptors can detect.

4 What sort of signal passes along a nerve fibre?

7.2 The nervous system

The nervous system plays a vital role in our response to stimuli. The main function of the nervous system is to carry impulses (signals) from one part of the body to another. These impulses consist of tiny electric pulses which travel rapidly through the nervous system.

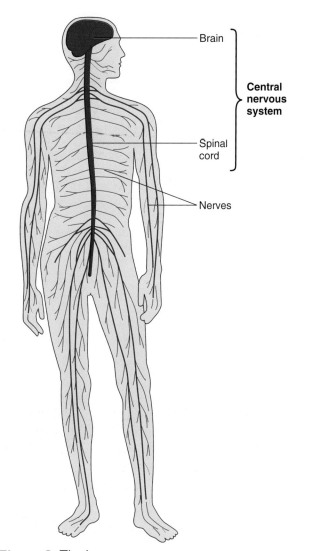

Brain

Central
nervous
system

Spinal
cord

Nerves

Figure 2 The human nervous system

The nervous system consists of two parts:

I the **central nervous system** (CNS) –
the brain and spinal cord

2 a **network of nerves** linking the CNS
with the different parts in the body.

The brain is enclosed within the skull. The
spinal cord runs down the centre of the
backbone. So, the whole of the CNS is well
protected by bone. Some nerves come out of
the brain and go to the sense organs and
muscles in the head. Other nerves come out
of the spinal cord and go to our arms, legs
and the rest of our body.

Figure 3 shows the structure of a typical
nerve cell.

Nerve cells are called **neurones**.

Long neurones like that in Figure 3 link our
sense organs (eyes, skin, etc.) to the spinal
cord and the brain.

The main part of a neurone is the **cell body**
which contains the nucleus. Part of the
cytoplasm of the cell body is extended into a
long thin nerve fibre. A nerve fibre, called a
dendron, links receptors in the sense organ
to the cell body. A second nerve fibre called
an **axon** then links the cell body to the spinal
cord or the brain.

Nerve cells differ from other cells in having
branches called **dendrites**. Dendrites at the
end of a dendron pick up stimuli in sense
organs and then transmit impulses to the
spinal cord or brain. Dendrites in the brain
link up with other nerve cells to form a
complex network.

Three types of neurone come into play when
we respond to a stimulus.

I **Sensory neurones** like that in Figure 3
carry impulses from sense organs to the
brain or spinal cord.

2 **Motor neurones** carry impulses from
the spinal cord to muscles and other
organs.

3 **Relay (connector) neurones** in the
spinal cord and the brain connect
sensory neurones to motor neurones
and pass on (relay) signals. The main
function of relay neurones is to allow a
large number of cross connections,
rather like a telephone exchange.

Relay neurones are quite short, but sensory
and motor neurones can be very long indeed.
For example, the sensory neurone linking the
tip of your finger to your spinal cord may be
half a metre long.

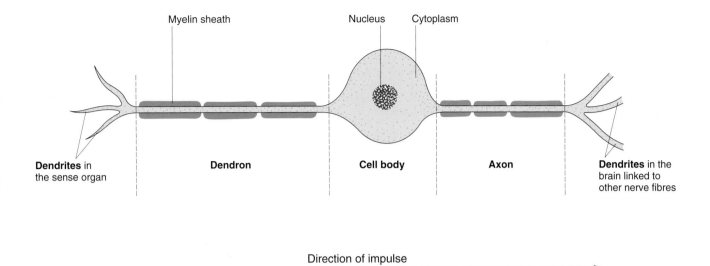

Figure 3 The structure of a typical nerve cell (neurone) linking a sense organ to the brain

Nerve fibres are grouped together into bundles called **nerves** (Figure 4). The **myelin sheath** is a layer of fatty tissue around each nerve fibre. This insulates it from neighbouring fibres. It also prevents impulses crossing from one fibre to another. It is rather like the insulation round the wires in an electric cable.

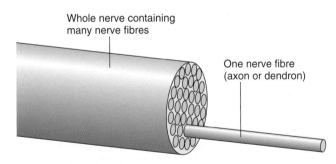

Figure 4 Bundles of nerve fibres in a nerve

5 Name the **two** parts of the central nervous system.

6 Name the **three** types of neurone.

7 What is the job of the myelin sheath?

7.3   Reflex actions

If you touch something hot, you pull your hand away. If your nose tickles, then you sneeze. You don't have to think. Each of these actions is automatic. Your responses are spontaneous and out of your control.

Rapid and automatic responses to stimuli are called **reflex actions**.

Reflex actions are rapid because the nervous impulses travel by the shortest route in your body. These shortest routes are called **reflex arcs**. The reflex arc involved in responding to a hot flame is shown as a flow diagram in Figure 5 (over the page).

★ The heat from the flame acts as a **stimulus**.

★ **Receptors** in the skin detect the stimulus.

★ Impulses pass along a **sensory neurone** from the skin to the central nervous system.

★ Impulses pass via a **relay neurone** in the CNS to a motor neurone.

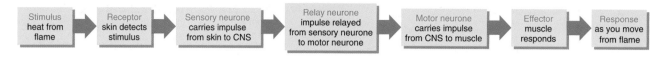

Figure 5 A flow diagram showing the pathway for a simple nervous response (reflex arc)

★ Impulses pass along **motor neurones** to muscles (**effectors**) which allow you to move.

★ The final **response** is to move away from the flame.

Effectors which bring about responses are either muscles or glands.

Muscles usually respond by contracting, whereas glands respond by secreting chemicals (hormones). The actions of hormones are described in Chapter 8.

You can see the reflex arc which causes you to pull your finger away from a flame in Figure 6.

As soon as you touch the flame, heat and pain receptors in your finger create nervous impulses. These pass along sensory nerve fibres to the spinal cord. Here, the sensory neurones connect with relay neurones. The relay neurones then transfer the impulses to motor neurones. Finally, impulses carried by the motor neurones make the muscle contract, pulling your finger away from the flame.

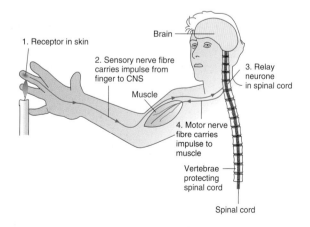

Figure 6 The reflex arc used in pulling your finger away from a flame

Notice that the brain is not involved in reflex actions. This makes the responses much quicker because impulses have less distance to travel.

You may have had your reflexes tested like this young woman. The doctor is tapping her leg just below the knee. This is done to check the condition of her spinal cord.

Many of our actions are not automatic. They are **conscious actions**.

Conscious actions involve the brain as well as the spinal cord.

During conscious actions, impulses travel to the spinal cord and then up to the brain. The brain co-ordinates a response. Return impulses start at the brain, travel down the spinal column and then to the muscles. So, you can see that conscious actions take longer routes.

7.4 The structure of the eye

Our eyes enable us to see things. They can respond to changes in light (section 7.5). They can focus on things at different distances. Figure 7 shows the structure of an eye.

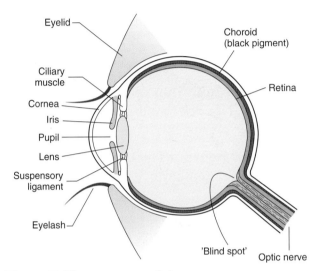

Figure 7 The structure of the eye

Labels: Eyelid, Ciliary muscle, Cornea, Iris, Pupil, Lens, Suspensory ligament, Eyelash, Choroid (black pigment), Retina, 'Blind spot', Optic nerve

★ The **cornea** is a transparent skin at the front of the eye. Light enters the eye through the cornea.

★ The **iris** can become larger or smaller depending on how much light passes through the cornea.

★ The **pupil** is the gap at the centre of the iris. Light goes into the eye through the pupil. The pupil looks black becaues of the black pigment (choroid) inside the eye.

★ The **lens** is held in position by the suspensory ligaments and ciliary muscles. The lens and ciliary muscles help us to focus.

★ The **retina** contains receptor cells. These are sensitive to light.

★ The **optic nerve** carries impulses from the retina to the brain along sensory neurones.

There are very few light-sensitive cells (receptors) at the point where the optic nerve leaves the retina. This area is called the **blind spot**.

7.5 How do our eyes respond to light?

The iris, pupil and retina help us to control the amount of light entering our eyes.

Light passes through the pupil and acts on receptors in the retina. These receptors pass signals (impulses) to the brain. The brain then passes messages back to the muscles in the iris to control the size of the pupil.

In bright light, muscles in the iris make the pupil smaller so that less light enters the eye (Figure 8a). In poor light, muscles in the iris make the pupil larger so that more light can enter the eye (Figure 8b).

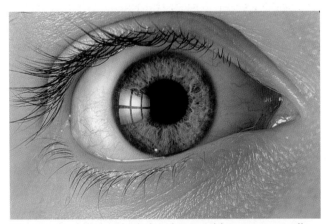

Figure 8 a) In bright light, the pupil becomes smaller

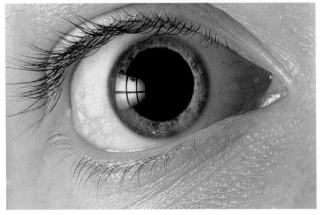

Figure 8 b) In poor light, the pupil becomes larger

8 What controls the amount of light entering the eye?

9 Draw an iris and pupil on
a) a bright day and b) a dull day.

Summary

1 We depend on our **senses** and **sense organs** in order to survive. We have five sense organs. They are:

   ★ eyes to see

   ★ ears to hear

   ★ nose to smell

   ★ tongue to taste

   ★ skin to touch and feel temperature.

   Our sense organs have special cells called **receptors**. They are sensitive to changes around us. These changes are called **stimuli**.

2 When receptors detect a stimulus, they send a signal to the brain. The signal is a tiny **electrical impulse** which travels along **nerve fibres**.

3 There are two parts to the nervous system:

   ★ the central nervous system (CNS) – the brain and spinal cord

   ★ thousands of nerves linking the CNS to every part of our bodies.

4 Nerve cells are called **neurones**. Each neurone has a **cell body** with a nucleus somewhere along a long, thin nerve fibre. Neurones provide a link between receptors in our sense organs and the central nervous system.

5 When we respond to a stimulus, three things happen:

   ★ **Sensory neurones** carry impulses from the sensory organ to the CNS.

   ★ **Motor neurones** carry impulses from the CNS back to muscles, glands and other organs.

   ★ **Relay neurones** make short cuts between sensory neurones and motor neurones.

6 When the telephone rings, you hear it and then go to answer it. This **response** involves impulses (messages) going to your brain. It is called a **conscious action**. When you accidentally touch a hot flame, your response is much quicker. This is called a **reflex action**. In this case, the impulse travels by a shorter route – sensory neurone → relay neurone → motor neurone. This route is called a **reflex arc**. This time your brain isn't involved. You don't have to think. Your hand comes away immediately.

7 We see things with our **eyes**. They respond to the stimulus of light. Our eyes can respond to changes in light. When it is dark, the pupil gets bigger to let more light in.

1 The diagram shows a reflex pathway in a human.

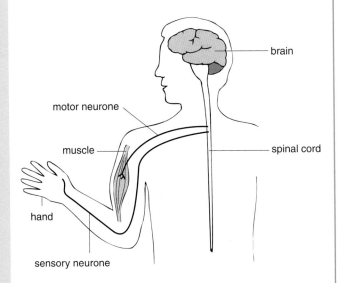

a) What is the *receptor* on the diagram? *(1)*

b) What is the *effector* on the diagram? *(1)*

c) (i) Suggest a stimulus to the hand that could start a reflex response. *(1)*

(ii) Describe the response that this stimulus would cause. *(1)*

d) Copy the diagram and put arrows on your copy to show the direction of the path taken by the nerve impulses. *(1)*

[AQA (SEG) 1999]

2 a) Copy the table about receptors. Fill in your copy. The first answer has been done for you.

Receptors in the	Sensitive to
Eyes	Light
Skin	
	Sound
Tongue	

(3)

b) The diagram shows a section through the eye.

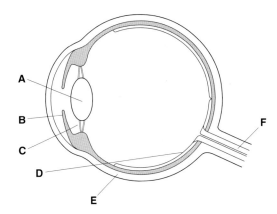

Which of the letters, A to F, on the diagram is:

(i) the iris;

(ii) the sclera;

(iii) the retina? *(3)*

c) Describe, in as much detail as you can, how information is transmitted from light receptors in the retina to the brain. *(3)*

[AQA (NEAB) 1999]

3 The graph below shows the size of the pupil in a student's eye in different light intensities.

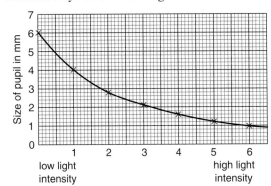

a) Use the graph to answer the questions below.

(i) How many readings were taken to produce the data for the graph? *(1)*

(ii) What was the size of the pupil at a light intensity of 1.5? *(1)*

(iii) What does the graph show about pupil size as the light gets brighter? *(1)*

b) (i) Name the part of the eye which changes the size of the pupil. *(1)*

(ii) Explain why changing the size of the pupil is important. *(3)*

[Edexcel 1998]

Hormones and control

8.1 Our hormones and hormonal control

Many processes in our bodies are controlled by chemicals called **hormones**. Hormones are produced by organs called **glands** and then passed into the bloodstream.

When a particular hormone is needed, it passes into the bloodstream in tiny amounts and then spreads to other parts of the body.

Figure 1 The hormonal system in humans showing the hormones released and their effects.

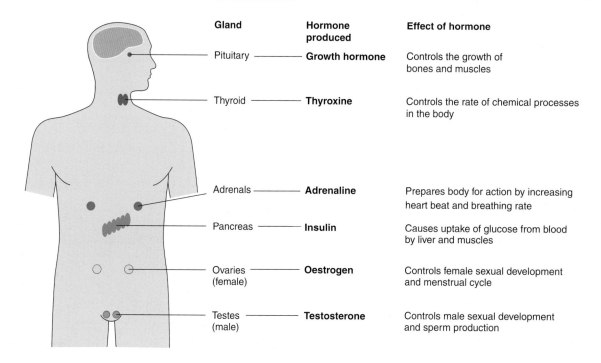

Gland	Hormone produced	Effect of hormone
Pituitary	**Growth hormone**	Controls the growth of bones and muscles
Thyroid	**Thyroxine**	Controls the rate of chemical processes in the body
Adrenals	**Adrenaline**	Prepares body for action by increasing heart beat and breathing rate
Pancreas	**Insulin**	Causes uptake of glucose from blood by liver and muscles
Ovaries (female)	**Oestrogen**	Controls female sexual development and menstrual cycle
Testes (male)	**Testosterone**	Controls male sexual development and sperm production

Usually, the hormone only affects certain cells which are described as its **target cells**. So, hormones carry messages from one part of the body to another. They are sometimes called **chemical messengers**.

The hormone system consists of a number of glands. The positions of these glands, the hormones which they produce and the effects of these hormones are shown in Figure 1.

The monthly release of an egg from a woman's ovaries is controlled by hormones from her pituitary gland and ovaries. So fertility in women can be controlled by giving:

★ hormones that prevent eggs developing (contraceptive pills)

★ hormones that stimulate the release of eggs from the ovaries (fertility drugs).

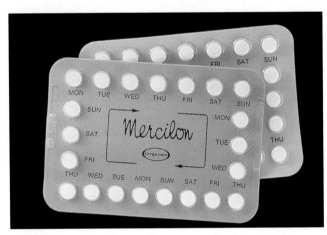

Contraceptive pills usually contain the hormone, oestrogen. The packet shows the pills to take day by day. Oestrogen in these pills stops any eggs from developing.

Look at Figure 1.

Adrenaline has an effect on various organs. It causes cells to respire faster and produce more energy. It causes the heart to beat faster. This increases the blood supply to our muscles so that they are ready for action. The extra blood supply to our muscles also involves cutting down the flow of blood to other organs like the gut.

This explains how you feel in an emergency. Your heart is racing and there is a sinking feeling in your stomach.

Oestrogen is a female sex hormone produced by the ovaries. **Testosterone** is the male sex hormone produced by the testes.

These hormones promote the development of secondary sexual characteristics during puberty. These include the growth of body hair, the development of breasts in girls and larger muscles in boys. Oestrogen controls egg production and the menstrual cycle in women. Testosterone controls sperm production in men.

Hormones play a major part in controlling body processes. Like the central nervous system, they allow 'messages' to be sent from one part of the body to another.

★ The central nervous system controls our actions and responses very rapidly, second by second.

★ The hormone system controls our body processes much more slowly. This happens over hours, days or even years as in the case of growth or the development of secondary sexual characteristics.

8.2 Controlling glucose levels in blood

Starchy foods like bread are broken down by enzymes in saliva and in the stomach to produce glucose. Glucose is then absorbed into the blood and broken down further in our cells. In the cells, energy is released and carbon dioxide and water are made.

Our bodies and cells work best when the level (concentration) of glucose in the blood is constant. Too much glucose can damage our kidneys. Too little glucose makes us feel tired and faint. Fortunately, our bodies can control the level of glucose in the blood. This control is carried out by the pancreas, the liver and the hormone **insulin** (Figure 2).

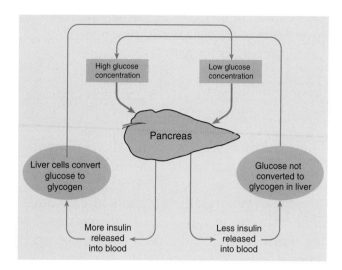

Figure 2 The control of glucose levels in the blood

If the glucose concentration in the blood is too high (red box in Figure 2), the pancreas releases more insulin into the blood. The insulin makes liver cells change glucose into insoluble glycogen. The glycogen is stored in the liver and the blood glucose level falls.

If the blood glucose level becomes too low (blue box in Figure 2), the pancreas releases less insulin. Glucose is no longer converted to glycogen and the concentration of blood glucose rises.

This control of insulin output involves the feedback of information to the pancreas about glucose levels in the blood. It is known as **feedback control**.

This is an example of **homeostasis** (section 8.3).

Diabetes

Some people cannot produce enough insulin to keep their glucose level steady. These people are called **diabetics** and their condition is called **diabetes**. Without treatment, their glucose level becomes too high. This makes them weak and dizzy. They could die if they go into a coma.

In order to enjoy a normal life, diabetics must control the level of glucose in their blood. They must watch their diet carefully.

They must have regular meals with just enough carbohydrate (glucose). Many diabetics have to inject insulin to keep their glucose levels at the right level. Sometimes, they need to test a sample of their blood just before injecting so that they can work out the right amount of insulin.

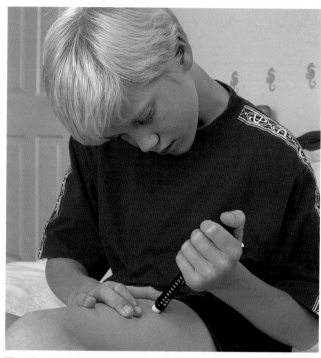

This boy is injecting insulin under his skin

1 What happens to the insulin level if the glucose concentration in the blood is too high?

2 What happens to the insulin level if the glucose concentration in the blood is too low?

3 What problem do diabetics have?

4 How do diabetics control this problem?

<table>
<tr><td>8.3</td><td>

Maintaining control – homeostasis

</td></tr>
</table>

Our bodies cannot work properly unless certain conditions inside our cells are under control. These conditions such as temperature, pH and the level of glucose must be fairly constant.

If the temperature inside your body increases too much, reactions in your cells will not work properly. To get round this, our bodies have a temperature control system. It works like a thermostat which controls the temperature of a room. The thermostat acts as a sensor.

If the temperature is too high (red box in Figure 3), the thermostat switches the heater off. This allows the temperature to fall.

If the temperature becomes too low (blue box in Figure 3), the thermostat switches the heater on. This causes the temperature to rise.

This 'feedback' of information to control the heater is called **feedback control**.

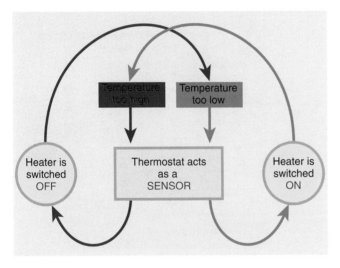

Figure 3 Feedback control in maintaining the temperature in a room using a heater and thermostat.

Our blood and skin act as sensors of temperature rather like a thermostat. If the temperature rises or falls, our blood and skin 'feedback' information to the brain. The brain then passes messages to our muscles, hairs, arteries and sweat glands to put things right.

This 'feedback' control of machines and organisms which tries to keep conditions constant is called **homeostasis**.

The word 'homeostasis' comes from two Greek words – *homeo* meaning constant (the same) and *status* meaning state or condition.

There are many examples of homeostasis. Some of these are shown in Table 1.

| 8.4 | **Controlling our body temperature** |

Our body temperature must stay close to 37°C. Variations in our body temperature alter the activity of enzymes. These control our body processes.

It is very dangerous to fall through the ice of a frozen pond. If this happens, the body temperature falls very quickly. When it reaches 27°C, the person becomes unconscious. The heart stops beating at 25°C. This drop in body temperature is called **hypothermia**.

Variable being controlled	Sensor which 'senses' (monitors) the variable	Actuator which changes conditions (puts things right)
room temperature	thermostat	heater
body temperature	skin and blood	muscles, hairs, sweat glands
glucose in blood	pancreas/brain	insulin
water content of body	brain	kidneys (and to a lesser extent lungs and skin)

Table 1 Some examples of homeostasis

If a person is suffering from a bad infection, his or her body temperature can rise to 40°C. The heart will have to beat very fast and the person becomes very ill and may die without treatment.

There are three main ways in which our bodies gain heat and three ways in which they lose heat.

Gain of heat

1. Respiration in our cells is an **exothermic reaction**, giving out energy.

2. Our bodies are warmed directly by the Sun and by indoor heating systems.

3. Hot meals and hot drinks help us to warm up.

Loss of heat

1. When we breathe out, we lose warm gases.

2. We lose heat when we excrete warm urine and warm faeces.

3. We lose heat to the surroundings, especially on cold days.

Our bodies have important control systems to counteract these gains and losses of heat. These systems keep our internal body temperature at 37°C.

The **skin** is our main contact with the environment. It plays an important part in controlling our body temperature.

Temperature receptors in the skin send impulses (messages) to the brain. The brain then returns 'messages' to the skin. The skin can respond and control body temperature in four ways.

I Variable blood flow

Blood flows through capillaries in the skin which are close to the surface. Heat from the blood is therefore lost to the skin and then to the air (Figure 4).

In cold weather, blood vessels and capillaries near the surface of our skin contract. This is called **vasoconstriction**. Less blood flows through the narrower (constricted) capillaries and less heat is lost from the blood.

In warm weather, our surface blood vessels and capillaries expand. This is called **vasodilation**. This enables more blood to flow through them and more heat can be lost from the body.

Our body temperature rises when we go for a run. This makes us sweat. As sweat evaporates, it takes heat from the skin. This cools us down.

2 Shivering

When we shiver, our muscles contract. This activity increases respiration in our muscle cells. Respiration is an exothermic process, so heat is produced to warm us up.

3 Sweating

When our blood temperature rises above normal, we begin to sweat. Sweat glands secrete sweat (mainly water) onto our skin. As the sweat evaporates, it takes the heat needed for evaporation from the skin. This cools us down.

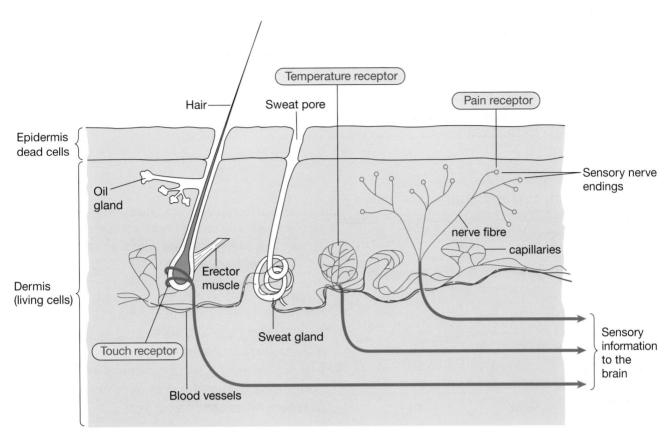

Figure 4 The structure of human skin

4 Hairs and muscle activity

Each hair can be raised or lowered by its own tiny **erector muscle** (Figure 4). The erector muscle joins the bottom of the hair to the top of the dermis.

In cold weather, the muscle contracts. This lifts the hair away from the surface of the skin. The raised hairs trap more air which is a very poor conductor. The layer of air acts as an insulator and heat loss from the body is reduced.

In warm weather, the erector muscles relax. Less air is trapped close to the body and heat loss is less restricted.

The clothes we wear affect our body temperature.

★ Clothing traps air. This acts as an insulator and prevents heat loss. Fleeces are very good at this.

★ Light, thin clothing reduces the amount of trapped air. It helps us to lose heat in hot weather.

★ White clothes reflect heat (radiation) from the Sun. This reduces the amount of heat absorbed. This is why tennis players often wear white.

5 What is hypothermia?

6 Name **two** ways the body can gain heat.

7 What is our usual body temperature?

8 How do our bodies keep cool in hot weather?

9 How do our bodies keep warm in cold weather?

Getting rid of waste – excretion

In Chapter 2, we learnt how food is broken down (digested). Then, in Chapters 3 and 4 we learnt how this digested food plus oxygen is made available to the cells in our bodies via the bloodstream.

After using the digested food and oxygen, our bodies produce waste products. These waste products of metabolism must be removed (**excreted**).

Most of the waste products of metabolism are removed by the lungs and the kidneys.

★ Carbon dioxide and water are produced during respiration in our cells. These diffuse into the blood and then into the lungs. Finally, they are breathed out (see section 3.3).

★ Urea, excess water and excess salt are removed from the blood by the kidneys. They are excreted in the urine (next section).

★ Water and salts are also lost from the skin when we sweat.

| 8.6 | ## Controlling the water content of our bodies – the kidneys

The main job of the kidneys is to control the water and salt content of our bodies. We take in water and salts when we eat and drink. We lose water and salts from our bodies in urine and sweat.

Urine is mainly water. Sometimes, it is almost colourless. When it contains more waste products, it looks yellow.

Urea is the other major waste product in urine. Urea is produced when proteins are metabolised. Proteins are first broken down into amino acids. Most of these amino acids are used for growth and the repair of body tissues. Excess amino acids are broken down in the liver to form urea (Figure 5).

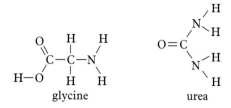

glycine   urea

Figure 5 The chemical structures of glycine (the simplest amino acid) and urea. Excess glycine is broken down to urea. Which parts of their structures are the same?

Urea is poisonous. It must be removed from the body. It dissolves in the blood surrounding the liver cells and is then removed from the blood by the kidneys. Figure 6 shows how the kidneys are connected to the blood system and the **urinary excretory system**.

The kidneys

We have two kidneys at the back of our body, just above the waist. The kidneys have an excellent supply of blood through the **renal arteries** from the aorta (Figure 6). Blood is carried back to the heart via the **renal veins** and the vena cava.

As the renal arteries pass into the kidneys, they divide into a complex network of blood capillaries. As the blood flows through the tiny capillaries, water, salt, urea and other waste products are filtered out first. Water and other substances, including sugars and salts, are then re-absorbed to meet the body's needs. This leaves urea, excess salt and excess water which are excreted via the **ureters**.

The ureters (one from each kidney) carry urine to the **bladder** (Figure 6). The bladder expands as urine collects in it. Urine is excreted from the bladder via the **urethra**. The urethra runs to an opening in front of the vagina in a female and down the centre of the penis in a male.

The kidneys produce dilute urine if there is too much water in the blood and concentrated urine if there is too little water in the blood.

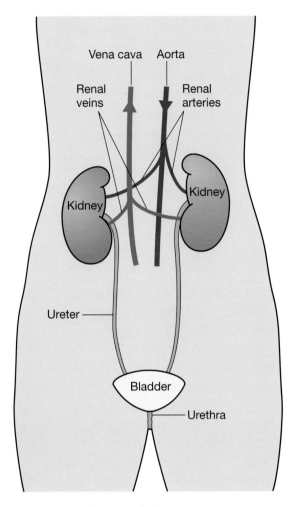

Figure 6 The kidneys and the urinary excretory system

10 Which **two** organs remove waste from the body?

11 What is the major waste in urine?

12 Where are the kidneys found in the human body?

13 Where is urine stored in the body?

14 What things can cause the concentration of urine to change?

| 8.7 | **Drugs – helpful and harmful** |

Drugs are chemicals which affect our metabolism and behaviour. Almost all drugs affect the way we feel and behave. When drugs are prescribed by a doctor, they are usually helpful. If drugs are not used properly, they can be very dangerous.

Drugs which affect the central nervous system can be classified as four types.

1 Sedatives, like alcohol.
2 Stimulants, like caffeine in coffee.
3 Painkillers, like aspirin.
4 Hallucinogens, like cannabis.

Sedatives (**depressants**) slow down the brain and the nervous system. Valium is a sedative. It is prescribed to help people suffering from anxiety. Alcohol is another example of a sedative. It does not take much alcohol to slow down our brain. This is why you must never drink and drive.

Don't drink and drive!

Stimulants speed up the nervous system and make you more alert. They include caffeine in tea and coffee, 'pep pills' and cocaine.

Painkillers (analgesics) include aspirin and paracetamol. They are taken to reduce the feeling of pain such as toothache. Morphine is prescribed to reduce intense pain. Heroin is used illegally to dull the senses.

Drug	Effect on behaviour and health
Nicotine in tobacco	Tobacco smoke hinders the action of cilia and kills cells which line the air passages and the lungs. This causes bronchitis, emphysema and lung cancer. Low levels of oxyhaemoglobin in the blood (see section 3.4) put a strain on the heart and the circulatory system.
Alcohol	Alcohol affects the nervous system. Reactions are slowed down, and walking becomes unsteady. A really drunk person may become unconscious. Long-term abuse causes liver and brain damage.
Solvents in glues, sprays, polishes, etc.	Inhaling these substances affects the nervous system and key areas of metabolism. This causes damage to the brain, heart, lungs and liver.
Cannabis	This drug affects the brain and the nervous system. Long-term use damages the brain and the reproductive system.

Table 2 The harmful effects of some drugs

Hallucinogens, such as cannabis (pot, dope, joints) and LSD cause weird and unusual sensations. Someone using these drugs may be irresponsible and act dangerously.

8.8 Hormones in plants

Which one of these cress plants has been grown with light from only one side?

Have you noticed how plants on a window ledge grow towards the light? The stems bend towards the window and the leaves and flowers turn to the Sun.

These responses of plants are called **tropisms**. Tropisms in plants occur much more slowly than responses in animals.

The responses of plant roots and shoots to light, gravity and moisture are caused by chemicals. These chemicals control cell growth and development. They are **plant hormones** which act in a similar way to hormones in animals.

Plants respond to three major stimuli – **light**, **gravity** and **moisture**.

★ **Phototropism** is the name for a plant's response to light. Plant shoots grow towards the stimulus of light and are described as **positively phototropic**. On the other hand, plant roots grow away from the light so they are **negatively phototropic**.

★ **Geotropism** is a plant's response to gravity. Plant roots grow towards the stimulus of gravity and so they are described as **positively geotropic**. On the other hand, plant shoots are **negatively geotropic** (Figure 7).

★ Plant roots also grow towards moisture. This is another example of positive tropism.

These responses to stimuli are helpful to plants. As roots grow towards gravity and moisture, they will anchor the plant firmly in the soil and take up water for photosynthesis. Shoots growing towards the light photosynthesise better and grow faster.

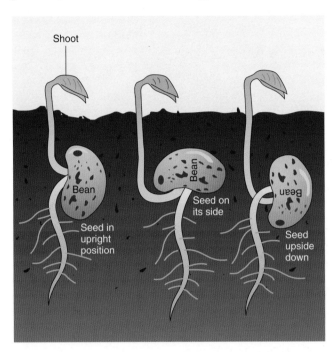

Figure 7 When a bean seed grows, the shoots are always negatively geotropic. The roots are always positively geotropic.

The growth in roots and shoots is controlled by plant hormones called **auxins**. Auxins and other plant hormones are now produced commercially and used by gardeners and horticulturists.

★ Hormone rooting powders are chemicals which promote the growth of roots in plant cuttings.

★ Selective weedkillers are synthetic growth substances. They make broad-leaved weeds like dandelions and daisies grow very fast. The plant grows too fast for its supply of water and nutrients and then dies.

★ Growth substances are sprayed on unpollinated flowers to make them produce fruits without seeds. This is how seedless grapes and oranges are produced.

These two cuttings were taken at the same time from the same plant. The cutting on the left has been treated with hormone rooting powder. The one on the right was untreated.

15 What is a *tropism*?

16 Name the **three** major stimuli that plants respond to.

17 Describe **three** ways gardeners use plant hormones.

18 Copy and complete this table. Part of it has been done already.

Part of the plant	Phototropic	Geotropic
shoot	positive	
root		

The dock plant in the photo on the right has been sprayed with selective weedkiller.
Hormones in the weedkiller speed up the plant's metabolism. The plant grows too
fast for its supply of water and nutrients and then dies.

Summary

1   **Hormones** in our bodies are produced by **glands**. They are released into the bloodstream as **chemical messengers**. They control our growth, our sexual characteristics and how our digested food is used.

2   The level of glucose in our blood must be kept steady. This is done by the hormone, **insulin**. When the glucose concentration in the blood is too high, more insulin is released into the blood. This causes the liver to store glucose as glycogen. When the glucose levels are too low, the release of insulin stops. This is an example of **feedback control**.

3   Some people are unable to control glucose amounts in their blood. They are called **diabetics**. They need to eat regular meals with no sugary foods. Some diabetics have to inject insulin before a meal.

4   Our body temperature should stay close to 37°C. To do this we may need to gain heat or to lose heat. There are four ways in which our skin tries to keep our body temperature constant.

   ★ **Blood capillaries** in the skin dilate (expand) when we're hot. This cools us down as we lose more heat. When we are cold, the skin capillaries contract to cut down the loss of heat.

   ★ **Shivering** makes heat because muscle cells respire more.

   ★ **Sweating** causes cooling. As sweat evaporates, heat is taken away from the skin.

   ★ In cold weather, **hairs** on the skin stand up when muscles at their roots contract. These hairs trap air to keep the body warm.

   Keeping our temperature and other body conditions in a steady state is called **homeostasis**.

Summary

5 After our cells have used nutrients in the blood, waste and unwanted materials have to be removed. This is done by our kidneys which filter out:

- ★ urea – waste from protein
- ★ salts
- ★ water

} to form urine

The urine passes down the **ureters** and collects in the **bladder**. Urine is excreted through the **urethra**.

6 There are four types of drugs which affect our central nervous system:

- ★ sedatives – slow us down
- ★ stimulants – speed us up
- ★ painkillers
- ★ hallucinogens – cause weird and unusual sensations.

7 Plants also have hormones. They control the way in which:

- ★ plant shoots lean towards the light – **phototropism**
- ★ plant roots grow down because of gravity – **geotropism**.

Plant growth hormones are called **auxins**.

Exam questions for Chapter 8

1 The diagram shows the human skin.

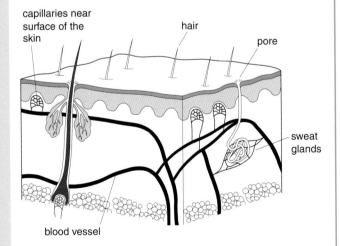

capillaries near surface of the skin

hair

pore

sweat glands

blood vessel

a) (i) In hot weather the diameters of the capillaries in the skin change. Explain how this change keeps us cool. *(3)*

(ii) Give **one** other way that the skin can keep us cool. *(1)*

b) Give **one** other function of the skin. *(1)*

[AQA (SEG) 1999]

2 The table shows four ways in which water leaves the body, and the amounts lost on a cool day.

| | Water loss (cm³) | |
	Cool day	Hot day
Breath	400	the same
Skin	500	
Urine	1500	
Faeces	150	

a) (i) Copy the table. Fill in your table to show whether on a hot day the amount of water lost would be

less   more   the same

The first answer has been done for you. *(3)*

(ii) Name the process by which we lose water from the skin. *(1)*

b) On a cool day the body gained 2550 cm³ of water. 1500 cm³ came directly from drinking. Give **two** other ways in which the body may gain water. *(2)*   **[AQA (NEAB) 1999]**

3 The diagram below shows part of the human urinary system.

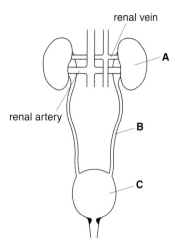

renal vein

A

renal artery

B

C

a) Name the parts **A**, **B** and **C**. *(3)*

b) Blood leaving a kidney contains less urea than blood entering it.

   The kidney has taken urea out of the blood. Describe what happens to this urea. *(3)*

c) Give **two** ways in which a person can be treated if the kidneys stop working. *(2)*

[Edexcel 1998]

4 Some drugs are listed below.

   barbiturate   alcohol   amphetamine   aspirin
   caffeine   heroin   LSD   penicillin

Copy the table below. Write the name of **each** drug, in the correct column, in your table. Each drug should be used **once** only. One has been done for you. *(7)*

Type of drug	Example
Antibiotic (kills bacteria or prevents their reproduction)	
Painkiller (stops some nerve impulses)	
Depressant (slows down nerve impulses)	barbiturate
Stimulant (speeds up nerve impulses)	
Hallucinogen (person sees things which are not really there)	

[Edexcel 1998]

5 This question is about how body reactions are affected by alcohol.

Mr Jones took part in a survey. His reaction time was measured using an electronic timer. Mr Jones drank an alcoholic drink, then waited for ten minutes. His reaction time was measured again. This was repeated five times.

a) (i) Mr Jones waited ten minutes after his drink. Explain why he was asked to wait. *(2)*

The table show the number of drinks Mr Jones drank and his reaction times.

Number of drinks	Reaction times in seconds
0	0.2
1	0.3
2	0.5
3	0.8
4	1.4
5	1.9
6	2.6

(ii) Copy the graph below and plot all the points on your graph. The first two points have been done for you. *(2)*

(iii) Finish the graph by drawing the best curve. *(1)*

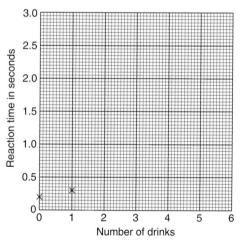

(iv) What is the link between the amount of alcohol and Mr Jones's reaction time? *(2)*

b) If Mr Jones drinks too much alcohol it can damage his brain. Alcohol damages other organs of the body. Write down the name of **one** of them. *(1)*

[OCR 1999]

CHAPTER

9

Chains and cycles

9.1	Ecosystems	9.4	Microbes and decomposers
9.2	Food chains	9.5	The carbon cycle
9.3	Food webs		

9.1 Ecosystems

Look at a field, or a garden or even a single rose bush. Notice that organisms live together in groups and not by themselves. Usually, there are several rabbits in a field, two or three blackbirds in a garden and hundreds of greenfly on a rose bush.

Groups of organisms of the same species which live together are called **populations**.

Usually there are populations of lots of different animals and plants in one area. Just think of the different populations in a wood – oak trees, bluebells, brambles, squirrels, etc.

Different populations which live together are called a **community**. The place where a community lives is called its **habitat** (Figure 1).

The animals and plants which live together in one community will be different to those in another community. So, the community in a pond will be very different to a forest community.

A habitat plus its community is called an **ecosystem**. The study of ecosystems is known as **ecology**.

For example:

ecosystem = habitat + community
(pond)   (water, mud,   (tadpoles, frogs,
             stones)   beetles, pondweed)

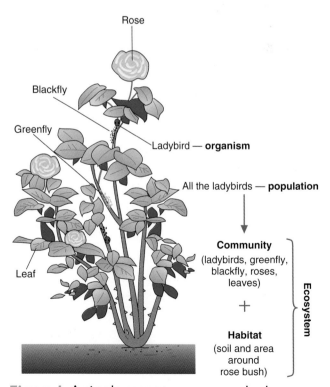

Figure 1 A simple ecosystem on a rose bush

The simple ecosystem on a rose bush is shown in Figure 1 (on the previous page).

Some animals link one ecosystem to another. For example, the ladybirds, greenfly and blackfly in the ecosystem shown in Figure 1 might well fly to other nearby ecosystems. On a much larger scale, ecosystems in different continents can be linked by migrating birds, fish and other animals.

This swallow links ecosystems in Europe and Africa

9.2   Food chains

All living things need food. Food gives them energy and the chemicals they need to grow.

In any ecosystem, the animals and plants will interact with each other. One way in which they do this is through feeding.

Plants are the only organisms which can make (produce) their own food. Because of this, plants are called **producers**.

Animals and micro-organisms must feed on other living things in order to live. They must eat (consume) other animals or plants. They are called **consumers**. So, all animals are consumers because they rely on plants and other animals for food.

Figure 2 shows how grass provides food for rabbits and then foxes feed on rabbits.

Flow diagrams of producers to consumers such as: grass → rabbit → fox are called **food chains**.

Food chains show which organisms feed on other organisms.

This rabbit was eating grass before it was taken by the fox

Three more food chains are shown in Table 1.

Producer	First consumer	Second consumer	Third consumer
grass	snail	thrush	cat
rose bush	greenfly	ladybird	
seaweed	crab	seagull	

Table 1 Examples of food chains

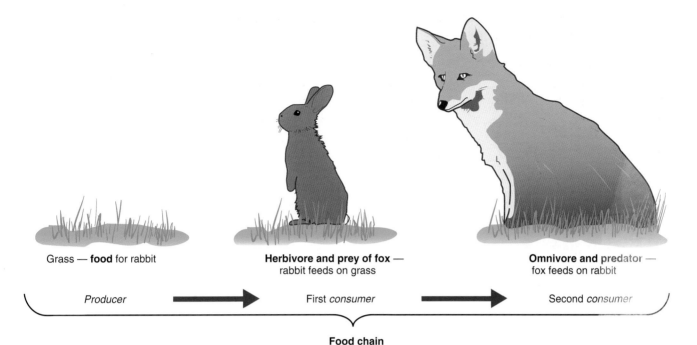

Grass — **food** for rabbit

Herbivore and prey of fox —
rabbit feeds on grass

Omnivore and predator —
fox feeds on rabbit

Producer → First *consumer* → Second *consumer*

Food chain

Figure 2 Producers and consumers in a food chain

In any food chain:

★ energy in the food is transferred along the chain from one organism to the next

★ the producers are always plants

★ the first consumers are often **herbivores** – animals that eat only plants

This lion is a predator. It's prey is the zebra.

★ the second consumers are either **carnivores** – animals that feed only on other animals, or **omnivores** – animals that eat both plants and animals.

Animals, such as foxes, which kill and eat other animals are called **predators**. The animals, like rabbits, which they kill and eat are their **prey**.

9.3 Food webs

Most animals eat more than one kind of food. So, feeding patterns are not usually as simple as those in Figure 2 and Table 1. For example, thrushes will eat greenfly and ladybirds as well as snails. Crabs will consume snails as well as seaweed.

This means that living things can be in more than one food chain. Often there are links between the food chains.

Food chains which are interlinked are known as **food webs**.

A food web for a garden community is shown in Figure 3, over the page.

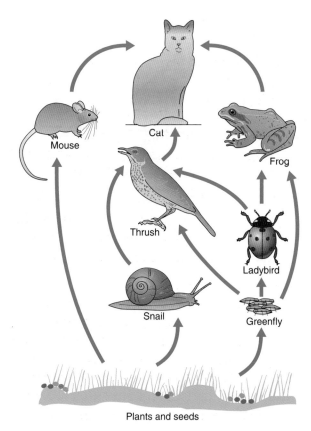

Figure 3 A food web for a garden community

As energy is transferred along a food chain, most of it is lost to the environment as heat. Plants and animals must respire to stay alive. Respiration converts the chemical energy in food to other forms of energy including heat. Most of the heat is lost to the environment. So, there is less to pass on to the next consumers. At each step, large amounts of energy are lost and this limits the number of steps in a food chain.

Pyramids of numbers

When biologists study food chains, they sometimes show the number of organisms at each step. These results are shown in diagrams called **pyramids of numbers**. Figure 4 shows a pyramid of numbers for one food chain. It takes 100 000 leaves to feed 1000 insects. These insects feed ten blackbirds which are prey to one cat. Each level of pyramid is represented by a separate section. The size of each section represents the number of organisms at that level.

As you pass along a food chain, the number of organisms usually gets less. This gives a pyramid like that in Figure 4. Millions of plants provide food for fewer (perhaps thousands) of first consumers. These provide food for fewer second consumers and so on.

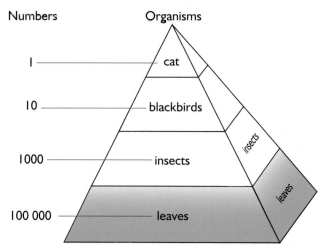

Figure 4 A pyramid of numbers for a food chain in a small garden

Pyramids of biomass

Pyramids of numbers only tell you the *number* of organisms in a food chain. They do not tell you *how much* food is eaten at each stage. We can work out how much food is being eaten at each stage if we know the total mass of each organism. This is called **biomass**.

Table 2 shows how we can calculate the biomasses of organisms in the following food chain:

leaves → greenfly → ladybirds.

Number		Mass of one organism in grams	Biomass in grams
leaves	1000	1	1000
greenfly	500	0.01	5
ladybirds	10	0.1	1

Table 2 The calculation of biomass of organisms in a food chain

Using the biomasses in Table 2, we can draw a **pyramid of biomass** (Figure 5). Pyramids of biomass are usually very neat with the biomass decreasing from one level to the next. This decrease in biomass shows that only a fraction of the total food, and therefore the total energy, passes from one stage to the next.

Loss of energy along the food chain occurs because:

★ Organisms respire and use up food (energy). The energy is needed to keep them warm and help them to move. Warm blooded animals and birds also lose heat to their surroundings.

★ Energy and materials are lost in an organism's waste products. Animals breathe out carbon dioxide as a warm gas. Heat is also lost from the body when urine or faeces pass out.

Organism	Biomass of organism in grams	Pyramid of biomass
ladybirds	1	
greenfly	5	ladybirds 1g / greenfly / 5g / leaves / 1000g
leaves	1000	

Figure 5 A pyramid of biomass for leaves, greenfly and ladybirds in a food chain

1 How is a food web different from a food chain?

2 Look at the food web in Figure 3. The gardener put out snail pellets which killed all the snails. What will happens to the thrushes in the garden?

3 Why is it rare for food chains to be longer than four consumers?

9.4 Microbes and decomposers

Living things take materials from the environment in order to live and grow. For example, plants take carbon dioxide and oxygen from the air. They also take water and minerals containing nitrogen from the soil. Animals take in oxygen, water and food. These materials are then used to build up (synthesise) carbohydrates and proteins.

As plants and animals respire and grow, they make waste. The waste materials include carbon dioxide, water and urea.

Water, carbon dioxide and nitrogen are also returned to the environment when animals and plants die and decay (**decompose**). Dead animals and plants decay because they are broken down by **decomposers**. Fungi, microbes like bacteria, small invertebrates like earthworms and large scavengers like crows are important decomposers.

Decomposers feed on dead plants and animals producing carbon dioxide, water and nitrogen.

Microbes are making this fruit go rotten

Microbes are tiny living things like bacteria. They can only be seen with a microscope. There are millions and millions of them in the air, in the soil and everywhere.

If the conditions are right, microbes grow, divide and multiply rapidly. Microbes rot things faster if it is:

★ warm – microbes grow best at 37°C

★ damp – microbes need water

★ airy – most microbes need oxygen.

Microbes are very active in sewage works. Here they decompose human waste to water, carbon dioxide, methane and sludge. The sludge can be used as a fertiliser

Microbes also play an important role in breaking down dead plants in a compost heap. The decay processes produce water, carbon dioxide, nitrogen and rich compost. Plants grow much better in soil that has been enriched with compost.

Elements such as carbon, hydrogen, oxygen and nitrogen are recycled by living things.

Materials containing these elements are taken in by living things and then returned to the environment when they die and decay. The materials can be used over and over again.

Decomposers and decay are crucial in the recycling of elements. In an ecosystem, the processes which take materials from the environment are balanced by decay processes which return materials to the environment.

Without decomposers, recycling would be impossible. The Earth would be littered with dead plants and animals. Fungi are important decomposers. Look at this huge fungus growing on a dead tree.

Carrion crows play their part as decomposers by eating dead animals

Decomposers on faeces. These flies are busy eating (decomposing) and recycling the elements in cow dung.

4 Name **three** types of decomposer.

5 Under what conditions do microbes grow best?

6 What materials are made when dead plants decay?

7 If decay did not happen, what would the Earth look like?

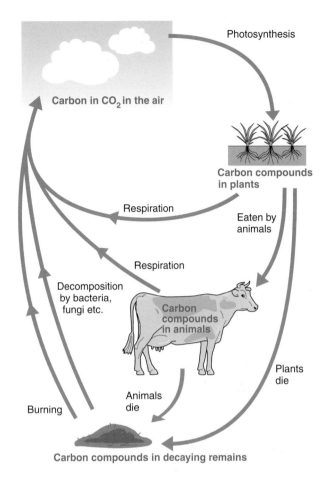

Figure 6 Important processes in the carbon cycle

9.5 The carbon cycle

As plants and animals grow and die, the elements in them are recycled. Carbon is one of these elements which is used over and over again. The processes in which carbon is recycled are called the **carbon cycle** (Figure 6).

Plants and animals need a steady supply of carbon to make important compounds like carbohydrates and proteins.

Look carefully at the key stages in Figure 6.

★ Plants make their carbon compounds by photosynthesis. The carbon comes from carbon dioxide in the air.

★ Animals get their carbon compounds by eating plants and other animals.

★ When plants and animals respire, carbon is returned to the air as carbon dioxide.

★ Carbon dioxide is also returned to the air when decaying plants and animals are decomposed by bacteria.

★ Carbon dioxide is returned to the air when decaying plants and animals are burnt.

★ When plants and animals die, their carbon compounds begin to decay. In some cases, the decaying remains get trapped underground as fossil fuels.

Grass and leaves in this compost heap are decaying. Carbon dioxide and water are two of the products. In this case, the reaction produces so much heat that water comes off as steam.

This peat bog has formed from plants that died hundreds (possibly thousands) of years ago. A similar process occurs over millions of years when fossil fuels form.

8 Name **one** process that takes carbon dioxide out of the air.

9 Name **three** processes which put carbon dioxide into the air.

10 How were fossil fuels, such as coal, oil and peat, formed?

11 What is happening to the level of carbon dioxide in the atmosphere? What effect does this change cause?

Summary

1 ★ Imagine a group of rabbits living together in a warren on a hillside. This is a **population** of rabbits.

★ These rabbits live alongside worms, insects and grasses. This is a **community** made up of several populations.

★ The hillside is called the **habitat** for this community.

★ The community of plants and animals living on the hillside is called an **ecosystem**.

2 ★ Plants can make their own food. They are called **producers**.

★ Animals consume (eat) plants and other animals. They are called **consumers**.

★ A **food chain** always starts with a producer. For example, grass (a producer) is eaten by rabbits (consumers). A fox (second consumer) may eat the rabbits.

3 Usually, living things are part of more than one simple food chain. These linked food chains are called **food webs**.

Summary

4 ★ We can look at food chains as **pyramids of numbers**. For example, thousands of blades of grass are eaten by lots of rabbits. But only one fox may feed on the rabbits.

★ A **pyramid of biomass** shows the total mass of plants and animals at each stage.

★ Large amounts of energy are wasted at each step in a food chain. This is why food chains are usually short.

5 Recycling happens naturally in the environment. Waste products, dead plants and dead animals are broken down by **decomposers**. For example, leaves die in the autumn. They fall and become leaf mould because of the action of microbes. This leaf mould enriches the soil for other trees and plants.

6 The **carbon cycle** is an example of recycling. Carbon dioxide in the air is taken in by plants during photosynthesis to make food. Plants are eaten by animals. These animals excrete waste products. The plants and animals die and decay under the action of decomposers. One of the main products from the action of decomposers is carbon dioxide. Animals also respire and breathe out carbon dioxide. The cycle starts all over again using this carbon dioxide.

Exam questions for Chapter 9

1 The diagram below shows a woodland food web.

a) Using the information below:

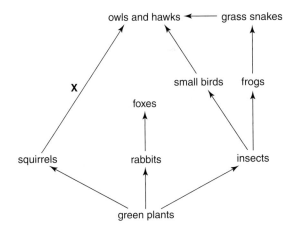

(i) Name a herbivore. *(1)*

(ii) Name a carnivore. *(1)*

(iii) What is the source of energy for **all** the living organisms in the food web? *(1)*

(iv) Name **two** effects on the food web if all the frogs were killed. *(2)*

(v) Explain fully what the arrow at **X** means. *(1)*

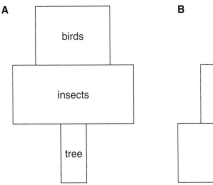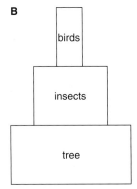

b) Which of the diagrams given above represents:

(i) a pyramid of numbers;

(ii) a pyramid of biomass? *(2)*

[WJEC 1998]

2 The diagram shows some of the stages by which materials are cycled in living organisms.

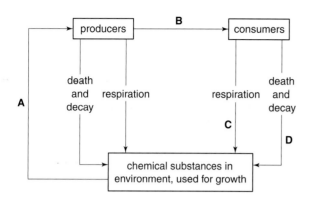

a) In which of the stages, **A**, **B**, **C** or **D**:

   (i) are substances broken down by microbes;

   (ii) is carbon dioxide made into sugar;

   (iii) are plants eaten by animals? *(3)*

b) In an experiment, samples of soil were put into four beakers. A dead leaf was put onto the soil in each beaker. The soil was kept in the conditions shown.

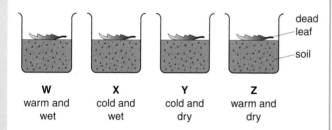

In which beaker, **W**, **X**, **Y** or **Z**, would the dead leaf decay quickest? *(1)*

[AQA (NEAB) 1999]

3 Several animals live in a National Park. The table shows what they eat.

Animal	Food
bighorn sheep	green plants
elk	green plants
marmots (small mammals)	green plants
mountain lions	bighorn sheep, elk, snowshoe hares
snowshoe hares	green plants
wolves	elk, marmots, mountain lions

a) Which organism in the table is a producer? *(1)*

b) Copy the food web and complete it for the animals listed in the table. *(4)*

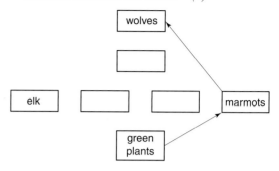

c) Many tiny fleas live in the fur of the wolf.

Draw a pyramid of numbers for this food chain:

green plants → marmots → wolves → fleas *(2)*

[AQA (NEAB) 1999]

4 a) Copy the boxes with gaps. Use the words in the box to fill in the gaps labelled **A**, **B**, **C** and **D** in the diagram. You may use each word once or not at all.

carbon	burning	decay	eaten
nitrogen	oxygen	pollution	respiration

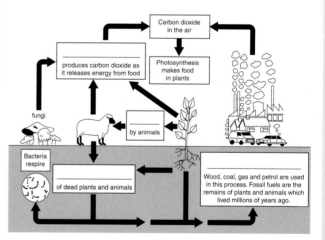

(4)

b) (i) Why are fungi called decomposers? *(1)*

   (ii) Give **one** other type of decomposer. *(1)*

c) Explain how cars and factories can cause acid rain. *(4)*

[AQA (SEG) 1999]

Reproduction and genetics

10.1 Human reproduction

Human beings make babies by 'having sex'. The correct term for this is **sexual intercourse**. When sexual intercourse leads to a new baby, the process is called **reproduction**.

During sexual intercourse, a man's penis becomes stiff. This is because it contains special erectile tissue. Thousands of capillaries in the tissue fill with blood and make the penis hard. If sexual intercourse continues, the man's penis is inserted into the woman's vagina. Semen containing sperms may spurt out of the penis.

Fertilisation

For fertilisation to happen, a **sperm cell** from the male joins (fuses) with an **egg cell** from the female. This usually happens in the **oviduct** (egg tube).

At monthly intervals, an egg is released from one of a woman's ovaries. If the woman has sexual intercourse when an egg is in the oviduct, sperms may reach it and one sperm may fertilise it (Figure 1).

If one of the sperms gets through the membrane of the egg, its nucleus will fuse with the nucleus of the egg cell.

This fusing of the nucleus of the sperm and the nucleus of the egg cell is called **fertilisation**.

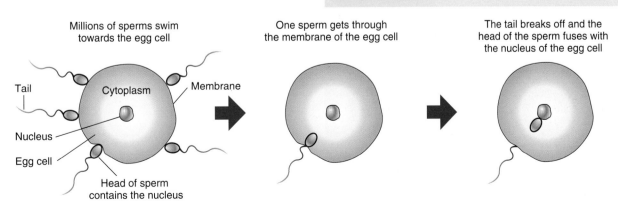

Figure 1 Fertilisation of an egg by a sperm

Notice in Figure 1 that sperm cells are much smaller than egg cells. Sperm cells have a 'tail' which allows them to move in search of an egg cell.

If fertilisation occurs, the fertilised egg is called a **zygote**.

Once a sperm gets through the membrane of the egg cell, changes in the membrane prevent other sperms getting in.

The zygote grows by dividing into two cells, then into four cells and so on.

In time, a ball of cells is formed. This is called an **embryo**.

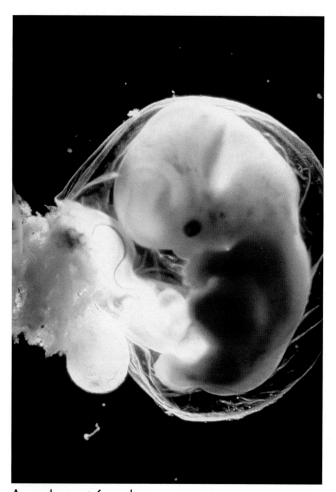

An embryo at 6 weeks

Sometimes, an embryo forms two groups of cells at an early stage. Each group of cells then develops separately producing two babies. These babies have developed from the same zygote. They have the same genes (section 10.2) and are called **identical twins**.

Sometimes, two eggs are released at the same time and both of these may be fertilised by sperms. In this case, the embryos develop from different eggs and different sperms. The babies have different genes and they are called **non-identical twins**.

10.2   Chromosomes and genes

The largest part of a cell is usually its nucleus. The nucleus contains important structures called **chromosomes**.

Chromosomes carry the information which allows your cells to divide and makes your body work. Chromosomes carry information about all your features – your height, your hair colour, etc.

Chromosomes also store the information which passes from parents to offspring during fertilisation.

When a cell is studied through a microscope, the chromosomes look like fine threads. The chromosome threads have different lengths and different thicknesses. All organisms have a fixed number of chromosomes in the nuclei of their cells. This is called the **chromosome number**. Different organisms have a different chromosome number. For example, human cells have 46 chromosomes, hen cells have 36 and pea cells have 14.

These chromosomes can be arranged in pairs which look alike. The members of each pair control the same characteristics in an organism. They are called **homologous pairs**.

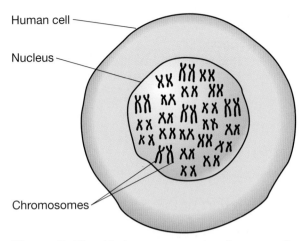

Figure 2 The 46 chromosomes in a human cell are made up from 23 homologous pairs.

So, humans have 23 homologous pairs. That means 46 chromosomes altogether (Figure 2). In each of these homologous pairs, one chromosome comes from the father and the other from the mother.

The structure of chromosomes

Chromosomes are made of a complex polymer called **DNA**. The long DNA molecules can be divided into sections called **genes** (Figure 3). Chromosomes and genes can be copied by cells and passed on to the next generation. This explains why parent animals and plants can pass on features to their offspring.

These twins are identical. They have grown from the same fertilised egg. So, they have the same chromosomes, the same genes and the same features.

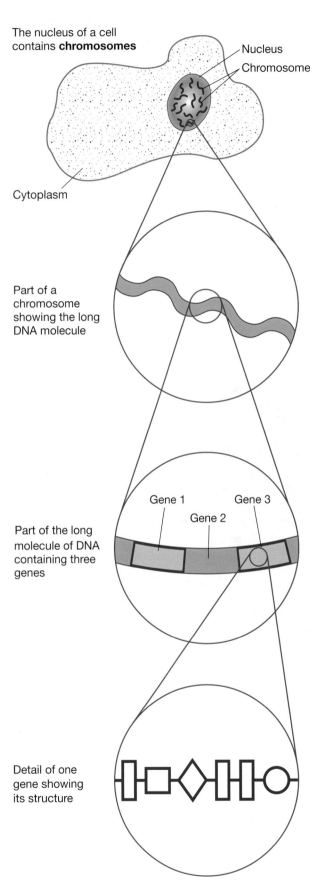

Figure 3 A cell showing the nucleus, chromosomes, DNA and genes

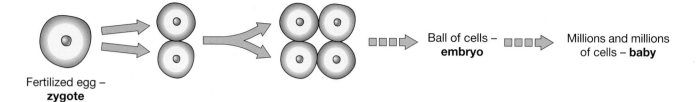

Fertilized egg –
zygote

Ball of cells –
embryo

Millions and millions
of cells – **baby**

Figure 4 Simple cell division

Simple cell division

As soon as an egg is fertilised, it begins to grow and then split into two cells. Each of these cells has a full set of chromosomes. The two cells then split to form four cells, then eight cells and so on. Each time the cells divide, every cell gets a full set of chromosomes. As the embryo gets larger, groups of cells specialise to form different organs. Eventually, a baby is formed containing millions and millions of cells (Figure 4).

All the cells in your body (except sperms or eggs) contain 46 chromosomes. Scientists can treat the chromosomes and produce a picture like this photo. The picture is different from one person to another. These DNA pictures are called 'genetic fingerprints'. They can be used to identify criminals.

1 In which part of the cell are chromosomes found?

2 How many chromosomes do human brain cells have?

3 What are chromosomes made of?

4 What is a *gene*?

5 What can genetic fingerprints be used for?

10.3 Genetic engineering

During the last twenty years, scientists have discovered ways in which they can isolate a gene from one particular organism and then insert it into the DNA of another organism. This technique is called **genetic engineering**.

Genetic engineering involves extracting the DNA from one particular species and breaking it into smaller fragments using enzymes. Selected fragments are then isolated and attached to the DNA of a 'carrier'. The carrier organisms are usually bacteria. By culturing ('growing') these carrier bacteria on a large scale, commercial quantities of proteins and other chemicals associated with the inserted fragment of DNA are produced.

Figure 5 shows how human insulin for diabetics can be produced by genetic engineering.

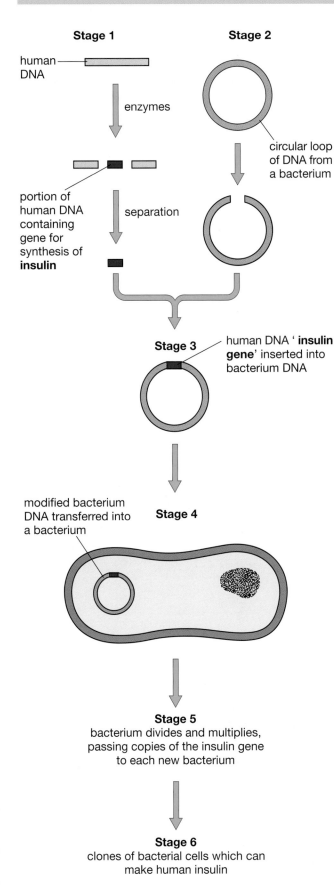

Stage 1

human DNA

enzymes

portion of human DNA containing gene for synthesis of **insulin**

separation

Stage 2

circular loop of DNA from a bacterium

Stage 3 — human DNA '**insulin gene**' inserted into bacterium DNA

modified bacterium DNA transferred into a bacterium

Stage 4

Stage 5
bacterium divides and multiplies, passing copies of the insulin gene to each new bacterium

Stage 6
clones of bacterial cells which can make human insulin

Figure 5 Producing human insulin by genetic engineering

Genetic engineering could bring many benefits:

★ Bacteria containing human genes can produce chemicals like insulin and growth hormones to treat human diseases.

★ Genes can be transferred between plants and bacteria to improve crops and food production. This might involve the development of plants which are resistant to disease, which grow faster or which produce larger fruits.

The human genome project

Early in 2000, scientists in Britain and the USA finally identified the position of every gene on the 46 human chromosomes. This was called the **human genome project**.

In the future, this information could be used to:

★ enable cures to be found for certain diseases

★ allow scientists and doctors to predict which children are at risk of inheriting certain diseases from their parents

★ lead to the replacement of 'faulty' genes with normal genes.

Some of the scientists and their companies working on the human genome project have patented the genes they have discovered. They hope to recover some of their costs by charging those who benefit from their discoveries. These developments and the ethics of tampering with human genes are very controversial.

10.4 Sexual and asexual reproduction

Living things can reproduce in two different ways – by sexual reproduction or by asexual reproduction.

Sexual reproduction

Reproduction in most animals, including humans, is sexual. It involves sexual intercourse or mating of a male and a female. Some plants also reproduce sexually.

Sexual reproduction is similar for all organisms. It involves the formation of sex cells, called **gametes** followed by **fertilisation**.

Female gametes are the **egg cells** produced in the **ovary** of the female animal or plant. **Male gametes** are either **sperms** in animals or **pollen** in plants.

Sperm carry genetic information from the father. Egg cells carry genetic information from the mother. So, sexual reproduction results in offspring with genetic information from *two parents*. Sexual reproduction therefore results in a mixing of genetic information (**genetic variation**).

Asexual reproduction

Most plants can reproduce asexually. This means that male and female gametes are not necessary. Part of the plant is separated and then grows and develops on its own. Plants which reproduce asexually usually do so by forming bulbs, tubers or runners.

Unlike sexual reproduction, asexual reproduction requires only *one parent*. The new plant forms cells with the same genetic information as the parent plant.

The runners on this strawberry plant will root and start new plants with the same genes as the parent plant. These new plants are clones of the parent plant.

Asexual reproduction produces identical offspring called **clones**.

Look at Figure 6 which compares sexual and asexual reproduction.

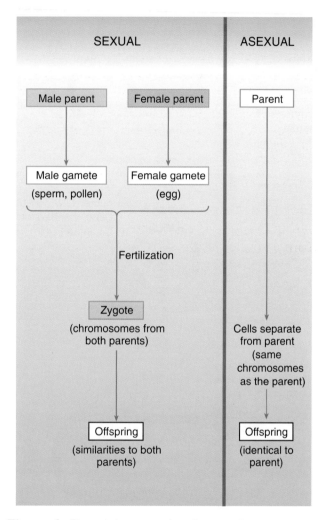

Figure 6 Comparing sexual and asexual reproduction

10.5 Cloning

All the clones from one plant have identical chromosomes. So, they have the same genes and look very similar. There are various methods of producing clones. Four of these are described below. The first example occurs naturally. The second and third methods are used by gardeners. The fourth method has been developed in recent years.

1 Binary fission

This method occurs in simple, single-cell organisms such as amoeba and bacteria. In this case, the 'parent' amoeba or bacterium divides to produce two identical 'daughter' cells. These daughter cells will also divide.

2 Cuttings

A short stem with a few leaves can be cut from a parent plant such as a geranium. The gardener may use hormone rooting powder to encourage root growth. The cutting is planted in damp soil and a cloned geranium plant will grow.

3 Tissue culture

Look at Figure 7. Using tissue culture, large numbers of identical plants can be grown from a single parent in a relatively short time. This is sometimes called **micro-propagation**. Micro-propagation is used by commercial growers.

Seedlings of Douglas Fir trees produced by micro-propagation.

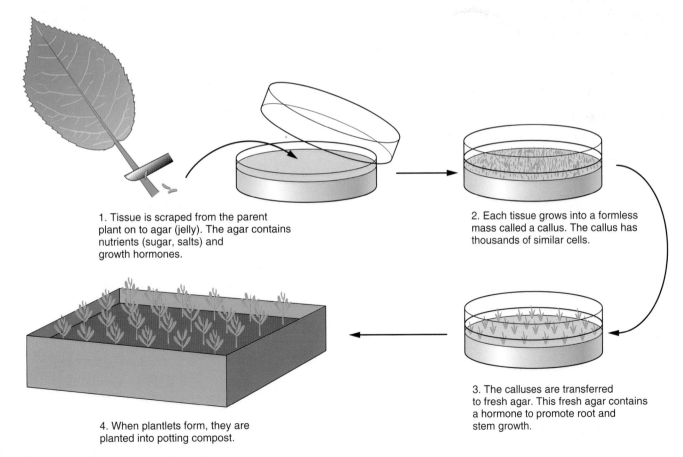

1. Tissue is scraped from the parent plant on to agar (jelly). The agar contains nutrients (sugar, salts) and growth hormones.

2. Each tissue grows into a formless mass called a callus. The callus has thousands of similar cells.

3. The calluses are transferred to fresh agar. This fresh agar contains a hormone to promote root and stem growth.

4. When plantlets form, they are planted into potting compost.

Figure 7 Using tissue culture for micro-propagation

4 Embryo Transplants

Identical copies of animals like Dolly the sheep, can be produced by splitting apart the cells of an embryo before they become specialised. These embryonic cells are then implanted into the uterus of a host mother, where they develop.

Dolly, the sheep, was the first clone to develop into an adult animal. This photo was taken in February 1997 when Dolly was 7 months old.

6   Name a male gamete.

7   Name a female gamete.

8   Copy and complete the following.

Sperm cells carry genetic information from the _____ . _____ cells carry genes from the mother. Babies have genes from both their _____ and their _____ . This mixing of genetic information is called _____ .

9   What is a *clone*?

10 Name **two** ways a gardener can make clones.

Summary

1   A human baby is born nine months after its mother and father have had sex and the mother's **egg cell** has been fertilised by a **sperm** from the father. This is called **sexual reproduction**.

2   When an egg is **fertilised** by a sperm, it is called a **zygote**. The zygote divides into two cells, then into four cells, then eight and so on. The cells begin to specialise to make organs and limbs. This is called an **embryo**. The embryo will grow and will become a baby girl or a baby boy.

3   The nucleus of every cell in your body contains long, threadlike structures called **chromosomes**.

   ★   Chromosomes carry information to allow our cells to divide and work properly.

   ★   Chromosomes store information which passes from parents to their offspring.

   ★   Chromosomes are arranged in pairs called **homologous pairs**. One chromosome of the pair comes from the mother and the other from the father.

   ★   Chromosomes are made of long molecules of DNA which contain **genes**.

4   Most plants and a few simple animals are able to reproduce **asexually**. This means that new organisms are made without the mating of a male and female. For example, when one daffodil bulb is planted, it makes side bulbs which produce flowers in the spring. These new daffodils are exactly the same as the first daffodil and have the same chromosomes. They are called **clones**.

1   The diagram shows the urinary and reproductive organs of a woman.

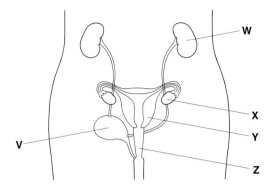

a) Use words from the list to label the organs **V**, **W**, **X**, **Y** and **Z** on the diagram.

> bladder   kidney   ovary   vagina
> womb (uterus)   *(5)*

b) List A gives the names of five organs shown on the diagram. List B gives the jobs of these organs in a different order.

List A   List B

Bladder   where eggs are made

Kidney   where sperm is placed by the penis

Ovary   removes poisonous substances from the blood

Uterus   stores poisonous substances and surplus water

Vagina   where embryo grows before birth

Write down List A and List B. Draw a straight line from each organ in List A to its job in List B. One has been done for you. *(4)*

c) The drawing shows a sperm cell.

On a copy of the drawing, use guidelines to label

(i)   cytoplasm,

(ii)   cell membrane.   *(2)*

d) (i)   Describe how a sperm cell moves.   *(1)*

(ii)   Describe how a sperm cell carries information so that a baby is partly like its father.   *(1)*

[AQA (NEAB) 1997]

2   These young rabbits look like their parents. This is because information about characteristics such as fur colour is passed from parents to their young.

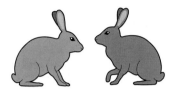

Copy the sentences below and choose words from this list to complete your sentences.

> body   genes   chromosomes   nucleus   clones
> sex   cytoplasm

Information is passed from parents to their young in _____ cells.

Each characteristic, e.g. fur colour, is controlled by _____ .

The structures which carry information for a large number of characteristics are called _____ .

The part of the cell which contains these structures is called the _____ .   *(4)*

[AQA (NEAB) 1999]

3   A market gardener produces large numbers of attractive, large flowered geranium plants.

a) Give **two** advantages to the gardener of producing geraniums from cuttings rather than from seeds.   *(2)*

b) Gardeners often cover trays of cuttings with large polythene bags.

Suggest **one** advantage of this.   *(1)*

[AQA (NEAB) 1998]

4   A bacterium reproduces asexually by dividing into two.

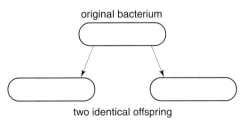

Why are the two offspring identical to the original bacterium?   *(2)*

[Edexcel 1998]

Genetics and evolution

11.1 Passing on genes

Our **genes** control how we grow and what we look like. Each gene controls a single characteristic. There are thousands of genes on each **chromosome**. There are 46 chromosomes in the nucleus of each of our cells. The chromosomes in our parents are passed to their sons or daughters when a sperm fuses with an egg to form a zygote. All genes occur in pairs, one from each parent. These pairs of genes are called alleles.

Figure 1 shows what happens to the chromosomes when eggs and sperms are produced. Each egg and each sperm is a single cell. **Egg cells** are made in the **ovaries** and **sperm cells** are made in the **testicles**. They are called **sex cells** or **gametes**.

Sex cells are very different from ordinary body cells. They have half the number of chromosomes in a body cell.

A nucleus in a cell like a nerve cell will have 46 chromosomes. These 46 chromosomes can be sorted into 23 pairs. A sex cell has only 23 single chromosomes.

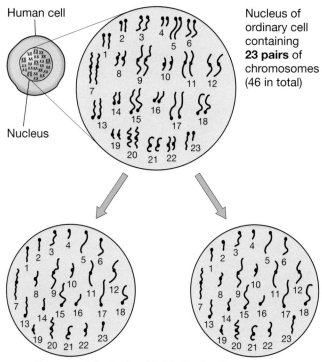

Human cell

Nucleus

Nucleus of ordinary cell containing **23 pairs** of chromosomes (46 in total)

Two sex cells each with **23 single** chromosomes

Figure 1 Paired chromosomes separate when eggs and sperms are produced.

When a sperm fuses with an egg, 23 chromosomes in the sperm cell join the 23 chromosomes in the egg cell. This produces a fertilised egg with 46 chromosomes. The zygote has a full set of chromosomes so it can develop and grow into a baby.

1 Where are egg cells made?

2 What sex cells are made in the testicles?

3 How many pairs of chromosomes are there in an ordinary human cell?

4 What is a *zygote*?

5 Copy and complete the following.

Children inherit _____ their chromosomes from their mother and half from their _____ . Each child is a unique mix of g _____ , showing some characterisitics from each p _____ .

11.2 Genetics and sex

Genetics is the branch of science which studies genes.

When a baby is born, we all want to know whether the baby is a boy or a girl. What decides the sex of a baby? The answer lies in its genes and chromosomes.

One of the pairs of chromosomes determines our sex. These are called the **sex chromosomes**.

Unlike the other pairs, the sex chromosomes are not always identical. There are two types of sex chromosomes.

1 A long one called the **X chromosome** – this contains the usual number of genes.

2 A short one called the **Y chromosome** – this contains only a few genes.

All females have two X chromosomes, written as XX.

All males have one X and one Y chromosome, written as XY.

Figure 2 shows what happens to the sex chromosomes when eggs and sperms are produced and when the eggs and sperms fuse to produce a fertilised egg.

All the eggs from the mother contain one X chromosome. But half the sperms from the father have one X chromosome and the other half have one Y chromosome.

So, there is an equal chance that an egg will be fertilised by an X sperm or by a Y sperm.

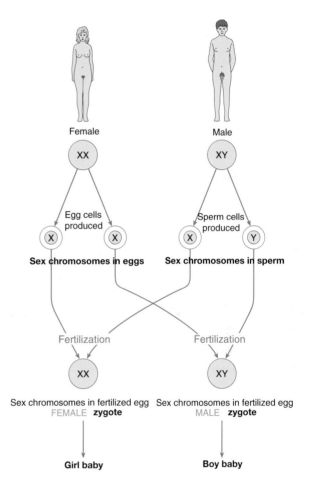

Figure 2 Sex chromosomes decide if a baby is a boy or a girl.

If an X sperm fertilises an egg, the zygote will contain two X chromosomes, XX. This zygote will develop into a girl. If a Y sperm fertilises an egg, the zygote will contain an X and a Y chromosome, XY. This zygote will develop into a boy.

XX pairs of chromosomes are just as likely as XY pairs. So, there are about equal numbers of boys and girls.

Notice in Figure 2 how a baby's sex depends on the father. If the baby gets an X chromosome from the father, it is a girl. If the baby gets a Y chromosome from the father, it is a boy.

The zygote copies its chromosomes and then divides into two identical cells. The cells copy and divide again and again to form an embryo. More and more divisions occur and the embryo develops into a baby. Usually, the process goes to plan, but sometimes the chromosomes are not copied exactly. Bits of chromosomes may be lost or the atoms in their structure may be different. These changes in the chromosome structure lead to changes in genes.

This formation of changed genes is called **genetic mutation**. The genes are also known as **mutant genes**.

Most mutations are harmful. Some mutations have no effect. In rare cases, a mutation can help and benefit an animal or plant.

Down's syndrome in humans is an example of genetic mutation. In this case, the zygote gets 24 chromosomes from the egg, not the usual 23. The embryo develops with 47 chromosomes rather than the normal 46. This leads to abnormal mental and physical development.

Mutations can occur naturally. In our modern world, the chance of a mutation is increasing because of powerful radiations and dangerous chemicals. For example, nicotine in tobacco smoke can cause mutations. These mutations lead to abnormal cells and cancers.

6 Copy and complete this table to show which sex chromosomes a boy and a girl have.

	Boy	Girl
Sex chromosomes		

This photo shows the inside of a patient's bronchus. The normal cells covered with cilia (hairs) have been invaded by lumpy cancer cells. These cancer cells have been caused by a mutation.

7 What fraction of the sperm carry a Y chromosome?

8 What is a genetic mutation?

9 List **two** things which can cause a mutation.

11.3 Inherited diseases

Some diseases can be passed on (inherited) from parents to their children even though the parents do not have the disease themselves.

Inherited diseases are caused by faulty genes.

Cystic fibrosis, sickle cell anaemia, haemophilia and colour blindness are all inherited.

Cystic fibrosis

This is a rare disease. It is caused by a faulty gene in one pair of chromosomes. The faulty gene causes a very, very thick and sticky mucus to be produced in the lungs. This thick mucus must be coughed up every day because it would block the air passages in the lungs. A person can only have the disease if they inherit the faulty gene from both parents. The parents are healthy because they have one normal gene and one faulty gene. The parents are **carriers** of the disease.

Sickle cell anaemia

This is another inherited disease. Sufferers have inherited faulty genes from both parents. As a result, they have fewer normal red blood cells. Some of their red blood cells are curved like a sickle. The reduced number of normal cells makes the person pale, weak and tired. We say the person is anaemic. The abnormal sickle cells block tiny capillaries and the blood does not clot as well as it should. The heart may be affected and may start to fail.

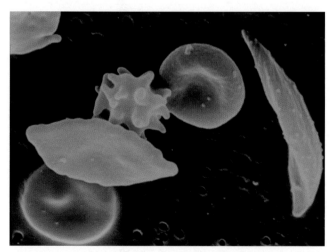

Normal red blood cells and sickle-shaped cells in the blood of a person suffering from sickle cell anaemia.

Inherited diseases linked to the sex chromosomes

Some diseases, including haemophilia and colour blindness, are much more common in males than in females.

This is because the diseases are caused by faulty genes on the X chromosome. Males with an XY chromosome pair are more likely to have these diseases than females with two X chromosomes as an XX pair. This is because the female would have to have the faulty gene on both X chromosomes to have the disease. A male only has to have it on his one X chromosome. Figure 3 (over the page) shows the possible chromosome pairs for males and females who carry the normal and faulty genes associated with these diseases.

Haemophiliacs cannot make an essential substance for blood clotting. This is very serious. Once the sufferer starts bleeding, it will not stop in the usual way. Fortunately, haemophiliacs can now be given Factor VIII . This prevents constant bruising and bleeding.

Sufferers of **colour blindness** cannot tell the difference between reds and greens. Both colours appear to them as shades of grey.

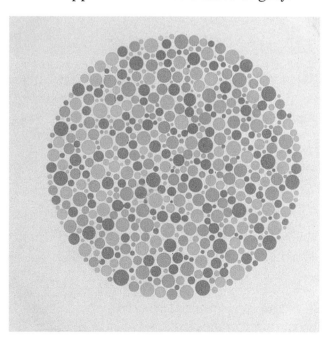

Cards like this are used to test for colour blindness. Someone suffering from red–green colour blindness would not see the number 16.

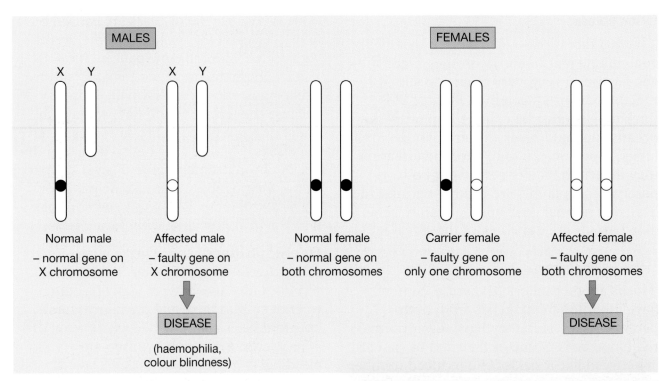

Figure 3 The possible chromosome pairs for males and females carrying the normal and faulty genes causing haemophilia and colour blindness.

11.4 Selective breeding

Farmers, animal breeders and gardeners have been using genetics for centuries. Year by year and generation by generation, they have selected particular animals and plants and controlled their breeding.

For example they have selected:

★ cows with a higher milk yield

★ sheep which give better quality wool

★ wheat which is resistant to disease

★ apples with better flavour.

Nowadays, scientists can advise growers on ways to improve yields, flavour and appearance. Selective breeding has brought large economic benefits.

This tiny Yorkshire Terrier and the massive Great Dane are in the same species. They are both dogs. Their differences have resulted from selective breeding over thousands of generations.

11.5 Variations in a species

Look at the boys and girls in your class. They have differences in their height, weight, skin colour, hair colour and hair texture. But, these boys and girls are all the same species – *Homo sapiens*.

The differences between individuals are called **variations**.

All these children were born in the same year. What variations can you see in them?

Variations in a species can arise in two ways:

★ from genetic (inherited) causes

★ from environmental causes.

Many human characteristics including birth weight, height, skin colour and hair colour are determined by the genes we inherit from our parents. However, we are certain to be different from our parents because of three processes.

1 **Formation of sex cells.** When eggs and sperms are formed, the chromosome pairs separate in a random fashion (section 11.1).

2 **Fertilisation** brings together an entirely new set of 46 chromosomes – 23 from the father and 23 from the mother (section 11.1).

3 A **mutation** is a change in the chemical structure of a gene (section 11.2).

Although many human characteristics are inherited (genetic), they can be affected by our environment. For example, your body weight is affected by your diet. Your skin colour may depend on the climate. Your hair style may change with the latest fashion.

The environment can also affect plants. Those grown with plenty of sunlight and water are very different to those grown in darkness or drought.

Two trays of pea seedlings. One was grown in the dark and the other in good light. Which is which?

11.6 Natural selection and evolution

The variation of individuals in a species means that some are taller, others are stronger and some can run faster.

These variations allow some organisms to survive longer in a harsh environment. In many places, animals and plants struggle to survive. For example:

★ they have to avoid **predators**

★ they have to stay free of **disease**

★ they are in **competition** with others for food, water and shelter

★ they have to survive the **climate**.

Some animals and plants survive better than others. They are usually the fittest. If they can run fast, they may be better at escaping their predators. If they are fitter, they are less likely to suffer from disease. They can compete more successfully for food and shelter. They can withstand harsh weather conditions. This survival of animals and plants best adapted to the conditions in their environment is described as the '**survival of the fittest**'.

The photos in Figure 4 show four examples of how animals and plants are adapted for survival.

Organisms with the characteristics which make them better suited to their environment will survive and reproduce. This means that those genes which give the most favourable characteristics will be passed on to their offspring and become more common.

A fit, strong zebra can escape from the lion.

Ospreys with better eyesight, stronger wings and sharper talons will catch more fish.

In the 1960s, thousands of rabbits died from myxomatosis. A few rabbits had genes that helped them to survive.

Alpine sunflowers grow close to the ground. They are only 10 cm tall. This helps them to survive at high altitudes in very cold weather. Ordinary sunflowers are usually about 1 metre tall.

Figure 4 Examples of the ways in which animals and plants are better adapted to survive.

Over many generations, the population slowly changes and becomes better adapted to survive in that particular habitat.

This process by which a population slowly changes over many generations to become better adapted for survival is known as **natural selection**. The process of natural selection leads to the **evolution** of a species.

In some cases, the organisms in a species cannot adapt to changing conditions. The organisms find it difficult to survive. If they all die, the species will become **extinct**.

One of the best examples of natural selection and evolution concerns the peppered moth. This moth lives in woodland areas. Most of the time, the peppered moth rests on tree trunks. During the 1840s, a dark form of the peppered moth appeared for the first time. It was the result of a mutation (Figure 5).

Figure 5 The dark and light forms of the peppered moth on the trunk of a tree

In unpolluted areas, the lighter form of the moth is well camouflaged on clean tree trunks. The darker form is easily seen and taken by predators like thrushes. In polluted areas, where tree trunks are darkened by soot, the darker mutant moth is better camouflaged. This form is now more likely to survive. In polluted areas, the darker mutant moth has evolved as the usual form of the species.

Darwin's theory of evolution

In 1831, **Charles Darwin** was a naturalist on a world-wide scientific expedition. The expedition visited Africa and America where Darwin studied animals and plants. From his observations, Darwin suggested that different species had evolved through a slow process of natural selection.

In 1859, Darwin published his theory of evolution by natural selection in a book called *The Origin of Species*.

The key ideas in Darwin's theory are shown in Figure 6 (over the page).

10 Explain what *survival of the fittest* means.

11 What does *extinct* mean?

11.7 Evidence for evolution

The first living things to inhabit the Earth were very simple organisms. Over 3000 million years, these simple creatures and plants evolved into thousands of different organisms. Some organisms adapted and evolved. Others like dinosaurs and dodos have become extinct (died out).

The best evidence for evolution comes from **fossils**. When a plant or animal dies, it may be eaten or it may decay. Decay is caused by bacteria, fungi and oxygen in the air. In some cases, dead animals and plants have not been eaten and their decay has been slowed down and almost stopped.

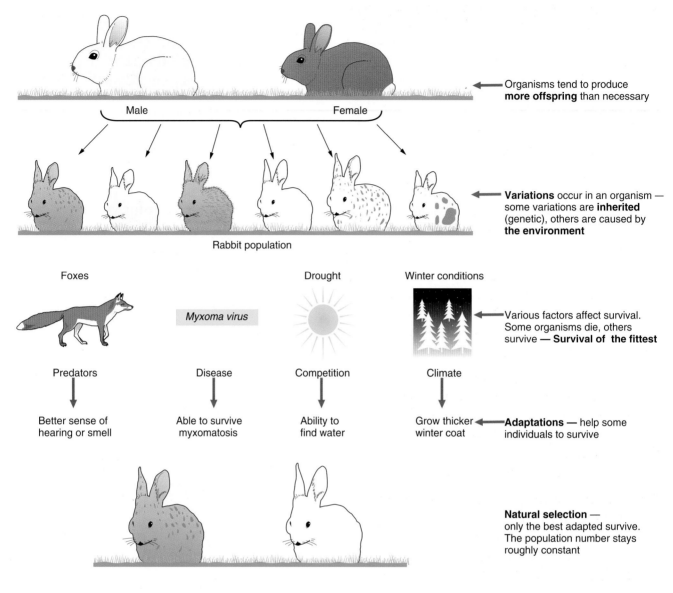

Organisms tend to produce **more offspring** than necessary

Male   Female

Variations occur in an organism — some variations are **inherited** (genetic), others are caused by **the environment**

Rabbit population

Foxes

Myxoma virus

Drought

Winter conditions

Various factors affect survival. Some organisms die, others survive — **Survival of the fittest**

Predators   Disease   Competition   Climate

Better sense of hearing or smell

Able to survive myxomatosis

Ability to find water

Grow thicker winter coat

Adaptations — help some individuals to survive

Natural selection — only the best adapted survive. The population number stays roughly constant

Figure 6 The key ideas in Darwin's theory of evolution.

In some areas, dead organisms have been covered by the sea, by sediment or by rocks. In these places, the material has decayed in the absence of oxygen. Instead of rotting away, it has been compressed leaving bones or woody tissue trapped in rocks for millions of years.

Dodos inhabited Mauritius until the end of the 17ᵗʰ century. The last dodo was killed by hunters.

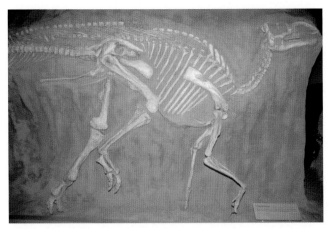

These fossilised dinosaur bones are a few million years old.

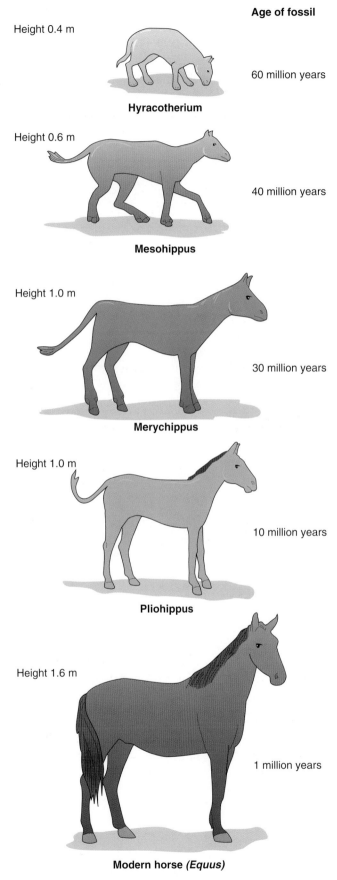

Age of fossil

Height 0.4 m

60 million years

Hyracotherium

Height 0.6 m

40 million years

Mesohippus

Height 1.0 m

30 million years

Merychippus

Height 1.0 m

10 million years

Pliohippus

Height 1.6 m

1 million years

Modern horse *(Equus)*

In other areas, dead organisms have been preserved in ice and covered by layers of snow. The temperature is so low that decay is almost halted.

The conditions for fossil formation are rare. This is why we don't find many fossils. Scientists who study fossils can work out what the animal or plant was like when it was living. Using radioactive dating (section 32.7), the age of a fossil can be worked out.

By looking at fossils, a picture can be built up which shows how animals and plants have changed since life began on Earth. We can also see how animals and plants have adapted, evolved and sometimes become extinct.

Figure 7 shows how horses have evolved from their prehistoric ancestors to become the modern horse that we know today.

12 How do scientists know how the horse has evolved?

Figure 7 The evolution of present day horses from their prehistoric ancestors.

Summary

1 The nucleus of all cells (except sex cells) in our bodies have 23 pairs of chromosomes. Sex cells (egg cells and sperm) have 23 single chromosomes. Chromosomes are like long threads. They are divided into **genes**.

2 The study of genes is called **genetics**. Genes are passed on from parents to their offspring. They control how we grow and what we look like.

3 One pair of chromosomes determines our sex – whether we are male or female. These are called the **sex chromosomes**. All males have one X and one Y sex chromosomes (XY). All females have two X chromosomes (XX).

4 All egg cells have one X chromosome, but sperms may have either one X or one Y chromosome. At fertilisation:

★ if the father's Y chromosome joins the mother's X chromosome to make an XY pair, the baby will be a boy.

★ if the father's X chromosome joins the mother's X chromosome to make a XX pair, the baby will be a girl.

5 Faulty genes may be passed from parents to their children. This can cause a disease like cystic fibrosis. The parents are healthy, but the mixing of genes after fertilisation causes the baby to have the disease.

6 We are all humans, but we live in a world of very different people. These differences in humans and other organisms are called **variations**. Variations occur because:

★ we inherit characteristics from our parents, such as the colour of our skin (our genes)

★ where we live and how we live affects us (our environment).

7 We are different from our parents. When an egg is fertilised by a sperm, the chromosomes from the mother and the chromosomes from the father are mixed in a random way.

8 Some organisms in a species are better adapted to survive than others. There is a **natural selection** of the fittest. Changes in the characteristics of a particular species happen over millions of years. This is called **evolution**. Organisms that are unable to adapt, like dinosaurs, eventually die out. They become **extinct**.

Exam questions for Chapter 11

1 The sex of a person is controlled by chromosomes **X** and **Y**.

a) Where are chromosomes **X** and **Y** found in a cell? *(1)*

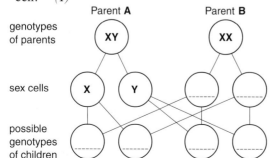

b) Copy the genetic diagram. Complete your copy to show how sex chromosomes are passed on from parents to their children. *(3)*

c) Mrs Smith is pregnant.

(i) Which two sex chromosomes does Mrs Smith have? *(1)*

(ii) What is the chance that her baby will be a girl? *(1)*

(iii) Mrs Smith already has two children, Bill and Harry. They are identical twins. Bill weights 35 kg and Harry weights 41 kg. Suggest two reasons for this difference. *(2)*

[Edexcel 1999]

2 Many years ago nearly all wheat plants had very long stalks. Then big improvements were made in the number and size of seed grains.

Long stalks made the tops of the plants heavy and caused them to bend over.

To solve this problem, scientists used artificial selection to develop plants with short stalks.

a) Put the sentences **A–D** below into the correct order in a flow diagram so that they tell you how to develop short-stalked wheat plants. (You can use just the letters if you want to.)

A Repeat this for many generations.

B Select plants with shorter stalks.

C Grow the seeds into new plants.

D Breed these together to produce seeds. *(3)*

b) Suggest a reason why farmers wanted wheat plants with short stalks in our British climate. *(1)* **[AQA (NEAB) 1999]**

3 Modern humans belong to the species *Homo sapiens*. Many people think that modern humans evolved from more primitive species. Three of these primitive species were *Australopithecus*, *Homo habilis* and *Homo erectus*. These three species are now extinct. The graph shows the brain size of several specimens from each of the species.

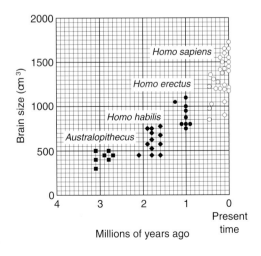

a) Using information from the graph:

(i) give the time period when *Homo habilis* individuals lived on Earth, (e.g. from _____ to _____ millions of years ago); *(1)*

(ii) describe how brain size changed during the evolution of modern humans; *(1)*

(iii) estimate the mean brain size of *Homo habilis*. *(1)*

b) Suggest how we know about the brain size of *Australopithecus*. *(2)*

[AQA (NEAB) 1999]

4 a) Copy the sentences below. Use words from the list to complete your sentences.

alleles   chromosomes   gametes   genes
mutations

The nucleus of a cell contains thread-like structures called _____ .

The characteristics of a person are controlled by _____ which may exist in different forms called _____ . *(3)*

b) The drawing shows some of the stages of reproduction in horses.

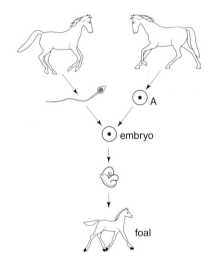

(i) Name this type of reproduction. *(1)*

(ii) Name the type of cell labelled **A**. *(1)*

c) When the foal grows up it will look similar to its parents but it will **not** be identical to either parent.

(i) Explain why it will look similar to its parents. *(1)*

(ii) Explain why it will **not** be identical to either of its parents. *(2)*

[AQA (NEAB) 1999]

CHAPTER 12

Our effect on the environment

12.1 Populations and communities

Living things can only survive if they are well adapted to their habitat. The population will increase if the conditions are favourable and will fall when conditions are difficult.

Herds of bison in Yellowstone National Park, U.S.A. These herds travel hundreds of miles every year to find good grazing.

Five important factors affect the size of populations.

1 The supply of food and water

In a community, the number of animals is limited by the amount of food and water. When there is plenty of food and water, animals are in good condition and produce healthy young. A rich supply of food makes a difference in the offspring of predators. Ospreys rear strong fledglings if fish are in good supply. A pack of wolves will rear more cubs if there is a ready supply of deer and elk. Plants will grow and reproduce when there is adequate rainfall and plenty of sunshine.

2 Climate

In many areas, the climate controls the supply of food and water. In drought conditions, plants die back and there is no food for herbivores.

The temperature also plays an important part in controlling the size of both plant and animal populations. Like rainfall, temperature also varies from season to season. This affects the size of populations from year to year.

A good food supply has given these wolf cubs a successful start in life.

3 Space (territory)

Given more space, populations usually increase in size. If there is too little space, overcrowding happens and there is competition. Plants grow weak and 'leggy' in their search for light. Some animals, such as robins and wolves, fight to keep their territory. Female rats will not breed if they have contact with too many males.

This male robin is strongly defending his space (territory).

4 Waste products

If an animal population increases to a high level, waste products such as faeces and urine pollute the surrounding area. Disease and sickness may result. Animals die young and few are able to reproduce. The population will then decrease in size.

5 Predators

Look closely at the graph in Figure 1. This shows the population numbers of the arctic lynx and snowshoe hares in Northern Canada.

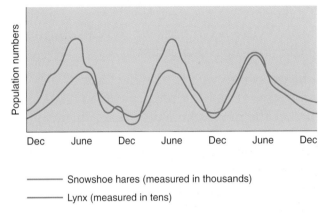

———— Snowshoe hares (measured in thousands)

———— Lynx (measured in tens)

Figure I The changing populations of arctic lynx and snowshoe hares in Northern Canada.

Notice that:

★ as the population of snowshoe hares (prey) increases, the population of lynx (predators) also increases.

★ as the population of lynx reaches a high value, the population of hares decreases.

In general, biologists have found that:

★ if the population of prey increases, food is plentiful for predators and their population also increases.

★ if the population of predators increases, they need more food and so the population of prey decreases.

1 List **five** factors which affect the size of a population.

2 What happens to a population when there is plenty of food?

3 What happens to a population during a drought?

4 Why do robins defend their territory so strongly?

If a garden is neglected, weeds appear in the flower beds and in the lawn. Gradually, the garden becomes a meadow.

The grass and weeds may die back in the winter months, but they grow even taller and thicker the next year. Seeds from shrubs and trees will germinate. In time, saplings (small trees) will become tall trees.

The plant population in a neglected garden is a good example of competition in nature. At first, grass on the lawn and garden flowers compete with weeds for light, space, water and nutrients in the soil. But, without a gardener, the flowers lose out in competition with the weeds.

Later, the weeds have to compete with the canopy of leaves from shrubs and trees. The weeds die because of poor light and lack of water.

> Life on Earth is a **competition**. Both plants and animals experience competition for food (nutrients), water and space.

Competition occurs in many ways. Organisms may experience competition from members of their own species. This often leads to survival of the fittest. In addition, organisms may be in competition with different species. For example, frogs compete for mates, robins compete for territory and squirrels compete with finches for pine cones.

Adapt and survive

> Many organisms have developed features which help them to survive better in their normal environment. This is called **adaptation**.

Plants growing in a meadow are often eaten by herbivores such as cows and sheep. Some plants, like dandelions and daisies, have adapted by growing leaves which lie flat on the ground (Figure 2).

In a garden, lawn grass and flowers are in competition with weeds. With the help and care of a gardener, the lawn and flowers can win!

Figure 2 Daisies and dandelions have adapted to grazing animals. They have flat leaves which lie low on the ground.

There are thousands of adaptations in nature. Here are some others.

★ Animals such as rabbits, wildebeest and antelope can run fast. This helps them to evade their predators. They live in groups or herds so that during a hunt, only the oldest and weakest are caught. The animals that survive stay alert at all times and use warning signals.

★ Animals such as monkeys and squirrels are good at climbing trees. This helps them to escape from predators.

★ Polar bears survive in the Arctic by having a thick layer of insulating fat and a thick, hairy coat.

★ Some plants, such as cacti are specially adapted for arid (dry) conditions. They have a thicker, tough cuticle and fewer stomata to reduce water loss through transpiration.

★ Certain plants warn off animals which might eat them. They may have spikes and needles or produce poisons and stings when they are touched.

5 Name **two** things which plants compete for.

6 Name an animal which competes with finches for pine cones.

7 How are antelopes adapted to survive in the wild?

8 How are polar bears adapted to survive in the Arctic?

| 12.3 | **The human population** |

Some organisms are more adaptable than others. Probably the most adaptable organisms of all are humans. We can survive in almost any habitat on Earth, from freezing arctic wastes to hot, scorching deserts. Why are we so adaptable? The reasons are our intelligence and because we can share and pass on our knowledge.

Our adaptability has led to increases in the human population since the Middle Ages (Figure 3).

A polar bear in an icy wilderness

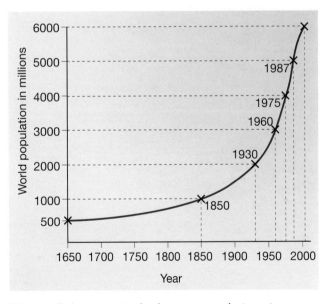

Figure 3 Increase in the human population since 1650

There are about 6000 million people in the world today. In 1930, the world population was 2000 million and in 1850, it was only 1000 million. Notice in Figure 3 how the human population has grown since the middle of the 19th century.

This population 'explosion' has created:

★ an increased demand for food, raw materials and energy

★ an increased destruction of wildlife habitats in order to build houses, factories, roads and farm the land

★ an increased need for the disposal of vast amounts of waste

★ increased pollution of the Earth.

Population growth varies from one country to another. In many developed countries, such as Britain, France and the USA, methods of birth control have almost brought populations to a steady level. But in Asia and Africa, the population continues to grow and grow. This population 'explosion' cannot go on forever. We must take steps to limit this increasing demand for food, land and energy.

Eventually, one of the limiting factors listed in section 12.1 will cause the world population to level off. This may involve shortages of food or water, overcrowding, pollution or disease. Many people believe that the only way to avoid a disaster is to introduce reliable methods of birth control throughout the world.

Many people protested about the building of a motorway through the quiet countryside of Twyford Down in Hampshire. Planning permission was eventually granted and another unspoilt area was changed forever.

More people, more pollution!

In some highly populated areas, our activities are leading to serious pollution problems.

Air pollution

Air pollution is caused by the release of poisonous gases into the air. These gases harm living things. Most air pollution is caused by the burning of fossil fuels in our homes, in power stations and in our vehicles.

The harmful substances released into the air by these processes are listed in Table 1. The table also shows their harmful effects and possible methods of control.

Acid rain has affected these trees and made lake water acidic in the Liesjarvi National Park in Finland.

Air pollutant	Source	Effects	Methods of control
Soot and smoke	Burning fuels	Deposit soot on buildings Make clothes and fabrics dirty	Use of smokeless fuels Improved supply of air to burning fuels
Carbon dioxide	Burning fuels	Increased concentrations of carbon dioxide in the air have caused more heat to be retained by the Earth. This affects our climate leading to the 'greenhouse effect'	Burn less fossil fuels by: • improving home insulation • making vehicles more efficient
Carbon monoxide	Burning fuels – particularly in vehicles	Poisonous to humans and animals Prevents haemoglobin in the blood from carrying oxygen	Making vehicle engines burn fuel more efficiently Fit catalytic converters
Sulphur dioxide	Burning fuels – particularly coal. Small amounts of sulphur in coal and oil burn to form sulphur dioxide. This reacts with rainwater to form sulphurous acid ('acid rain')	Acid rain – harms plants – gets into rivers and lakes and harms fish – attacks the stonework of buildings	Burn less coal and oil Remove sulphur dioxide from waste gases
Nitrogen oxides	Vehicle exhaust gases. These react with rainwater to form nitrous and nitric acids ('acid rain')		Adjust vehicle engines so that nitrogen oxides do not form. Fit catalytic converters to vehicle exhaust systems

Table 1 Harmful substances causing air pollution

12.5   The greenhouse effect

The increasing use of fossil fuels has led to a small but significant increase in the concentration of carbon dioxide in the air. Cutting down forests (deforestation) to provide timber has also led to increased carbon dioxide in the air. Vast forests in Brazil, Malaysia and other parts of the world have been felled. Before this deforestation, the trees could remove carbon dioxide from the atmosphere as they photosynthesised.

Molecules of carbon dioxide are larger and heavier than the molecules of oxygen and nitrogen in clean air. The relative molecular mass (M_r) of CO_2 is 44. $M_r(O_2)$ is 32 and $M_r(N_2)$ is only 28.

Radiant heat (energy waves) cannot pass through carbon dioxide as easily as it passes through clean air. So, as the concentration of carbon dioxide in the atmosphere rises, less heat escapes from the Earth and the temperature slowly rises.

Carbon dioxide traps heat in the Earth's atmosphere just like the glass in a greenhouse. We call it the **greenhouse effect**.

Global warming

The greenhouse effect is leading to **global warming**. This involves an increase in average temperatures throughout the Earth.

The following changes back up the view that global warming is taking place.

★ **Changes in the climate are occurring**. Higher temperatures than ever are being recorded in some areas. There are changes in the pattern of rainfall. There seem to be more violent storms. The higher average temperatures in Britain are causing birds to make nests and lay eggs earlier in the spring.

Bird watchers in Britain have studied nest building and egg laying trends. They have found that magpies are now starting to nest 17 days earlier than they did in the 1940s. Is this evidence for global warming?

★ **Patterns of food production are changing**. In certain parts of the world, particularly in East Africa, rainfall has decreased and crops are failing more frequently than in the past.

★ **Sea levels are rising**. Coastal flooding is causing more damage due to the melting of the polar ice caps.

A number of countries, including Britain and the USA, are now committed to reducing the levels of carbon dioxide emitted into the atmosphere. They have set targets for reductions by specified dates.

9   What was the world's population in
    a) 1850 b) 2000?

10 What effect has this change had on the Earth's rivers and seas?

11 Name **two** gases which cause acid rain.

12 What effect does acid rain have on life in a lake?

13 What evidence is there that global warming is really happening?

12.6 Water pollution

The main pollutants of our rivers, lakes and oceans are shown in Table 2. The table also shows and sources the damaging effects of these pollutants.

Sewage

The main cause of water pollution is sewage. At one time, sewage was simply piped into rivers or into the sea. This poisoned living things in the water and led to disease. Today, sewage plants treat the waste before it is returned to rivers, to the sea or to the land. Sewage is first pumped into large tanks. Here it is aerated (mixed with air). This helps bacteria (decomposers) to convert it to harmless products – carbon dioxide, water and nitrogen (section 9.4).

In February 1996, the Sea Empress oil tanker ran aground near the Texaco oil refinery at Milford Haven, South Wales. 70 000 tonnes of crude oil spilled into the sea coating thousands of birds in oil, and causing many to die.

Fertilisers have leaked into this river from agricultural land. The nitrates in the fertilisers have caused green algae to grow rapidly. The algae then use up all the oxygen in the water and cause fish and plants to die.

Water pollutant	Source	Damaging effects
Sewage	Homes, schools, factories	Bacteria grow on nutrients in sewage. This uses up dissolved oxygen in the water. Lack of oxygen causes the bacteria, fish and water plants to die. The decaying matter makes the water smelly.
Oil	Refineries and oil spills from tankers	Pollutes beaches and destroys habitats. Sea birds are covered in oil and die in large numbers.
Fertilisers	Rainwater washes fertilisers from farmland into rivers and lakes	Bacteria and water plants grow rapidly because of fertilisers. They use up the dissolved oxygen and then die. The decaying matter makes the water stink like a sewer. This enrichment of rivers and lakes with nutrients, such as fertilisers, is called **eutrophication**.
Pesticides	Insecticides, herbicides & fungicides used by farmers and gardeners	Pesticides kill helpful and harmless organisms (e.g. pollinating insects, decomposers, pet animals) as well as pests. They get into food chains where they harm organisms further along the chain.

Table 2 The main water pollutants

Fertilisers

Problems can arise when fertilisers get into water courses and pollute them. But we do need to use fertilisers in order to feed the world's population.

Chemical pesticides

Chemical pesticides benefit crop yields but they kill helpful organisms as well as the pests. They are easy to use as powders or granules and they act rapidly. In order to prevent damage to organisms and ecosystems, more use is now being made of **biological methods of pest control**. These include the use of:

★ natural predators, such as cats, to control rats and mice and ladybirds to control aphids on plants

★ sterile males to reduce the population of pests.

| 12.7 | **Conservation of wildlife and the countryside** |

In some parts of the world, our effects on the environment has been disastrous. Agricultural methods, industrial pollution and the hunting of animals have destroyed habitats and caused the **extinction** of entire species. The dodo is probably the best known extinct animal, but there are many others. In addition to these species which have disappeared forever, there are hundreds of **endangered species**. These animals and plants are in real danger of becoming extinct.

There are successful **conservation projects** throughout the world and regulations are working well. These include:

Regulations to reduce air pollution
The Clean Air Acts made in Britain in the1960s led to the reduction of soot in the atmosphere. Laws have reduced the amounts of lead in petrol. Agreements are in place to try to reduce the emissions of carbon dioxide.

In parts of central Africa, the elephant has been hunted to extinction. Hunters kill the animals to obtain their tusks which are made of ivory.

Reclaimed areas damaged by mining and quarrying
In the Thames Valley, gravel pits have been reclaimed and converted into water sports areas. In South Yorkshire and South Wales, mining tips have been landscaped and turned into parks and gardens.

Strict management of habitats, nature reserves and National Parks
Many countries are making a big effort to protect areas where wildlife can flourish.

Restriction on the number of animals taken for food in any one year
This applies particularly to fish and whales in areas where there has been over-fishing in the past.

Red kites had almost died out in England in the 1960s. A few pairs were introduced into the Chilterns in Buckinghamshire in the 1970s. They are now fairly common.

Summary

1 Five important factors affect the size of populations of living things.

* the supply of food and water

* climate

* space (territory)

* waste products

* predators

2 Life on Earth is a **competition**. Both plants and animals experience competition for food (nutrients), water and space.

3 Many organisms have developed features which help them to survive better in their normal environment. This is called **adaptation**.

4 Increase in the human population has resulted in:

* an increased demand for food

* an increased destruction of habitats

* an increased need to dispose of waste

* increased population.

5 Air pollution is caused by the release of poisonous gases. These include carbon dioxide, carbon monoxide, sulphur dioxide and nitrogen oxides.

6 Pollution of the air from the burning of fossil fuels has led to **acid rain**, the **greenhouse effect** and **global warming**.

7 Water pollution has affected our lakes and oceans. The main water pollutants are sewage, oil, fertilisers and pesticides.

8 In the future, it is important that we preserve habitats and protect endangered species.

1 A population of rabbits lived on a small island. The graph shows their population over the last 50 years.

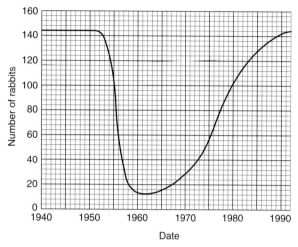

a) (i) How many rabbits were there on the island in 1950? *(1)*

(ii) Give **one** year when there were 88 rabbits on the island. *(1)*

b) (i) Calculate the decrease in rabbit population between 1950 and 1960. *(1)*

(ii) Suggest a reason why the rabbit population fell in these years. *(1)*

c) The most rabbits on the island is always about 140. Suggest a reason for this. *(1)*

[AQA (SEG) 1999]

2 Beavers live in the streams of northern forests. They cut down lots of trees. They use some trees for food and some to make dams. The dams form large deep ponds. In the middle of these ponds the beavers build their homes. These homes have underwater entrances.

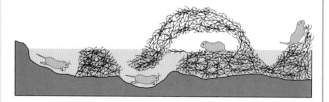

a) Explain how each of the following features makes beavers well adapted for living in water and cutting down trees:

- large paddle-shaped tails
- thick, waterproof fur
- front teeth which never stop growing *(3)*

b) Suggest **two** ways in which the design of the beaver's home protects it from predators. *(2)*

[AQA (NEAB) 1999]

3 People have burned fossil fuels, eg. coal, in Britain for hundreds of years. Until about two hundred years ago the effects of this could only be seen in large towns where buildings became blackened with soot.

Now we can see other effects. For example animals are being killed in lakes in country areas far from towns and cities. This is because the water there has become much more acidic. Gases produced by burning fossil fuels are the cause of this.

a) Name **two** of these gases. *(2)*

b) These gases are produced in towns. Explain how they can make lakes much more acidic in country areas. *(2)*

c) The effects of burning fossil fuels are much greater now than they were two hundred years ago. Explain why. *(2)*

[AQA (NEAB) 1999]

4 The gemsbok is a large herbivore that lives in herds in desert areas of South Africa. Gemsboks feed on plants that are adapted to living in dry conditions. There are not many rivers, lakes or ponds that can provide drinking water for the animals. The desert areas are hot during the day but cool at night. As the air cools at night it becomes moist, and the plants absorb the moisture.

a) A few lions live in the desert areas. They hunt and feed on the gemsboks.

Use information from the drawing of the gemsbok to suggest **two** ways in which it could avoid being killed by lions. *(2)*

b) The graph show the water content of the desert grass and the times of day that the gemsboks feed.

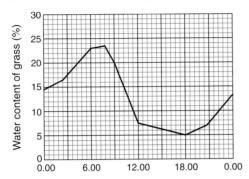

(i) Describe how the water content of the grass changes during the day. *(1)*

(ii) Suggest why the water content of the grass changes. *(1)*

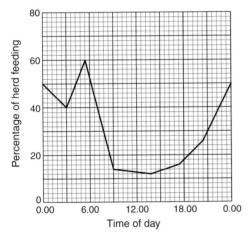

c) (i) Between which times of day are more than 25% of the herd feeding? *(1)*

(ii) Suggest an advantage to the gemsbok of feeding mainly at these times. *(2)*

[AQA (NEAB) 1998]

This photo shows light reflected from the shiny metal alloy in a catalytic converter. Metals are discussed in Chapter 15 and 18. Catalysts and reaction rates are studied in Chapter 20. The whole of this section is about Chemistry – the study of materials and their properties.

Materials and their properties

Mixtures, elements and compounds

13.1 Materials

We use the word 'material' in different ways. Sometimes it is used to describe the fabrics which are used to make clothes. In science, a 'material' is something which is used to *make* things. There are millions of different materials in the universe. Just look around you. How many different materials can you see at the moment? Can you see any wood, any paper, ink, water or steel?

Classifying materials

There are different types of materials. Some materials, like sand, air, wood and water, can be found all around us. We can get them from the ground, from the air, from plants or from the sea. They are called **naturally-occurring materials** or **raw materials**. Naturally-occurring materials are often used to make more useful materials like paper and steel. Most of the materials that we use have been made or manufactured from raw materials. These materials are called **man-made materials**.

Figure 1 What materials are these cups, mugs and glasses made from? One is metal, one is plastic, one is ceramic, one is glass and one is fibre. Which is which?

Most of the objects on this table are man-made. Which naturally-occurring materials did they come from?

A second way of sorting or classifying materials is by their **properties**. We can classify materials into five important types – **metals**, **plastics**, **ceramics**, **glasses** and **fibres**.

For example, we can sort food containers very neatly into these five types of material:

★ cans made from **metals**

★ polythene wrappings and bags made of **plastics**

★ bottles and jars made from **glass**

★ paper and wooden boxes made from **fibres**

★ china jars and crockery made from **ceramics**.

Fibres are materials that have long, thin strands. These include cotton, wool, cellulose in paper and polyester in clothes.

Ceramic materials are made from clay. They include crockery, bricks, tiles, concrete and pottery.

Type of material	Examples	What raw materials are they made from?	Typical properties	Useful products
Metals	Iron, aluminium, copper, steel	Rocks and ores	• hard and strong • high density • good conductors • malleable (can be hammered and bent into different shapes) • high melting point	
Plastics	Polythene, PVC, polystyrene	Crude oil	• flexible • low density • easily moulded and coloured • poor conductors • melt easily and may burn on heating	
Fibres	Cotton wool, paper, wood, polyester	Fibres from plants, animals and crude oil	• flexible • low density • may burn on heating • have long threads or strands	
Glasses	Bottle glass, crystal glass	Mainly sand	• hard but brittle • medium density • very high melting point • very unreactive – do not burn • transparent	
Ceramics (pottery)	China, concrete, bricks, tiles	Mainly clay	• the same as glasses – but not transparent	

Figure 2 Useful products from metals, plastics, fibres, glasses and ceramics.

Look carefully at Figure 2, on the previous page. This shows the five types of materials, their properties and some useful products we get from them.

Notice two things from Figure 2.

1 Ceramics and glasses have very similar properties.

2 Plastics and fibres have similar properties. In fact, plastics and some fibres belong to a larger group of materials called **polymers** (Chapter 22).

Choosing materials for different jobs

When we choose materials for different jobs, we need to ask two key questions.

1 Does it have the right properties?

You wouldn't put a paper roof on your house or make a wooden window. The material you use must have the right property for the job.

These properties include **physical properties** like hardness, strength, conductivity, density amd melting point. They also include **chemical properties** of the material. For example, does the material burn, does it corrode, does it react with water? If these properties are wrong, the material will be useless or it may be unsafe.

2 Is the cost reasonable?

The cost of raw materials and the cost of manufacture are also important in choosing materials for different uses.

1 List **four** naturally-occurring materials.

2 List **four** man-made materials.

3 What are fibres? Give **two** examples.

4 Give reasons why each of these materials is used for the job shown:

a) mercury in thermometers

b) glass for windows.

| 13.2 | **Separating materials** |

Most naturally-occurring materials are mixtures. For example, sea water is a mixture of water and salt. Materials like water, salt, steel and oxygen which we can put a name to are called **substances**.

Sometimes, mixtures have to be separated so that we can use the materials in them. The methods that we choose to separate mixtures depend on the different properties of the substances in them. When scientists separate mixtures, they often use similar equipment to cooks.

Separating an insoluble solid from a liquid

We can do this by **filtering**. This is like using a sieve to strain water from peas or making filter coffee (Figure 3). Filtering is also used to collect the dust in a vacuum cleaner.

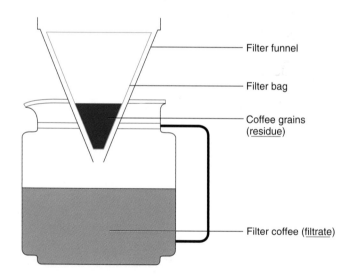

Filter funnel

Filter bag

Coffee grains (residue)

Filter coffee (filtrate)

Figure 3 Filtering coffee. The filter bag is made of filter paper. It has tiny holes that let the liquid through, but these holes are too small for the solid particles to pass through. The liquid that runs out of the filter is called the **filtrate**. The solid left behind is called the **residue**.

Sometimes, the solid particles are so small that they can pass through the filter paper. The tiny solid particles float in the liquid as a **suspension**. When this happens, the solid can be separated by **centrifuging**. The mixture is poured into a tube and spun round very fast in a centrifuge. This forces the denser solid particles to the bottom of the tube and the liquid can be poured off easily.

Centrifuging is used in dairies to separate cream from milk. It is used in hospitals to separate blood cells from blood plasma.

Separating a soluble solid from a liquid

Tap water is not pure. It contains dissolved gases, such as oxygen from the air, and dissolved solids from the soil and river beds. Tap water is a **solution**.

Sea water is also a solution. It contains salt (the **solute**) dissolved in water (the **solvent**). The easiest way to separate a soluble solid (such as the salt in sea water) is by **evaporation**. When sea water is left in the sun, the water evaporates and a white salt is left behind.

This process in which a liquid turns to a vapour is called **evaporation**.

Evaporation is used to obtain salt from sea water in hot countries

If the solvent evaporates slowly from a solution, the solute is left behind as large, well-shaped crystals.

Getting crystals by evaporating the solvent from a solution is called **crystallisation**.

Usually, evaporation is speeded up by boiling the solution. In this case, the solute is left behind as small, poorly-shaped crystals.

Separating a solvent from a solution

Sometimes, the part of a solution that you want is the liquid solvent and *not* the solute. In this case, **distillation** can be used.

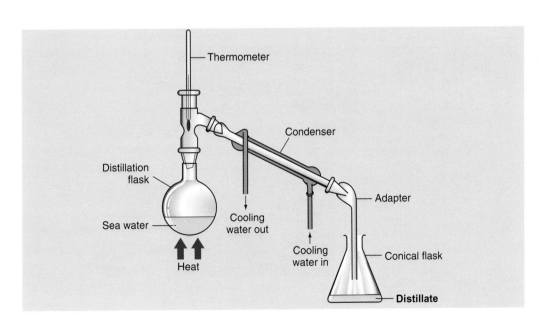

Figure 4 Separating pure water from sea water by distillation. The pure water (liquid) which collects after distillation is called the **distillate**.

We can use distillation to separate pure water from sea water (Figure 4, on previous page). The sea water is boiled and water evaporates off as steam. The steam passes into a cold container called a **condenser**. Here the steam turns back to water.

This process in which a vapour changes to a liquid is called **condensation**.

Notice from Figure 4 that:

distillation = evaporation + condensation

Distillation is an important process in:

★ making 'spirits' such as whisky, gin and vodka from weaker alcoholic liquids

★ obtaining pure drinking water from sea water.

Separating liquids which mix completely

If alcohol is added to water, the two liquids mix completely to form a single layer.

Liquids like these which mix completely are described as **miscible**.

Miscible liquids can be separated by a special form of distillation called **fractional distillation**.

The method works because the different liquids have different boiling points. When the mixture is heated, the liquid with the lowest boiling point is collected first. As the other liquids boil off, they are condensed separately.

Fractional distillation is important in:

★ separating the different fractions in crude oil (section 22.2)

★ separating oxygen and nitrogen from liquid air.

Separating similar substances

Chromatography can sometimes be used to separate very similar substances. For example, it is used to separate dyes in ink, different sugars in urine and drugs in the blood.

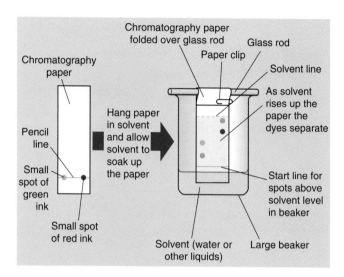

Figure 5 Separating the dyes in inks by chromatography. How many dyes are there in a) the green ink b) the red ink?

Figure 5 shows how the dyes in inks can be separated by chromatography. As the solvent moves up the paper, the dyes separate. The dyes that dissolve more easily in the solvent will travel further up the paper.

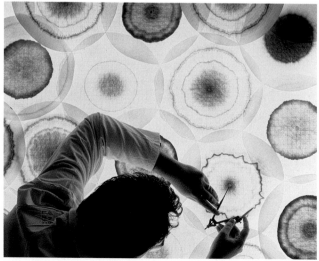

This scientist is studying industrial dyes using paper chromatography.

5 Give an example of using filtering.

6 How can blood cells be separated from blood plasma?

7 What is evaporation? Give an example of how it can be used in separating mixtures.

8 How can you make pure water from sea water?

9 If you cool air to a very low temperature, the gases turn to liquid. This liquid is a mixture of nitrogen, oxygen and carbon dioxide. How can you separate these three?

13.3 Elements – the simplest substances

There are millions of different substances in the universe. All these substances can be put into one of three groups – **elements**, **mixtures** or **compounds**.

Elements are the simplest substances. They cannot be broken down into simpler substances.

So, elements are the building blocks for all other substances. They are the simplest possible materials.

So far, we know of 106 elements. These include iron, copper, aluminium, gold, carbon and oxygen. Every substance in the universe is made from one or more elements. For example, sand is made of silicon and oxygen, and water is made of hydrogen and oxygen.

Classifying elements – types of elements

There are two types of element – **metals** and **non-metals**.

Metals have very different properties from non-metals. The major differences between metals, such as iron and copper, and non-metals, such as oxygen and nitrogen, are shown in Table 1.

The easiest way of checking whether an element is a metal or a non-metal is to see if it conducts electricity. This can be done using the apparatus in Figure 6.

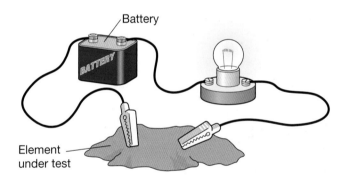

Figure 6 How does this apparatus show you the difference between a metal and a non-metal?

Property	Metals (e.g. iron, copper, aluminium)	Non-metals (e.g. oxygen, nitrogen, sulphur)
State at room temperature	Usually solids	Mostly gases
Appearance	Shiny solids	
Density	Usually high	Usually low
Melting point and boiling point	Usually high	Usually low
Conduction of heat and electricity	Good	Poor (except graphite)
Effect of hammering (malleability)	Bent into different shapes – malleable	Solids are brittle or soft

Table 1 Comparing the properties of metals and non-metals

13.4   Elements and compounds

When charcoal (carbon) is heated strongly, it burns with a pale blue flame to form a colourless gas. The colourless gas is carbon dioxide. The carbon has **reacted** (combincd) with oxygen in the air to make carbon dioxide. The carbon dioxide is a new substance. Changes which make new substances are called **chemical reactions**. The substances which react, in this case carbon and oxygen, are called **reactants**. The new substance which forms is called the **product** of the reaction. The reaction can be summarised in a word equation.

carbon + oxygen ⟶ carbon dioxide
(charcoal)

⎵ **reactants**   ⎵ **product**

Carbon and oxygen are elements. They have combined to form a compound called carbon dioxide.

A **compound** is a substance which contains two or more elements combined together.

Charcoal (carbon) burning on a barbecue

When two elements react together to form a compound, the name of the compound ends in **-ide**.

For example:

carbon + oxygen   → carbon diox**ide**

iron + sulphur   → iron sulph**ide**

aluminium + chlorine → aluminium chlor**ide**

When a metal reacts with a non-metal, the non-metal forms the -ide part of the name of the compound. When two non-metals react, the more reactive non-metal forms the -ide part of the name.

When elements combine to form compounds, the reaction is an example of **synthesis**.

Synthesis is the building up of more complex substances by joining together simpler substances.

Compounds can be split into simpler substances. For example, sodium chloride can be split into sodium and chlorine when electricity is passed through molten sodium chloride.

electricity
sodium chloride ⟶ sodium + chlorine

When a compound is split into simpler substances, the reaction is an example of **decomposition**.

Decomposition is the breaking down of more complex substances into simpler substances.

Notice that decomposition is the reverse of synthesis.

synthesis
sodium + chlorine ⇄ sodium chloride
decomposition

Another example of decomposition is the effect of heat on limestone (calcium carbonate). When limestone is heated the products are quicklime (calcium oxide) and carbon dioxide.

$$\text{calcium carbonate} \rightarrow \text{calcium oxide} + \text{carbon dioxide}$$

This reaction is brought about by heating, so it is called a **thermal** decomposition.

When chemical reactions occur, we do not lose any matter. All the mass of the reactants goes into forming the products. We say that all the mass is conserved. This is summarised in the **law of conservation of mass**.

This says:

In any chemical change, the total mass of the products equals the total mass of the reactants.

10 What is made when carbon and oxygen react?

11 What is a compound?

12 Copy and complete these sentences.

When elements combine together, they make a new compound. This process is called _____ . When a compound is split into simpler substances, the process is called _____ .

13.5 Mixtures and compounds

Most materials are mixtures. They may be:

★ *mixtures of elements*, like air which contains mainly oxygen and nitrogen

★ *mixtures of compounds*, like sea water which contains water and salt (sodium chloride)

★ *mixtures of elements and compounds*.

The label on this carton says 'Pure orange juice'. The orange juice is not really pure because it contains more than one substance.

A **mixture** is two or more substances which are *not* combined together chemically.

Look at the four points in Table 2.

Mixtures	Compounds
1 Contain two or more substances just mixed together.	1 Contain just one pure substance.
2 Properties are similar to the substances in them.	2 Properties are very different from the elements in them.
3 Substances in them can often be separated easily.	3 Elements in them can only be separated by a chemical reaction.
4 The percentages of substances in the mixture can vary, i.e. a mixture can have a variable composition.	4 The percentages of elements in a compound are constant, i.e. a compound has a constant composition represented by a formula.

Table 2 The differences between mixtures and compounds

These points show the differences between mixtures and compounds.

1 This is the most important difference between a mixture and a compound. A mixture contains more than one substance, but a compound is one pure substance. In a mixture there are two or more substances which are not combined together.

2 The properties of a mixture are a 'kind of average' for the substances in it. So, salt water is both salty like sodium chloride (salt) and wet like water.

3 Substances in a mixture can often be separated easily.

4 Compounds have constant compositions which can be shown by formulas. (Formulas are discussed in the next chapter.)

13.6 Hazard symbols

Different chemicals and different materials have very different properties. Some chemicals and materials can cause hazards. For example, petrol is very flammable, concentrated sulphuric acid will burn (corrode) your skin and chlorine is poisonous (toxic). It is very important that anyone using dangerous substances is aware of the possible hazards.

Many of these substances are also transferred around the country. This means it is necessary to have a system of labelling the containers of dangerous substances. This system must be easily understood by everyone. If there is an accident involving a hazardous chemical, the police and fire service need to know if it is flammable, if it is poisonous and, in particular, how to deal with any spillage.

Hazard symbol	Oxidizing 	Toxic 	Harmful 
What does the symbol mean?	These substances provide oxygen. This allows other materials to burn more strongly.	These substances can cause death. They may cause problems when swallowed or breathed.	These are similar to toxic substances, but less dangerous.
Examples	Potassium manganate (VII) Sodium nitrate	Chlorine Sulphur dioxide	Aspirin Iodine Ethanol (alcohol)
Hazard symbol	Corrosive 	Irritant 	Highly flammable 
What does the symbol mean?	These substances attack and destroy living tissues, including eyes and skin.	These substances are not corrosive, but can redden or blister the skin.	These substances easily catch fire.
Examples	Concentrated sulphuric acid Sodium hydroxide	Dilute sulphuric acid Iodine solution Sodium hydroxide solution	Petrol Ethanol (alcohol) Magnesium

Figure 7 The main hazard symbols

A series of **Hazard Symbols** are used to label chemicals that might cause problems. The main hazard symbols are shown in Figure 7 with examples of the substances to which they apply. The symbols have been chosen so that everyone can understand them and know what they mean.

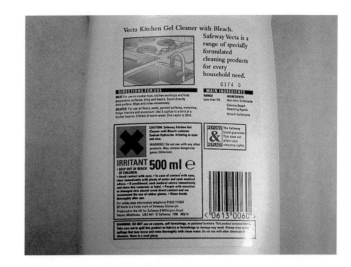

This kitchen cleaner with bleach can harm your skin. Its container has the **irritant** hazard symbol.

Summary

1 A **material** is a form of matter which can be used in some way.

2 Some materials such as sand and water are found in the world around us. We say that they are **naturally-occurring** or **raw materials**. These materials can be made into useful materials such as cement. We say that these materials are **man-made**.

3 There are five important types of materials:

★ **metals** e.g. copper, steel

★ **plastics** e.g. polythene, PVC

★ **ceramics** or pottery e.g. china, bricks

★ **glasses** e.g. bottle glass, window glass

★ **fibres** e.g. wood, paper

4 In choosing materials for different uses, we need to ask:

★ Does it have the right property for the job?

★ Is the cost reasonable?

5 Most naturally-occurring materials are **mixtures**. For example, sea water is a mixture of two substances, water and salt.

6 It is often necessary to separate mixtures. The method used depends on a difference in properties of the substances being separated.

7 We can separate materials by:

★ **Filtering** – to separate a solid which has not dissolved in a liquid e.g. coffee grains (the residue) are separated by a filter bag, leaving the coffee-flavoured water (the filtrate) in the jug ready for us to drink.

★ **Centrifuging** – to separate really tiny particles of solid from a liquid e.g. a milk centrifuge spins rapidly, forcing the denser milk below the cream.

★ **Evaporating** – to separate a soluble solid from a liquid e.g. sea water is salt (the solute) dissolved in water (the solvent). By heating the water so that water evaporates, crystals of salt are left behind.

★ **Distilling** – to separate a liquid from a soluble solid e.g. to obtain pure water from sea water, the sea water is boiled. The steam then passes into a cooled container called a condenser. Here, the steam condenses forming water which is pure.

Summary

★ **Fractional distillation** – to separate liquids which mix completely e.g. the different substances in crude oil are separated by fractional distillation. This allows the different liquids which boil at different temperatures to be condensed separately.

★ **Chromatography** – to separate similar substances such as dyes in ink.

8 **Elements**, such as iron and carbon, are the simplest substances. They cannot be broken down. Elements are divided into **metals** such as iron and **non-metals** such as carbon.

9 **Compounds** are substances containing two or more elements combined together. The elements carbon and oxygen can react (combine) to form carbon dioxide. This is a **chemical reaction**. Carbon and oxygen are called the **reactants**. Carbon dioxide is the **product**.

10 A **synthesis reaction** occurs when simpler substances combine to form a more complex substance.

A **decomposition reaction** is when compounds are split into simpler substances.

11 Most materials are **mixtures**. Unlike compounds, the substances in a mixture are not combined chemically. A compound is one pure substance. Mixtures contain more than one substance.

Exam questions for Chapter 13

1 a) The list below gives six substances.

aluminium   beer   copper   milk   pure water
sodium chloride

Copy the table below. Put each substance in the correct column of your table.

Elements	Compounds	Mixtures

(3)

b) Elements can be divided into two groups, metals and non-metals. The list below gives some properties of elements.

★ brittle
★ can be hammered into shape
★ dull
★ good conductors of electricity
★ poor conductors of electricity
★ shiny

Copy the table below. Put each property into the correct column of your table.

Properties of metals	Properties of non-metals

(3)

[AQA (NEAB) 1997]

2 Distillation has been used in some parts of the world to obtain drinking water from sea water. The diagram shows a small scale distillation apparatus that could be used to demonstrate this process in a school laboratory.

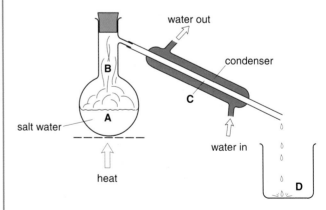

a) Explain, as fully as you can, how the apparatus makes drinking water from salt water. You may use the letters **A**, **B**, **C** and **D** to help with your answer. (4)

b) Why is this method of making drinking water very expensive? (1)

[AQA (NEAB) 1997]

3 This label has been taken from a stick of *Rock*. It was bought at a sweet shop in Pwllheli, North Wales. The E-numbers refer to colours.

a) State the number of colours present in this *Rock*. *(1)*

b) A student carried out an experiment to find out if the *Rock* contained this number of colours. Read what the student did and answer the questions which follow.

The student crushed some of the *Rock*. The crushed *Rock* was placed in a small beaker. A very small amount of water was added and the mixture was stirred to make a solution.

A pencil line was drawn on a piece of filter paper. A spot of the solution was placed on the line.

The student placed some water in a large beaker. The apparatus was then set up as shown below. It was left for half an hour.

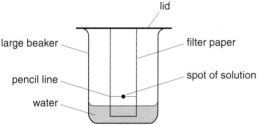

(i) Suggest why the line should be drawn using pencil rather than ink. *(1)*

(ii) The spot must **not** be below the water level at the start of the experiment. State the reason for this. *(1)*

(iii) After half an hour the water had risen to the top of the filter paper. State what the student would see if the *Rock* contained the number of colours suggested in part (a). *(1)*

(iv) Name this method of separation. *(1)*

c) The student was given a solution of pure E102. The student used the same apparatus to show that the *Rock* solution contained this colour. Describe how the student could do this. What would be seen? *(2)*

[AQA (NEAB) 1997]

4 John Dalton was a famous chemist who lived 200 years ago. He made a list of substances he thought were elements. He gave symbols to these elements. Here is a copy of his table.

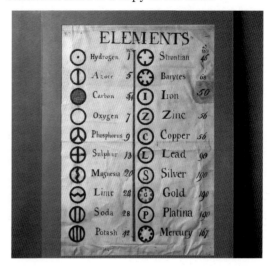

a) We now know that some substances (such as hydrogen, carbon, oxygen and zinc) are elements. Write down the **names** of two other substances in his list that we now know are elements. *(2)*

b) Here are three compounds shown using Dalton's symbols. Write down the names of the compounds. One has been done for you.

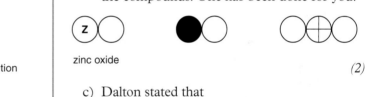

zinc oxide

(2)

c) Dalton stated that

1 All elements are made up of atoms.

2 Atoms cannot be split up into simpler particles.

We now know that atoms contain smaller particles. Describe the structure of an atom such as carbon. *(4)*

[OCR 1999]

Particles, reactions and equations

14.1 Solids, liquids and gases

Scientists classify (sort) materials and substances in several ways. They can sort them into groups of naturally-occurring materials and those which are man-made. Another useful way is to sort them into **solids**, **liquids** and **gases**.

Concrete and ice are solids, petrol and water are liquids, air and steam are gases.

Solids, liquids and gases are called the **three states of matter**.

The important properties of solids, liquids and gases are shown in Table 1.

14.2 Changes of state

Most substances can exist in all three states. Usually, this depends on the temperature. Different materials change state at different temperatures.

Water, for example, is a solid (ice) below 0°C, a liquid between 0°C and 100°C and a gas (steam) above 100°C.

We can change the state of a substance by heating it or cooling it. An icy snowball melts to liquid water from the heat of your hands. Water which is put in an ice-tray in the fridge will change to ice cubes. A summary of the different changes of state is shown in Figure 1.

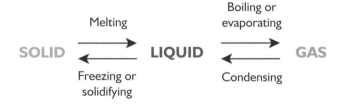

Figure 1 Changes of state

Remember, liquids can turn to gases by **boiling** or by **evaporating**. Liquids can evaporate at temperatures well below their boiling point. This is what happens when water evaporates from puddles.

	Solids	Liquids	Gases
Density	Have high densities, usually greater than 2 gm/cm^3	Have medium densities about 1 gm/cm^3	Have low densities
Shape	Keep the same shape	Flow easily and take the shape of their container	Flow easily and take the shape of their container
Volume	Keep the same volume	Keep the same volume	Take the volume of their container
Compressibility (squashability)	Cannot be compressed (squashed) into a smaller volume	Can be compressed (squashed) very slightly	Can be compressed (squashed) into a much smaller volume
Example	Rocks show all the properties of a solid	Water shows all the properties of a liquid	Air inside balloons shows all the properties of a gas

Table 1 The important properties of solids, liquids and gases

1 Name the **three** states of matter.

2 Copy and complete this table.

Material	Solid, liquid or gas
ice	
steam	
tap water	
lava in a volcano	
coal	
crude oil	

3 How can you change solid aluminium into liquid aluminium?

14.3 Particles in motion

How does the smell of frying bacon spread all through the house? Why can a tiny amount of curry powder flavour a whole dish of food?

We can answer these questions if we use the idea that **all substances are composed of tiny, invisible particles**.

If you put a tiny pinch of curry powder into a soup, every spoonful tastes of curry. This means that the curry powder must contain tiny bits or particles which have spread through the whole dish.

Evidence for moving particles comes from studies of **diffusion**.

Diffusion explains how you can smell frying bacon well away from the kitchen. Particles of gas are released from the frying bacon. These particles mix with air particles and move away from the frying bacon.

This moving and mixing of particles is called **diffusion**.

Gases consist of tiny particles moving very fast. These particles collide with each other and with the walls of their container.

Sooner or later, gases like those from the frying bacon will diffuse into all the space they can find.

Diffusion also takes place in liquids, but occurs much more slowly than in gases (Figure 2). This tells us that the particles in liquids move around more slowly than the particles in gases. Diffusion does not happen in solids.

Two drops of blackcurrant juice

Water

1 week later

Figure 2 Add 2 drops of blackcurrant juice to a glass of water. The juice colours a small part of the water purple. Leave the glass in a safe place where it cannot be disturbed. The purple juice moves away from the top of the water. After a week or so all the water is a pale lilac colour. The purple juice particles have moved about and mixed with the water particles.

Diffusion is important in living things. It explains how the food you eat gets into your bloodstream, where it is transported all round your body. After a meal, food passes into your stomach. Here, large particles in the food are broken down into smaller particles (section 2.2). These smaller particles can **diffuse** through the walls of the intestine into your bloodstream.

The kinetic theory

The idea that all substances contain very small moving particles is called the **kinetic theory of matter**.

The word 'kinetic' comes from a Greek word meaning moving.

The main points of the kinetic theory are:

★ All matter is made of tiny, invisible moving particles. These particles are actually atoms, molecules and ions (section 14.5).

★ The particles of different substances have different sizes. Particles of elements like iron, copper and sulphur are very small. Particles of compounds like petrol and sugar are larger. Particles of some complex compounds, such as polythene, PVC and proteins, are much, much larger but still far too small to see.

★ Small particles move faster than larger particles at the same temperature.

★ As the temperature rises, the particles have more energy and move around faster.

Look at Figure 3. Notice that particles in solids, liquids and gases differ in:

★ how close they are packed
★ how they move about.

4 What is *diffusion*?

5 In which states of matter does diffusion happen?

SOLID	LIQUID	GAS
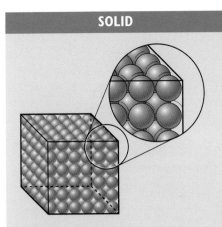	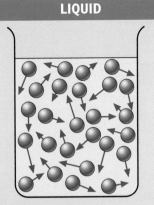	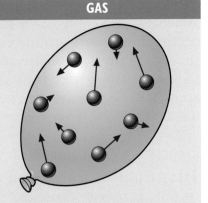
In a solid, the particles are very close. There are strong forces between the particles. This explains why:	**In a liquid**, the particles are further apart. Forces between particles are not as strong as in solids.	**In a gas**, the particles are very far apart. Forces between particles are almost zero.
	This explains why:	This explains why:
• solids are denser than liquids and gases	• liquids are not as dense as solids	• gases have very low densities
• solids cannot be compressed (squashed).	• liquids can be compressed (squashed) slightly.	• gases are very compressible (squashable).
Solid particles can only vibrate. They cannot move from their positions.	Liquid particles can roll around each other.	Gas particles move very fast in all the space they can find.
This explains why:	This explains why:	This explains why:
• solids cannot flow	• liquids flow easily	• gases flow easily
• solids keep a fixed volume and a fixed shape.	• liquids keep a fixed volume but can change their shape.	• gases fill the whole of their container.

Figure 3 Particles in solids, liquids and gases

6 Give **two** examples of diffusion in everyday life.

7 Put these particles in order of size, starting with the smallest.

polythene   petrol   iron

The forces between particles in steel are so strong that thin steel cables can be used to lift heavy loads.

14.4   Using the kinetic theory

We can use the kinetic theory to explain changes of state.

Melting

When a solid is heated, its particles gain energy. The particles vibrate faster and faster until they break away from their fixed positions. The particles begin to roll around each other. The solid has **melted** to a liquid. The temperature at which the solid melts is called the **melting point**.

Freezing

When a liquid cools down, the particles lose energy. They move around each other more slowly. On further cooling, the particles are moving so slowly that they can only vibrate about one position. At this point, the liquid has **frozen** to form a solid.

Evaporation

The particles in a liquid can move around each other. Some particles near the surface may have enough energy to escape from the liquid into the air. When this happens, the liquid **evaporates** to form a gas.

If the liquid is heated, its particles move faster. This gives more of them enough energy to escape from the surface. Evaporation increases as the temperature of the liquid rises.

Boiling

With more heating, the temperature rises and the particles gain more energy. The liquid particles now move so rapidly that bubbles of gas form in the liquid. The temperature at which this evaporation occurs in the bulk of the liquid is the **boiling point**. Boiling points tell us how strongly the particles are held together in liquids. Some liquids, like petrol, evaporate easily and boil at low temperatures. They have weak forces between their particles. We say these liquids are **volatile**.

Condensation

When a gas is cooled, its particles lose energy. The particles move around slower and slower. In time, the particles do not have enough energy to bounce off each other when they collide. The particles cling together as a liquid. The gas has condensed to a liquid. This process is called **condensation**.

Pressure in gases

Figure 4 shows how the pressure in a gas can be explained using the kinetic theory.

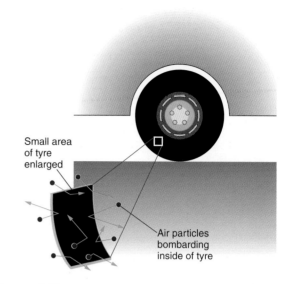

Small area of tyre enlarged

Air particles bombarding inside of tyre

Figure 4 If we pump more air into tyres and balloons, they inflate (blow up). We add millions of air particles which hit the inside of the tyre every second. This causes a pressure on the inside of the tyre. The tyre is also hit by air particles on the outside, but the pressure inside is greater than the pressure outside. The greater pressure inside keeps the tyre inflated (blown up).

Dissolving

When one substance dissolves in another, their particles mix completely. So, when sugar dissolves in water, the tiny sugar particles break away from the solid sugar. The sugar particles then mix with tiny water particles. We can't see any of the sugar.

State symbols

Icebergs off the coast of Antarctica

This photo shows water in three different states – solid ice, liquid water and gaseous water vapour. All three states are the same substance with the same formula, H_2O.

This could be confusing. So, chemists use **state symbols** after a formula to show the state of a substance:

(**s**)   means the substance is a solid

(**l**)   means the substance is a liquid

(**g**)   means the substance is a gas

(**aq**) means the substance is in the aqueous state – it is dissolved in water.

So, ice is written as $H_2O(s)$. Liquid water is $H_2O(l)$. Water vapour (steam) is $H_2O(g)$. Sea water (sodium chloride solution) is $NaCl(aq)$.

> **8** What happens to the particles in a solid as it melts?
>
> **9** What happens to the particles in a liquid as it boils?
>
> **10** What happens to sugar particles when they dissolve in water?
>
> **11** Copy and complete this table.

Symbol	State
l	
g	
s	
aq	

14.5   Atoms, molecules and ions

All substances and materials can be classified in two ways:

1 as **solids**, **liquids** and **gases** (section 14.1)

2 as **elements**, **compounds** and **mixtures** (Chapter 13).

★ **Elements** are substances that cannot be broken down any further.

★ **Compounds** contain two or more elements that are combined together. Compounds can be broken down into the elements they contain.

★ **Mixtures** contain two or more different substances which are just mixed together. The substances in mixtures are not combined.

For example, air is a mixture. The main parts are nitrogen and oxygen. Sea water is a mixture of mainly salt (sodium chloride) and water.

In this chapter, you have learnt that all substances and all materials are made of particles. There are only three *kinds* of particle – **atoms**, **molecules** and **ions**.

What is an atom?

An **atom** is the smallest particle of an element.

The word 'atom,' comes from a Greek word meaning 'indivisible' or 'unsplittable'. At one time, scientists thought that atoms could not be split. We now know that atoms can be split. But, if an atom of one element is split, it is no longer the same element.

Elements contain only one kind of atom. Compounds contain more than one kind of atom and their atoms are combined together chemically.

So, copper contains only copper atoms, and carbon contains only carbon atoms. But water contains both hydrogen and oxygen atoms combined together.

In 1807, John Dalton put forward his **atomic theory of matter**. Dalton was the first scientist to use the word atom for the smallest particle of an element.

Dalton also suggested **symbols** to represent atoms. The modern symbols which we use are based on his suggestions.

Table 2 gives a list of the symbols for some elements. Notice that most elements have two letters in their symbol. The first letter is always a capital, the second letter is always small.

Some symbols come from the English name, for example O for oxygen and C for carbon.

Other symbols come from the Latin name. For example the Latin word for gold is *aurum*. So the symbol for gold is Au. The Latin word for copper is *cuprum*. So the symbol for copper is Cu.

What is a molecule?

A **molecule** is a particle with two or more atoms chemically joined together.

The atoms in molecules are not just mixed together. They are held together by **chemical bonds**. For example, a molecule of water contains two atoms of hydrogen joined to one atom of oxygen. A molecule of carbon dioxide contains one atom of carbon combined with two atoms of oxygen (Figure 5).

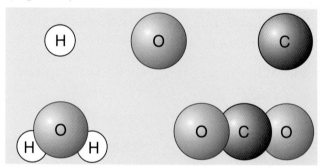

Figure 5 Atoms of hydrogen, oxygen and carbon above molecules of water and carbon dioxide.

Element	Symbol	Element	Symbol	Element	Symbol
Aluminium	Al	Hydrogen	H	Oxygen	O
Argon	Ar	Iodine	I	Phosphorus	P
Bromine	Br	Iron	Fe	Potassium	K
Calcium	Ca	Krypton	Kr	Silicon	Si
Carbon	C	Lead	Pb	Silver	Ag
Chlorine	Cl	Magnesium	Mg	Sodium	Na
Chromium	Cr	Mercury	Hg	Sulphur	S
Copper	Cu	Neon	Ne	Tin	Sn
Gold	Au	Nickel	Ni	Uranium	U
Helium	He	Nitrogen	N	Zinc	Zn

Table 2 The symbols for some elements

When the atoms of different elements join together, they form **compounds**. The symbols in Table 2 can also be used to represent compounds. For example, water is represented as H_2O, two hydrogen atoms (H) and one oxygen atom (O). Carbon dioxide is written as CO_2, one carbon atom (C) and two oxygen atoms (O).

H_2O and CO_2 are called **chemical formulas**.

> A chemical formula shows the numbers of atoms of the different elements in a molecule.

When there are two or more atoms in a formula, their number is written after the symbol. The number is written as a subscript (at a lower level) than the symbol. Some other pictures of molecules and their formulas are shown in Figure 6.

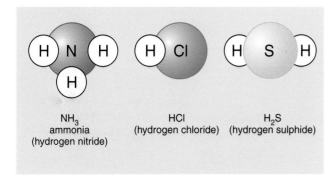

NH_3
ammonia
(hydrogen nitride)

HCl
(hydrogen chloride)

H_2S
(hydrogen sulphide)

Figure 6 Pictures of three molecules and their formulas

Some molecules are very simple like hydrogen chloride (HCl) and water (H_2O). Others are more complex like alcohol (C_2H_6O) and octane (C_8H_{18}). Others are very complicated like chlorophyll ($C_{51}H_{72}O_4N_4Mg$).

Atoms and molecules of elements

Most elements, like iron (Fe), aluminium (Al) and copper (Cu), can be represented by their symbols because they contain single atoms. This is not the case with oxygen, hydrogen, nitrogen or chlorine.

These elements exist as molecules containing two atoms combined together. So, oxygen is best represented as O_2 and not O, hydrogen as H_2 not H, nitrogen as N_2 and chlorine as Cl_2.

What is an ion?

Compounds containing only non-metals, like water (H_2O), carbon dioxide (CO_2) and ammonia (NH_3), consist of molecules.

Compounds which contain metals and non-metals are made up of **ions**, not molecules. These compounds containing ions are called **ionic compounds**.

> An **ion** is a charged particle. It is formed from an atom which has lost or gained one or more electrons.

(There is more about electrons in sections 16.3, 16.4, and 17.4.)

The atoms of all elements are neutral (uncharged). But, when metal atoms react with non-metal atoms, the compound formed contains ions (charged particles). The ions can have a positive electrical charge or a negative electrical charge.

> Metal ions always have a positive charge. Non-metal ions (except hydrogen) always have a negative charge.

When sodium reacts with chlorine, sodium chloride is formed. This contains sodium ions (Na^+) and chloride ions (Cl^-). The formula of sodium chloride is Na^+Cl^-, or just NaCl if we leave out the charges.

Table 3 (on the next page) shows a list of some common ions with their charges.

Positive ions (cations)		Negative ions (anions)	
Aluminium	Al^{3+}	Bromide	Br^-
Calcium	Ca^{2+}	Carbonate	CO_3^{2-}
Chromium	Cr^{3+}	Chloride	Cl^-
Copper(I)	Cu^+	Hydroxide	OH^-
Copper(II)	Cu^{2+}	Iodide	I^-
Hydrogen	H^+	Nitrate	NO_3^-
Iron(II)	Fe^{2+}	Nitride	N^{3-}
Iron(III)	Fe^{3+}	Oxide	O^{2-}
Lead	Pb^{2+}	Sulphate	SO_4^{2-}
Magnesium	Mg^{2+}	Sulphide	S^{2-}
Nickel	Ni^{2+}	Sulphite	SO_3^{2-}
Potassium	K^+		
Silver	Ag^+		
Sodium	Na^+		
Zinc	Zn^{2+}		

Table 3 Some common ions and their charges

Notice the following points from Table 3.

★ **Many ions have more than one unit of charge**.

★ **Copper can form two ions, Cu^+ and Cu^{2+}**. We show this in the names of its compounds by writing copper(I) (pronounced 'copper-one') and copper(II) (pronounced 'copper-two'). So, copper forms two oxides, two chlorides, two sulphates, etc. The correct names for its oxides are copper(I) oxide which is red and copper(II) oxide which is black (Figure 7). Most of the common copper compounds are copper(II) compounds.

★ **Iron can also form two different ions, Fe^{2+} and Fe^{3+}**. We use the names iron(II) and iron(III) for their compounds.

★ **Most metal ions have a charge of 2+**.

The only common metal ions with a charge of 1+ are Ag^+, Na^+ and K^+ (say 'AgNaK' to remember this).

Figure 7 The oxides and chlorides of copper. Pure copper(I) chloride is white, but samples of it are usually pale green as it often contains some copper(II) chloride.

The only common metal ions with a charge of 3+ are Cr^{3+}, Al^{3+} and Fe^{3+} (say 'CrAlFe' to remember this).

★ **Some negative ions contain more than one kind of atom**. For example, hydroxide, OH^-, contains one oxygen and one hydrogen atom, whilst nitrate, NO^{3-}, contains one nitrogen and three oxygen atoms.

Iron tablets are really iron(II) sulphate. Why are pregnant women advised to take iron tablets? What is the formula of iron(II) sulphate?

Balancing charges

In ionic compounds, the charges on the positive ions must balance the charges on the negative ions. So, as the sodium ion is Na^+ and the chloride ion is Cl^-, we can predict that the formula of sodium chloride will be Na^+Cl^-. In this case, the one positive charge on Na^+ is balanced by one negative charge on Cl^-.

Farmers often put lime on the soil. Lime is an ionic compound. Its chemical name is calcium oxide. What is its formula?

By balancing charges we can predict that the formula of calcium chloride will be $Ca^{2+}(Cl^-)_2$ or simply $CaCl_2$. Two positive charges on one Ca^{2+} balance two negative charges on two Cl^- ions. The formula of aluminium oxide is $(Al^{3+})_2(O^{2-})_3$ or simply Al_2O_3. In this case, the six positive charges on two Al^{3+} ions are balanced by six negative charges on three O^{2-} ions.

There is more about ionic structures in section 19.5.

12 What is an atom?

13 What is a molecule?

14 Give the chemical formula of three molecules.

15 What is an ion?

16 Name **three** metal ions which have a charge of 1+.

14.6	**Comparing the masses of atoms**

Atoms are incredibly small. Atoms of chlorine are about one hundred millionth (1/100 000 000) of a centimetre in diameter. So, if you put 100 million of them in a straight line, they would still only measure one centimetre. Figure 8 (on the next page) will also help you to understand how small atoms are.

Atoms are so small that it is impossible to weigh single atoms on a balance. But, scientists can compare the masses of different atoms relative to one another. They use an instrument called a **mass spectrometer**. Streams of atoms are deflected (bent) using a magnetic field. The heavier an atom, the less it is deflected. So, by comparing the deflections of different atoms, it is possible to compare their masses. This gives a list of their relative masses. The relative masses which scientists use for different atoms are called **relative atomic masses**.

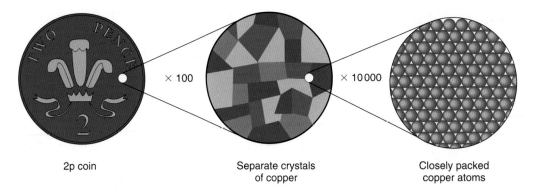

2p coin   Separate crystals of copper   Closely packed copper atoms

Figure 8 If a 2p coin is magnified one hundred times using an ordinary microscope, it is possible to see separate crystals of copper. If these crystals are now magnified 10 000 times, it is possible to measure individual copper atoms. Altogether, the coin would have been magnified first 100 times, then 10 000 times, which equals one million times in total (100 × 10 000).

The element carbon is the standard for relative atomic masses. Carbon atoms are given a relative mass of exactly 12.

The relative masses of other atoms are then found by comparing them with carbon. For example, carbon atoms are 12 times as heavy as hydrogen atoms. So, the relative atomic mass of hydrogen is 1.0. Magnesium atoms are twice as heavy as carbon atoms. So, the relative atomic mass of magnesium is 24.0. A few relative atomic masses are listed in Table 4.

Element	Symbol	Relative atomic mass
Carbon	C	12.0
Hydrogen	H	1.0
Magnesium	Mg	24.0
Oxygen	O	16.0
Aluminium	Al	27.0
Iron	Fe	55.8
Copper	Cu	63.5

Table 4 Some relative atomic masses

The symbol for relative atomic mass is A_r. So, we write A_r (C) = 12.0, A_r (Fe) = 55.8, or simply C = 12.0, Fe = 55.8.

Relative formula masses

We can use relative atomic masses to compare the masses of atoms in different elements. Relative atomic masses can also be used to compare the masses of molecules in different compounds. These relative masses of molecules are called **relative formula masses**.

The relative formula mass of a compound is obtained by adding up the relative atomic masses of all the atoms in the formula. For example:

Relative formula mass of water (H_2O)

= 2 × relative atomic mass of hydrogen + relative atomic mass of oxygen

= 2 × 1 + 16

= 18

Relative formula mass of iron(III) oxide (Fe_2O_3)

= $2 \times A_r(Fe) + 3 \times A_r(O)$

= 2 × 55.8 + 3 × 16.0

= 159.6

17 How many chlorine atoms would fit across a gap of 1 cm?

18 What instrument is used to compare the mass of atoms?

19 Which element has a relative atomic mass of 12?

20 What is the relative formula mass of water?

21 What is the relative formula mass of carbon dioxide?

14.7 Reactions and equations

A **chemical equation** is a summary of the starting substances (reactants) and the products in a chemical reaction.

The sparks from a sparkler are bits of burning magnesium. Let's find the equation for this reaction.

When magnesium burns in air, it reacts with oxygen to form magnesium oxide. The **word equation** for this is

magnesium + oxygen → magnesium oxide

In this reaction, magnesium and oxygen are the **reactants**. Magnesium oxide is the **product**.

Chemists usually write symbols and formulas rather than names in equations. So for the word equation above, we should write Mg for the element magnesium, O_2 for oxygen and $Mg^{2+}O^{2-}$ (or simply MgO) for magnesium oxide.

$$Mg + O_2 \rightarrow MgO$$

But notice that this equation does not balance. There are two oxygen atoms in O_2 on the left and only one oxygen atom in MgO on the right. So MgO must be doubled to give:

$$Mg + O_2 \rightarrow 2MgO$$

Unfortunately, the equation still doesn't balance. There are now two Mg atoms on the right in 2MgO, but only one on the left in Mg. This is easily corrected by writing 2Mg on the left to give:

$$2Mg + O_2 \rightarrow 2MgO$$

The numbers of different atoms are now the same on both sides of the arrow. This is a **balanced chemical equation**.

Writing equations

If you know the reactants and products of a reaction, it is possible to write a balanced equation. The following example shows the three steps involved.

Step 1 Write a word equation.

e.g. hydrogen + oxygen → water

Step 2 Write symbols and formulas for the reactants and products.

e.g. $H_2 + O_2 \rightarrow H_2O$

Remember that oxygen, nitrogen, hydrogen and chlorine are always written as O_2, N_2, H_2 and Cl_2. All other elements are shown as single atoms, for example, Zn for zinc, C for carbon.

Step 3 Balance the equation by making the number of atoms of each element the same on both sides.

e.g. $2H_2 + O_2 \rightarrow 2H_2O$

You must *never change a formula* to make an equation balance. The formula of water is always H_2O and never HO_2 or H_2O_2. You can only balance an equation by putting numbers in front of symbols or in front of a whole formula, that is, $2H_2$ and $2H_2O$.

Balanced chemical equations are more useful than word equations because they show:

★ the symbols and formulas of the reactants and products

★ the relative numbers of atoms and molecules of the reactants and products.

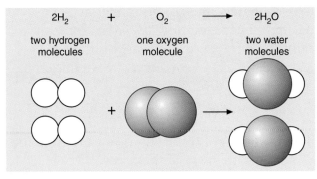

2H₂ + O₂ ⟶ 2H₂O

two hydrogen molecules   one oxygen molecule   two water molecules

Figure 9 Using models to represent the reaction between hydrogen and oxygen to form water.

Balanced equations also help you to see how the atoms are re-arranged in a reaction. You can see this even better using models as in Figure 9.

22 Write down the balanced chemical equations for the following reactions:

a) carbon + oxygen → carbon dioxide

b) hydrogen + oxygen → water

c) zinc + oxygen → zinc oxide

Summary

1 The **three states of matter** are **solids**, **liquids** and **gases**. We can change the state of a substance by heating or cooling it. Different substances change state at different temperatures.

2 The **kinetic theory of matter** tells us that substances are made up of incredibly small moving **particles**.

3 ★ **In a solid**, the particles are very close with strong forces between them. Solid particles can only vibrate.

★ **In a liquid**, the particles are further apart and the forces between them are not as strong as in solids. Liquid particles can roll round each other.

★ **In a gas**, the particles are very far apart and the forces between them are almost zero. Gas particles move very fast and can fill all the space they can find.

4 In different substances, the particles are either **atoms**, **molecules** or **ions**.

In copper, the particles are atoms.

In water, the particles are molecules.

In salt, the particles are ions.

Na⁺   and   Cl⁻

As the temperature rises, the particles have more energy and move faster.

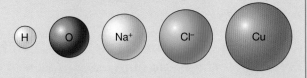

H   O   Na⁺   Cl⁻   Cu

5 Atoms, ions and molecules can be represented using **symbols** for different elements.

★ An **atom** is the smallest particle of an element.

an atom of chlorine, Cl   Cl

★ A **molecule** has two or more atoms chemically joined together.

a molecule of chlorine, Cl₂   Cl   Cl

★ An **ion** is formed from an atom by the loss or gain of one or more electrons.

a chlorine ion, Cl⁻   Cl⁻

Summary

6 When non-metals react, they form compounds containing molecules.

e.g. H_2O, CO_2.

When metals react with non-metals, they form compounds containing ions.

e.g. Na^+Cl^-, $Cu^{2+}SO_4^{2-}$.

All metal ions are positive.

All non-metal ions (except H^+) are negative.

7 Atoms of carbon are given a **relative atomic mass** of exactly 12. The relative atomic masses of other atoms are obtained by comparison with carbon.

The relative atomic mass of chlorine is 35.5 and that of copper is 63.5.

8 A **chemical equation** is a summary of the **reactants** and **products** in a reaction.

e.g. sodium + water $\rightarrow$ sodium hydroxide + hydrogen

Balanced chemical equations can be obtained from word equations by:

★ writing symbols and formulas

e.g. $Na + H_2O \rightarrow NaOH + H_2$

★ then balancing the number of atoms of each element on both sides of the equation.

$2Na + 2H_2O \rightarrow 2NaOH + H_2$

Exam questions for Chapter 14

1 a) Copy the sentences below. Complete your sentences using words from the box.

> atom   compound   formula   metal   mixture   property

An element contains only one type of
_____.

When elements combine, they form a
_____.

Iron combines with sulphur to form iron sulphide. This is not magnetic because it has a different physical _____ to iron.

Iron sulphide is represented as FeS. This is its _____. (4)

b) The diagram shows an atom of boron.

(i) How many electrons are in this atom? (1)

(ii) How many neutrons are in this atom? (1)

[Edexcel 1999]

2 The table shows some chemical reactions.

These reactions take place at different rates.

Choose from the list below a description for the rate of each reaction **A, B, C** and **D**.

You can use each answer only once.

explosive   fast   slow   very slow   (3)

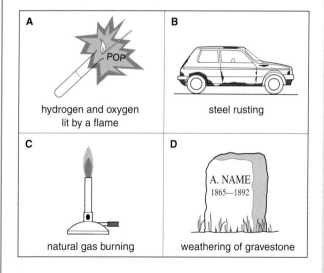

[OCR 1998]

3 The list below gives some properties of materials.

- can be squeezed into a much smaller space
- spread out into all the space available
- have a definite shape
- take up the shape of the container into which they are put
- have a definite volume

a) Copy the table below and complete your table by choosing properties from the list above.

Put two properties of solids in the first column, two properties of liquids in the second column and one property of gases in the third column. One property has been put in the table for you.

You will need to use one property twice.

Properties of solids	Properties of liquids	Properties of gases
		can be squeezed into a much smaller space

(5)

b) Underwater divers carry a cylinder filled with compressed air so that they can breathe under water.

The air in the cylinder has been squeezed so that it takes up much less space.

Explain **in terms of particles** why air can be squeezed up. *(1)*

[AQA (NEAB) 1997]

4 a) The diagrams show the particles present in four samples of gas. Each circle represents an atom. Circles of the same size and shading represent atoms of the same element.

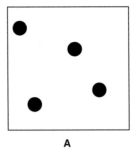

A

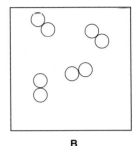

B

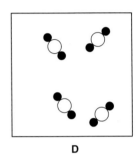

C

D

Which diagram represents:

(i) oxygen, O_2 *(1)*

(ii) steam, $H_2O(g)$ *(1)*

(iii) a mixture of gases *(1)*

(iv) a monatomic gas? *(1)*

b) Draw circles, in a copy of the box below, to represent the arrangement of particles in a solid element. One particle has been drawn for you.

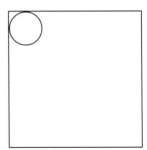

c) Describe how the arrangement and movement of particles in a solid change when it is heated until it is liquid. *(3)*

[Edexcel 1999]

15

Metals and the reactivity series

15.1 The properties and uses of metals

Metals are very important and useful materials. Just look around you. Notice the uses of different metals, for example, knives and forks, handles and locks for doors, radiators, cars, girders and bridges.

The photographs in Figure 1 show three important uses of different metals. Why are the particular metals chosen for these uses? What properties of the metals make them ideal for these uses?

Why is steel used for the girders in this bridge?

Why is copper used for these hot water pipes?

Why is aluminium used to cover this joint of meat during cooking?

Figure 1 Important uses of metals

1 Name **five** objects made of metal.

2 Name **three** metals used in your home.

3 Why is steel used to make bridges?

4 Why is copper used in electrical wires?

15.2 How do metals react with air (oxygen)?

Sodium is stored under oil. As soon as it comes into contact with air, its shiny surface starts to go dull. This is because the sodium reacts very rapidly with oxygen in the air. It forms white sodium oxide.

sodium + oxygen → sodium oxide

Other metals, like zinc, react more slowly. Steel gates and buckets are often coated with zinc to stop them going rusty. This process is called **galvanising**. The shiny zinc surface takes several weeks before it goes dull. The dull layer is white zinc oxide. Zinc has reacted with oxygen in the air.

zinc + oxygen → zinc oxide
$2Zn +$ O_2 → $2ZnO$

Unreactive metals, like copper, take months or even years before they go dull. Shiny copper coins take months to become darker. Copper in the coins reacts slowly with oxygen in the air. It forms a thin layer of black copper oxide.

copper + oxygen → copper oxide
$2Cu +$ O_2 → $2CuO$

We can summarise these reactions of metals with oxygen as:

metal + oxygen → metal oxide

Very unreactive metals, like gold, do not react with oxygen. They stay shiny for hundreds of years.

Unreactive metals like gold are sometimes called 'noble metals'.

The gold on Tutankhamun's face mask has stayed shiny for more than 3000 years.

Chemists can study the reactions of metals with oxygen. They heat the metals in air or in pure oxygen. They find out which are more reactive. Then they arrange the metals in order of reactivity (Figure 2).

The order of reactivity for metals is like a league table. It is usually called the **reactivity series**.

Metals at the top of the reactivity series, such as sodium and calcium, are the most reactive. Metals at the bottom of the series, like silver and gold, are the least reactive.

The reactivity series can be used to predict other reactions of metals. As expected, reactive metals like sodium also react strongly with non-metals such as chlorine and sulphur. Unreactive metals, like gold, react very little with non-metals. So, unreactive metals do not form compounds so readily.

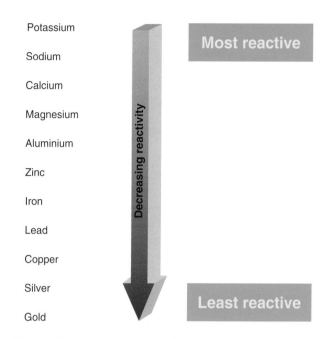

Figure 2 The reactivity series

Reactions with oxygen

When substances react with oxygen, they form new substances (products) called **oxides**.

When magnesium burns in air, it reacts very quickly with oxygen. The product is magnesium oxide.

These reactions in which a substance gains oxygen are called **oxidations**.

Sometimes, it is possible to remove oxygen from oxides. If mercury oxide is heated strongly, it will decompose to mercury and oxygen.

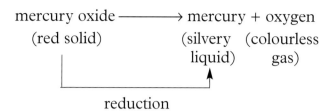

Reactions like this in which a substance loses oxygen are called **reductions**.

Oxidation is the **gain** of oxygen.
Reduction is the **loss** of oxygen.

5 Why is sodium stored under oil?

6 Why is steel sometimes coated in zinc?

7 Why do copper coins and pipes go dull?

8 Why is gold such a good metal for jewellery and coins?

9 What is the difference between an oxidation reaction and a reduction reaction?

15.3	**How do metals react with water?**

Metals which are keen to react with oxygen also react with water. The metals take oxygen from water (H_2O) to form their oxides. Hydrogen gas (H_2) is also a product. For example:

sodium + water → sodium oxide + hydrogen

$$2Na + H_2O \rightarrow Na_2O + H_2$$

Table 1 (on the next page) shows the reactions of six metals with water.

Look at the results in Table 1. Work out the order of reactivity of the metals with water. Check your order with the order of reactivity of metals with air (oxygen) in Figure 2. The two orders of reactivity are the same.

Metal	Reaction with water
Calcium	Sinks in the water. Steady stream of hydrogen produced. The solution becomes alkaline and cloudy.
Copper	No reaction
Iron	No reaction. (Iron will only react with cold water if air (oxygen) is also present for rusting.)
Magnesium	Tiny bubbles of hydrogen appear on the surface of the magnesium after a few minutes. The solution slowly becomes alkaline.
Potassium	A violent reaction occurs. A globule of molten potassium skates over the water surface. The globule burns with a lilac flame. Hydrogen and potassium hydroxide form.
Sodium	A vigorous reaction occurs. A globule of molten sodium skates about the water surface. Hydrogen and sodium hydroxide form.

Table 1 The reactions of six metals with water

Why is this hot water tank made of copper rather than steel (iron)?

Only the most reactive metals, from potassium down to magnesium in Figure 2, react with *cold* water. Metals below magnesium, such as zinc and iron, will not react with cold water, but they will react with *hot* water or steam. For example:

$$zinc + water \rightarrow zinc\ oxide + hydrogen$$
$$Zn + H_2O \rightarrow ZnO + H_2$$

The reactions of metals with water can be summarised as:

$$metal + water \rightarrow metal\ oxide + hydrogen$$
$$(hydrogen\ oxide)$$

In these reactions, the metal is oxidised to metal oxide. The water (hydrogen oxide) is reduced to hydrogen.

The boilers in steam trains are made from iron (steel). What is the disadvantage in using iron (steel)? Why is copper not used?

15.3 How do metals react with acids?

Various foods contain acids. These include vinegar, oranges, lemons and rhubarb. Have you noticed that acids in food can attack metal saucepans? Figure 3 shows what happened when five different metals were added to cold dilute hydrochloric acid at 20°C. This acid is more reactive than the acids in food. But it shows how different metals are attacked. If you try this experiment, you must wear safety spectacles.

Notice in Figure 3 that aluminium does not react at first. This is because it has a surface layer of aluminium oxide. The oxide reacts slowly with the acid. When the oxide has reacted away, the aluminium reacts more vigorously. The metals used most often for pans and cutlery are iron (in the form of stainless steel), aluminium and copper.

Copper is the only one which does not react with acids in food. But copper is very expensive. The thin oxide layer on aluminium pans protects it from some weak acids in food. But acids in rhubarb and in vinegar react with the oxide and 'clean' the pan during cooking. Iron (stainless steel) which is used for cutlery and pans is also attacked by acids in food.

Foods which contain acids are best stored in unreactive glass or plastic containers. Tin cans may contain acidic foods like pineapple pieces. They are made of steel coated on both sides with tin and then lacquered on the inside. The lacquer forms an unreactive layer between the tin and its contents.

All the metals in Figure 3, except copper, react with the dilute hydrochloric acid. The metals take chlorine from the hydrochloric acid (HCl) to form metal chlorides. Hydrogen is also produced. This is what forms the bubbles.

metal + hydrochloric acid $\longrightarrow$ metal chloride + hydrogen

magnesium + hydrochloric acid $\longrightarrow$ magnesium chloride + hydrogen

$$Mg + 2HCl \longrightarrow MgCl_2 + H_2$$

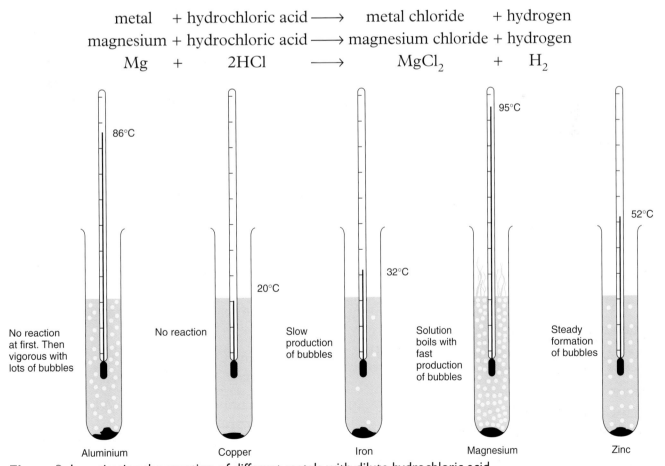

Figure 3 Investigating the reaction of different metals with dilute hydrochloric acid

These reactions are similar to the reactions of metals with water. With water, the metals are taking oxygen from H_2O. With hydrochloric acid, the metals are taking chlorine from HCl. A similar reaction occurs between metal and dilute sulphuric acid. In this case, the products are a metal sulphate and hydrogen.

The reactions of metals with acids can be summarised as:

> metal + acid → metal compound + hydrogen
> (salt)

Metal compounds such as metal chlorides and metal sulphates are usually called **salts**. The best known salt is sodium chloride which is table salt.

10 Put these metals in the order of their reactivity with water. Put the most reactive first.

calcium   iron   copper
sodium   zinc

11 Copy and complete this word equation.

metal + acid → metal _____ + _____

12 Copy and complete this table.

acid used	salt made
sulphuric acid	
	chloride

15.5	**Exothermic and endothermic reactions**

When metals react with acids, heat (energy) is given out. The temperature of the mixture rises (Figure 3). In time this heat is lost to the surroundings.

Changes in temperature often occur when chemical reactions are taking place. The changes in temperature are evidence that a reaction has occurred.

The changes in temperature occur because of energy differences between the reactants and the products.

Exothermic reactions

Reactions like those between metals and acids which *give out heat* are called **exothermic reactions**.

The burning of fuels, like natural gas on a gas hob and petrol in cars, are obvious exothermic reactions. When the fuel burns, it reacts with oxygen in the air. Carbon dioxide and water are produced. Lots of heat (energy) is given out.

> fuel + oxygen → carbon dioxide + water

Heat is given out from exothermic reactions in a campfire. This heat is used to cook the food.

Endothermic reactions

When calcium carbonate (limestone) is heated, it decomposes into calcium oxide (quicklime) and carbon dioxide. We need heat for the reaction to go. The reaction *takes in heat*.

$$\text{calcium carbonate} \xrightarrow{\text{heat}} \text{calcium oxide} + \text{carbon dioxide}$$

These reactions which *take in heat* are called **endothermic reactions**.

15.6 Limestone – an important raw material

Limestone is an important raw material for the construction and chemical industries. It is quarried throughout the U.K. and used as a building material.

This limestone rock in Yorkshire has been attacked by rainwater to form a flat pavement.

Limestone aggregate is used as a base for roads before tarmac is laid on top.

Powdered limestone is used to neutralise acidity in soils and lakes. It is also used to manufacture iron (section 16.2), cement and glass.

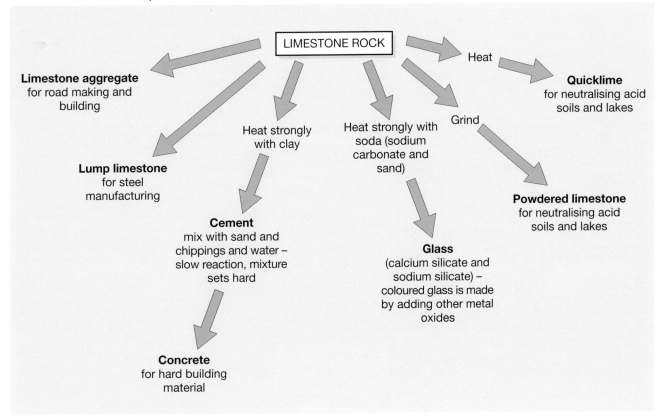

LIMESTONE ROCK

Limestone aggregate
for road making and building

Lump limestone
for steel manufacturing

Heat strongly with clay

Cement
mix with sand and chippings and water – slow reaction, mixture sets hard

Concrete
for hard building material

Heat strongly with soda (sodium carbonate and sand)

Glass
(calcium silicate and sodium silicate) – coloured glass is made by adding other metal oxides

Grind

Powdered limestone
for neutralising acid soils and lakes

Heat

Quicklime
for neutralising acid soils and lakes

Figure 4 Uses of limestone

Reactions of limestone (calcium carbonate)

Limestone is fairly pure calcium carbonate. It is heated in huge kilns to produce quicklime (calcium oxide).

calcium carbonate → calcium oxide + carbon dioxide
(limestone) (quicklime)

$$CaCO_3 \rightarrow CaO + CO_2$$

Quicklime (calcium oxide) reacts exothermically with water to produce slaked lime (calcium hydroxide).

calcium oxide + water → calcium hydroxide
(quicklime) (slaked lime)

$$CaO + H_2O \rightarrow Ca(OH)_2$$

Calcium hydroxide is slightly soluble in water. The solution is usually called 'lime water'. How is lime water used as a test for carbon dioxide?

Quicklime and slaked lime are both used, like powdered limestone, to neutralise excess acidity in soils and in lakes affected by acid rain.

Figure 5 summarises the reactions of calcium carbonate (limestone)

A helicopter drops powdered calcium carbonate (quicklime) into a lake. The lime will neutralise the acids in the water from acid rain.

There are economic advantages but also environmental problems in quarrying for limestone. The balance between advantages and disadvantages is not always clear. The key issues to consider are similar to those involved in mining metal ores (Table 1 in Chapter 16, on page 156).

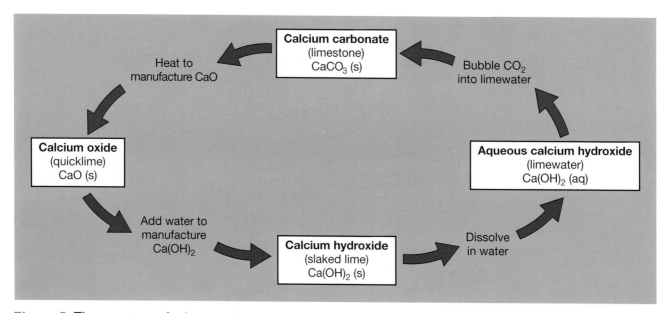

Calcium carbonate (limestone) $CaCO_3$ (s)

Heat to manufacture CaO

Bubble CO_2 into limewater

Calcium oxide (quicklime) CaO (s)

Add water to manufacture $Ca(OH)_2$

Aqueous calcium hydroxide (limewater) $Ca(OH)_2$ (aq)

Calcium hydroxide (slaked lime) $Ca(OH)_2$ (s)

Dissolve in water

Figure 5 The reactions of calcium carbonate

15.7 Displacing metals

Earlier in this chapter, we studied the reactions of metals with acids. Metals above copper in the reactivity series react with acids to form a salt and hydrogen. For example:

$$\text{zinc} + \underset{\text{acid}}{\text{sulphuric}} \rightarrow \underset{\text{sulphate}}{\text{zinc}} + \text{hydrogen}$$

$$\text{Zn} + \text{H}_2\text{SO}_4 \rightarrow \text{ZnSO}_4 + \text{H}_2$$

In this case, zinc has *displaced* hydrogen (H_2) from H_2SO_4. If zinc can displace H_2 from H_2SO_4, it may be able to displace Cu from CuSO_4. This is because zinc is more reactive (higher up the reactivity series) than copper. Let's look at some more displacement reactions.

Figure 6 shows what happens when strips of zinc are placed in solutions of different metal compounds. Notice that:

★ Zinc displaces lead from lead nitrate solution, copper from copper sulphate solution and silver from silver nitrate solution.

★ Zinc does not displace magnesium from magnesium sulphate solution.

When zinc is placed in copper sulphate solution, the zinc gets coated with red-brown copper. At the same time, the blue colour of the solution fades.

$$\text{zinc} + \underset{\text{sulphate}}{\text{copper}} \rightarrow \underset{\text{sulphate}}{\text{zinc}} + \text{copper}$$

$$\text{Zn} + \text{CuSO}_4 \rightarrow \text{ZnSO}_4 + \text{Cu}$$

In the reaction, zinc has displaced copper from the solution. Copper has been deposited on the zinc. Zinc ions have replaced copper ions in the copper sulphate solution.

Table 2 (on the next page) summarises the results of the experiment in Figure 6. It also shows the results of four other experiments in which magnesium, iron, lead and copper were used in place of zinc.

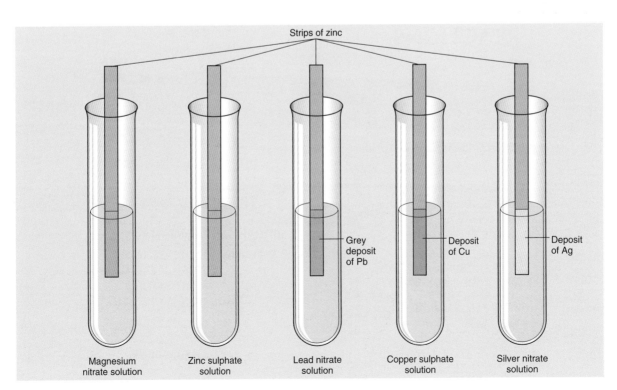

Figure 6 Investigating displacement reactions with zinc.

Notice two things in Table 2.

1 The deposits form if the metal added displaces the second metal from a solution of its ions. Reactions like these in which one metal displaces another are usually called **displacement reactions**.

2 The metals and their solutions are written in the order of the reactivity series. **Each metal only displaces metals which are below it in the reactivity series**. So, zinc can displace lead, copper and silver, but not magnesium. Lead can displace copper and silver, but not magnesium and zinc.

These experiments confirm that magnesium is more reactive than the other metals in Table 2. Magnesium reacts and forms its ions as it displaces the other metals from a solution.

$$Mg + Zn^{2+} \rightarrow Mg^{2+} + Zn$$

So, magnesium is higher in the reactivity series than the other metals in Table 2. In the same way, zinc is more reactive than lead, copper and silver, but less reactive than magnesium. So, zinc is above lead, copper and silver in the reactivity series, but below magnesium. These results provide further evidence for the order of metals in the reactivity series.

Metal used	Results with an aqueous solution of:				
	magnesium nitrate	zinc sulphate	lead nitrate	copper sulphate	silver nitrate
Mg		Dark grey deposit of zinc	Grey deposit of lead	Red-brown deposit of copper	Black deposit of silver
Zn	**NO REACTIONS**		Grey deposit of lead	Red-brown deposit of copper	Black deposit of silver
Fe			Grey deposit of lead	Red-brown deposit of copper	Black deposit of silver
Pb				Red-brown deposits of Cu forms slowly	Grey-black deposit of silver
Cu					Black deposit of silver

Table 2 The results of some displacement reactions with metals

Summary

1 The uses of metals depend on their properties.

2 metal + oxygen → metal oxide

3 metal + water → metal oxide + hydrogen (hydrogen oxide)

4 metal + acid → metal + hydrogen compound (salt)

5 The **reactivity series** shows the order of reactivity for metals. It provides a helpful summary of all the reactions of metals.

6 ★ **Oxidation** is the **gain** of oxygen.

   ★ **Reduction** is the **loss** of oxygen.

7 ★ **Exothermic** reactions **give out** heat.

   ★ **Endothermic** reactions **take in** heat.

Summary

8 A metal will **displace** from solution any metal below it in the reactivity series.

9 The table shows a summary of the reactions of metals based on the reactivity series. The order of reactivity for metals is the same with air (oxygen), water and dilute acids.

Reactivity series	Reaction with oxygen when heated in air	Reaction with water	Reaction with dilute acids	Reactions with solutions of metal salts	Symbols
Potassium Sodium Calcium Magnesium	Burn with decreasing reactivity down the series to form their oxide	React with water with decreasing reactivity down the series forming hydrogen	React with dilute HCl and dilute H_2SO_4, less and less vigorously down the series, producing hydrogen	Each metal will displace metals below it in the reactivity series from solutions of their salts	K Na Ca Mg
Aluminium Zinc Iron		React with steam, but not water forming hydrogen			Al Zn Fe
Lead Copper	Only form a layer of oxide	Do not react with water or steam			Pb Cu
Silver Gold	Do not react		Do not react with dilute acid		Ag Au
General equation	$2M + O_2 \rightarrow 2MO$	$M + H_2O \rightarrow MO + H_2$	$M + 2HCl \rightarrow MCl_2 + H_2$ $M + H_2SO_4 \rightarrow MSO_4 + H_2$		

Exam questions for Chapter 15

1 a) Drinks are often sold in cans.

Three metals are used to make these cans. The table gives information about these metals.

Metal	Cost of 10 kg (£)	Amount in Earth's crust (%)
Aluminium	7.5	8
Iron (steel)	1.5	5
Tin	90	0.0002

The cans are made either from **aluminium** or from **steel coated with tin**.

(i) Use the information in the table to give **two** reasons why it is important to recycle tin. *(2)*

(ii) It is more difficult to recycle the tin from cans than to recycle the aluminium from cans. Why? *(1)*

b) Scientists arrange metals into a reactivity series. The diagram shows five metals in order of reactivity.

aluminium
iron
tin   decreasing reactivity
copper
gold

(i) Early in the last century, aluminium could only be made by reacting aluminium salts with sodium.

aluminium salt + sodium → sodium salt + aluminium

Suggest why sodium can be used to displace aluminium from an aluminium salt. *(1)*

(ii) Some metals such as gold and copper have been in use for a few thousand years, but aluminium has only been used on a large scale during this century.

Use the information in the reactivity series to help you to explain this.   *(3)*

[Edexcel 1998]

2   Four powdered metals **A**, **B**, **C** and **D** are placed in dilute acid. The diagram shows what happens.

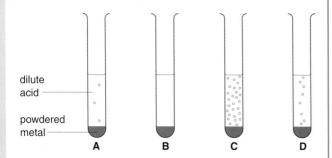

a) Use the information in the diagram to put the metals **A**, **B**, **C** and **D** in order of reactivity, from most reactive to least reactive.   *(2)*

b) A test tube of the gas produced was collected. What test could you do to show that the gas is hydrogen? Give the result of this test.   *(2)*

c) Another student placed the same four powdered metals in dilute acid, but measured the temperature rise in each tube. The student forgot to make a note of which metal was used in each tube. Copy the table below. Put metals **A**, **B**, **C** and **D** in the correct place in your table.

Metal	Temperature rise °C
	0
	16
	32
	25

(2)

[AQA (NEAB) 1998]

3   a) (i) Three metals are:

copper   iron   magnesium

List them in order of reactivity, starting with the **most** reactive.   *(2)*

(ii) Which **one** of the three metals does **not** react with dilute hydrochloric acid?   *(1)*

b) (i) A small piece of sodium is dropped into a large beaker of water. It reacts to form sodium hydroxide solution and a gas. Describe **three** things you would **see**.   *(3)*

(ii) Give the name of the gas formed by this reaction.   *(1)*

(iii) Sodium hydroxide solution is alkaline. Suggest the pH of the solution.   *(2)*

(iv) How would the temperature of the water change during the reaction?   *(2)*

[Edexcel 1999]

4   The diagram shows some magnesium ribbon burning.

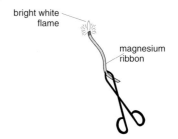

a) Copy the sentences below. Choose words from the list to complete your sentences.

electrical   heat   light   kinetic

an endothermic   an exothermic
    a neutralisation   a reduction

When magnesium burns, it transfers _____ and _____ energy to the surroundings. We say that it is _____ reaction.   *(3)*

b) Complete a copy of the word equation for the reaction.

magnesium + _____ → magnesium oxide
(1)

[AQA (NEAB) 1999]

5   The uses of metals are linked to their properties. Copy the table below which shows the uses and properties of some metals. Complete the spaces in your table.

Metal	Property	Use
Aluminium		Manufacture of saucepans
Copper	Very unreactive	
	Low melting point	In solder

(3)

[NICCEA 1998]

16

Extracting metals

16.1 From rocks to metals

16.3 Extracting aluminium by electrolysis

16.2 Extracting iron from iron ore

16.4 Purifying copper by electrolysis

16.1 From rocks to metals

Most metals are too reactive to exist on their own. They are usually found in rocks as compounds with non-metals. The rocks which contain metal compounds are called **ores**.

A few metals, like gold and silver, are very unreactive. They occur in the ground as uncombined metals.

A few metals, like gold, occur in the ground as the uncombined metal. This picture shows a prospector panning for gold in California in the late 19th century. He is looking for small bits of shiny gold in the sediment and stones.

Extracting metals from their ores usually involves three stages:

1 mining and concentrating the ore

2 converting the ore to the metal

3 purifying the metal.

Let's look at these three stages in more detail.

1 Mining and concentrating the ore

In order to obtain metal ores, we need to dig tunnels or make quarries. The ores we get are mixed with impurities such as rocks and soil. These impurities must be removed before the ore is converted to the metal.

Metal ores are usually much denser than soil and rocks. The rocks containing the ore are first crushed. The powder is then passed into a liquid. The heavy ore sinks and the waste material floats away. The process is called **flotation**.

Gold being separated from crushed rock at a mine in Canada. The sloping metal table vibrates, washing dense particles of gold to the bottom.

Metals are very useful, but the mines, quarries and waste heaps can cause problems. Table 1 lists some of the advantages and disadvantages of mining for metal ores.

Advantages	Disadvantages
Metals are produced and used to manufacture **thousands of useful articles**	Mining **damages the environment** with spoil heaps, quarries and mines
Mining ores and the manufacture of metal articles **creates jobs**	Mining often **destroys wildlife habitats**
The sale of ores, metals and metal products can **increase the wealth of a community**	Mining can cause **subsidence** which affects land and buildings

Table 1 Advantages and disadvantages of mining for metal ores

2 Converting the ore to the metal

Table 2 shows the ores from which we get some important metals.

Metal	Name of the ore	Name and formula of metal compound in the ore
Sodium	Rock salt	Sodium chloride, $NaCl$
Aluminium	Bauxite	Aluminium oxide, Al_2O_3
Zinc	Zinc blende	Zinc sulphide, ZnS
Iron	Iron ore (haematite)	Iron(III) oxide, Fe_2O_3
Copper	Copper pyrites	Copper sulphide and iron sulphide $CuS + FeS$ ($CuFeS_2$)

Table 2 The ores from which we get some important metals.

Notice in Table 2 that metal ores are often oxides, sulphides and chlorides. This is because oxygen, sulphur and chlorine are reactive non-metals.

The method used to get a metal from its ore depends on two factors:

★ The position of the metal in the reactivity series.

★ The cost of the process.

i) Heating the ore in air

This is the cheapest way to extract a metal. But, it only works with the compounds of metals at the bottom of the reactivity series. These can be reduced to the metal fairly easily. For example, copper is extracted from copper sulphide (copper pyrites) by heating the ore in air.

$$\text{copper sulphide} + \text{oxygen} \rightarrow \text{copper} + \text{sulphur dioxide}$$

$$CuS + O_2 \rightarrow Cu + SO_2$$

This vast copper mine is near Salt Lake City, USA

ii) Reduction with carbon and carbon monoxide

Metals in the middle of the reactivity series, like zinc, iron and lead, cannot be extracted simply by heating their ores in air. They are obtained by **reducing** their oxides with carbon (coke) or carbon monoxide.

For example

$$\text{zinc oxide} + \text{carbon (coke)} \rightarrow \text{zinc} + \text{carbon monoxide}$$

$$ZnO + C \rightarrow Zn + CO$$

Sometimes, these metals exist as sulphide ores. These ores can be converted to oxides before reduction. This is done by heating the sulphides in air.

$$\text{zinc sulphide} + \text{oxygen} \rightarrow \text{zinc oxide} + \text{sulphur dioxide}$$

In section 16.2, we will see how iron is obtained from iron ore.

iii) Electrolysis of molten compounds

Metals like sodium, magnesium and aluminium are at the top of the reactivity series. They cannot be obtained by reduction of their oxides with carbon or carbon monoxide. This is because the temperature needed to reduce their oxides is too high. We use electricity to get these metals from their ores. The process is called **electrolysis**.

But the process cannot use *aqueous* solutions. This is because electrolysis would decompose the water in the solution and not the metal compound.

The only way to extract these reactive metals is by electrolysis of their *molten* compounds ('molten' means melted). Potassium, sodium, calcium and magnesium are obtained by electrolysis of their molten chlorides. Aluminium is obtained by electrolysis of its molten oxide. This is described in section 16.3.

Table 3 (over the page) summarises the methods used to obtain different metals. Notice that the method used depends on the metal's position in the reactivity series.

Reactivity series of metals	Method used to obtain metal from its ore
Potassium Sodium Calcium Magnesium Aluminium	Electrolysis of molten ore
Zinc Iron Lead	Reduction of ore using carbon or carbon monoxide
Copper Mercury	Heating ore in air
Silver Gold	Metals occur uncombined in the ground

Table 3 A summary of the methods used to get metals from their ores.

3 Purifying the metal

After a metal has been extracted from its ore, it needs to be purified. The copper which comes straight from the furnace contains about 3% impurities. Sheets of this copper are purified by electrolysis with copper sulphate solution (section 16.4).

Similarly, iron obtained directly from the furnace contains about 7% impurities. This impure iron is called **pig-iron**. The purification of pig-iron is described in the next section.

1 What is an *ore*?

2 Name **two** metals which are found uncombined in rocks.

3 What are the **three** stages in extracting metals from their ores?

4 What method is used to get:

 (a) copper from its ores
 (b) sodium from its ores?

16.2 Extracting iron from iron ore

We get iron from iron ore (haematite). This is impure iron(III) oxide. Iron ore is changed into iron in special furnaces called **blast furnaces**. These furnaces are built as towers about 15 metres tall. Blasts of hot air are blown in at the bottom of the furnace. This keeps the temperature high.

Figure 1 shows a diagram of a blast furnace with a summary of the process involved.

Why is limestone used in the furnace?

Iron ore contains impurities like soil and sand (silicon dioxide, SiO_2). Limestone helps to remove these impurities as slag. The molten slag falls to the bottom of the furnace. Here, it floats on the molten iron. The molten slag can be tapped off separately and used in building materials and in cement making.

Large blocks of red-hot steel produced from pig-iron at a modern steel-making plant.

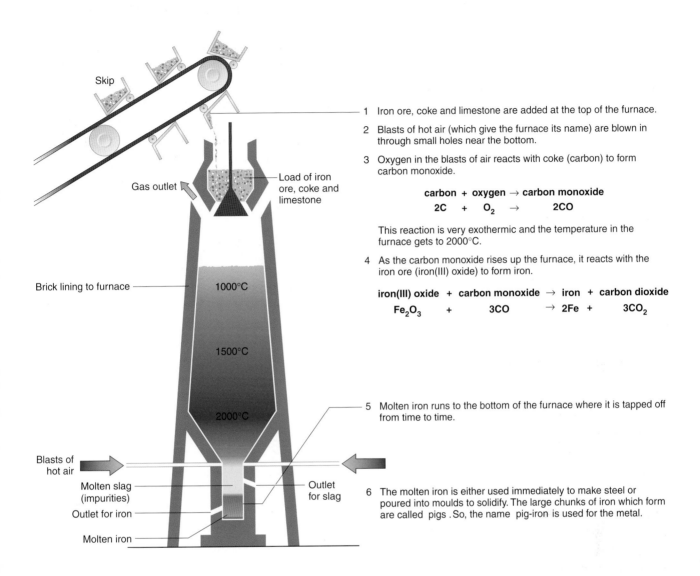

1 Iron ore, coke and limestone are added at the top of the furnace.

2 Blasts of hot air (which give the furnace its name) are blown in through small holes near the bottom.

3 Oxygen in the blasts of air reacts with coke (carbon) to form carbon monoxide.

$$\text{carbon} + \text{oxygen} \rightarrow \text{carbon monoxide}$$
$$2C + O_2 \rightarrow 2CO$$

This reaction is very exothermic and the temperature in the furnace gets to 2000°C.

4 As the carbon monoxide rises up the furnace, it reacts with the iron ore (iron(III) oxide) to form iron.

$$\text{iron(III) oxide} + \text{carbon monoxide} \rightarrow \text{iron} + \text{carbon dioxide}$$
$$Fe_2O_3 + 3CO \rightarrow 2Fe + 3CO_2$$

5 Molten iron runs to the bottom of the furnace where it is tapped off from time to time.

6 The molten iron is either used immediately to make steel or poured into moulds to solidify. The large chunks of iron which form are called pigs. So, the name pig-iron is used for the metal.

Figure 1 Extracting iron from iron ore in a blast furnace

From pig-iron to steel

Pig-iron contains about 7% of impurities. The main impurity is carbon. This makes pig-iron very brittle compared to pure iron and steel. Pig-iron could not be bent to make things like car bodies.

To make pig-iron into steel, the amount of carbon must be reduced to about 0.15%. To do this, oxygen is blown onto hot, molten pig-iron. The oxygen converts the carbon to carbon dioxide which escapes as a gas.

5 Why is the furnace used to make iron called a blast furnace?

6 Why is limestone added to the blast furnace?

7 Give **two** differences between pig-iron and steel?

<table>
<tr><td>16.3</td><td></td></tr>
</table>

16.3	### Extracting aluminium by electrolysis

Aluminium is manufactured by the electrolysis of molten aluminium oxide. We get aluminium oxide from an ore called bauxite.

Electrolysis involves the decomposition of compounds by electrical energy.

The compound which is decomposed is called an **electrolyte**.

The electric current enters and leaves the electrolyte through terminals called **electrodes**.

The electrode connected to the positive of the battery is called the **anode** and the electrode connected to the negative of the battery is called the **cathode**.

Aluminium is obtained from bauxite, impure aluminium oxide. The photo shows bauxite being mined.

Pure aluminium oxide is not used as the electrolyte because it does not melt until 2045 °C. This would make the electrolysis very expensive. Instead, the aluminium oxide is dissolved in molten cryolite (Na_3AlF_6) which melts below 1000 °C. Figure 2 shows a diagram of the electrolytic process.

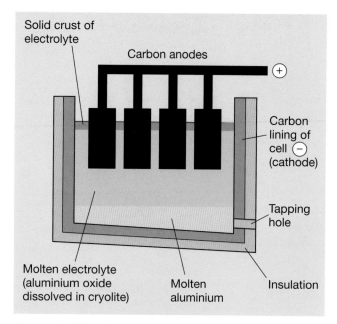

Figure 2 The electrolytic cell for aluminium manufacture

During electrolysis, positive aluminium ions in the electrolyte are attracted to the negative carbon cathode which lines the cell. Here, they combine with electrons to form neutral aluminium atoms.

Cathode (−)

$$Al^{3+} + 3e^- \rightarrow Al$$

Each aluminium ion, Al^{3+}, has three positive charges. So it needs three electrons, each with one negative charge, to form an aluminium atom.

Molten aluminium collects at the bottom of the cell and is tapped off at intervals. It takes about 16 kilowatt-hours of electricity to produce 1 kg of aluminium. The extraction plants are therefore built near sources of cheap electricity, such as hydro-electric power stations.

8   What is the main ore of aluminium?

9   What is the negative electrode called?

10   Why is cryolite used to make aluminium?

11   Where does the aluminium metal collect?

The statue of Eros is made of pure aluminium. It was placed in Piccadilly Circus, London in 1893. At that time, aluminium was almost as expensive as gold.

12 Why is aluminium so expensive to make?

<table>
<tr><td>16.4</td><td>**Purifying copper by electrolysis**</td></tr>
</table>

When copper sulphate is electrolysed with copper electrodes, copper is deposited on the cathode and the copper anode loses weight (Figure 3).

The copper sulphate solution contains copper ions (Cu^{2+}) and sulphate ions (SO_4^{2-}). During electrolysis, positive Cu^{2+} ions are attracted to the negative cathode. Here they gain electrons and form neutral copper atoms. This copper is deposited on the cathode.

Cathode (−)

$$Cu^{2+} + 2e^- \rightarrow Cu$$

During electrolysis, sulphate ions (SO_4^{2-}) are attracted to the positive anode. But they are so stable they do not react. Instead, copper atoms, which make up the anode, each give up two electrons to form Cu^{2+} ions. The Cu^{2+} ions then go into solution.

Anode (+)

$$Cu \rightarrow Cu^{2+} + 2e^-$$

The overall result is that the anode loses copper and the cathode gains copper. Copper metal goes into solution at the anode and copper metal is deposited on the cathode.

This method is used in industry to purify copper. The impure copper is the anode of the cell. The cathode is a thin sheet of pure copper. The electrolyte is copper sulphate solution. The impure copper anode 'dissolves' away and pure copper deposits on the cathode.

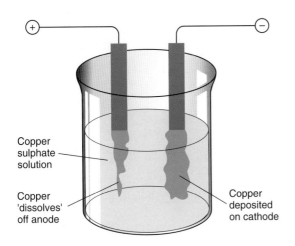

Copper sulphate solution

Copper 'dissolves' off anode

Copper deposited on cathode

Figure 3 Purifying copper by electrolysis

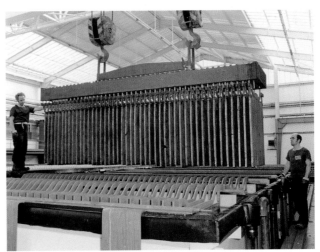

Impure copper anodes being transferred to an electrolysis tank for purification.

Summary

1   Metals occur in rocks as impure compounds called **ores**.

2   Metals are extracted from their ores.

3   Extracting metals from their ores involves three stages:

  ★   mining and concentrating the ore

  ★   converting the ore to the metal

  ★   purifying the metal.

4   Metals higher in the reactivity series are harder to extract than those lower down.

  ★   Metals high in the reactivity series (like sodium and aluminium) are extracted by **electrolysis**.

★   Metals in the middle of the reactivity series (like zinc and iron) are extracted by **reduction** with carbon or carbon monoxide in **blast furnaces**.

★   Metals low in the reactivity series (like copper) are extracted by heating in a furnace.

★   Metals at the bottom of the reactivity series (like gold and silver) occur uncombined.

5   **Electrolysis** involves the decomposition of compounds by electrical energy.

  The compound which is decomposed is called an **electrolyte**.

Exam questions for Chapter 16

1   Copper is extracted from the ore called copper pyrites.

  a) Copper pyrites contains copper and another metal. Name the other metal in copper pyrites. *(1)*

  b) One of the important reactions in the extraction of copper is shown in the symbol equation below.

  $$Cu_2S_{(l)} + O_{2(g)} \rightarrow 2\,Cu_{(l)} + SO_{2(g)}$$

  (i) Complete a copy of the word equation for this reaction.

  Copper sulphide + _____ → _____ + _____ *(2)*

  (ii) When copper is formed in this reaction, is it a solid, a liquid or a gas? *(1)*

  c) The copper obtained from the reaction in part (b) is impure. Copper used in electrical wiring must be very pure.

  Explain how pure copper is different from impure copper. *(1)*

  d) The diagram shows a method for changing impure copper into pure copper.

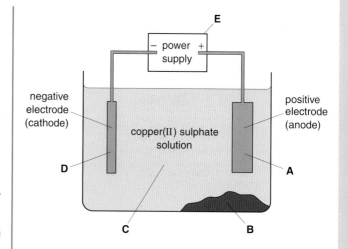

  Which of the places labelled **A, B, C, D** or **E** is where:

  (i) the impure copper is placed;

  (ii) the impurities collect;

  (iii) the pure copper collects? *(3)*

  e) The solution shown in the diagram contains copper(II) sulphate.

  Work out the formula of copper(II) sulphate. *(1)*

  [AQA (NEAB) 1998]

2 Copy the passage below. Choose words from the list to complete the passage about the extraction of aluminium. Words may be used **once** only.

> carbonate   chloride   chlorine   cryolite
> electrolysis   graphite   negative   neutralisation
> oxide   oxygen   positive   steel

The main ore of aluminium is bauxite. This is an impure form of aluminium _____ and has the formula Al_2O_3. The ore is purified and then dissolved in molten _____ . Aluminium is extracted by the process of _____ . The electrodes are made of _____ which is a form of carbon. Aluminium is produced at the _____ electrode. The gas called _____ is produced at the other electrode.   *(6)*

[AQA (NEAB) 1998]

3 Aluminium is made from aluminium oxide by electrolysis.

a) Aluminium oxide is an ionic compound.

(i) What is the formula of an aluminium ion?   *(1)*

(ii) What is the formula of an oxide ion?   *(1)*

b) The diagram shows an electrolysis cell used to make aluminium.

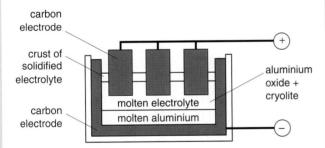

(i) Why must the electrolyte be molten?   *(1)*

(ii) Why is the aluminium oxide mixed with cryolite?   *(1)*

(iii) Why is aluminium formed at the negative electrode?   *(1)*

(iv) The positive electrodes have to be replaced frequently. What causes them to burn away?   *(1)*

c) Aluminium is a reactive metal but it resists corrosion. This is because it is covered in a layer of aluminium oxide. To give extra protection the thickness of this layer can be increased by electrolysis. Explain briefly how this is done.   *(3)*

[AQA (NEAB) 1999]

4 The 'Iron Age' began about 3000 years ago. Before the 'Iron Age' was the 'Bronze Age'. The 'Bronze Age' began when people melted copper and tin together to produce the alloy bronze.

a) Describe how copper metal can be obtained from copper oxide.   *(2)*

b) Two other metals which were available to 'Bronze Age' people were gold and silver. Suggest why they were available at that time.   *(2)*

c) The table below gives the dates of discovery of some metals.

Metal	Date of discovery
Potassium	1807
Sodium	1807
Calcium	1808
Magnesium	1808
Aluminium	1827

Explain why these metals were not discovered much earlier.   *(2)*

d) Nowadays, iron is extracted from its ore in blast furnaces.

Name the other raw materials needed at **A**, **B** and **C** and the products formed at **D**, **E** and **F**.   *(6)*

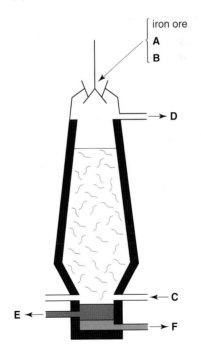

[Edexcel 1998]

CHAPTER 17

Atomic structure

17.1 Metals, non-metals and metalloids

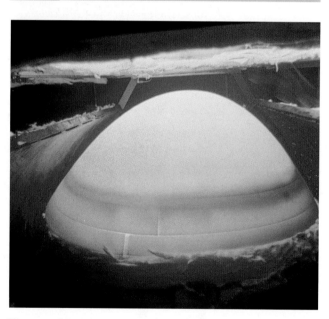

The graphite nose cone of a space shuttle. The nose cone is being tested in a furnace. Why is graphite used for the nose cone?

One way to classify elements is as metals and non-metals (section 13.3). But a few elements cannot be classified easily as either metals or non-metals. For example, graphite has a high melting point and a high boiling point (like metals), but a low density (like non-metals).

Graphite conducts electricity better than non-metals but not as well as metals.

Elements, like graphite, with some properties like metals and other properties like non-metals are called **metalloids**.

This difficulty in classifying some elements has led to further studies of elements.

17.2 Patterns of elements

During the 19th century, several chemists looked for patterns in the properties of elements. The most successful scientist was the Russian chemist Dmitri Mendeléev.

★ In 1869, Mendeléev made a list of all the elements he knew in order of their relative atomic masses.

★ Then, he put the elements in horizontal rows in a table so that elements with similar properties were in the same vertical column.

Figure 1 shows part of Mendeléev's table. Notice that elements with similar properties, such as sodium (Na) and potassium (K), fall in the same vertical column. Which other pairs of similar elements fall in the same vertical column in Mendeléev's table?

Groups

	I	II	III	IV	V	VI	VII	VIII
Period 1	H							
Period 2	Li	Be	B	C	N	O	F	
Period 3	Na	Mg	Al	Si	P	S	Cl	
Period 4	K	Ca	*	Ti	V	Cr	Mn	Fe Co Ni
	Cu	Zn	*	*	As	Se		

Figure 1 Mendeléev's periodic table

Mendeléev called his table a **periodic table** because of the *periodic* repetition (repeating) of similar elements.

In the periodic table:

★ the vertical columns of similar elements are called **groups**

★ the horizontal rows of elements are called **periods**.

Mendeléev had two clever ideas in setting out his periodic table.

1 He left gaps in his table so that similar elements were in the same vertical group. Three of these gaps are shown as asterisks in Figure 1.

2 He predicted the properties of elements to fill these gaps. He did this by looking at the properties of elements above and below the gaps in his table. Within 15 years, the three missing elements had been discovered. They were called scandium, gallium and germanium. Their properties were very similar to Mendeléev's predictions.

This made chemists realise that Mendeléev's periodic table was a very helpful summary of the properties of elements.

Dmitri Mendeléev was the first chemist to put elements in a periodic table.

1 Who developed the first periodic table?

2 How did he decide the order in which to put the elements?

3 What are the vertical columns called?

4 What are the horizontal columns called?

5 Name the **three** missing elements in the first periodic table.

17.3 The modern periodic table

The modern periodic table is based on Mendeléev's. It shows all the elements numbered along each period, starting with period 1, then period 2, etc. The number given to each element is called its **atomic number**. Thus, hydrogen has an atomic number of 1, helium 2, lithium 3, etc. You will learn more about atomic numbers in section 17.4.

Notice the following points about the modern periodic table.

★ The big difference between modern periodic tables and Mendeléev's is the position of the **transition elements**. These have been taken out of the simple groups and placed between group II and group III. Period 4 is the first to contain a series of transition elements.

Transition elements which belong to period 4 include chromium, iron, copper and zinc.

★ Some groups have names as well as numbers. These names are shown below the group numbers in Figure 2.

★ Metals are clearly separated from non-metals. The 20 or so non-metals are packed into the top right-hand corner above the thick stepped line in Figure 2. Some elements close to the steps are classed as metalloids.

★ From left to right across each period, the elements change from metals, through metalloids to non-metals.

★ In each group of the periodic table, the elements have similar properties. But, there is a gradual change in properties from the top to the bottom of a group.

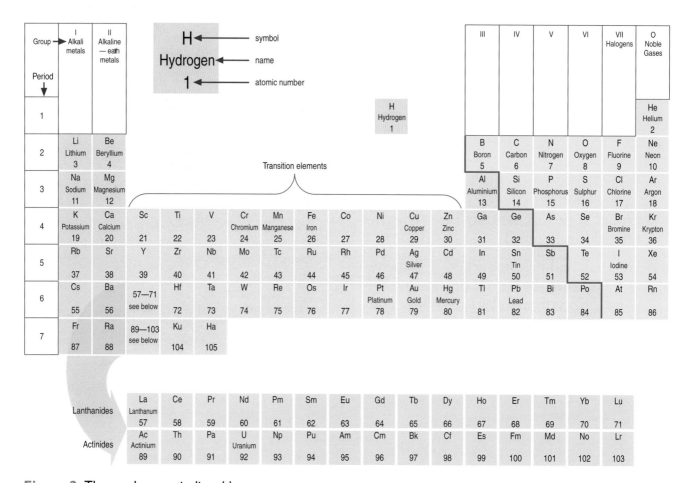

Figure 2 The modern periodic table

★ Apart from noble gases, the most reactive elements are near the left and right-hand sides of the periodic table. The least reactive elements are in the centre. Sodium and potassium, two very reactive metals, are on the left-hand side. The next most reactive metals, like calcium and magnesium, are in group II. Less reactive metals (like iron and copper) are in the centre of the table. Carbon and silicon, unreactive non-metals, are also in the centre of the periodic table. Sulphur and oxygen, which are nearer the right-hand edge, are more reactive. Fluorine and chlorine, the most reactive non-metals, are very close to the right-hand edge.

★ The periodic table shows all the elements arranged in order of atomic number.

Use the modern periodic table to answer these questions.

6 Name **two** elements from group I.

7 Name **two** transition metals.

8 In which part of the table do you find:

a) non-metals

b) the most reactive metals?

9 Which element has an atomic number of 16?

17.4 Atomic structure

A century ago, scientists thought that atoms were hard, solid particles like tiny marbles. Early in the 20th century, experiments led to a clearer picture for the structure of atoms.

★ All atoms are built from just three particles – **protons**, **neutrons** and **electrons**.

★ The centre of an atom is called the **nucleus**. This contains the protons and neutrons. The nucleus takes up less than 1% of the volume of an atom.

★ Protons and neutrons have the same mass. The proton and neutron are each given a relative mass of one.

★ Protons have a positive charge, but neutrons are neutral (i.e. they have no charge).

★ More than 99% of an atom is empty space occupied by moving **electrons**.

★ An electron has a mass about 2000 times less than that of a proton or a neutron.

★ Electrons have a negative charge. The negative charge on one electron just cancels the positive charge on one proton.

★ Electrons move around very rapidly. They occupy layers or **shells** at different distances from the nucleus.

The key points about atomic structure are summarised below in Table 1.

Protons, neutrons and electrons are the building blocks for all atoms. Hydrogen atoms are the simplest atoms. Each hydrogen atom has one proton and one electron (Figure 3a, over the page). The next simplest atoms are those of helium with two protons, two electrons and two neutrons. After helium comes lithium, with three protons, three electrons and four neutrons (Figure 3b).

Particle	Position in the atom	Relative mass	Relative charge
Proton	Nucleus	1	+1
Neutron	Nucleus	1	0
Electron	Shells	$\frac{1}{2000}$	−1

Table 1 Protons, neutrons and electrons in atomic structure

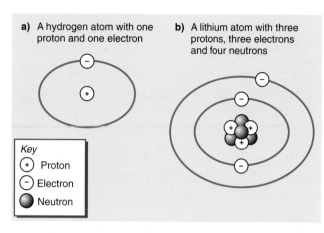

a) A hydrogen atom with one proton and one electron

b) A lithium atom with three protons, three electrons and four neutrons

Key
(+) Proton
(−) Electron
(●) Neutron

Figure 3 The atomic structure of a hydrogen atom and a lithium atom

Some of the heaviest atoms have large numbers of protons, neutrons and electrons. For example, uranium atoms have 92 protons, 92 electrons and 143 neutrons.

Notice in all these examples, that **an atom always has the same number of protons and electrons**. This ensures that the positive charges on the protons balance the negative charges on the electrons. This keeps the atom neutral overall.

Suppose the nucleus of an atom was enlarged to the size of a pea and placed on the top of Nelson's Column. The electrons furthest away would be like specs of dust on the pavement.

10 Draw and label an atom of helium.

11 Which particle has no charge?

12 How many times bigger is a proton compared to an electron?

13 How many protons, neutrons and electrons are found in a uranium-235 atom?

17.5	**Atomic number and mass number**

The only atoms with one proton are those of hydrogen.
The only atoms with two protons are those of helium.
The only atoms with three protons are those of lithium and so on.
So, the number of protons in an atom tells you which element it is.

The number of protons in an atom is called its **atomic number**.

Hydrogen atoms have one proton. So, hydrogen has an atomic number of one, helium has an atomic number of two, lithium three, and so on.

Remember also that the order of the element in the periodic table tells you its atomic number (Figure 2). So, chlorine, the seventeenth element in the periodic table with 17 protons and 17 electrons, has an atomic number of 17.

The mass of the electrons in an atom is tiny compared to the mass of protons and neutrons in an atom (Table 1). Therefore the mass of an atom will depend on the number of its protons plus neutrons. This number is called the **mass number** of the atom.

Atomic number = number of protons

$$\text{Mass number} = \frac{\text{number of}}{\text{protons}} + \frac{\text{number of}}{\text{neutrons}}$$

So, aluminium atoms, with 13 protons and 14 neutrons, have an atomic number of 13 and a mass number of 27. Figure 4 shows how the mass number and atomic number are often shown with the symbol of an element.

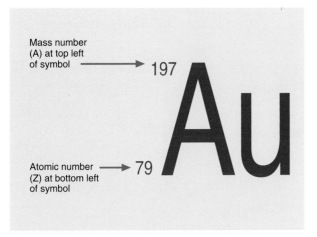

Mass number (A) at top left of symbol → 197

Atomic number (Z) at bottom left of symbol → 79

Au

Figure 4 The mass number and the atomic number for gold (Au). How many protons, neutrons and electrons are there in a gold atom?

17.6 Isotopes and relative atomic mass

Some elements have relative atomic masses which are whole numbers. For example, the relative atomic mass of carbon is 12.0, that of fluorine is 19.0 and that of sodium is 23.0. This is not surprising. The mass of an atom depends on the mass of its protons and neutrons and both of these have a relative mass of 1.0. We could calculate the relative mass of fluorine as follows:

One $^{19}_{9}F$ atom has:

9 protons – relative mass   = 9.0

9 electrons – relative mass = 0.0

10 neutrons – relative mass = 10.0

∴ relative atomic mass of a $^{19}_{9}F$ atom = 19.0

Some other elements have relative atomic masses that are nowhere near whole numbers.

For example, the relative atomic mass of chlorine is 35.5 and that of copper is 63.5. These unexpected results were explained in 1919. In that year, W.F. Aston built the first mass spectrometer. Using his mass spectrometer, Aston found that one element could have atoms with different masses. These atoms have the same number of protons, but have different numbers of neutrons.

These atoms of the same element with different masses are called **isotopes**. Each isotope has a relative atomic mass which is a whole number, but the average relative atomic mass for the mixture of isotopes is not always a whole number.

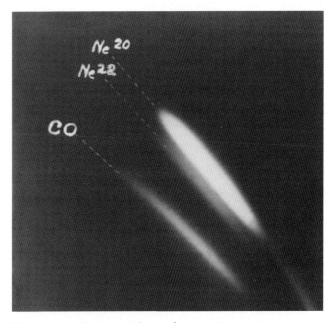

This photo shows evidence for two isotopes in neon, neon-20 and neon-22. The trace for neon-20 is much thicker than that for neon-22. This means there are more neon-20 atoms. What does CO represent?

Chlorine is a good example of an element with isotopes (Figure 5, over the page). Naturally-occurring chlorine contains two isotopes, $^{35}_{17}Cl$ called chlorine-35 and $^{37}_{17}Cl$ called chlorine-37. Each of these isotopes has 17 protons and 17 electrons. Therefore, both isotopes have the same atomic number. They also have the *same chemical properties* because these are determined by the number of electrons.

However, one isotope ($^{35}_{17}$Cl) has 18 neutrons and the other ($^{35}_{17}$Cl) has 20 neutrons. Therefore, they have different mass numbers. This gives them different masses and hence *different physical properties* because these depend on the masses of the atoms

Chlorine-35	Chlorine-37
Mass number = 35 **Cl**	Mass number = 37 **Cl**
Atomic number =17	Atomic number =17
17 protons	17 protons
17 electrons	17 electrons
18 neutrons	20 neutrons

Figure 5 Isotopes of chlorine

The similarities and differences between isotopes of the same element are summarised in Table 2.

Isotopes have the same	Isotopes have different
Number of protons	
Number of electrons	Numbers of neutrons
Atomic number	Mass numbers
Chemical properties	Physical properties

Table 2 The similarities and differences between isotopes

Isotopes are atoms with the same atomic number but different mass numbers.

14 What is meant by:

   a) the atomic number of an atom

   b) the mass number of an atom

   c) isotopes?

15 Why do isotopes of an element have the same chemical properties?

16 Describe the atomic structure of the two isotopes of chlorine.

Summary

1 Some elements, like graphite, are difficult to classify as metals or non-metals. They have some properties like metals and some properties like non-metals. These elements are known as **metalloids**.

2 The periodic table shows that **the properties of elements are closely related to their atomic number**. Elements with similar properties fall in the same vertical column in the periodic table.

3 In the periodic table:

   ★ the vertical columns are called **groups**

   ★ the horizontal rows are called **periods**.

4 All atoms are built up from **protons**, **neutrons** and **electrons**. The proton and the neutron have a mass of one unit. The electron has a mass of $\frac{1}{2000}$ th of a unit. The proton has a positive charge, the electron has a negative charge and the neutron has no charge.

5 The **atomic number** of an atom

   = the number of protons

   = the order of the element in the periodic table.

   The **mass number** of an atom

   = number of protons + number of neutrons.

6 Isotopes have the same
   - number of protons
   - number of electrons
   - atomic number
   - chemical properties

   Isotopes have different
   - numbers of neutrons
   - mass numbers
   - physical properties

1 The diagram represents an atom. Choose words from the list for each of the labels **A**, **B** and **C**.

electron   ion   neutron   nucleus   *(3)*

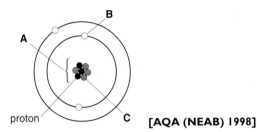

proton   **[AQA (NEAB) 1998]**

2 This question is about elements and atoms.

a) About how many different elements are found on Earth? Choose the correct number.

40   50   60   70   80   90   *(1)*

b) The following are parts of an atom:

electron   neutron   nucleus   proton

Choose from the list the one which:

(i) has no electrical charge;

(ii) contains two of the other particles;

(iii) has very little (negligible) mass.   *(3)*

c) Scientists have been able to make new elements in nuclear reactors. One of these new elements is fermium. An atom of fermium is represented by the symbol below.

$$^{257}_{100}\text{Fm}$$

(i) How many protons does this atom contain?

(ii) How many neutrons does this atom contain?   *(2)*   **[AQA (NEAB) 1999]**

3 Part of the periodic table which Mendeléev published in 1869 is shown at the bottom of the page.

Use the periodic table on page 166 to help you to answer this question.

a) (i) Give the symbols of **two** elements in group 1 of Mendeléev's periodic table which are **not** found in group 1 of the modern periodic table.   *(1)*

(ii) Name these **two** elements.   *(2)*

b) Which group of elements in the modern periodic table is missing on Mendeléev's table?   *(1)*

c) Mendeléev left several gaps in his periodic table. These gaps are shown as asterisks(*) on the table.

Suggest why Mendeléev left these gaps.   *(1)*

d) Complete a copy of the following sentence.

In the **modern** periodic table the elements are arranged in the order of their _____ numbers.   *(1)*

e) Mendeléev placed lithium, sodium and potassium in group 1 of his periodic table. This was because they have similar properties.

Some properties of elements are given in the table. **Four** of them are properties of lithium, sodium and potassium. One of these properties has been ticked for you. Write down the other **three** properties.   *(3)*

Property	
They react with water to give alkaline solutions	
They are gases.	
They are non-metals.	
They form an ion with a 1+ charge.	
They react with water and give off hydrogen.	✓
They form an ion with a 1– charge.	
They are metals.	
They react with water to give acidic solutions.	

f) What happens when a small piece of sodium reacts with water?

You should describe what you would see and state what substances are formed.   *(3)*

	Group 1	Group 2	Group 3	Group 4	Group 5	Group 6	Group 7
Period 1	H						
Period 2	Li	Be	B	C	N	O	F
Period 3	Na	Mg	Al	Si	P	S	Cl
Period 4	K	Ca	*	Ti	V	Cr	Mn
	Cu	Zn	*	*	As	Se	Br
Period 5	Rb	Sr	Y	Zr	Nb	Mo	*
	Ag	Cd	In	Sn	Sb	Te	I

[AQA (NEAB) 1999]

CHAPTER

18

The periodic table

18.1 Types of elements and the periodic table

18.2 The alkali metals – reactive metals

18.3 The halogens – reactive non-metals

18.4 The noble gases – unreactive non-metals

18.5 The transition metals – useful metals

18.1 Types of elements and the periodic table

The periodic table is a simple way to summarise the properties of all elements.

The table can be divided into four blocks of elements. Each block contains similar elements. The four blocks of similar elements are shown in Figure 1.

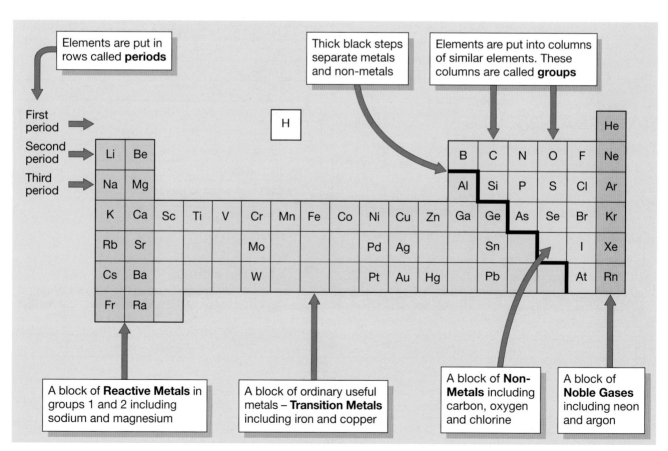

Figure 1 Blocks of similar elements in the periodic table.

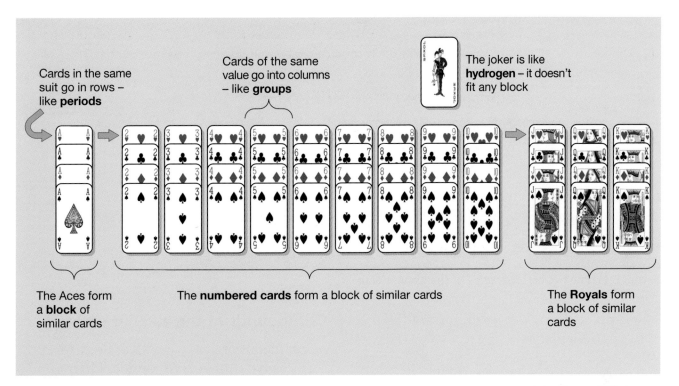

Figure 2 A pack of playing cards is like the periodic table of elements.

The periodic table is like a pack of playing cards (Figure 2). The periodic table has four blocks of similar elements. A pack of cards has four sets of similar cards – hearts, clubs, diamonds and spades.

In the next four sections we will look at the properties of some elements. Each section looks at elements in one of the four blocks.

18.2 **The alkali metals – reactive metals**

The first block contains the elements from groups I and II. They are reactive metals.

The elements in group I are called **alkali metals** (Figure 3). They are called alkali metals because they react with water to form alkaline solutions. The alkali metals are very reactive. They must be stored under oil. This prevents them reacting with oxygen and water vapour in the air. Some of the properties and reactions of the alkali metals are summarised in Table 1 (over the page).

Notice three important points from Table 1.

1 All alkali metals have very similar properties and reactions.

2 The alkali metals are softer and have much lower melting points, boiling points and densities than other metals.

3 The reactions of the alkali metals with air and water show that the elements get more reactive from lithium to potassium. They become more reactive with an increase in their relative atomic mass.

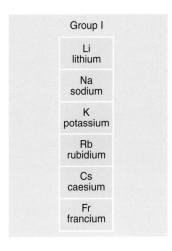

Group I

Li lithium
Na sodium
K potassium
Rb rubidium
Cs caesium
Fr francium

Figure 3 The alkali metals

Property	Property/reaction
Appearance	Shiny when freshly cut. Then reacts quickly with oxygen in the air to form a dull layer of oxide.
Hardness	Soft metals. Li, Na and K can be cut with a knife.
Melting and boiling points	Low compared with other metals.
Density	Low compared with other metals. Li, Na and K will float on water.
Reaction with air	Burn to form white oxides, e.g. sodium + oxygen → sodium oxide The metals get more reactive from Li down the group.
Reaction with water	Li reacts steadily, sodium vigorously, potassium violently. The products are an alkaline solution of the metal hydroxide and hydrogen e.g. sodium + water → sodium hydroxide + hydrogen

Table 1 Properties and reactions of the alkali metals.

These points bring out an important feature of the periodic table.

Elements in the same group of the periodic table have similar properties. There is a gradual change in the properties of the elements from the top to the bottom of the group.

We can use this idea to predict the properties of different elements.

Potassium reacts violently with water. Potassium hydroxide and hydrogen gas are formed. The reaction produces so much heat that the hydrogen gas catches fire. The hydrogen burns with a violet flame because potassium gas is present.

Compounds of the alkali metals

Alkali metals are very reactive. They react very easily to form compounds. Their compounds are made up of positive ions from the alkali metals (e.g. Na^+) and negative ions from non-metals (e.g. Cl^-).

The solid compounds of the alkali metals are white. These compounds are soluble (dissolve) in water. They form colourless solutions unless the negative ion in the compound is coloured. The most important sodium compounds are sodium chloride (Na^+Cl^-) and sodium hydroxide (Na^+OH^-).

Rock salt being mined in the USA

The yellow glow from this street light is produced by a sodium vapour lamp

Sodium chloride is an important raw material for the chemical industry.

Sea water contains sodium chloride (salt). In hot countries, sea water is allowed to evaporate and the salt is collected when dry. Sodium chloride also occurs in salt beds below the ground. Impure salt is used for treating icy roads. Pure salt is used in cooking. We put salt on our chips to make them taste better.

Sodium metal is obtained by electrolysis of molten sodium chloride. We use it in street lamps. The sodium vapour lamps have a yellow glow.

Sodium hydroxide is used to remove gums and resins from wood pulp. The pure pulp is then made into paper.

Sodium hydroxide is manufactured by the electrolysis of *aqueous* sodium chloride (brine). Chlorine is produced at the same time.

Sodium hydroxide is used in large amounts in industry. It is used to make soap, paper and rayon. Paper and rayon are made from wood. The wood is ground up into pulp and soaked in sodium hydroxide solution. This removes gums and resins, leaving the natural fibres.

Soaps and soap powders are made by boiling oils and fats with sodium hydroxide. The oils and fats are converted to complex sodium compounds which make up soap. Sodium hydroxide is also used in oven and drain cleaners because it reacts with and removes fats and grease. It will also react with our skin. We must be very careful when we use oven and drain cleaners.

Oven cleaner containing sodium hydroxide being used. The user is wearing rubber gloves and eye protection.

1 In which group are the alkali metals?

2 Which is the most reactive alkali metal?

3 Name **two** uses of sodium chloride.

4 Name **three** uses of sodium hydroxide.

18.3 The halogens – reactive non-metals

Let's now look at another block of elements in the periodic table. They are the elements in group VII. They are called **halogens** (Figure 4). They form a group of reactive non-metals. The halogens are so reactive that they never occur naturally as elements. They are always combined with metals in salts such as sodium chloride (NaCl), calcium fluoride (CaF_2) and magnesium bromide ($MgBr_2$). The name halogen means 'salt-former'.

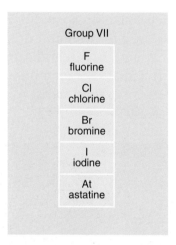

Group VII
F fluorine
Cl chlorine
Br bromine
I iodine
At astatine

Figure 4 The halogens

Trends in properties

Table 2 lists some physical properties for the common halogens, which are chlorine, bromine and iodine. Look at Table 2. Let's see how properties change as the relative atomic mass increases from chlorine to iodine.

We can look at four properties:

1 state at room temperature
2 colour
3 melting point
4 boiling point.

All the halogens exist as **simple molecules**, Cl_2, Br_2, I_2. Strong bonds hold the two atoms together as a molecule. But, the bonds which separate the molecules are very weak. This means that the molecules are easily separated. As a result, the halogens have low melting points and low boiling points.

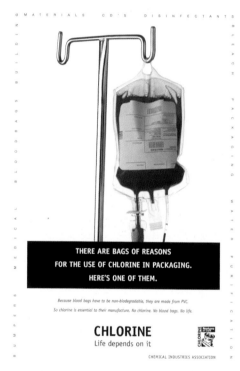

THERE ARE BAGS OF REASONS
FOR THE USE OF CHLORINE IN PACKAGING.
HERE'S ONE OF THEM.

Because blood bags have to be non-biodegradable, they are made from PVC.
So chlorine is essential to their manufacture. No chlorine. No blood bags. No life.

CHLORINE
Life depends on it

CHEMICAL INDUSTRIES ASSOCIATION

Chlorine is a very important chemical. It is used in bleaches, degreasing agents, pesticides, disinfectants and in the manufacture of PVC. Blood bags are made of PVC. The plastic is not biodegradable. It keeps the blood in good condition.

Element	Relative atomic mass	State at room temperature	Colour	Structure	Melting point (°C)	Boiling point (°C)
Chlorine	35.5	Gas	Pale green	Cl_2 molecules	−101	−35
Bromine	79.9	Liquid	Red brown	Br_2 molecules	−7	58
Iodine	126.9	Solid	Dark grey	I_2 molecules	114	183

Table 2 Some properties of chlorine, bromine and iodine

As we move down the group, the halogen molecules get larger and heavier. Therefore, from chlorine to iodine, they are gradually more difficult to melt and vaporise. This results in higher melting points and boiling points.

Reactions of the halogens

The chemical reactions of the halogens are similar, but there are gradual changes from one element to the next down the group. Fluorine is the most reactive of all non-metals. Chlorine is also very reactive. Iodine is only moderately reactive.

Chlorine is the most important element in group VII. Some of the uses of chlorine are shown in Figure 5.

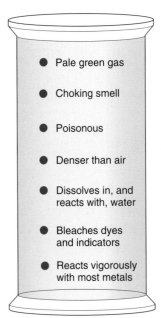

- Pale green gas
- Choking smell
- Poisonous
- Denser than air
- Dissolves in, and reacts with, water
- Bleaches dyes and indicators
- Reacts vigorously with most metals

Figure 6 Important properties of chlorine

Chlorine is added to tap water in very small quantities to kill bacteria and viruses

Chlorine is added to water in swimming pools to kill bacteria and viruses

Bleach for cleaning toilets and drains contains chlorine and chlorine compounds

Chlorine is used to make various pesticides e.g. DDT

Chlorine is used to make PVC (polyvinyl chloride) – for suitcases, furniture, clothes

Various solvents are made from chlorine – tetrachloroethene (dry cleaning clothes)

Figure 5 Important uses of chlorine

Soldiers wore gas masks to protect them from chlorine and other poisonous gases during the First World War.

The important properties of chlorine are summarised in Figure 6. Remember that chlorine is **poisonous** (toxic) and it has a choking smell. It was used as a poison gas in the First World War. Always treat chlorine with care! Experiments with chlorine should always be done in a fume cupboard.

Reactions with water

The halogens react with water to form an acidic solution. Chlorine reacts to form a strongly acidic solution:

chlorine + water → hydrochloric acid + hypochlorous acid

$$Cl_2 + H_2O \rightarrow HCl + HClO$$

Bromine reacts much less with water. The solution which forms is less acidic. Iodine reacts only slightly with water. The solution is only slightly acidic.

We can use this reaction as a test for chlorine.

Chlorine bleaches the colour from moist litmus paper.

If blue litmus paper is used, this turns red at first (because chlorine is reacting with water to form an acidic solution). Then the paper goes white.

Reactions with sodium

Sodium will burn fast and vigorously in chlorine (Figure 7). The product is sodium chloride.

$$\text{sodium} + \text{chlorine} \rightarrow \text{sodium chloride}$$
$$2Na \quad + \quad Cl_2 \quad \rightarrow \quad 2NaCl$$

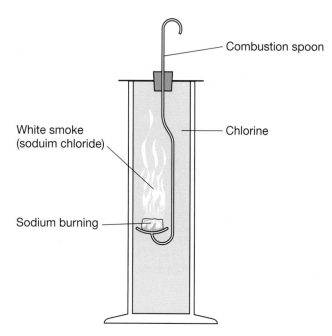

Figure 7 Sodium burning in chlorine.

Sodium also burns in bromine vapour, but much less vigorously. The product is sodium bromide.

$$\text{sodium} + \text{bromine} \rightarrow \text{sodium bromide}$$
$$2Na \quad + \quad Br_2 \quad \rightarrow \quad 2NaBr$$

Notice that the halogens react with sodium and with other metals to form salts, which are called chlorides, bromides and iodides.

Notice that **the halogens get less reactive as their relative atomic mass increases**. This is opposite to the trend in group I where the alkali metals get more reactive with increasing atomic mass.

5 In which group are the halogens?

6 Which is the most reactive halogen?

7 Which halogen is used to make bleaches?

8 What is the test for chlorine?

9 Copy and complete these word equations.

_____ + chlorine → sodium _____

sodium + _____ → _____ bromide

18.4 The noble gases – unreactive non-metals

Figure 8 shows the noble gases in group 0 of the periodic table. The most common noble gas is argon which makes up almost 1% of dry air. Neon, krypton and xenon occur in smaller quantities in the air. These four noble gases are obtained industrially during fractional distillation of liquid air. There are only small traces of helium in the air.

Properties of the noble gases

The noble gases are all colourless and very unreactive. They have very low melting points, boiling points and densities. These show a steady increase as their relative atomic mass increases. The graph in Figure 9 shows the trend in their boiling points and densities with increasing relative atomic mass.

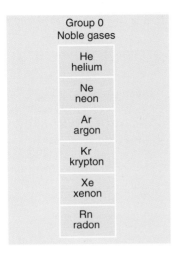

Figure 8 The noble gases in group 0 of the periodic table

The noble gases exist as separate single atoms. Until 1962, no compounds of the noble gases were known. Chemists thought they were completely unreactive. This is why they were called the *inert* gases. Nowadays, several compounds of them are known. The name *inert* has been replaced by noble. Remember, the unreactive metals such as gold are called **noble metals**.

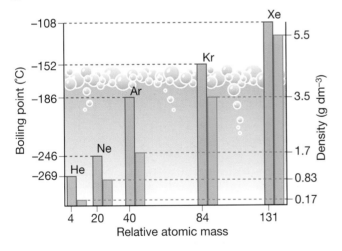

Figure 9 A graph showing the increase in boiling point and density of the noble gases with relative atomic mass.

Uses of the noble gases

Neon lights in Piccadilly

An advertising balloon filled with helium. Notice the ropes holding the balloon to the ground.

Noble gas	Use	Reason for the use
Helium	In weather balloons and advertising airships	Very low density, non flammable
Neon	In neon advertising lights	Neon gives a bright glow when an electric spark passes through it
Argon	During welding and in lasers	Argon covers the very hot materials during the welding or laser process so that there is no reaction with oxygen in the air
Argon and krypton	In electric light bulbs	White hot tungsten wires (filaments) in electric lights will not react with argon or krypton

Table 3 Important uses of the noble gases

Table 3 shows some important uses of the noble gases with reasons for these uses.

10 Which is the most common noble gas?

11 Why are these gases called noble gases?

12 Name **one** use of helium.

13 Name **one** noble gas used in light bulbs.

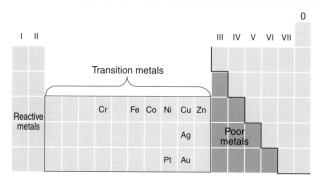

Figure 10 The position of transition metals in the periodic table

18.5 The transition metals – useful metals

The final block of the periodic table we shall look at is that containing the **transition metals**.

Figure 10 shows the position of transition metals in the periodic table. They lie between the reactive metals in groups I and II and the poor metals in groups III and IV. Symbols of the more common transition metals are also shown in Figure 10.

All the transition metals have similar properties. Unlike other parts of the periodic table, there are similarities *across* the periods as well as *down* the groups.

Uses of the transition metals

The transition metals are very useful metals. The most important transition metals are iron and copper. Iron is the most widely used metal. More than 700 million tonnes of it are manufactured each year. Almost all of this is converted to steel which is hard, strong and relatively cheap. Steel is used in girders, in engines and in tools.

After iron and aluminium, copper is the third most widely used metal. About 10 million tonnes are manufactured each year. Copper is a good conductor of heat and electricity. It is also malleable (bends easily), so it can be made into different shapes and drawn into wires. Copper is used in electrical wires and cables and in hot water pipes and car radiators.

The Howrah Bridge, Calcutta, India. Large amounts of iron (steel) are used to build bridges.

Distillery vessels like this are made of copper. Why is copper used rather than steel?

Copper is also used in **alloys** with other metals. Alloys of copper and zinc produce brass which is harder and stronger than pure copper. Alloys of copper and tin produce bronze. This is stronger than copper and easier to cast into moulds.

Properties of transition metals

Some properties of iron and copper are shown in Table 4. Compare them with the properties of group I metals in Table 1.

The information in Table 4 shows the characteristic properties of transition metals. We can summarise them as follows:

★ **High melting points** and **high boiling points** – much higher than alkali metals.

★ **High densities** – much higher than alkali metals.

★ **Unreactive with water** – unlike alkali metals. None of the transition metals react with cold water. Some of them, like iron, react slowly with steam.

Element	Melting point (°C)	Boiling point (°C)	Density (g cm^{-3})	Reaction with water	Formulas of oxides	Symbols of ions	Colour of salts
Iron	1540	3000	7.9	Does not react with pure water but reacts slowly with steam	FeO Fe$_2$O$_3$	Fe^{2+} Fe^{3+}	Fe^{2+} salts are green Fe^{3+} salts are yellow or brown
Copper	1080	2600	8.9	No reaction with water or steam	Cu$_2$O CuO	Cu$^+$ Cu^{2+}	Cu^{2+} salts are blue or green

Table 4 Some properties of iron and copper

★ **More than one ion**. Most of the transition metals form more than one stable ion. Each ion has its own set of compounds. For example, iron forms Fe^{2+} and Fe^{3+} ions resulting in iron(II) and iron(III) compounds. Copper forms Cu^+ and Cu^{2+} ions resulting in copper(I) and copper(II) compounds. Alkali metals form only one stable ion with a charge of 1+.

★ **Coloured compounds**. Transition metals usually have coloured compounds due to the colour of their ions. In contrast, alkali metals form white compounds with colourless solutions, unless the negative ion is coloured.

★ **Catalytic properties**. Transition metals and their compounds can act as catalysts.

For example, iron or iron(III) oxide is a catalyst in the Haber process (see section 23.3). Platinum or vanadium(V) oxide is a catalyst for the manufacture of sulphuric acid. Nickel is a catalyst for the production of margarine from vegetable oils.

14 We use some metals more than others. Put these metals in order of amounts used.

aluminium   copper   iron   tin.

15 Why is copper used in electrical wires?

16 What is brass made from?

17 How many ions does copper form?

18 Name the metal used as a catalyst in the Haber process.

Summary

1 The periodic table can be divided into **four blocks of similar elements**:

   ★ reactive metals (e.g. alkali metals)
   ★ transition metals
   ★ non-metals (e.g. halogens)
   ★ noble gases.

2 The **alkali metals** in group I

   ★ are reactive metals with similar properties
   ★ have lower melting points, lower boiling points and lower densities than other metals
   ★ react rapidly with oxygen in the air to form oxides
   ★ react rapidly with water to form alkaline solutions
   ★ become more reactive with increase in relative atomic mass.

3 The **halogens** in group VII

   ★ are reactive non-metals with similar properties

   ★ have low melting points and boiling points
   ★ change from gas (Cl_2), to liquid (Br_2) to solid (I_2) with increase in relative atomic mass
   ★ become less reactive with increase in relative atomic mass.

4 The **noble gases** in group 0

   ★ are very unreactive non-metals with similar properties
   ★ have very low melting points and boiling points
   ★ are all gases at room temperature.

5 The **transition metals**

   ★ have similar properties
   ★ have high melting points, high boiling points and high densities
   ★ are unreactive with cold water
   ★ form more than one ion (e.g. copper forms Cu^+ and Cu^{2+})
   ★ have coloured compounds
   ★ can act as catalysts (as elements or compounds).

1 a) Choose from the names of elements in the box the answers to the questions which follow.

> aluminium   carbon   chlorine   copper
> helium   iron   magnesium   sodium

Give the name of:

(i) an alkali metal   *(1)*

(ii) a halogen   *(1)*

(iii) a noble gas   *(1)*

b) The alkali metals are in group 1 of the periodic table. The elements in group 1 have a number of similar properties.

(i) Describe **one chemical** property which they have in common.   *(1)*

(ii) Describe **one physical** property which they have in common.   *(1)*

[AQA (SEG) 1999]

2 a) The table below contains information about three elements.

Write down the correct colour and physical state at room temperature for each element.

Physical state	Element	Colour
Gas	Bromine	Green
Liquid	Chlorine	Grey
Solid	Iodine	Red

(4)

b) Use the periodic table to find the atomic number of bromine.   *(1)*

c) To which group of elements do bromine, chlorine and iodine belong?   *(1)*

d) An atom of chlorine contains 17 protons, 18 neutrons and some electrons.

(i) How many electrons does this atom of chlorine contain?   *(1)*

(ii) What is the mass number of this atom of chlorine?   *(1)*

(iii) What **two** particles are found in the nucleus of the atom of chlorine?   *(2)*

(iv) Which **two** of the particles in the chlorine atom have the same mass?   *(1)*

[Edexcel 1998]

3 The diagram shows some of the elements in groups 1 and 7 of the periodic table.

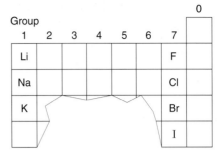

a) The elements in group 1 have similar chemical properties. Describe **one** chemical reaction which shows that lithium, sodium and potassium react in the same sort of way.

You should say what you would react them with and what substances would be produced.   *(3)*

b) All the elements in group 7 react with hydrogen. Fluorine reacts in the dark, explosively, at very low temperatures. Chlorine reacts explosively in sunlight, at room temperature. Bromine, in light, only reacts if heated to about 200°C.

Suggest the conditions needed for hydrogen and iodine to react.

Give a reason for your answer.   *(2)*

[AQA (NEAB) 1999]

4 The table shows information about three elements in group 0 of the periodic table.

Element	Symbol	Density (g/dm³)	Boiling point (°C)	Use
Helium	He	0.18	−269	To fill airships and weather balloons
Neon	Ne	0.90	−246	For advertising signs
Argon	Ar	1.78	−186	In light bulbs

a) State **one** reason why argon is suitable for use in light bulbs.   *(1)*

b) Why is helium better than argon for filling airships and weather balloons?   *(1)*

[Edexcel 1998]

19.1 Studying structures

What is the general shape of the salt (sodium chloride) crystals in this photo?

Look at the crystals of sodium chloride in the photo. Notice that all the salt crystals are roughly the same cubic shape. Scientists know that *all the crystals of one substance have similar shapes.* This suggests that the particles in the crystals are always packed in the same way to give the same overall shape. Sometimes, crystals grow unevenly and their shapes are not so perfect.

Even so, we can usually see their general shape.

Solids which have a regular packing of particles are called **crystalline**.

The particles may be atoms, ions or molecules. Figure 1 shows how cubic crystals and hexagonal crystals can form. If the particles are always placed in parallel lines or at 90° to each other, the crystal will be cubic. If the particles are placed at 120° in the shape of a hexagon, the final crystal will be hexagonal.

Crystals grow in the same way that a bricklayer lays bricks. If the bricks are always placed in parallel lines or at 90°, then the final buildings will be like cubes or boxes. If the bricks are laid at 120° to make hexagons, then the final buildings will be hexagonal.

The shape of a crystal only gives one clue to the way in which the particles are arranged. X-rays give us much better evidence.

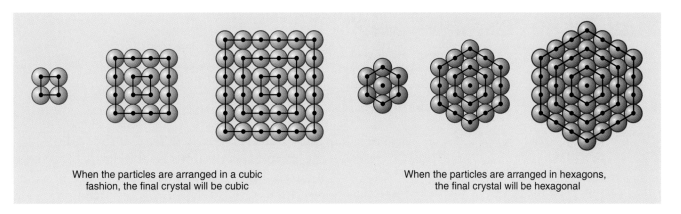

When the particles are arranged in a cubic fashion, the final crystal will be cubic

When the particles are arranged in hexagons, the final crystal will be hexagonal

Figure 1 When the particles are arranged in a cubic fashion, the final crystal will be cubic. When the particles are arranged in hexagons, the final crystal will be hexagonal.

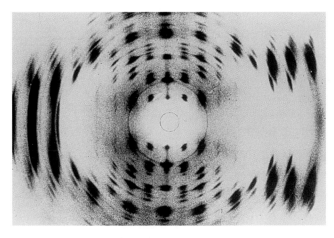

An X-ray diffraction photo of DNA. DNA is the substance that makes up our genes. Notice the general pattern in the dots.

Using X-rays to study crystals

Look through a piece of thin stretched cloth at a small bright light. You will see a pattern. This pattern is caused by the deflection of the light by threads of the fabric. This deflection of the light is called **diffraction** and the patterns produced are **diffraction patterns**. From the diffraction pattern which we *can* see, we can work out the pattern of the threads in the fabric which we *cannot* see. The same idea is used to work out how the particles are arranged in a crystal.

A narrow beam of X-rays is directed at the crystal (Figure 2). Some of the X-rays are diffracted by particles in the crystal onto X-ray sensitive film.

When the film is developed, a regular pattern of spots appears. This is the diffraction pattern for the crystal. From the diffraction pattern which we *can* see, it is possible to work out the pattern of particles in the crystal which we *cannot* see.

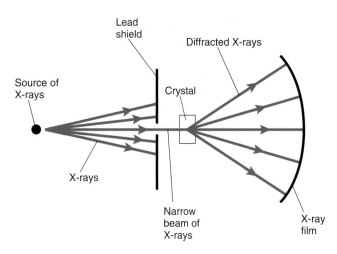

Figure 2 The diffraction of X-rays by a crystal

X-rays have been used in this way to study the structure of thousands of different solids.

1 What shape are crystals of sodium chloride?

2 What is the angle between particles in a hexagonal crystal?

3 What can the diffraction patterns made by X-rays tell us about a crystal?

19.2 The structure of substances

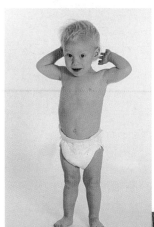

What properties must nappies have? What do you think the structure of nappy material is like?

Metal was used to make armour in the Middle Ages. Why was metal used?

All substances are made up of particles. If we know how particles are arranged (the **structure**) and how the particles are held together (the **bonding**), we can explain the **properties** of a substance. For example, copper is a good conductor of electricity because its metallic bonding allows electrons to move through the structure when it is connected to a battery.

The properties of a substance determine what it can be used for. Copper, for example, is used for electrical wires and cables because it is a good conductor.

Notice that:

★ the structure and bonding of a substance give its properties

★ the properties of a substance lead to its uses.

So, the links from structure and bonding to the properties of a material help us to explain its uses. They explain why metals are used as conductors, why diamonds are used in jewellery and why clay is used to make bricks.

From chapter 14, we know that:

★ all substances are made up from only three different particles – atoms, ions and molecules.

These three particles give rise to four different solid structures:

1 giant metallic structures
2 giant covalent (giant molecular) structures
3 giant ionic structures
4 simple molecular structures.

These four structures are studied in the next four sections.

Table 1 shows the particles in these four structures, the types of substances formed and examples of these substances.

19.3 Giant metallic structures

Look carefully at the photo on the next page. This shows the surface of galvanised iron (iron coated with zinc). Notice the irregular shaped areas separated by clear boundaries. The irregular shaped areas are called **grains** and the boundaries between them are called **grain boundaries**. The grains in zinc are often easy to see. The grains in other metals are usually too small to see with the naked eye.

Type of structure	Particles in the structure	Types of substance	Examples
Giant metallic	Atoms	Metals and alloys (mixtures of metals)	Na, Fe, Cu, steel, brass
Giant covalent	Very large molecules containing thousands of atoms	Non-metals or non-metal compounds	Diamond (carbon), polythene, sand (silicon dioxide, SiO_2)
Giant ionic	Ions	Compounds of metals with non-metals	Na^+Cl^- (salt), $Ca^{2+}O^{2-}$ (lime), $Cu^{2+}SO_4^{2-}$ (copper sulphate)
Simple molecular	Small molecules containing a few atoms	Non-metals or non-metal compounds	I_2 (iodine), O_2 (oxygen), H_2O (water), CO_2 (carbon dioxide)

Table 1 The four types of solid structure and the particles they contain

This box is made of steel covered (galvanised) with a thin layer of zinc. The grains (irregular shaped crystals of zinc) are easy to see in the close-up.

X-ray analysis shows that the atoms in metal grains are packed in a regular fashion. The grains are irregular-shaped crystals pushed tightly together. It is this close packing of atoms which gives most metals their high densities.

This arrangement is called **close packing**. Figure 3 shows a few atoms in one layer of a metal crystal.

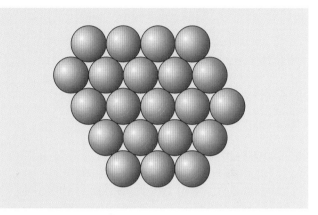

Figure 3 The close packing of atoms in one layer of a metal crystal.

Notice that each atom in the middle of the crystal touches six other atoms in the same layer. When a second layer is added, atoms in the second layer sink into the dips between atoms in the first layer (Figure 4). This means that an atom in the first layer can touch six atoms in its own layer, three atoms in the layer above it and three atoms in the layer below, that is, a total of twelve atoms in all. This is the closest possible arrangement.

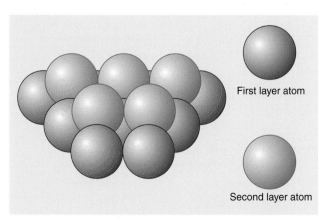

First layer atom

Second layer atom

Figure 4 Atoms in two layers of a metal crystal.

The properties of metals

The close packed structure of metals can explain their properties.

★ **High density** because the metal atoms are packed close together.

★ **High melting points** and **boiling points**

A lot of energy is needed to separate the metal atoms to form a liquid. Even more energy is needed to form a gas.

The structures of metals are described as **giant structures**. In a giant structure, there are strong bonds from one atom or ion to another in a vast network throughout the whole substance.

★ **Good conductivity**

The outermost electrons in metal atoms can move about freely. When a metal is connected in a circuit, the freely moving outer electrons move towards the positive terminal. At the same time, electrons move into the other end of the metal from the negative terminal (Figure 5). This flow of electrons through the metal forms the electric current.

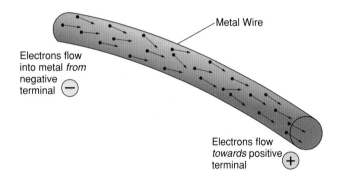

Figure 5 Electrons flowing along a metal wire form an electric current.

★ **Malleability**

The bonds between metal atoms are strong but they are not rigid. When a force is applied to a metal crystal, the layers of atoms can 'slide' over each other. This is known as **slip**.

After slipping, the atoms settle into close-packed positions again. Figure 6 shows the positions of atoms before and after slip. This is what happens when a metal is bent or hammered into different shapes.

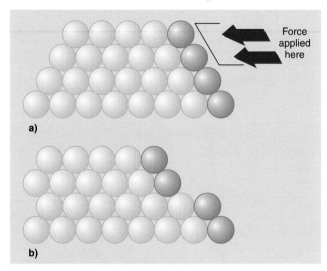

Figure 6 The positions of atoms in a metal crystal, a) before and b) after slip has occurred.

4 Name a giant metallic structure.

5 Describe the packing of atoms in a giant metallic structure.

6 Give **three** properties of giant metallic structures.

19.4 Giant covalent (giant molecular) structures

Diamond, graphite, polythene and sand (silicon dioxide) are giant covalent (giant molecular) structures. They have strong **covalent bonds** which join one atom to another. This results in very large molecules containing thousands or even millions of atoms.

In diamond, carbon atoms are joined to each other by strong covalent bonds. Inside the diamond structure, each carbon atom forms a covalent bond with four other carbon atoms. This is the case for the atom labelled X in Figure 7.

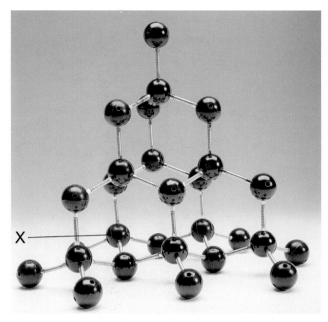

Figure 7 A model of the structure of diamond

In covalent bonds, atoms share the electrons in their outer shells. The positive nuclei of both atoms attract the shared negative electrons. This holds the atoms together as a covalent bond. In diamond, the covalent bonds extend through the whole structure forming a three-dimensional giant structure. So, each diamond is a single **giant molecule** or a **macromolecule**. Only a small number of atoms are shown in the model in Figure 7. In a real diamond, there are billions and billions of atoms.

The properties of diamond

★ **Diamond is very hard** because its carbon atoms are linked by very strong covalent bonds. In fact, diamond is the hardest natural substance that we know. Most of its industrial uses depend on this hardness.

★ **Diamond has a very high melting point**. Strong covalent bonds link carbon atoms in a giant structure. This means that the atoms cannot vibrate fast enough to break away from their neighbours until very high temperatures are reached.

★ **Diamond does not conduct electricity**. Unlike metals, diamond has no free electrons. All the electrons in the outer shell of each carbon atom are held firmly in covalent bonds. So, there are no free electrons in diamond to form an electric current.

Diamonds which are not good enough for jewellery are used in glass cutters and in diamond-studded saws. This photo shows a craftsman using a diamond cutter to make patterns on a glass dish.

7 Give **two** examples of a giant covalent structure.

8 Why are diamonds so hard?

9 Why do diamonds have such a high melting point?

10 Why don't diamonds conduct electricity?

19.5 Giant ionic structures

Chalk cliffs are composed of an ionic compound, calcium carbonate. This contains calcium ions (Ca^{2+}) and carbonate ions (CO_3^{2-}). Limestone is also calcium carbonate.

Ionic compounds form when metals react with non-metals. For example, when sodium burns in chlorine, sodium chloride is formed.

sodium	+	chlorine	→	sodium chloride
2Na	+	Cl_2	→	$2Na^+Cl^-$
2 sodium atoms	+	1 chlorine molecule	→	2 sodium ions plus 2 chloride ions

In solid ionic compounds, the ions are held together by the attraction between positive ions and negative ions. Figure 8 shows how the ions are arranged in one layer of sodium chloride. Figure 9 is a model of the structure of sodium chloride. Notice that Na^+ ions are surrounded by Cl^- ions and vice versa.

This kind of arrangement in which large numbers of ions are packed together in a regular pattern is another example of a **giant structure**.

> The force of attraction between oppositely-charged ions is called an **ionic** or **electrovalent bond**.

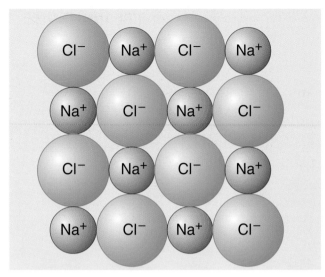

Figure 8 The arrangement of ions in one layer of a sodium chloride crystal

Strong ionic bonds hold the ions together very firmly. This explains why ionic compounds:

★ are **hard** substances

★ have **high melting points** and **high boiling points**

★ **do not conduct electricity** when solid because the ions cannot move freely. But, ionic compounds can conduct electricity when molten or dissolved in water as the charged ions can then move (see sections 16.3 and 16.4).

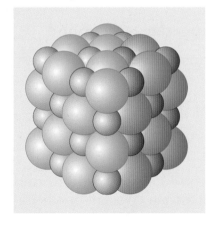

Figure 9 A 3-D model of the structure of sodium chloride. The larger green balls represent Cl^- ions ($A_r = 35.5$). The smaller red balls represent Na^+ ions ($A_r = 23.0$). In the middle of the structure, six Na^+ ions surround each Cl^- ion and six Cl^- ions surround each Na^+ ion.

19.6 Simple molecular substances

Oxygen and water are good examples of simple molecular substances. They have simple molecules containing a few atoms. Their formulas and structures are shown in Table 2. Most non-metals and non-metal compounds are made of simple molecules. For example, hydrogen is H_2, chlorine is Cl_2, iodine is I_2, carbon dioxide is CO_2 and methane in natural gas is CH_4. Sugar ($C_{12}H_{22}O_{11}$) has much larger molecules than these substances, but it still counts as a simple molecule.

In these simple molecular substances, the atoms are held together in each molecule by strong covalent bonds (Figure 10). But there are only weak forces between the separate molecules (Figure 11).

These weak forces between the separate molecules are called **intermolecular bonds** or **Van der Waals forces**.

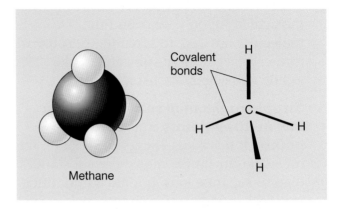

Methane

Figure 10 Methane (CH_4) is a simple molecular substance. In methane, the carbon atom and four hydrogen atoms are held together by strong covalent bonds.

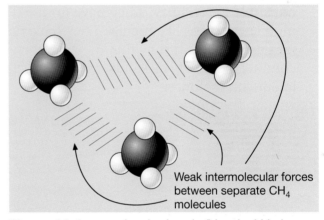

Weak intermolecular forces between separate CH_4 molecules

Figure 11 Intermolecular bonds (Van der Waals forces) in methane

Name	Molecular formula	Model of structure
Hydrogen	H_2	
Oxygen	O_2	
Water	H_2O	
Methane	CH_4	
Hydrogen chloride	HCl	
Iodine	I_2	
Carbon dioxide	CO_2	

Table 2 Formulas and structures of some simple molecular substances

The properties of simple molecular substances

The properties of simple molecular substances can be explained in terms of their structure and the forces between their molecules. In simple molecular substances, the forces between molecules are very weak. Some simple molecular substances, like iodine, sugar and water, do exist as liquids and solids so there must be some forces holding their molecules together.

★ **Simple molecular substances are soft**. The separate molecules in simple molecular substances are usually further apart than atoms in metals and ions in ionic structures. The forces between the molecules are only weak and the molecules are easy to separate. Because of this, crystals of these substances, like iodine and sugar, are usually soft.

★ **Simple molecular substances have low melting points and boiling points**. It takes less energy to separate the molecules in simple molecular substances than to separate ions in ionic compounds, or atoms in metals. So, simple molecular compounds have lower melting points and lower boiling points than ionic compounds and metals.

★ **Simple molecular substances do not conduct electricity**. They have no mobile electrons like metals. They have no ions either. This means that they cannot conduct electricity as solids, as liquids or in aqueous solution.

This butcher is using 'dry ice' (solid carbon dioxide) to keep meat cool during mincing. After mincing, the 'dry ice', which is a simple molecular substance, will evaporate rapidly without spoiling the meat.

Notice the following key points from the last four sections.

★ Substances with giant structures are often hard with high melting points and boiling points.

★ Substances with simple molecular structures are usually soft with low melting points and boiling points.

★ There are three types of strong force between particles in giant structures;

1 metallic bonds between metal atoms

2 covalent bonds between non-metal atoms

3 ionic bonds between positive metal ions and negative non-metal ions.

★ In simple molecular substances there are only weak forces between the separate molecules.

11 Copy and complete these sentences using the words below.

covalent   oxygen   weak   water

_____ and _____ are good examples of simple molecular substances. In these substances, atoms are held in each molecule by strong _____ bonds. But there are only _____ forces between separate molecules.

12 a) Are simple molecular substances hard or soft?

b) Do simple molecular substances have high or low melting points?

c) Do simple molecular substances conduct electricity?

13 What are Van der Waals forces?

Summary

1 ★ The **structures** of substances can be studied using X-rays.

★ A beam of X-rays is directed onto a crystal of the substance. Some of the X-rays are **diffracted** by the particles in the crystal onto X-ray sensitive film.

★ From the **diffraction pattern** on the X-ray film, it is possible to work out the arrangement of particles in the crystal.

2 The **uses** of a substance depend on its **properties**.

The **properties** of a substance depend on its **structure and bonding**.

3 All substances are made up from only three different particles – **atoms**, **molecules** and **ions**.

4 There are four different kinds of solid – **giant metallic**, **giant covalent**, **giant ionic** and **simple molecular**.

Table 3 summarises the particles, bonding and properties of these four different solid structures.

Type of structure	Particles in the structure	Type of substance	Bonding	Properties	Structure
Giant metallic	**Atoms** close-packed	Metals e.g. Na, Fe, Cu and alloys such as steel	Atoms are held in a close-packed giant structure by the attraction of positive ions for outer electrons	• high melting points and boiling points • conduct electricity • high density • hard but malleable	
Giant covalent	**Very large molecules** containing thousands of atoms (giant molecules)	A few non-metals (e.g. diamond, graphite) and some non-metal compounds (e.g. polythene, PVC, sand)	Large numbers of atoms are joined together by strong covalent bonds to give a giant structure as a 3D network or a very long, thin molecule	• high melting points and boiling points • do not conduct electricity • hard but brittle (3D networks) or flexible (long, thin structures)	\n3D network\n\nlong, thin structures
Giant ionic	**Ions**	Metal/non-metal compounds e.g. Na^+Cl^-, $Ca^{2+}O^{2-}$, $Mg^{2+}(Cl^-)_2$	Positive and negative ions are held together by the attraction between their opposite charges	• high melting points and boiling points • conduct electricity when molten and in aqueous solution • hard but brittle • often soluble in water	
Simple molecular	**Small molecules** containing a few atoms	Most non-metals and non-metal compounds e.g. O_2, S_8, H_2O, CO_2, sugar	Atoms are held together in small molecules by strong covalent bonds. The bonds between separate molecules are weak	• low melting points and boiling points • do not conduct electricity • soft when solid	

Table 3 The particles, bonding and properties of the four solid structures

193

1 Magnesium oxide is an ionic compound

a) Describe how a magnesium **ion** is formed from a magnesium **atom**. *(2)*

b) Why is the magnesium ion attracted to the oxide ion in magnesium oxide? *(1)*

[NICCEA 1998]

2 The label below was on a tube of toothpaste.

> INGREDIENTS: water, sorbitol, hydrated silica, cellulose gum, sodium lauryl sulphate, aroma, sodium saccharin, methylparaben, sodium fluoride, sodium hydroxide.
>
> Contains 0.2% sodium fluoride.

a) Which of the ingredients is a strong alkali? *(1)*

b) Sodium lauryl sulphate has the formula shown below.

$C_{12}H_{25}SO_4Na$

(i) How many hydrogen atoms are in this formula? *(1)*

(ii) How many different elements does this compound contain? *(1)*

c) Sodium fluoride is added to help stop tooth decay.

(i) The toothpaste contains 0.2% sodium fluoride. What mass of sodium fluoride is present in 100 g of toothpaste? *(1)*

(ii) This label was on a bottle of pure sodium fluoride.

Suggest why only a small amount of sodium fluoride is added to toothpaste. *(2)*

(iii) The electronic structure of a sodium atom is shown below. Draw the electronic structure of a fluorine atom.

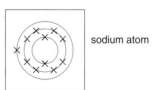

sodium atom

(iv) Sodium and fluorine can react to form sodium fluoride. The electronic structure of a fluoride ion is shown below. Draw the structure of a sodium ion.

fluoride ion (F⁻)

[AQA (NEAB) 1998]

3 The diagram below shows some stages in the manufacture of hydrochloric acid.

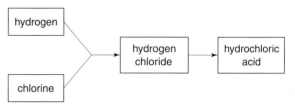

a) From the diagram above, give the name of:

(i) an element; *(1)*
(ii) a compound. *(1)*

b) What substance is mixed with hydrogen chloride to produce hydrochloric acid? *(1)*

c) Chlorine can be made by electrolysis. State the labels for the electrode, **A**, and electrode, **B**, on the diagram below. *(3)*

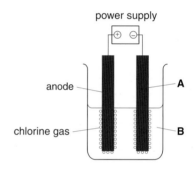

d) Hydrochloric acid contains hydrogen ions. Describe ONE similarity and ONE difference between a hydrogen atom (H) and a hydrogen ion (H⁺), in terms of protons, neutrons and electrons. *(2)*

e) Describe how a hydrogen molecule is formed from hydrogen atoms and name the type of bond formed. *(3)*

f) The diagram below shows the apparatus used to dissolve hydrogen chloride gas in water in the laboratory.

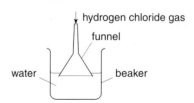

(i) Explain why this apparatus is used. *(2)*

(ii) What colour would Universal indicator become when added to the solution formed? *(1)*

[Edexcel 1998]

20

Reaction rates

20.1 How fast? – different reaction rates

Our lives are affected by the rates of chemical reactions. We need to know, for example,

★ how quickly we can make toast
★ how long it takes to cook rice
★ how fast paint will dry
★ how quickly milk goes sour.

Different reactions happen at very different rates.

The reactions which happen when food is cooked go at a steady rate.

Limestone reacts very slowly with carbonic acid in rain water. It has taken a hundred years for the limestone in these gravestones to get so 'weathered' and eaten away.

An explosion is an extremely fast reaction. This explosion is being used to break up rocks in a quarry.

195

The rates of most reactions fall somewhere between those described in the photos. The reactions which take place when fuels burn, and when food is cooked are good examples of reactions which occur at steady rates.

Why are reaction rates important?

Chefs and cooks know the importance of reaction rates. They know that reaction rates are affected by **temperature**. Kitchens have a cooker and a fridge. Preparing a meal can involve lots of reactions. The cooker is used to speed up some reactions. The fridge is used to slow down other reactions.

Food cooks faster if it is cut up into small pieces. This gives a larger surface area for reactions. So, rashers of bacon cook much faster than a bacon joint. Scones bake faster than a large fruit cake.

Most reactions in our bodies would never happen if the reacting substances were just mixed together. Fortunately, the reactions in our bodies are helped along by **catalysts** (section 20.6). Catalysts allow substances to react more easily. The catalysts in living things are called **enzymes**. Without enzymes, the reactions in our bodies would stop and we would die.

One of these enzymes is **amylase** (carbohydrase). Amylase is present in saliva. It speeds up the breakdown of starch in foods such as bread, rice and potatoes.

Industrial chemists are not satisfied with just turning one substance into another. They want to carry out reactions faster and cheaper. Speeding up reactions makes them more economical because saving time usually saves money.

The key reaction in the manufacture of ammonia is the Haber process (section 23.3). This involves converting nitrogen and hydrogen to ammonia.

$$\text{nitrogen} + \text{hydrogen} \rightarrow \text{ammonia}$$
$$N_2(g) + 3H_2(g) \rightarrow 2NH_3(g)$$

This reaction will not happen unless:

★ the temperature is raised to 400°C

★ a catalyst of iron is used

★ the **concentrations** of nitrogen and hydrogen are increased to give a pressure of about 200 atmospheres.

These examples show that there are four important factors which affect the rates of chemical reactions:

★ **surface area**
★ **concentration**
★ **temperature**
★ **catalysts**

These factors will be studied in more detail later in this chapter.

A mechanic fitting a special catalyst section to the exhaust system of a car. The catalyst removes carbon monoxide and nitrogen oxides from the exhaust fumes.

1 Give an example of a very slow chemical reaction.

2 Give an example of an extremely fast chemical reaction.

3 Why do small scones bake faster than a large fruit cake?

4 What are catalysts in living things called?

20.2 Measuring reaction rates

During a reaction, reactants are being used up and products are forming. The amounts of the reactants fall and the amounts of the products rise. We can use these changes to measure the **reaction rate**. We do this *by calculating how much reactant is used up or how much product forms in a given time.* Therefore:

$$reaction\ rate = \frac{amount\ of\ reactant\ used\ up}{time\ taken}$$

OR

$$reaction\ rate = \frac{amount\ of\ product\ formed}{time\ taken}$$

For example, when 0.1 g of magnesium was added to dilute hydrochloric acid, the magnesium reacted and disappeared in 10 seconds. Therefore:

reaction rate

$$= \frac{amount\ of\ magnesium\ used\ up}{time\ taken}$$

$$= \frac{0.1\ g\ magnesium\ used\ up\ per\ second}{10}$$

$$= 0.01\ g\ per\ second$$

In this case, we have calculated the reaction rate as a change in mass with time. Reaction rates can also be measured as changes in concentration with time.

Calculating reaction rates

The rate of reaction between small marble chips (calcium carbonate, $CaCO_3$) and dilute hydrochloric acid was studied using the apparatus in Figure 1.

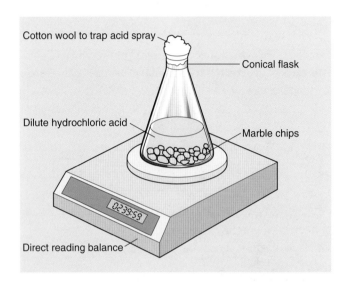

Cotton wool to trap acid spray

Conical flask

Dilute hydrochloric acid

Marble chips

Direct reading balance

Figure 1 Studying the rate of reaction between marble chips and hydrochloric acid. (**Wear eye protection if you try this experiment**.)

As the reaction occurs, carbon dioxide is produced. This escapes as a gas and so the mass of the flask and its contents decrease.

calcium carbonate (marble chips) + hydrochloric acid → calcium chloride + carbon dioxide + water

The decrease in mass is due to the carbon dioxide produced. The results of one experiment are given in Table 1 (over the page). These results have been plotted on a graph in Figure 2, which is shown on the next page.

Time (minutes)	Mass of flask and contents (g)	Decrease in mass (g)
0	78.00	0
2	75.50	2.50
4	74.60	3.40
6	74.33	3.67
8	74.30	3.70

Table 1 The results of an experiment to measure the rate of reaction between marble chips and dilute hydrochloric acid.

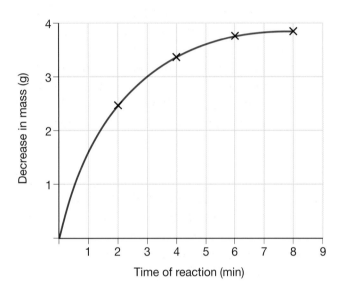

Figure 2 A graph showing the decrease in mass against time when marble chips react with hydrochloric acid.

During the first two minutes, there is a decrease in mass of 2.5 g as carbon dioxide escapes.

∴ average rate of reaction in the first two minutes

$$= \frac{\text{change in mass}}{\text{time taken}}$$

$$= \frac{2.5 \text{ g}}{2 \text{ min}}$$

= 1.25 g of carbon dioxide per minute

(Notice that the units for reaction rate are grams per minute this time.)

During the next 2 minutes (from time = 2 minutes to time = 4 minutes), 0.9 g of carbon dioxide escapes.

∴ average rate of reaction in the next 2 minutes

$$= \frac{0.90 \text{g}}{2 \text{ min}}$$

= 0.45 g of carbon dioxide per minute

These calculations and the graph show that the reaction is fastest at the start of the reaction when the slope of the graph is steepest. During the reaction, the rate of reaction falls and the slope of the graph levels off. Eventually, the reaction stops (reaction rate = 0.0 g/min). At this stage, the graph becomes flat (gradient or slope = 0).

This mechanic is tuning the car engine to adjust the rate at which petrol burns in the cylinders. The car's performance depends on the rate of this reaction.

20.3 Surface area and reaction rates

It is much easier to light a campfire using sticks rather than logs. The main reason for this is that the sticks have a greater surface area. There is a larger area of the sticks in contact with oxygen in the air, so they burn more easily.

Reactions go faster when there is more surface area to react.

The reaction between marble chips (calcium carbonate) and dilute hydrochloric acid can also be used to study the effect of surface area on reaction rate.

The results are shown in Figure 3. In experiment I, 30 *small* marble chips (with a total mass of 10 g) reacted with 100 cm^3 of dilute hydrochloric acid. In experiment II, six *large* marble chips (with the same total mass of 10 g) reacted with 100 cm^3 of the same hydrochloric acid.

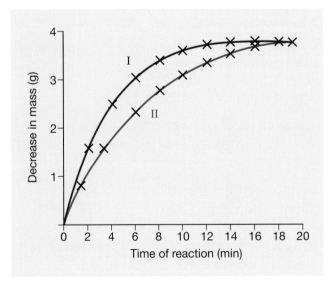

Figure 3 Studying the effect of surface area on reaction rate

Look closely at Figure 3.

5 Why is the overall decrease in mass the same in both experiments?

6 Why do the graphs become flat?

7 Which graph shows the greater decrease in mass per minute at the start of the experiment?

8 Which experiment begins at the faster rate?

9 Why is the reaction rate different in the two experiments?

20.4 Concentration and reaction rates

Substances that burn in air burn much faster in pure oxygen. Charcoal in a barbecue normally burns very slowly with a red glow. If you blow on it so that it gets more air and therefore more oxygen, it glows brighter. It may burst into flames. When red hot charcoal is put into oxygen it burns with a bright flame.

Chemical reactions occur when particles of the reacting substances collide. This is called the **collision theory**. Increasing the concentration of the reactants increases the number of collisions per second. This increases the reaction rate.

When charcoal burns, collisions occur between carbon atoms and oxygen molecules. These occur more frequently when oxygen is used instead of air. So, the reaction happens faster. It gives off more heat and produces flames when the concentration of oxygen is increased. Pure oxygen is also used to help the recovery of some hospital patients. Pure oxygen is especially helpful to patients suffering from breathing difficulties.

When gases react, the concentration of each gas can be increased by increasing its pressure. Some industrial processes use very high pressures. For example, in the Haber process (section 23.3), nitrogen and hydrogen are made to react at a reasonable rate by increasing the pressure to 200 times atmospheric pressure.

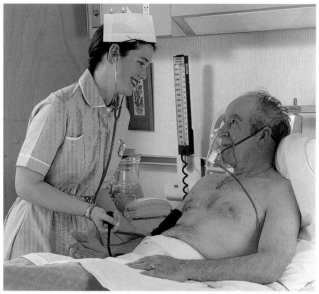

Pure oxygen is used to help the recovery of patients who have difficulty in breathing.

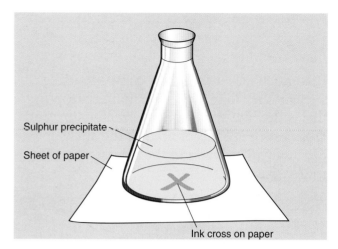

Figure 4 Investigating the effect of temperature on reaction rate.

20.5 Temperature and reaction rates

Milk will keep for several days in a cool fridge, but it turns sour very quickly on a hot day. Foods which 'go off' easily, like strawberries and cream, go bad more quickly left on a kitchen top on a hot, sunny day.

This is because:

Chemical reactions go faster at higher temperatures.

The effect of temperature on reaction rates can be investigated using the reaction between sodium thiosulphate solution and dilute hydrochloric acid. When the reactants are mixed, the solution becomes cloudy. This is because sulphur is produced (Figure 4).

As the precipitate gets thicker, the ink cross on white paper below the flask slowly disappears. We can find the reaction rate by mixing hydrochloric acid with sodium thiosulphate solution and then measuring the time for the cross to disappear.

Table 2 shows the results when Katie and Luke did the experiment at four *different* temperatures. To make the tests fair, they kept everything else the same in all four experiments.

Temperature (°C)	20	30	40	50
Time for cross to disappear (seconds)	162	80	41	20

Table 2 The results of Katie and Luke's experiment at different temperatures.

Notice from the results in Table 2 that:

★ the cross disappears more quickly at higher temperatures because the reaction goes faster.

★ if the temperature rises by 10°C, the reaction rate is about twice as fast. For example, at 20°C, the cross disappears in 162 seconds whilst at 30°C, it disappears in about half the time (80 seconds).

Why do reactions go faster at higher temperatures?

Most processes are speeded up by increasing the temperature. The chemical reactions in baking and cooking would never happen unless the food was heated at a high temperature.

For a reaction to take place, two things must happen. First, the particles must collide. At higher temperatures, particles move faster. Secondly, when they collide, they must have enough energy for the bonds to break. At a high temperature, there are more particles with enough energy for bonds to break.

So, there are two reasons why reactions go faster at higher temperatures.

★ The particles collide more often.

★ The particles collide with more energy.

Food can be stored in a freezer for long periods. Reaction rates for food 'going off' are almost zero at −18°C.

10 Copy and complete the following.

a) Reactions go faster when there is a _____ surface area.

b) Increasing the concentration of reactants _____ the number of collisions. This _____ the reaction rate.

c) Reactions go faster at _____ temperatures because there are more _____. Also the particles _____ with more energy.

20.6 Catalysts and reaction rates

One very important application of catalysts is in catalytic converters in car exhaust systems. Car exhaust fumes contain two poisonous gases, nitrogen oxide and carbon monoxide. Catalytic converters cause most of these poisonous gases to react. The products are nitrogen and carbon dioxide which are less harmful. This reduces air pollution.

$$\text{nitrogen oxide} + \text{carbon monoxide} \rightarrow \text{nitrogen} + \text{carbon dioxide}$$

The catalyst in catalytic converters is an expensive alloy containing platinum. Fortunately, the platinum alloy is not used up in the reaction.

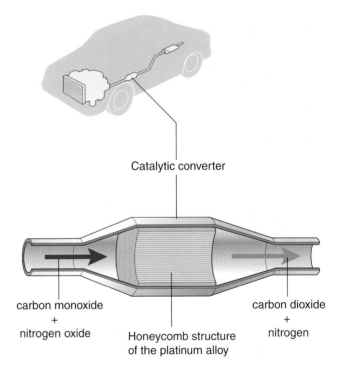

Catalytic converter

carbon monoxide + nitrogen oxide

Honeycomb structure of the platinum alloy

carbon dioxide + nitrogen

This catalytic converter in a car exhaust system changes poisonous carbon monoxide and nitrogen oxide into less harmful carbon dioxide and nitrogen. The reaction occurs on the surface of the platinum catalyst. A large surface area for the reaction is provided by the honeycomb structure.

Catalysts are substances which speed up chemical reactions without being used up during the reaction.

Different reactions need different catalysts and catalysts play an important part in the chemical industry. Petrol (section 22.4), margarine and ammonia (section 23.3) are all produced by processes which use catalysts. The catalysts in many of these important industrial processes are transition metals or their compounds. Iron is the catalyst for the manufacture of ammonia in the Haber process and nickel is the catalyst in the production of margarine.

Catalysts speed up reactions and allow substances to react more readily. They help bonds to break more easily. So, the particles need less energy to react and the reaction is faster.

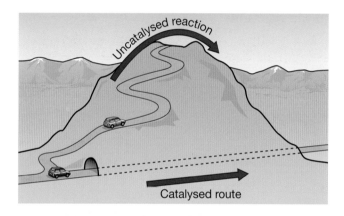

Figure 5 Using a catalyst for a slow reaction is like building a tunnel under a mountain. Tunnels are made so that there is a shorter, easier route for a journey. Catalysts provide a shorter, easier path for the reaction which needs less energy.

| 20.7 | **Enzymes – biological catalysts** |

The catalysts for biological processes are called **enzymes**.

Enzymes catalyse the breakdown of our food. They also catalyse the reactions which synthesise important chemicals like proteins in our muscles and DNA in our genes.

Enzymes are crucial for life. Without enzymes, the reactions in our bodies would stop and we would die.

More and more industrial processes are being developed which use enzymes. These processes include baking, brewing (section 3.6), cheese making and the manufacture of fruit juices, yoghurt and vitamins. The enzymes for these processes are often extracted from living material such as animal tissues, plants, yeast and fungi.

Biological washing powders contain enzymes. The enzymes break down the chemicals in food, grease and dirt.

Another important use of enzymes is in biological detergents and washing powders. These break down the stains on clothes from food, blood and other biological substances. The advantage of biological washing powders is that they work at relatively low temperatures. So, they are useful for washing delicate fabrics. We can save on the cost of electricity to heat the water. The disadvantage of biological washing powders is that some people are allergic to them.

The effect of temperature on enzyme-catalysed reactions

Hydrogen peroxide is produced in the cells of animals and plants. As the hydrogen peroxide forms, it decomposes to water and oxygen due to the presence of the enzyme, catalase.

This decomposition of hydrogen peroxide is also catalysed by manganese dioxide.

$$\text{hydrogen peroxide} \xrightarrow[\text{manganese dioxide}]{\text{catalase or}} \text{water + oxygen}$$

The sketch graph in Figure 6 shows how the rate of decomposition of hydrogen peroxide changes with temperature (i) using manganese dioxide (MnO_2) as the catalyst and (ii) using the enzyme, catalase, as the catalyst.

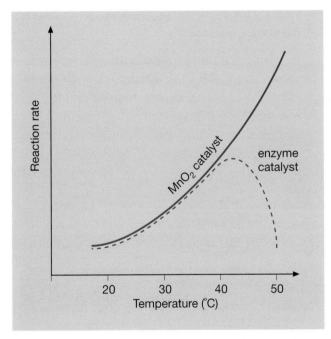

Figure 6 The rate of decomposition of hydrogen peroxide at different temperatures with (i) manganese dioxide as catalyst (ii) the enzyme catalase, as catalyst.

Most catalysed reactions go faster as the temperature rises, like the graph for manganese dioxide in Figure 6. This means that the reaction rate steadily increases with temperature, as expected.

The reaction of enzyme-catalysed reactions increases at fairly low temperatures. But, above about 40°C their reaction rate decreases rapidly as the temperature rises.

This is because enzymes are proteins. Their structure is damaged as the temperature rises above 40°C. This damage to the protein structure is called **denaturation**. As the protein is denatured, it becomes less and less effective as a catalyst. So, the enzyme-catalysed reaction goes slower and eventually stops.

This is why enzyme (biological) washing powders will not work in water above 40°C.

11 What is an enzyme?

12 Give **two** uses of enzymes in our bodies.

13 Give **two** advantages of biological washing powders.

14 Give **one** disadvantage of biological washing powders.

15 Why don't enzymes work well above 40°C?

Summary

1 Chemical reactions occur at different rates.

2 The rates of chemical reactions are affected by:
   - ★ surface area
   - ★ concentration
   - ★ temperature
   - ★ catalysts

3 During a reaction, reactants are being used up and products are forming. We can use these changes to measure the **reaction rate**.

$$\text{reaction rate} = \frac{\text{amount of reactant used up}}{\text{time taken}}$$

OR

$$\text{reaction rate} = \frac{\text{amount of product formed}}{\text{time taken}}$$

4 Chemical reactions occur when particles of the reacting substances collide. This is called the **collision theory**.

   - ★ Reactions go faster when there is more **surface area** because there are more particles in the surface for collisions.

   - ★ Reactions go faster when the **concentration** of reactants increases because there are more collisions per second.

   - ★ Reactions go faster at **higher temperatures**. At higher temperatures, particles move about faster. So, they collide more often and they collide with more energy. Energy is needed to break bonds.

   - ★ Reactions go faster with **catalysts**. Catalysts provide a shorter, easier path for the reaction.

5 Catalysts are substances which speed up chemical reactions without being used up. They can take part in the reaction over and over again.

Catalysts are vital for many industrial processes including the production of ammonia, sulphuric acid and petrol.

The catalysts for biological processes are called **enzymes**. Almost every chemical reaction in living things has its own particular enzyme.

Enzymes are **denatured** at temperatures above about 40° C. Enzymes are important in baking, brewing, cheese making and in the manufacture of yoghurt, fruit juices and vitamins.

Exam questions for Chapter 20

1 Some types of filler go hard after a catalyst is added from a tube. A manufacturer tested this reaction to see what effect the amount of catalyst had on the time for the filler to harden. The results are shown in the table.

   a) Draw a graph of these results. Plot time for the filler to harden vertically and volume of catalyst added to filler horizontally. *(3)*

   b) Use your graph to suggest the time taken for the filler to harden using 5cm^3 of catalyst. *(1)*

   c) What is the effect of the catalyst on the rate of this reaction? *(1)*

Volume of catalyst added to filler (cm^3)	Time for the filler to harden (minutes)
1	30
2	15
3	10
4	7
6	4

[AQA (NEAB) 1999]

2 a) The graph below shows the volume of carbon dioxide gas formed during a reaction between a lump of **solid** calcium carbonate and dilute hydrochloric acid.

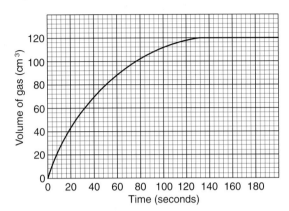

Use the graph to answer questions (i), (ii) and (iii) below.

(i) What volume of gas is produced in the first 50 seconds of the reaction? *(1)*

(ii) After how long did the reaction stop? Explain your answer. *(2)*

(iii) Between which of the following time ranges is the reaction fastest? *(1)*

0–20 seconds   20–40 seconds
40–60 seconds 60–80 seconds

(iv) State **three** ways in which this reaction could be made to go faster. *(3)*

b) During fermentation, carbon dioxide gas is produced by the action of **enzymes** in yeast on sugar solutions.

Using the same quantities each time, the volume of gas produced at different temperatures was measured. The results are shown in the table below.

Temperature (°C)	15	25	35	45	55
Volume of gas in first 15 mins (cm³)	10	20	40	0	0

(i) Draw a graph of the results. Plot volume of gas (cm³) along the vertical axis and temperature (°C) on the horizontal axis. *(2)*

(ii) Use your graph to find the volume of gas produced in 15 minutes at 30°C. *(1)*

(iii) Describe how the rate of the reaction changes with an increase in temperature. *(2)*

[WJEC 1998]

3 When a catalyst such as manganese oxide is added to hydrogen peroxide solution, H_2O_2, the hydrogen peroxide decomposes to give off oxygen.

a) (i) Describe how to test for oxygen. *(2)*

(ii) Complete and balance a copy of the equation for the decomposition of hydrogen peroxide.

$$2H_2O_2 \rightarrow \underline{\hspace{1.5cm}} + \underline{\hspace{1.5cm}}$$ *(3)*

b) The graph shows the volume of gas given off during an experiment using hydrogen peroxide solution and manganese oxide. Copy the graph.

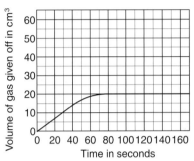

Draw, on your graph, a line to show the result you would expect if the volume of hydrogen peroxide solution had been the same, but it was **twice** as concentrated. *(3)*

[AQA (SEG) 1999]

4 The chart shows how you can make yoghurt.

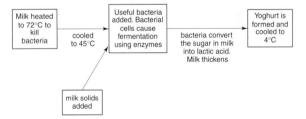

Use the information in the chart and your knowledge of fermentation, to answer the questions below.

a) Complete a copy of these sentences.

Bacteria use catalysts called _____ to change milk to yoghurt. These catalysts are damaged by temperatures above about _____°C. *(2)*

b) A sample of yoghurt turned universal indicator from green to red.

What is there in yoghurt that makes this happen? *(2)*

[AQA (NEAB) 1999]

21

Earth science

21.1 The Earth – our source of raw materials

Look around you. Notice the variety of useful materials:

★ wood to make chairs, tables and desks

★ fibres to make curtains, carpets and clothes

★ glass for windows, jars and ornaments

★ metals to make cutlery and vehicles.

All these useful materials have been made from raw materials we get from the Earth. Most of these useful materials have been made by chemical reactions. These chemical reactions convert raw materials into useful products.

Figure 1 shows the major sources of our raw materials:

★ the Earth's crust provides minerals, rocks and fossil fuels

★ the seas provide water, salt and other minerals

★ the air provides important gases

★ living things provide timber, food and fibres.

Most of our really important raw materials come from the Earth as fossil fuels, minerals and rocks.

A **mineral** is a single substance which has a chemical name and a formula.

Limestone and rock salt are good examples of minerals. Pure limestone is calcium carbonate, $CaCO_3$. Pure rock salt is sodium chloride, $NaCl$.

Minerals are usually impure when they are dug from the Earth. Mixtures of different minerals form rocks. So, impure limestone and impure rock salt are normally classed as rocks.

A **rock** is a mixture of different minerals.

Rock salt and sea water contain sodium chloride. They are used to manufacture (make) chlorine, sodium hydroxide and hydrogen.

Limestone is used to manufacture glass and cement. It is also used to remove earthy impurities in the manufacture of iron.

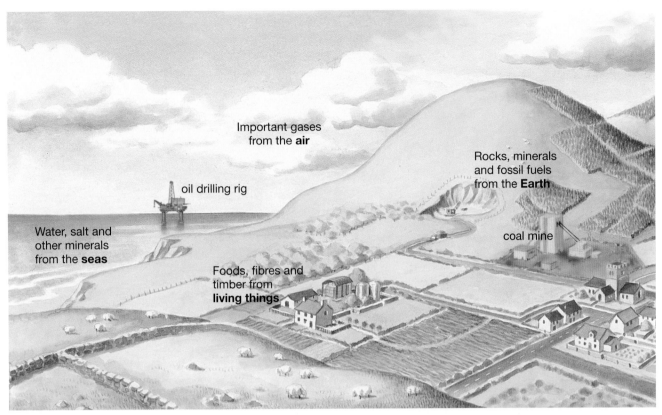

Figure 1 Sources of our raw materials

This cottage is built from two important rocks. It has limestone walls and a slate roof.

1   Name **four** useful materials whch are made from raw materials taken from the Earth.

2   What is a mineral? Give an example of a mineral.

3   What are rocks made of?

21.2	**How has the Earth changed (evolved)?**

4500 million years ago, the Earth was a ball of molten rock. As it cooled down, heavier metals sank to the centre. This has formed a **core** of dense molten iron, which has a temperature of about 4000°C (Figure 2). The core is surrounded by a thick band of quite dense solid and molten rock in the **mantle**. Here, the temperatures are between 1500 and 4000°C.

As the Earth cooled, less dense material floated and collected on the surface. It formed a thin, solid **crust** about 50 km thick. Where the crust is thickest, its surface is above sea level.

Outside and above the Earth is the **atmosphere**. This is a layer of gases about 100 km deep.

When the Earth was first forming, the atmosphere was mainly hydrogen and helium.

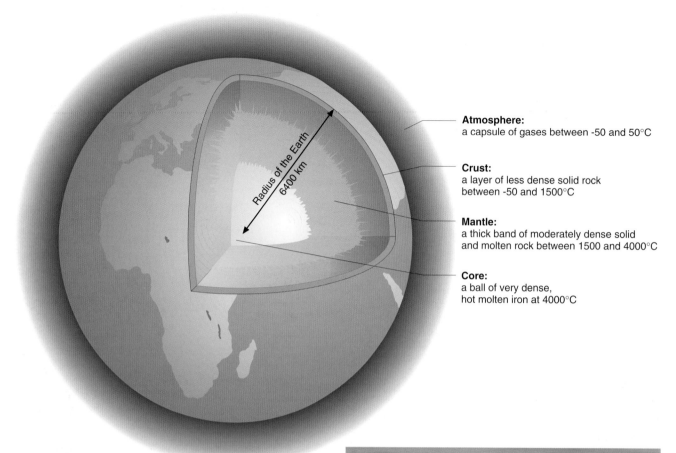

Atmosphere:
a capsule of gases between -50 and 50°C

Crust:
a layer of less dense solid rock
between -50 and 1500°C

Mantle:
a thick band of moderately dense solid
and molten rock between 1500 and 4000°C

Core:
a ball of very dense,
hot molten iron at 4000°C

Radius of the Earth
6400 km

Figure 2 Layers of the Earth. Notice how the temperature and density increase from the atmosphere to the core.

These gases had small molecules which escaped from the Earth's gravity into outer space. Later, when volcanic activity started on the Earth, other gases were added to the atmosphere.

These gases included water vapour, carbon dioxide, methane and ammonia. As the temperature of the Earth dropped even more, water vapour condensed to form rivers, lakes and oceans.

Plants appeared 3500 million years ago. They formed oxygen from water and carbon dioxide by photosynthesis. Flammable gases such as methane and ammonia burnt in the oxygen. This produced water, carbon dioxide and nitrogen.

Aerial photos such as this of Glen Canyon in Arizona, USA, help us to understand how water can change the Earth's surface.

Later, animals evolved and used the oxygen for respiration. At the same time, bacteria converted any remaining ammonia into nitrogen and nitrates. These processes helped to balance the nitrogen, oxygen and carbon dioxide in the atmosphere. The Earth's atmosphere has been more or less the same for the last 200 million years. The main constituents in dry air are shown in Table 1.

Element	% in dry air
Nitrogen	79
Oxygen	20
Argon	1

Table 1 The main constituents in dry air

The carbon cycle (section 9.5) also helps to maintain the composition of the atmosphere. Carbon dioxide and water vapour are removed from the atmosphere by photosynthesis. These gases are returned to the atmosphere when animals and plants respire and during combustion (burning). The amount of carbon dioxide in the atmosphere is also affected by the extent to which it dissolves in the water of the oceans.

Coral reefs form from the shells of sea organisms. Their shells are mainly calcium carbonate. This is formed from Ca^{2+} and CO_3^{2-} ions in sea water.

During the last century, we have burned more fossil fuels. This has led to a small but steady increase in the amount of carbon dioxide in the atmosphere. This increase in the amount of carbon dioxide is causing the 'greenhouse effect' and global warming (section 12.5).

21.3 The weathering of rocks

When rocks are exposed to the weather, they slowly break up and wear away.

The breaking up of rocks by wind, rain, ice and water is called **weathering**.

There are two types of weathering – **physical** and **chemical**.

Physical weathering

This is the cracking and breaking up rocks by physical means. There are two ways in which this happens.

1 By expansion and contraction of the rock

If you pour really hot water into a jam jar, it cracks. This is because the glass on the inside expands faster than that on the outside. This sets up forces in the glass causing it to crack. In the same way, the surface of a rock will expand and contract faster than the inside. The rock surface heats up and expands during the day and then cools and contracts at night. This may set up forces causing the rock to crack.

Large amounts of limestone rock scree have collected below Gordale Scar near Malham, Yorkshire. The scree is formed by physical weathering of the rock.

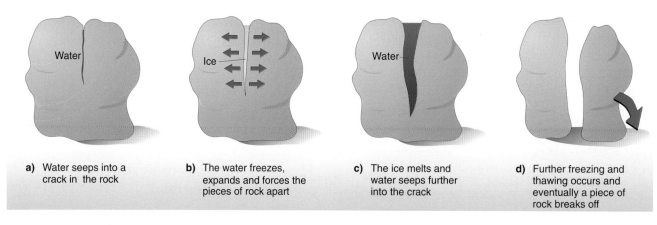

a) Water seeps into a crack in the rock

b) The water freezes, expands and forces the pieces of rock apart

c) The ice melts and water seeps further into the crack

d) Further freezing and thawing occurs and eventually a piece of rock breaks off

Figure 3 The physical weathering of a rock by repeated freezing and melting of water.

2 By the freezing of water

Once a rock cracks, water will seep into the joint (Figure 3). If the water filling a crack in a rock freezes, it expands. This pushes the pieces of rock apart. When the rock warms up, the ice melts and seeps further into the rocks.

Chemical weathering

This involves chemical reactions between the rocks and water. There are two important examples.

1 Reaction of water with feldspar in granite

Granite is a rock which contains different minerals. One of these minerals is called feldspar. Feldspar reacts slowly with water to form clay.

2 Reaction of rainwater with carbonates

Rocks containing carbonates react with chemicals in rainwater. The most important example of this is limestone (Figure 4).

As rain falls, it reacts with carbon dioxide in the atmosphere to form a dilute solution of carbonic acid.

$$\text{water} + \text{carbon dioxide} \rightarrow \text{carbonic acid}$$
$$H_2O(l) + \quad CO_2(g) \quad \rightarrow \quad H_2CO_3(aq)$$

In our wet climate, feldspar in the granite of this pit reacts with water to form clay. The soft wet clay is easily removed. It is used to manufacture high quality crockery.

This carbonic acid in rainwater reacts very slowly with insoluble calcium carbonate (limestone). It forms soluble calcium hydrogencarbonate. This dissolves in the water and is washed away.

$$\begin{array}{ccc} \text{carbonic} \\ \text{acid} \end{array} + \begin{array}{c} \text{calcium} \\ \text{carbonate} \end{array} \rightarrow \begin{array}{c} \text{calcium} \\ \text{hydrogencarbonate} \end{array}$$

$$H_2CO_3(aq) + \begin{array}{c} CaCO_3(s) \\ \text{(insoluble)} \end{array} \rightarrow \begin{array}{c} Ca(HCO_3)_2(aq) \\ \text{(soluble)} \end{array}$$

Figure 4 Look at these limestone statues on Rheims Cathedral, France. They have been weathered over the centuries by carbonic acid in rainwater.

4 Why does a glass jar crack when you pour boiling water into it?

5 How does freezing water break rocks?

6 What does feldspar turn into when it reacts with water?

7 What acid does carbon dioxide make with rainwater?

21.4 Rocks in the Earth

Rocks in the Earth are usually mixtures of different minerals. As the Earth cooled down, its molten crust solidified to form **igneous rocks**. At first, there were no other types of rock. Over millions of years, two other types of rock were created – **sedimentary rocks** and **metamorphic rocks**. Figure 5 shows how these three types of rock are being formed today.

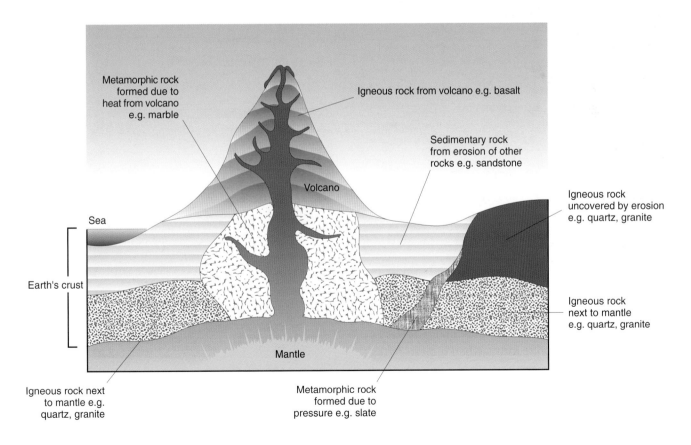

Figure 5 The formation of igneous, sedimentary and metamorphic rocks

Igneous rocks

Igneous rocks are formed when hot molten **magma** in the Earth's mantle cools and solidifies.

As the molten magma cools, it solidifies or crystallises as a mixture of different minerals. The crystals interlock in the solid. This rock is called igneous rock. Igneous means 'formed by fire'.

The size of the crystals in an igneous rock depends on the rate at which the magma has cooled and crystallised. Some igneous rocks are made when volcanoes erupt and the lava cools quickly in a matter of days. This produces rocks, such as basalt, with small crystals which are usually dark in colour.

Other igneous rocks are formed deep in the Earth's crust. Here the magma cools very slowly, possibly over centuries. This results in rocks with much larger crystals such as granite and quartz. These are usually light in colour.

This is a polished sample of granite – an igneous rock. Igneous rocks are formed from the cooling of very hot, molten rock. Granite forms when molten rocks cool slowly below the Earth's surface. The crystals in it are large.

Sedimentary rocks

When rocks are weathered, they form sediments and fragments such as sand and gravel. These sediments may be carried by rivers and deposited in the sea. As the sediment builds up over millions of years, the material below is compressed forming new, soft rocks such as mudstone, sandstone and shale.

Some sedimentary rocks, such as coal and chalk have formed by the decay of living things. Others, such as rock salt have formed by crystallisation from sea water.

If the layers are buried deeper, the soft sediments such as chalk get converted to harder sedimentary rocks like limestone.

All of these rocks are known as **sedimentary rocks** because they are formed by the build up of sediments.

The texture of most sedimentary rocks consists of small fragments of rock held together by cementing material. In some cases, these fragments contain fossils of plants or animals. These help us to date rocks.

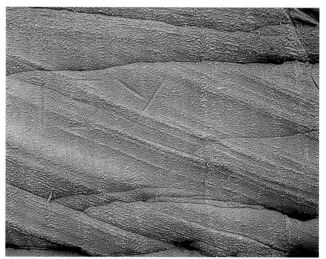

This is a sample of red sandstone – a sedimentary rock. It has formed from the erosion of granite. Very often, sedimentary rocks are formed in layers. Layers close to the surface are those which cut across other layers are usually younger.

Metamorphic rocks

Sometimes, sedimentary rocks are changed into harder rocks by very high pressures or temperatures. The new rock has a different structure from the original rock. It is therefore called **metamorphic rock** from a Greek word meaning 'change of shape'. Slate and marble are good examples of metamorphic rocks. Slate is formed when clay and mud are subjected to very high temperatures. Marble is formed when limestone is subjected to very high temperatures from hot igneous rock or molten magma.

This is a sample of impure marble – a metamorphic rock. It has formed from sedimentary rocks at high temperature and pressure.

8 What does the word *igneous* mean?

9 Copy out and complete these sentences.

When _____ cools slowly, the _____ rocks made have _____ crystals. _____ is an example of a rock made this way.

When _____ cools quickly, the _____ rocks made have _____ crystals. _____ is an example of a rock made this way.

10 What type of rock is made from sediments?

11 What is a fossil?

12 What type of rock are slate and marble?

13 How is limestone changed into marble?

Table 2 summarises the properties of igneous, sedimentary and metamorphic rocks. It will help you to decide whether a rock is igneous, sedimentary or metamorphic.

Property	Igneous	Sedimentary	Metamorphic
Is the rock hard or soft?	Hard	Soft (grains can be rubbed off)	Usually hard
What is the structure?	Interlocking crystals	Separate grains	Grains or crystals
Might the rock have layers?	No	Yes	Yes
Might the rock have fossils?	No	Yes	Yes
Might the rock fizz (give off CO_2) with dilute HCl?	No	Yes	Yes

Table 2 Identifying igneous, sedimentary and metamorphic rocks

21.5   The rock cycle

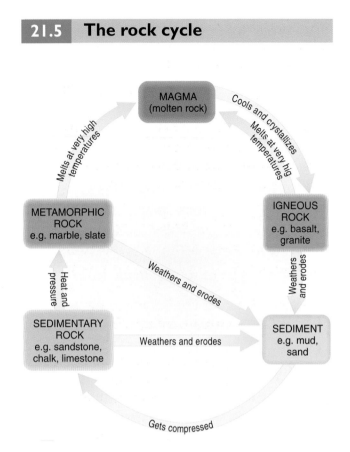

Figure 6 The rock cycle

Deep inside the Earth, the temperature reaches 4000°C. The temperature in the mantle ranges from 1500 to 4000°C. As rocks are buried below the Earth's surface, they eventually melt to form magma. In time, this magma may solidify as igneous rock and the sequence of events in the **rock cycle** begins again.

Figure 6 shows the main stages of the rock cycle. The complete cycle lasts hundreds of millions of years. Notice that sedimentary and metamorphic rocks can be weathered like igneous rock.

The rock cycle involves igneous, sedimentary and metamorphic processes which take place over very different **timescales**. Landslides, volcanoes and floods occur on *short* timescales of hours, days or possibly weeks. Other processes, such as the cooling of lava and the movement of fragments by rivers and glaciers, have *moderate* timescales which take months, years or even decades.

Some processes, such as the burial of fragments to form sedimentary rock and the effects of heat and pressure to form metamorphic rocks, are measured in *long* timescales of thousands or millions of years. These geological processes with very different timescales are all part of the rock cycle. They have been happening since the Earth was formed 4500 million years ago.

21.6   Layers of the Earth

The Earth's **shape** is like an orange – spherical but slightly flattened at the poles. The Earth's **structure** is like a cracked egg. The 'cracked shell' is like the Earth's thin crust, the egg 'white' is the mantle and the 'yolk' is the core. (See Figure 7).

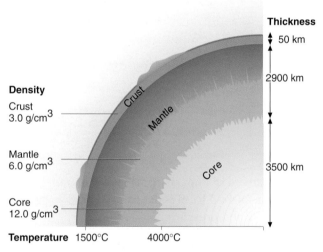

Figure 7 A cross section of the Earth showing the thicknesses, densities and temperatures in its internal structure.

Notice in Figure 7 that the three layers of crust, mantle and core increase in thickness, in density and in temperature towards the centre. The deepest mines in the Earth go to a depth of about 3 km. The temperature here is about 50°C.

Deep below the Earth's surface, miners work in temperatures like a hot summer's day

Below the crust, temperatures in the outer mantle are about 1500°C. This is hot enough to soften the rocks so that they behave like stiff plasticine. Within the mantle, temperatures are between 2000°C and 3000°C. The material is liquid.

In the Earth's core, the temperatures are even higher, reaching 4000°C. The main constituents in the core are iron and nickel.

There are two reasons why the core of the Earth is so hot.

1 When the Earth first formed, the temperatures inside were very high. Since then the outer layers of the Earth have helped to insulate the core, keeping the heat in.

2 Rocks in the Earth, and particularly granite, contain radioactive elements such as uranium, thorium and potassium. As these elements decay (break up), energy is released as heat. This energy helps to maintain temperatures inside the Earth.

21.7 Earth movements

The Earth's crust is cracked and broken into huge sections called **plates**. These vast plates float on the denser mantle below.

The plates fit together like a gigantic spherical jigsaw. The oceans and continents sit on top of these plates.

Over long periods of time, possibly millions of years, the plates move very slowly. This movement is caused by convection currents in the liquid mantle. When the plates slide past each other, move apart or push each other, various things can happen.

Plates slide past each other

When plates slide past each other, strains build up in the Earth's crust. This may cause the plates to bend. In some cases, the strains are released suddenly. The Earth moves, the ground shakes in an **earthquake** and huge cracks appear in the ground. These cracks in the ground, when plates slide past each other horizontally, are called **tear faults** (Figure 8). The San Andreas Fault in California and the Great Glen Fault in Scotland are examples of tear faults.

Tear fault between plates

Figure 8 A tear fault results when plates move past each other horizontally.

Plates move apart

When plates move apart, the crust is being stretched. Cracks sometimes appear in the Earth's surface. As the plates move further apart, surface rocks sink. This results in vertical faults. These faults produced by stretching forces are referred to as **normal faults**. When two vertical faults occur alongside each other, rift valleys are formed (Figure 9, over the page).

There is severe damage and often loss of life when an earthquake occurs. Roads are torn up and buildings collapse.

In some cases, hot molten rock (**lava**) escapes through cracks in the Earth's surface and erupts as a **volcano**.

After being quiet for nearly four centuries, the volcano on the Caribbean island of Montserrat erupted in 1995. The capital, Plymouth, had to be abandoned because of the flows of hot rock, ash and gases.

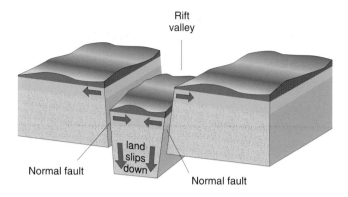

Figure 9 As plates move apart, the land on one side may sink into the crack. If there are two normal faults near each other, a **rift valley** may form.

Hell's Gate is a rift valley in Kenya

Plates push against each other

Folds in the Earth's crust at Stair Hole near Lulworth Cove in Dorset.

216

When plates push against each other, rocks are squeezed together. The forces push layers of the Earth's crust into a **fold**.

Sometimes, cracks appear as plates push against each other. One plate is then forced upwards and above the other (Figure 10). This is called a **reverse fault**.

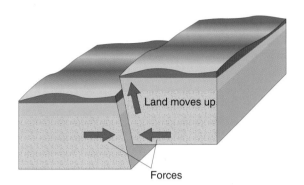

Figure 10 As plates move towards each other and collide, the Earth may crack with one layer moving over another as a reverse fault.

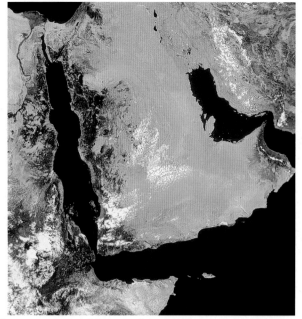

Many years ago, Africa and Arabia used to be joined together. They are now drifting apart, very, very slowly as the Red Sea gradually widens.

The study of the movement of the giant plates on the Earth's surface is called **plate tectonics**.

Every year, there are reports of serious earthquakes somewhere in the world. These earthquakes show that the Earth's crust is unstable. Earthquakes, folds and faults also show that the crust is subjected to very large forces when plates move. Over millions of years, movements of the giant plates can cause mountain ranges to form. These replace older mountains which have been worn away by weathering and erosion.

14 Copy out and complete these sentences.

The Earth's c_____ is cracked and broken into huge sections called plates.

These plates float on the m_____ .

They are moving slowly. There are three sorts of movement.

a) The plates s_____ past each other.

b) The plates move a_____ .

c) The plates squeeze together.

15 What is the study of the movement of plates called?

Summary

1 **The Earth is our source of raw materials**.

We get:

★ rocks, minerals and fossil fuels from the **Earth's crust**

★ water, salt and other minerals from the **seas**

★ important gases from the **air**

★ foods, fibres and timber from **living things**.

2 **Rocks** are mixtures of different minerals.

Minerals are single substances with a chemical name and a formula, e.g. pure sand is silicon dioxide, SiO_2.

3 **The Earth is made up of four layers**. The temperature and density of these layers increases from the atmosphere to the core.

★ The **atmosphere** is a covering of gases between −50 and 50°C.

★ The **crust** is a thin layer of less dense solid rock between −50 and 1500°C.

★ The **mantle** is a thick band of moderately dense molten and solid rock between 1500 and 4000°C.

★ The **core** is a ball of very dense molten iron at 4000°C.

4 **Weathering** is the breaking up of rocks. There are two kinds of weathering:

Physical weathering

★ by expansion and contraction of rocks as the temperature changes

★ by the freezing of water in cracks.

Chemical weathering

★ by the action of water on feldspar in granite

★ by the action of rainwater on carbonates (e.g. limestone)

5 There are **three different types of rock**:

	Igneous	Sedimentary	Metamorphic
How is it formed?	**Cooling of molten magma** underground or after a volcano	**Layers of sediment** in lakes or seas over millions of years	**Heat and pressure** on existing rocks over long periods
Structure	Various minerals in interlocking crystals	Grains cemented by salt crystals	Grains, layers or small crystals
Examples	Granite, basalt	Sandstone, limestone, chalk	Marble, slate

6 The Earth's crust is cracked and broken into vast sections called **plates**. These plates float on the dense liquid mantle. The plates move very, very slowly due to convection currents in the liquid mantle.

The study of the movement of the giant plates is called **plate tectonics**.

★ When plates slide past each other, **tear faults** and earthquakes occur.

★ When plates move apart, **normal faults**, rift valleys and volcanoes occur.

★ When plates push against each other, folds and **reverse faults** occur.

1 Portland cement was invented by Joseph Aspdin, a builder from Leeds. The flow diagram shows how cement is made.

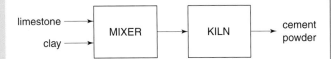

a) What are the **two** raw materials used to make cement? *(1)*

b) Cement is mixed with three substances to make concrete. Choose from the list the **three** substances used.

> crushed rock   slag   iron ore   soda
> quicklime   water   sand   *(3)*

[AQA (NEAB) 1999]

2 a) Use the types of rock in the box below to answer the questions that follow:

> Basalt   Granite   Limestone   Marble
> Sandstone   Slate

(i) Name **one** metamorphic rock. *(1)*

(ii) Name **one** igneous rock. *(1)*

b) (i) Describe how igneous rocks are formed. *(2)*

(ii) Explain why some igneous rocks have very small crystals and others have large crystals. *(1)*

[WJEC 1998]

3 Industrial chemists turn raw materials into useful products.

The list below gives some raw materials.

> coke   clay   iron ore   soda
> limestone   sodium chloride   crude oil   sand

Choose, **from the list**, the raw material or materials used to make each of the following products. You will need to use some of the raw materials more than once.

Which:

a) one raw material is used to make plastics;

b) two raw materials are used to make cement;

c) three raw materials are used to make glass;

d) one raw material is used to make chlorine;

e) three raw materials are used to make iron? *(7)*

[AQA (NEAB) 1999]

4 The diagram below shows part of a cliff face. Four different layers of sedimentary rock can be seen.

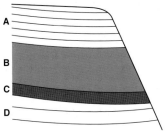

a) Which layer of sedimentary rock is probably the oldest? *(1)*

b) Three different stages which lead to the formation of sedimentary rock are listed below.

A Earth movement which made sediment become buried

B Movement of sediment by wind, rivers and tides

C Weathering of rock occurred

Place the three stages (**A**, **B** and **C**) in the order in which they occurred. *(1)*

c) When rock is buried, the increased pressure and temperature may cause it to change. Which type of rock is formed by this process? *(1)*

d) Large crystals are sometimes found in igneous rocks. Describe in detail how igneous rock is formed. *(4)* **[Edexcel 1998]**

5 a) Millions of years ago, the atmosphere contained:

> ammonia   carbon monoxide   methane
> nitrogen   oxygen   steam

The amounts of these gases have changed over millions of years.

(i) State **one** gas which has decreased. *(1)*

(ii) State **one** gas which has increased. *(1)*

b) What is the percentage of oxygen in the atmosphere today? *(1)*

c) Describe a test for carbon dioxide. *(2)*

d) Photosynthesis changes the amount of oxygen and carbon dioxide in the atmosphere. How does photosynthesis change the amount of:

(i) oxygen; *(1)* (ii) carbon dioxide? *(1)*

[Edexcel 1999]

22

Chemicals from crude oil

22.1 Crude oil

Coal, oil and natural gas are our most common fuels.

They are called **fossil fuels** because they have formed from the remains of dead animals and plants.

The oil that we use as fuel comes from crude oil. The crude oil has formed over millions of years. It is a **non-renewable** resource. Once used, it is gone forever. There is a finite amount of crude oil available, it is not a limitless supply.

This fossil of a prehistoric fish was left when the rest of it became crude oil.

Crude oil is our main source of fuel and organic chemicals. Crude oil comes to refineries in the UK from the North Sea and the Gulf area in the Middle East.

It is a sticky, smelly, dark brown liquid. You will have seen TV pictures of it on beaches when there has been an oil spill. Crude oil is a mixture containing hundreds of different compounds. These vary from simple substances like methane (CH_4) to complicated substances with long chains and rings of carbon atoms. Most of the substances in crude oil are **hydrocarbons**.

Hydrocarbons are substances containing only hydrogen and carbon.

A century ago, oil was almost unknown. Now, it is essential for our lifestyles. It is almost as important to our lives as air and water. In the UK, 70% of all organic chemicals come from oil. Antifreeze, brake fluid, lipstick, nylon, explosives and paint are all made from it.

Textiles, like nylon and polyester, are manufactured from chemicals in crude oil. All your clothes might be made of these textiles.

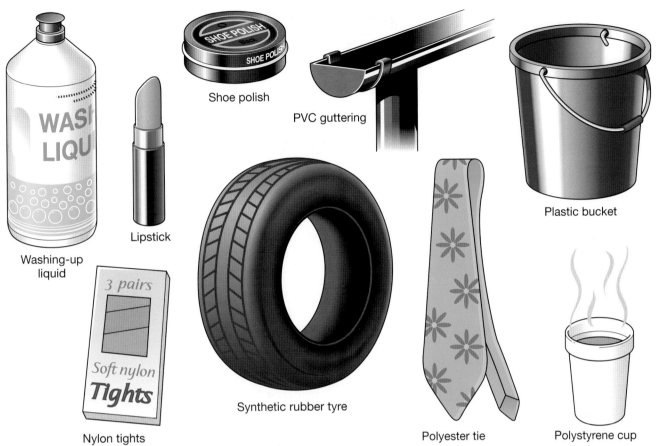

Figure 1 Some of the products from crude oil

An aerial view of the oil refinery at Pernis, Holland. Notice the fractionating towers and the storage tanks.

Without crude oil, there would be no petrol or diesel for cars, trains or aircraft. Transport would come to a standstill. Figure 1 shows some of the products we get from crude oil.

1 Name **three** fossil fuels.

2 What is a hydrocarbon?

3 Name **four** things made from crude oil.

| 22.2 | **Separating crude oil into fractions** |

The hydrocarbons in crude oil have different boiling points. This means that crude oil can be separated by boiling off portions over different temperature ranges.

These portions are called **fractions**. The process of boiling off the fractions is called **fractional distillation**.

Most of the fractions from crude oil are used as fuels. Figure 2 shows the small scale fractional distillation of crude oil. The ceramic wool, soaked in crude oil, is heated very gently at first and then more strongly. Distillate slowly drips into the collecting tube. Four fractions are collected. Their boiling ranges and properties are shown in Table 1 over the page.

Boiling range (°C)	Name of fraction	Colour	Viscosity (runniness)	How does it burn?
20–70	Petrol (gasoline)	Pale yellow	Runny	Easily with a clean yellow flame
70–120	Naphtha	Yellow	Fairly runny	Quite easily, yellow flame, some smoke
120–170	Paraffin (kerosene)	Dark yellow	Fairly viscous	Harder to burn, quite smoky flame
170–230	Diesel oils	Brown	Viscous	Hard to burn, very smoky flame

Table 1 The properties of fractions from the small scale fractional distillation of crude oil.

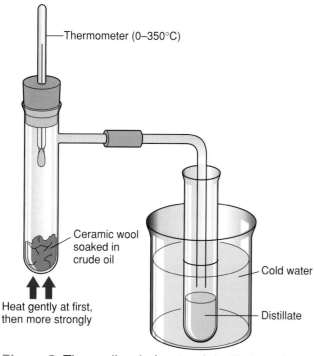

Figure 2 The small scale fractional distillation of crude oil

Table 1 also shows the industrial names of the fractions. Notice how the properties of the fractions gradually change in colour, viscosity (runniness) and ease of burning.

Figure 3 shows the temperatures and products at different heights in an industrial fractionating tower. Inside the tower there are horizontal trays at different levels. The crude oil is heated in a furnace and the vapours pass into the lower part of the tower. As the vapours rise up the column, the temperature falls.

Different vapours condense at different heights in the tower and are tapped off. Liquids like petrol, which boil at low temperatures, condense high up in the tower and have a small relative molecular mass. Liquids like fuel oils, which boil at higher temperatures, condense low down in the tower and have a larger relative molecular mass.

Each of the fractions from crude oil contain similar substances. The substances at each fraction are made up of roughly the same number of carbon atoms. Figure 3 also shows the uses of each fraction. The uses of the fractions depend on their properties. Petrol vaporises easily and is very flammable. It is ideal to use in car engines. Fuel oil and lubricating oil are very viscous. They are used in lubricants and in central heating. Tar (bitumen), which is solid but easy to melt, is used for waterproofing and on roads as tarmac.

Tar is mixed with stone chippings and used to surface roads

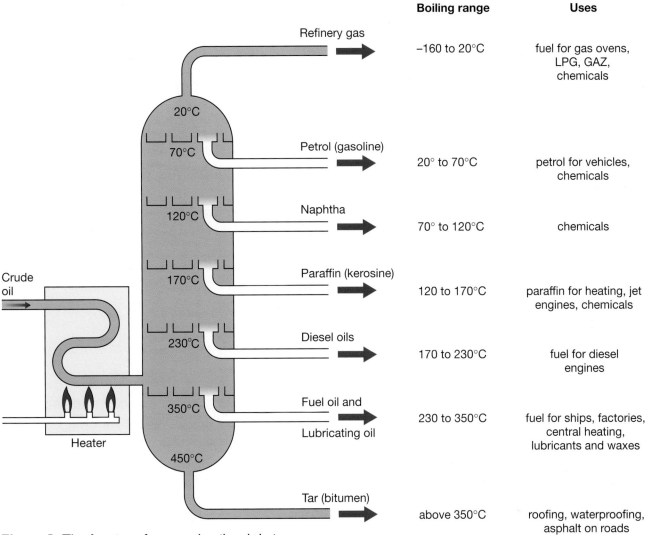

	Boiling range	Uses
Refinery gas	−160 to 20°C	fuel for gas ovens, LPG, GAZ, chemicals
Petrol (gasoline)	20° to 70°C	petrol for vehicles, chemicals
Naphtha	70° to 120°C	chemicals
Paraffin (kerosine)	120 to 170°C	paraffin for heating, jet engines, chemicals
Diesel oils	170 to 230°C	fuel for diesel engines
Fuel oil and Lubricating oil	230 to 350°C	fuel for ships, factories, central heating, lubricants and waxes
Tar (bitumen)	above 350°C	roofing, waterproofing, asphalt on roads

(Crude oil → Heater, with temperatures 20°C, 70°C, 120°C, 170°C, 230°C, 350°C, 450°C marked on the column)

Figure 3 The fractions from crude oil and their uses

4 Put these fractions in order of boiling points, starting with the highest.

   tar refinery gas fuel oil petrol diesel

5 What does the word *viscosity* mean?

6 Look at Figure 3.

   a) Give **two** uses of kerosene.

   b) Give **two** uses of fuel oil.

22.3   Natural gas and alkanes

Natural gas is a fossil fuel like crude oil. It has formed over millions of years from the remains of tiny dead sea animals, like plankton. The main constituent in natural gas is methane, CH_4. Methane is the simplest possible hydrocarbon with just one carbon atom per molecule. But carbon atoms can form strong covalent bonds with each other. This has led to thousands of other hydrocarbons with carbon atoms joined together in chains.

Name	Methane	Ethane	Propane	Butane
Molecular formula	CH_4	C_2H_6	C_3H_8	C_4H_{10}
Displayed formula	$$H-\underset{\underset{H}{\mid}}{\overset{\overset{H}{\mid}}{C}}-H$$	$$H-\underset{\underset{H}{\mid}}{\overset{\overset{H}{\mid}}{C}}-\underset{\underset{H}{\mid}}{\overset{\overset{H}{\mid}}{C}}-H$$	$$H-\underset{\underset{H}{\mid}}{\overset{\overset{H}{\mid}}{C}}-\underset{\underset{H}{\mid}}{\overset{\overset{H}{\mid}}{C}}-\underset{\underset{H}{\mid}}{\overset{\overset{H}{\mid}}{C}}-H$$	$$H-\underset{\underset{H}{\mid}}{\overset{\overset{H}{\mid}}{C}}-\underset{\underset{H}{\mid}}{\overset{\overset{H}{\mid}}{C}}-\underset{\underset{H}{\mid}}{\overset{\overset{H}{\mid}}{C}}-\underset{\underset{H}{\mid}}{\overset{\overset{H}{\mid}}{C}}-H$$
Models of the molecules (black balls for carbon, white balls for hydrogen)				

Table 2 Molecular and structural formulae of four hydrocarbons

The four simplest hydrocarbons are methane, ethane, propane and butane.

Table 2 shows the molecular formulas and displayed formulas for these four hydrocarbons. The displayed formulas show which atoms are attached to each other. There are four covalent bonds to each carbon atom. Each of these bonds consists of a pair of electrons shared by two atoms (section 19.4). Models of the molecules are shown in Table 2 below the formulas.

Methane, ethane, propane and butane are members of a series of compounds called **alkanes**. All other alkanes are named from the number of carbon atoms in one molecule. So, C_5H_{12} is *pen*tane, C_6H_{14} is *hex*ane, C_7H_{16} is *hep*tane and so on. The names of all alkanes end in *–ane*.

Look at the formulas of methane CH_4, ethane C_2H_6, propane C_3H_8 and butane C_4H_{10}. Notice that the difference in the number of carbon and hydrogen atoms between methane and ethane is CH_2. The difference between ethane and propane is CH_2 and the difference between propane and butane is also CH_2.

Properties of alkanes

Low melting point and boiling point

Alkanes are typical molecular (non-metal) compounds. They have low melting points and low boiling points. Alkanes with one to four carbon atoms in each molecule are gases at room temperature. Methane (CH_4) and ethane (C_2H_6) make up about 95% of natural gas. Propane (C_3H_8) and butane (C_4H_{10}) are the main constituents of 'liquefied petroleum gas' (LPG). The best known uses of LPG are 'Calor gas' and 'GAZ' for camping, caravans and boats.

A small blue butane (GAZ) cylinder used in camping

Alkanes with 5 to 17 carbon atoms are liquids at room temperature. Mixtures of these liquids are used in petrol, in paraffin and in lubricating and engine oils. Alkanes with 18 or more carbon atoms per molecule, such as tar, are solids at room temperature. Even so, they begin to melt on very hot days.

Notice that the alkanes change from gases to liquids and then to solids as their molecules get bigger.

Insoluble in water

Alkanes are insoluble in water, but they dissolve in solvents like petrol.

Burning (combustion)

The most important reactions of alkanes are burning. When there is plenty of oxygen, hydrocarbons burn completely producing carbon dioxide and water.

$$\text{methane} + \text{oxygen} \rightarrow \text{carbon dioxide} + \text{water}$$
(in natural gas)

$$CH_4 + 2O_2 \rightarrow CO_2 + 2H_2O$$

Burning reactions are very exothermic, that is, they give out lots of heat energy. So alkanes in natural gas and crude oil are used as fuels. When there is too little oxygen, incomplete combustion gives carbon (soot) and carbon monoxide as well as carbon dioxide. Carbon monoxide is very poisonous. So, it is dangerous to burn carbon compounds in a poor supply of air.

7 What is the main gas in natural gas?

8 Name the **four** simplest hydrocarbons.

9 Which alkane has seven carbon atoms?

10 What happens to the boiling point as the alkane molecules increase in size?

11 Write a word equation for methane burning in plenty of oxygen.

One of NASA's Lockheed aircraft being refuelled in flight. Paraffin (kerosene) is used as the fuel in aircraft.

22.4 Cracking – more petrol from crude oil

During the 1930s, the demand for petrol increased rapidly (Table 3, over the page). This meant that refineries were left with large, unwanted amounts of the heavier fractions. Fortunately, chemists found ways of converting the heavier fractions into petrol and other useful products.

One method of converting the heavier fractions into petrol is **catalytic cracking**.

Catalytic cracking involves breaking down larger hydrocarbon molecules into simpler hydrocarbons using a catalyst at high temperature.

Fraction	% in Crude oil	% in Everyday demand
Fuel gas	2	4
Petrol	6	22
Naphtha	10	5
Kerosene	13	8
Diesel oil	19	23
Fuel oil and bitumen	50	38

Table 3 Relative amounts of the different fractions in crude oil and the demand for each fraction.

How are molecules cracked?

Cracking is a chemical process. It involves breaking a strong covalent bond between two carbon atoms. This requires high temperatures and a catalyst. The catalyst is finely powdered aluminium oxide and silicon(IV) oxide. These substances do not react with the crude oil fractions. They provide a hot surface that speeds up the cracking process.

What are the products of cracking?

Look at the long molecule of decane ($C_{10}H_{22}$) on the left-hand side of Figure 4. It has a chain of 10 carbon atoms with 22 hydrogen atoms. Imagine that decane is cracked (split) between two of its carbon atoms. This cannot produce two smaller alkane molecules because there are not enough hydrogen atoms to go round.

But suppose that one product is the alkane, octane (C_8H_{18}). If C_8H_{18} is split off from $C_{10}H_{22}$, the molecular formula of the remaining part is C_2H_4. The chemical name for C_2H_4 is **ethene**. Notice in Figure 4 that ethene has a *double* bond between the two carbon atoms. This double bond allows all the carbon atoms in the products to have four bonds.

> Hydrocarbons such as ethene, which contain a double bond (C=C), are known as **alkenes**.

The names of alkenes come from the alkane with the same number of carbon atoms. But the alkene name has the ending *–ene* rather than *–ane*.

At one time lead compounds were added to petrol to help it burn smoother. As a result, the amount of lead in the environment increased. Most petrol is now unleaded because lead is poisonous to living things.

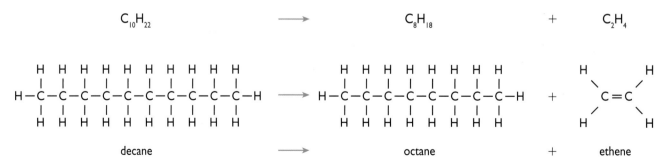

Figure 4 When decane undergoes catalytic cracking, it forms an **alkane**, like octane, and an **alkene**, like ethene.

Cracking is important because it can be used to produce more petrol. Larger alkanes are cracked to produce alkanes with about eight carbon atoms like octane. These are the main constituents in petrol. The petrol obtained in this way is better quality than that obtained by the fractional distillation of crude oil. Cracked petrol is therefore blended with other petrols to improve their quality.

Grangemouth oil refinery in Scotland.

12 What is *catalytic cracking*?

13 What is an *alkene*?

14 Which catalyst is used to crack alkanes?

15 What is the main alkane found in petrol?

Compounds, like ethene, which contain double bonds are called unsaturated compounds. Margarine and vegetable oil contain unsaturated fats.

Polythene

Alkenes, like ethene, are much more reactive than alkanes. Carbon compounds are more stable when they have single bonds between carbon atoms. The double bonds (C=C) make molecules like ethene very reactive.

If the conditions are right, molecules of ethene will join with each other. Double bonds break leaving single bonds as the molecules join together.

Polythene is made by heating ethene at high pressure with special catalysts.

22.5	**Polymers from alkenes**

Ethene is a very valuable substance for the chemical industry. Ethene and other alkenes are used to make important polymers because they are so reactive. They are used to manufacture polythene, PVC, polypropene, polystyrene and perspex.

Clingfilm is made from polythene.

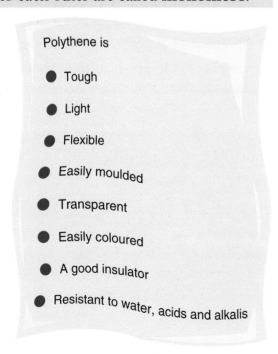

ethene molecules

part of the polythene molecule

Figure 5 Ethene molecules join to form poly(ethene)

The double bonds in the ethene molecule 'open up'. This allows carbon atoms on separate ethene molecules to join together forming polythene (see Figure 5). Polythene is short for poly(ethene). Poly means 'many'. So, poly(ethene) or polythene means 'many ethenes' joined together.

When ethene forms polythene, very long chains are produced. These long molecules contain between 1000 and 5000 carbon atoms.

This process is called **addition polymerisation**. Small molecules, like ethene, add to each other to form a giant molecule.
The giant molecule is called a **polymer**. The small molecules, like ethene, which add to each other are called **monomers**.

Polythene is

● Tough

● Light

● Flexible

● Easily moulded

● Transparent

● Easily coloured

● A good insulator

● Resistant to water, acids and alkalis

Figure 6 lists the properties of polythene. These have led to many different uses. Polythene is the most important plastic at present. It is used as thin sheets for packaging and coating materials. It is moulded into beakers, buckets and troughs. It is used to insulate wires and cables.

Other polymers

Two other polymers formed by addition polymerisation are shown in Table 4. The uses of these polymers are related to their structure and properties. Table 4 also shows the structure of the monomers and a section of the polymer structure.

These addition polymers have provided important new materials, but they have one big disadvantage. They are **non-biodegradable**. This means they are not decomposed (broken down) by bacteria. Plastic rubbish lies around for years, littering the environment.

In the last few years, biodegradable plastics have been developed. These are now being used for bags and other wrappings.

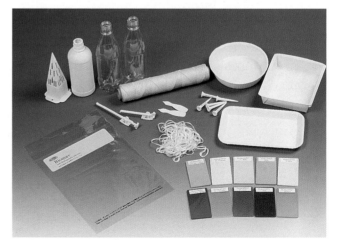

Figure 6 The properties of polythene

A range of products made from biodegradable plastic

Polymer	Name and structural formula of monomer	Section of polymer structure	Important uses of the polymer
PVC (polyvinylchloride)	vinyl chloride $$\begin{array}{c} Cl \qquad H \\ \diagdown C = C \diagup \\ H \qquad H \end{array}$$	$$\begin{array}{c} Cl\ H\ \ Cl\ H \\ \mid\ \ \mid\ \ \ \mid\ \ \mid \\ H-C-C-C-C-H \\ \mid\ \ \mid\ \ \ \mid\ \ \mid \\ H\ H\ \ H\ H \end{array}$$	Tough, water resistant plastic leads to use in rainwear, wallpaper, and as insulation for electric cables. Rigid PVC is used in CDs, guttering, pipes and flooring
Polystyrene	styrene $$\begin{array}{c} C_6H_5 \qquad H \\ \diagdown C = C \diagup \\ H \qquad H \end{array}$$	$$\begin{array}{c} C_6H_5\ H\ \ C_6H_5\ H \\ \mid\ \ \ \ \mid\ \ \ \ \ \mid\ \ \ \ \mid \\ -C-C-C-C- \\ \mid\ \ \ \ \mid\ \ \ \ \ \mid\ \ \ \ \mid \\ H\ \ H\ \ \ H\ \ H \end{array}$$	The bulky C_6H_5 group prevents close packing of the molecules. Hence the polymer has a low density and so is used in packaging and insulation

Table 4 The structure and uses of PVC and polystyrene

Summary

1 **Crude oil** is a **fossil fuel** like coal and natural gas.

 ★ Crude oil contains a mixture of hundreds of carbon compounds.

 ★ Most of the compounds in crude oil are **hydrocarbons**.

 ★ The hydrocarbons in crude oil can be separated into **fractions** using a process called **fractional distillation**.

 ★ The properties of these fractions differ and as a result they have different uses.

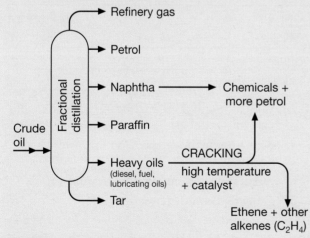

Figure 7 Processes from crude oil

2 Hydrocarbons are typical simple molecular compounds.

 ★ They contain only hydrogen and carbon.

 ★ Hundreds of carbon atoms may be joined together in one hydrocarbon.

 ★ They have low melting points and boiling points.

 ★ They are insoluble in water.

 ★ They burn in air to form carbon dioxide and water.

3 The simplest hydrocarbons are **alkanes**.

 ★ The simplest alkane is methane, CH_4.

 ★ Alkanes have strong C–C and C–H bonds so they have few reactions.

4 **Cracking** is used to produce petrol from the heavier fractions from crude oil. During cracking, alkane molecules are split into smaller alkanes plus **alkenes**.

5 Alkenes contain a carbon–carbon double bond (C=C).

 ★ Alkenes are much more reactive than alkanes because of their reactive double bond.

 ★ Alkenes undergo **addition polymerisation** to produce polymers e.g. polythene.

e.g. $$n\begin{array}{c} H\ \ H \\ \mid\ \ \mid \\ C=C \\ \mid\ \ \mid \\ H\ \ H \end{array} \xrightarrow[\substack{\text{high pressure} \\ + \\ \text{catalyst}}]{\substack{\text{high} \\ \text{temperature}}} \left(\begin{array}{c} H\ \ H \\ \mid\ \ \mid \\ C-C \\ \mid\ \ \mid \\ H\ \ H \end{array}\right)_n$$

1   Crude oil is a fossil fuel.

a) (i) Copy the sentence below. Complete your sentence by choosing the correct words from the box.

| energy   long   plants   rocks   short |

You may use each word once or not at all.

Fossil fuels were formed from the remains of _____ and animals over a _____ period of time. *(2)*

(ii) Give **one** other example of a fossil fuel. *(1)*

(iii) In the future there may be no fossil fuels left. Why? *(1)*

b) Crude oil is separated into useful fractions by fractional distillation. The fractions have the main uses given in the table.

Use	% of crude oil
Fuel for heating	35
Fuel for vehicles	29
Fuel for generating electricity	22
Manufacturing plastics and other chemicals	14

Use the information in the table to redraw and complete the bar chart. *(2)*

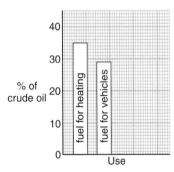

c) Crude oil is a mixture of hydrocarbons. One hydrocarbon, butane C_4H_{10}, is used as a fuel for heating. Complete a copy of the sentence.

A hydrocarbon is a compound of the elements _____ . *(2)*

d) Crude oil is a raw material used in the manufacture of plastics. One of the plastics manufactured is poly(ethene). Poly(ethene) is used to make carrier bags.

Give **one** advantage and **one** disadvantage of the use of poly(ethene) for carrier bags. *(2)*

[AQA (SEG) 1999]

2   The apparatus below is used to demonstrate the fractional distillation of crude oil.

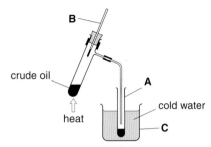

a) Name the pieces of apparatus labelled **A**, **B** and **C**. *(3)*

b) Suggest why this experiment should be carried out in a fume cupboard. *(1)*

c) Why is **cold** water placed in the apparatus labelled **C**? *(2)*

d) Describe how you would use the apparatus to collect the petrol fraction from crude oil. The petrol fraction boils between 40°C and 75°C. *(2)*

e) When fuels like petrol are burned they produce a large amount of carbon dioxide. Explain why it is thought that this carbon dioxide may affect the Earth's climate. *(2)*

[AQA (NEAB) 1998]

3   The table gives some information about seven hydrocarbons.

Name of hydrocarbon	Number of carbon atoms in one molecule	Boiling point (°C)
Methane	1	−164
Ethane	2	−89
Propane	3	−42
Butane	4	0
Pentane	5	36
Hexane	6	
Heptane	7	98

a) Which **one** of these hydrocarbons is the main part of natural gas? *(1)*

b) Name the hydrocarbon with the lowest boiling point. *(1)*

c) Suggest the boiling point of hexane. *(1)*

d) Copy and complete the sentence.

Hydrocarbons are compounds of carbon and _____ . *(1)*

e) Propane is used as a fuel. Copy and complete the word equation for the reaction that occurs when propane burns completely.

propane + oxygen → _____ + _____ *(2)*

[Edexcel 1999]

23

Ammonia and fertilisers

23.1 Reversible reactions

Baking a cake is an irreversible reaction

When you bake a cake, chemical reactions take place in the cake. Once the cake is baked, it is impossible to turn it back into flour, margarine, eggs and sugar.

The same applies when you burn charcoal in a barbecue. The charcoal, which is mainly carbon, reacts with oxygen in the air. The product is carbon dioxide.

$$\text{carbon} + \text{oxygen} \rightarrow \text{carbon dioxide}$$
$$\text{(charcoal)}$$
$$C(s) + O_2(g) \rightarrow CO_2(g)$$

No matter what you do, carbon dioxide cannot be turned back into charcoal and oxygen.

Reactions like this which cannot be reversed are called **irreversible reactions**.

Most of the reactions that we have studied so far are irreversible. But there are some processes which can be reversed. For example, ice turns into water on heating.

$$\text{ice} \xrightarrow{\text{heat}} \text{water}$$
$$H_2O(s) \xrightarrow{\text{heat}} H_2O(l)$$

231

If the water is now cooled, the ice reforms.

$$\text{water} \xrightarrow{\text{cool}} \text{ice}$$
$$H_2O(l) \xrightarrow{\text{cool}} H_2O(s)$$

These two parts of this reversible process can be combined in one equation as:

$$H_2O(s) \underset{\text{cool}}{\overset{\text{heat}}{\rightleftharpoons}} H_2O(l)$$

When solid ammonium chloride is heated, it decomposes to form two gases – ammonia and hydrogen chloride.

$$\text{ammonium chloride} \xrightarrow{\text{heat}} \text{ammonia} + \text{hydrogen chloride}$$
$$NH_4Cl(s) \xrightarrow{\text{heat}} NH_3(g) + HCl(g)$$

If these gases cool down and stay mixed, white clouds of powdery ammonium chloride reform.

$$NH_3(g) + HCl(g) \rightarrow NH_4Cl(s)$$

These two processes can be combined in one equation as:

$$NH_4Cl(s) \underset{\text{mix gases}}{\overset{\text{heat}}{\rightleftharpoons}} NH_3(g) + HCl(g)$$

These reactions which can be reversed are called **reversible reactions**.

Ice melts as it warms up in a drink. If the drink is chilled, ice will reform. This is a reversible process.

The reaction between nitrogen and hydrogen forming ammonia is also reversible. This can be demonstrated using the apparatus in Figure 1.

Caution! Your teacher may show you the experiment in Figure 1. You must **not** try the experiment yourself.

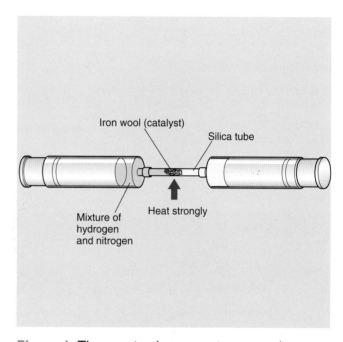

Figure I The reaction between nitrogen and hydrogen to form ammonia.

Using syringes, the mixture of hydrogen and nitrogen is pushed to and fro over the heated iron wool. The gases are then pushed out of the syringes on to damp red litmus paper. The litmus paper turns blue. This shows that ammonia has been produced. Ammonia is the only common alkaline gas.

$$\text{nitrogen} + \text{hydrogen} \rightarrow \text{ammonia}$$
$$N_2(g) + 3H_2(g) \rightarrow 2NH_3(g)$$

The experiment can be repeated, starting with ammonia in the syringes. This time, nitrogen and hydrogen are produced when ammonia gas is pushed to and fro over the heated iron wool.

$$2NH_3(g) \rightarrow N_2(g) + 3H_2(g)$$

These experiments show that the reaction between nitrogen and hydrogen to form ammonia is reversible. The reaction is the basis of the Haber process to manufacture ammonia (section 23.3).

1 Give **two** examples of irreversible reactions.

2 Give **two** examples of reversible reactions.

3 Write the word equation for the reaction between nitrogen and hydrogen to form ammonia.

4 Write the chemical symbol equation for the reaction between nitrogen and hydrogen to form ammonia.

23.2 Coming to equilibrium

During a reversible reaction, the reactants are sometimes *completely* changed to the products. But, in other cases, the reactants are *not completely* converted to the products.

For example, if ice and water are kept at 0°C, neither the ice nor the water seems to change. We say the two substances are in **equilibrium**. When two substances are in equilibrium like this, we replace the reversible arrows sign, $\rightleftarrows$ in the equation, with the equilibrium arrows sign $\rightleftharpoons$.

So, at 0°C,   ice $\rightleftharpoons$ water
$$H_2O(s) \rightleftharpoons H_2O(l)$$

In the same way, nitrogen and hydrogen will come to equilibrium with ammonia in the apparatus shown in Figure 1.

$$N_2(g) + 3H_2(g) \rightleftharpoons 2NH_3(g)$$

When equilibrium is reached, the concentrations of the reactants and products do not change any more.

23.3 Manufacturing ammonia – the Haber process

During the last century, the populations of Europe and America increased very rapidly. Increasing amounts of food were needed to feed the growing populations. This led farmers and gardeners to use nitrogen compounds as fertilisers (section 23.5). Initially, the main source of nitrogen compounds for fertilisers was sodium nitrate from Chile.

By 1900, the supplies of sodium nitrate in Chile were running out. Another supply of nitrogen had to be found or many people would starve. The obvious source of nitrogen was the air. But making nitrogen combine with hydrogen to form ammonia was difficult.

Several chemists began to work on this problem. The most successful was the German scientist, Fritz Haber. By 1908, Haber had found the ideal conditions to make ammonia from nitrogen and hydrogen on a large scale. By 1913, the **Haber process** had become the most important method of manufacturing ammonia.

In 1904, Fritz Haber began to study the reaction between nitrogen and hydrogen. It took him four years to find the ideal conditions to make ammonia. He had to use high temperature, high pressure and a catalyst. Ammonia from the Haber process is used to make ammonium salts and nitrates for fertilisers.

Raw Materials   Reactants   Product

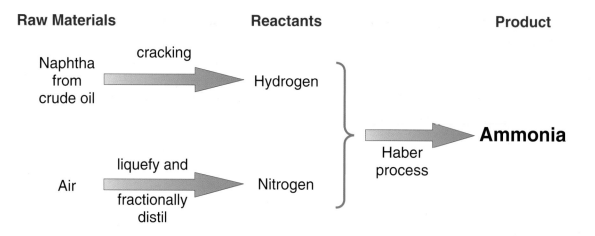

Naphtha from crude oil →(cracking)→ Hydrogen

Air →(liquefy and fractionally distil)→ Nitrogen

→(Haber process)→ **Ammonia**

Figure 2 A flow scheme for the Haber process.

A flow scheme for the modern Haber process is shown in Figure 2.

Notice that the raw materials for the process are:

★ naphtha from crude oil which is 'cracked' to produce hydrogen

★ air which is liquefied and then fractionally distilled to provide nitrogen.

The reaction is carried out under extreme conditions:

★ a pressure of 200 atmospheres

★ a temperature of 450°C

★ with a catalyst of iron.

The reaction for the Haber process can be summarised as:

$$N_2(g) + 3H_2(g) \xrightarrow[\text{450°C + iron catalyst}]{\text{200 atm}} 2NH_3(g)$$

Under these conditions, about 25% of the nitrogen and hydrogen are converted to ammonia. The hot gases from the converter are then cooled to liquefy the ammonia. The unreacted nitrogen and hydrogen are recycled.

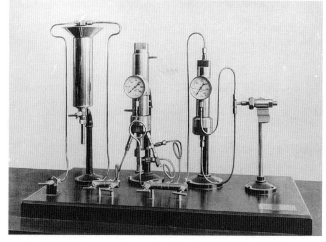

The original apparatus used by Fritz Haber to make ammonia.

5 Why are fertilisers so important?

6 What does the Haber process make?

7 Where does the hydrogen for the Haber process come from?

8 Which catalyst is used in the Haber process?

9 What pressure is used in the Haber process?

23.4	**Getting the most for your money**

Industrial chemists want to produce materials as fast and as cheaply as possible. They want to get the most product they can for the money they spend. In order to do this, they choose materials and conditions which:

1 use the cheapest materials and equipment

2 ensure the reaction happens as fast as possible.

The importance of these two points can be seen in the Haber process.

1 Cost of materials

The raw materials for the Haber process (Figure 2) are chosen so that ammonia is produced as economically as possible.

★ Air, which provides nitrogen, is plentiful and costs nothing.

★ Naphtha, which provides hydrogen, is plentiful and relatively cheap.

★ Iron, the cheapest metal, is used as the catalyst.

2 Fast reaction rate

Three conditions ensure a high reaction rate.

★ A pressure of 200 atmospheres which concentrates the nitrogen and hydrogen.

★ A temperature of 450°C.

★ A catalyst of iron.

Catalysts are essential for many industrial processes. By using a suitable catalyst, it is possible to carry out difficult reactions like the Haber process. Other processes can be carried out at lower temperatures and lower pressures when a catalyst is used. This makes them more economical.

23.5	**Ammonia**

Ammonia is an important chemical in industry and agriculture. Most ammonia is used to make fertilisers and nitric acid (see Table 1).

Use	Approx. %
Fertilisers	75
Nitric acid	10
Nylon	5
Wood pulp and organic chemicals	10

Table 1   The main uses of ammonia

The uses of ammonia depend on its properties. These are listed in Figure 3.

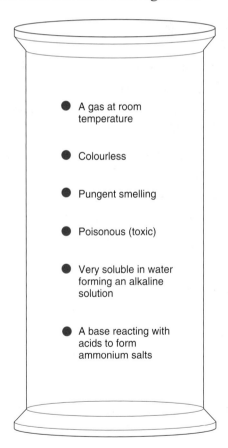

- A gas at room temperature
- Colourless
- Pungent smelling
- Poisonous (toxic)
- Very soluble in water forming an alkaline solution
- A base reacting with acids to form ammonium salts

Figure 3   Properties of ammonia

Ammonia is a strong smelling, poisonous (toxic) gas. You can smell it in household and lavatory cleaners. It is very soluble in water because it reacts with water to form an alkaline solution.

Testing for ammonia

Ammonia is the only common gas which is alkaline. So, we test for it using damp red litmus paper.

If ammonia is present, damp red litmus paper turns blue.

23.6	**Ammonia as a base – neutralisation reactions**

Ammonia is a base. It reacts with acids to form ammonium salts. This is how important fertilisers are made. For example, ammonium nitrate ('Nitram') is made by reacting ammonia with nitric acid.

This is an example of **neutralisation**. The base (ammonia) neutralises the acid (nitric acid) to produce a salt (ammonium nitrate).

$$base + acid \rightarrow salt$$
$$ammonia + nitric\ acid \rightarrow ammonium\ nitrate$$
$$NH_3 + HNO_3 \rightarrow NH_4NO_3$$

Ammonia also has a neutralisation reaction with sulphuric acid.

$$ammonia + \frac{sulphuric}{acid} \rightarrow \frac{ammonium}{sulphate}$$
$$2NH_3 + H_2SO_4 \rightarrow (NH_4)_2SO_4$$

This reaction is used to make ammonium sulphate for use as a fertiliser.

Metal oxides, metal hydroxides and metal carbonates can also act as bases. Like ammonia, they neutralise acids and form salts.

When metal oxides and hydroxides neutralise acids, the products are a salt and water.

For example:

$$\frac{copper}{oxide} + \frac{sulphuric}{acid} \rightarrow \frac{copper}{sulphate} + water$$
$$CuO + H_2SO_4 \rightarrow CuSO_4 + H_2O$$
$$\boxed{base} + \boxed{acid} \rightarrow \boxed{salt} + \boxed{water}$$

When metal carbonates neutralise acids, the products are a salt, water and carbon dioxide.

For example:

$$\frac{sodium}{carbonate} + \frac{hydrochloric}{acid} \rightarrow \frac{sodium}{chloride} + water + \frac{carbon}{dioxide}$$
$$Na_2CO_3 + 2HCl \rightarrow 2NaCl + H_2O + CO_2$$
$$\boxed{\frac{carbonate}{- base}} + \boxed{acid} \rightarrow \boxed{salt} + \boxed{water} + \boxed{CO_2}$$

Notice in these reactions that the salt produced depends on:

★ the metal in the base

★ the acid.

Neutralising hydrochloric acid produces chlorides.

Neutralising sulphuric acid produces sulphates.

Neutralising nitric acid produces nitrates.

10 Name **two** chemicals made from ammonia.

11 Is ammonia an acid or a base?

12 What is the test for ammonia?

13 Complete these two word equations.

a) ammonia + nitric acid → _____

b) ammonia + _____ → ammonium chloride

23.7	**Fertilisers**

Plants need various essential elements to grow well. These essential elements are called **nutrients**.

If crops are grown on the same land every year, these nutrients get used up. The soil becomes infertile. The plants which grow are stunted. Their leaves become yellow and seeds and fruit are small.

Carbon dioxide and water provide the carbon, oxygen and hydrogen which plants need. After these three elements, the most important nutrient for plant growth is nitrogen. So, shortages of nitrogen are soon noticed. For plants to grow well, there must be a good supply of nitrogen. This is ensured by adding fertilisers to the soil.

Different fertilisers are being mixed in this tank to give a blend of chemicals.

A solution of fertiliser being added to the soil. What are the advantages of using a solution of fertilisers rather than solid pellets?

Nitrogen fertilisers

Nitrogen fertilisers are usually nitrates or ammonium salts. Ammonium nitrate ('Nitram'), NH_4NO_3, is the most widely used fertiliser because it:

This farmer is using 'Nitram' fertiliser. Nitram is ammonium nitrate, NH_4NO_3

★ is soluble in water

★ can be stored and transported as a solid

★ contains a high percentage of nitrogen.

Ammonium nitrate (NH_4NO_3) contains ammonium ions (NH_4^+) and nitrate ions (NO_3^-) ions. Both these ions contain nitrogen. This explains the high percentage of nitrogen in ammonium nitrate.

Let's calculate the percentage of nitrogen in ammonium nitrate.

We know that:

the relative atomic mass of nitrogen, $A_r(N) = 14.0$

the relative atomic mass of hydrogen, $A_r(H) = 1.0$

the relative atomic mass of oxygen, $A_r(O) = 16.0$

So, the relative formula mass of ammonium nitrate (NH_4NO_3)

$= A_r(N) + 4 \times A_r(H) + A_r(N) + 3 \times A_r(O)$

$= 14 + 4 \times 1 + 14 + 3 \times 16 = 80$

So the formula mass of NH_4NO_3 is 80 g and this contains 2×14 g = 28 g nitrogen.

% of nitrogen in NH_4NO_3 = $\dfrac{28}{80} \times 100$ = 35%

Other nitrogen fertilisers are ammonium sulphate and 'nitrochalk'. 'Nitrochalk' is a mixture of ammonium nitrate and chalk (calcium carbonate). The chalk in this helps to reduce soil acidity.

> Fertilisers are substances which increase the yield from crops.

Fertilisers are now essential. We cannot feed everyone in the world at present. Every year we hear about people starving somewhere in the world. These problems would be ten times worse without fertilisers.

But, there are problems if fertilisers are over used (Figure 4).

★ They can change the soil pH and harm plants and animals in the soil.

★ They are washed into the ground causing pollution of drinking water.

Nitrogen fertiliser has been added to the soil on the left of this field. This has produced greener, taller and bushier wheat plants.

★ They are washed off the soil into streams and rivers. Fertilisers in the river cause water plants to grow very fast. The river becomes choked with plants. As they die and rot, they use up all the dissolved oxygen in the water. Fish and other water animals begin to die. This process which kills life in the water is called **eutrophication**.

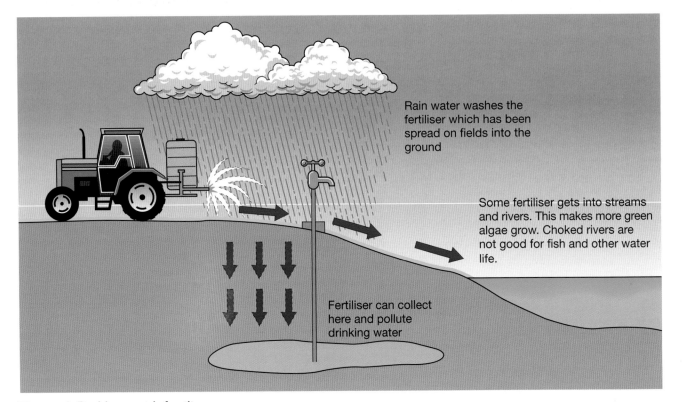

Rain water washes the fertiliser which has been spread on fields into the ground

Some fertiliser gets into streams and rivers. This makes more green algae grow. Choked rivers are not good for fish and other water life.

Fertiliser can collect here and pollute drinking water

Figure 4 Problems with fertilisers

Summary

1 An **irreversible reaction** is a reaction which, once it takes place, cannot be reversed.

   Reversible reactions can go in both directions.

   In some reversible reactions, the reactants are *completely* changed to the products.

   In other reversible reactions, the reactants are *not completely* changed to the products. This produces a mixture in which the concentrations of the reactants and products stay constant. We say the substances are in **equilibrium**.

2 Ammonia is made using the **Haber process**.

   nitrogen + hydrogen $\rightleftharpoons$ ammonia
   $$N_2 + 3H_2 \rightleftharpoons 2NH_3$$

   The raw materials for the process are:
   * air which provides nitrogen
   * naphtha, from crude oil, which is cracked to give hydrogen.

   These raw materials make the process *as cheap as possible*.

   The conditions used in the Haber process ensure *a fast reaction*:
   * a pressure of 200 atm
   * a temperature of 450°C
   * a catalyst of iron.

3 Ammonia is important in industry and agriculture.

   * It is used to make fertilisers, nitric acid and nylon.

   * Ammonia is a base (alkali). So, it neutralises acids to form salts. This is how nitrogen fertilisers are made. The reaction is an example of **neutralisation**.

   ammonia + nitric acid $\rightarrow$ ammonium nitrate
   $$NH_3 + HNO_3 \rightarrow NH_4NO_3$$
   base   acid   salt

   * Test for ammonia – ammonia turns damp red litmus blue.

4 Fertilisers

   * After carbon, oxygen and hydrogen, nitrogen is the most important element for plants to grow well. Fertilisers are added to the soil to replace the nitrogen which plants use up.

   * Fertilisers increase the yield from crops.

   * Over-use of fertilisers can cause environmental problems.

1 Ammonia is a very important chemical.

a) The table shows the percentage of ammonia used to make different substances.

Substances made from ammonia	Percentage (%) of ammonia used
Fertilisers	75
Nitric acid	10
Nylon	5
Others	10

Copy the pie chart below. Shade on your pie chart the percentage of ammonia used to make nitric acid. *(1)*

nylon 5%

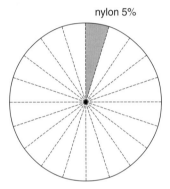

b) Ammonia gas is made by the reaction between nitrogen gas and hydrogen gas.

Write a word equation to represent this reaction using this layout.

_____ + _____ ⇌ _____ *(1)*

c) Nitrogen is one of the raw materials used to make ammonia. Nitrogen is obtained from air.

This pie chart shows the proportion of nitrogen, oxygen and other gases in air. Copy the pie chart. Label the area in your copy which represents the proportion of nitrogen in air. *(1)*

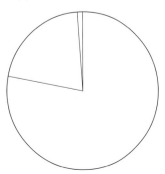

d) (i) Liquid ammonia is toxic. Road tankers carrying liquid ammonia must display a hazard warning symbol.

A   B   C   D   E

Which hazard warning symbol, **A** to **E**, should be displayed on the tanker? *(1)*

(ii) If liquid ammonia leaked from the tanker it would turn to gas. The diagram represents the particles in liquid ammonia.

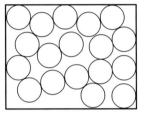

liquid ammonia

Copy and complete the diagram below to show the particles in ammonia gas. One particle has been drawn for you. *(1)*

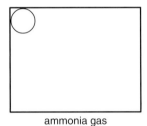

ammonia gas

e) An artificial fertiliser contains compounds with the formulas:

$$NH_4NO_3 \text{ and } KCl$$

(i) Name the elements in the compound NH_4NO_3. *(2)*

(ii) Name the compound KCl. *(1)*

f) (i) Ammonium nitrate is one type of artificial fertiliser.

Calculate the relative formula mass of ammonium nitrate NH_4NO_3.

(Relative atomic masses: H = 1, N = 14, O = 16.) *(1)*

(ii) Use your answer to part f)(i) to help you calculate the percentage by mass of nitrogen present in ammonium nitrate NH_4NO_3. *(2)*

[AQA (NEAB) 1999]

2 The bar chart shows the amounts of different gases in dry air.

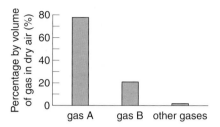

a) The list gives some of the gases present in air.

argon   nitrogen   carbon dioxide   oxygen
helium   xenon

Choose, **from the list**, the name of:

(i) gas A;   (ii) gas B.   *(2)*

b) Nitrogen from the air is used to make ammonia. Some facts about ammonia are given below.

- it has the formula NH_3
- it is a colourless gas
- it is very soluble in water
- it forms a **weak** alkaline solution in water

(i) Copy and complete the word equation for the reaction by which ammonia is made from its elements.

_____ + _____ → ammonia   *(2)*

(ii) Suggest a pH value for a solution of ammonia in water.   *(1)*

(iii) Ammonia solution reacts with nitric acid to make the salt called ammonium nitrate. Copy and complete your word equation for this reaction.

$\dfrac{\text{ammonia}}{\text{solution}} + \dfrac{\text{nitric}}{\text{acid}} \rightarrow \dfrac{\text{ammonium}}{\text{nitrate}} +$ _____   *(1)*

(iv) How would the pH number of the ammonia solution change as nitric acid is added?   *(1)*

(v) Ammonium sulphate can be made by adding a different acid to ammonia solution. Name this acid.   *(1)*

c) Ammonia, ammonium nitrate and ammonium sulphate can all be used as fertilisers.

(i) Calculate the formula mass (M_r) of ammonia. (Relative atomic masses: N = 14, H = 1)   *(1)*

(ii) Calculate the percentage by mass of nitrogen in ammonia.   *(2)*

Name of fertiliser	Formula of fertiliser	Percentage of nitrogen by mass in the fertiliser (%)
Ammonia	NH_3	
Ammonium nitrate	NH_4NO_3	35
Ammonium sulphate	$(NH_4)_2SO_4$	21

(iii) Suggest why it is an advantage to have as high a percentage by mass of nitrogen as possible in a fertiliser.   *(2)*

(iv) Suggest why ammonia is **not** often used as a fertiliser.   *(2)*   **[AQA (NEAB) 1998]**

3 The flow chart below shows the main stages in the production of ammonium nitrate.

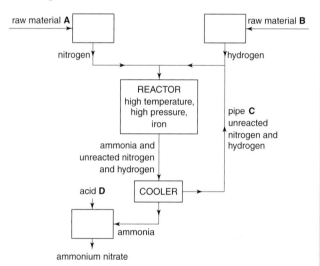

a) (i) Name the **two** raw materials shown in the flow chart as **A** and **B** by choosing words from the list.

air   coke   limestone   natural gas   *(2)*

(ii) Copy and complete the word equation for the reaction which makes ammonia.

_____ + _____ → ammonia   *(1)*

(iii) What is the purpose of the iron in the reactor?   *(1)*

(iv) What is the purpose of pipe **C**?   *(1)*

b) Look at the flow chart again. Give the name of acid **D** which is added to the ammonia to make ammonium nitrate.   *(1)*

c) (i) Explain why farmers add ammonium nitrate to the soil.   *(1)*

(ii) Explain how ammonium nitrate can cause pollution.   *(2)*

[AQA (NEAB) 1998]

A red dwarf star emits
light energy and
electromagnetic waves.
Energy transfers are
studied in Chapter 26
whilst electromagnetic
radiation and waves are
described in Chapters 30
and 31. The whole of this
section is about Physics –
the study of physical
processes involving forces,
energy and waves.

Physical processes

Movement and motion

24.1 Distance, speed and velocity	24.3 Speed and acceleration
24.2 Distance–time graphs	

24.1 Distance, speed and velocity

John and Duane walk 24 km from Whitford to Shawley in 8 hours.

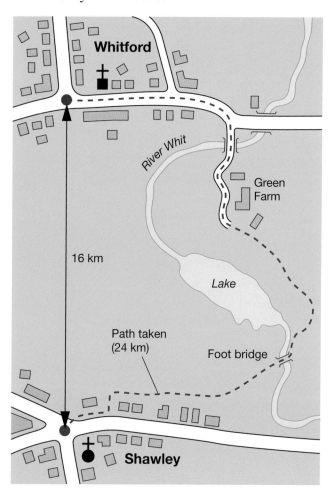

Figure 1 Map to show the route taken by John and Duane.

John and Duane want to know how fast they have walked.

To work out their speed, they can use the formula:

$$\text{speed} = \frac{\text{distance moved}}{\text{time taken}}$$

$$\text{speed} = \frac{24\ km}{8\ hr} = 3.0\ \text{km per hour}$$

In some cases, it is more convenient to measure speed in metres per second (m/s) rather than kilometres per hour.

Duane is a good runner. He can run the 200 metres in 25 seconds.

$$\text{His speed for the race} = \frac{\text{distance moved}}{\text{time taken}}$$
$$= \frac{200\ m}{25\ s}$$
$$= 8\ \text{m/s}$$

Sometimes, it is important to know the speed in a particular direction. John and Duane walked 24 km, but they moved in different directions during the 8 hours. Their speed was 3 km per hour, but it had no particular direction.

If we calculate their speed in a particular direction, it is called their **velocity**.

velocity = speed in a particular direction

Suppose Shawley is exactly 16 km south of Whitford.

John and Duane's velocity

$$= \frac{\text{distance moved south}}{\text{time taken}}$$

$$= \frac{16 \text{ km south}}{8 \text{ hr}}$$

$$= 2 \text{ km/hr south}$$

When a velocity is calculated, you must always show its direction as well as its size.

24.2 Distance–time graphs

Table 1 shows the distance that Kapil has run after every 5 seconds in a 400 metre race.

Kapil leads in the 400 m

Figure 2 shows a distance–time graph for Kapil's 400 metre run.

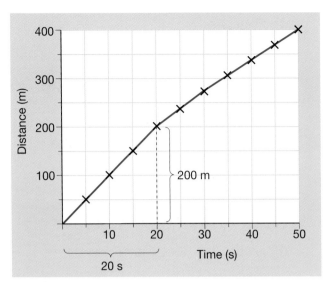

Figure 2 A distance–time graph for Kapil's 400 m run.

You can see from Table 1 that Kapil ran more quickly over the first 200 metres than he did over the second 200 metres. He was getting tired.

For the first 200 metres,

Kapil's speed $= \dfrac{\text{distance moved}}{\text{time taken}}$

$$= \frac{200 \text{ m}}{20 \text{ s}} = 10 \text{ m/s}$$

$$= \text{gradient (slope) of graph}$$

∴ **speed** = **the gradient of the distance–time graph**

What was Kapil's speed during the second 200 m?

Average speed

Kapil travelled at two different speeds during the race. Let's find his average speed.

average speed $= \dfrac{\text{total distance moved}}{\text{total time taken}}$

∴ Kapil's average speed $= \dfrac{400 \text{ m}}{50 \text{ s}} = 8 \text{ m/s}$

Distance sprinted (m)	0	50	100	150	200	233	267	300	333	367	400
Time taken (s)	0	5	10	15	20	25	30	35	40	45	50

Table 1

1 What units do we use to measure

a) speed b) velocity?

2 Explain the meaning of these words:

a) speed b) velocity.

3 Blackburn is 18 km east of Chorley. The distance by road is 24 km.

Dave, a keen cyclist, takes 1 hour to get to Blackburn from Chorley. The return journey takes 1.5 hours. What is:

a) his speed to Blackburn

b) his speed on the return journey

c) his average speed there and back?

Now work out:

d) his velocity on the journey to Blackburn

e) his velocity on the return journey

f) his average velocity for the whole journey to Blackburn and back to his starting point. (*Think carefully.*)

24.3 Speed and acceleration

This car is accelerating from the traffic lights.

A car moves away from the traffic lights and reaches a speed of 15 m/s in 5 seconds.

When things like cars increase their speed we say that they are **accelerating**. Table 2 shows the speed of the car each second after it left the traffic lights.

Time	Speed
0 s	0 m/s
1 s	3 m/s
2 s	6 m/s
3 s	9 m/s
4 s	12 m/s
5 s	15 m/s

Table 2

The car's speed goes up by 3 metres per second every second. We say that its acceleration is 3 metres per second per second. We can calculate acceleration using the formula below.

$$\text{acceleration} = \frac{\text{change in speed}}{\text{time taken}}$$

So, acceleration of the car

$$= \frac{15 \text{ m/s}}{5 \text{ s}} = \frac{3 \text{ m/s}}{\text{s}}$$

The car accelerates (increases its speed) by 3 m/s every second. This is usually written as 3 m/s^2.

Example

Vehicles must slow down as well as speed up. Suppose a car is travelling at 24 m/s. The driver applies the brakes and the car stops in 2 seconds. What is the acceleration?

Answer

$$\text{Acceleration} = \frac{\text{change in speed}}{\text{time taken}}$$
$$= -\frac{24 \text{ m/s}}{2 \text{ s}}$$
$$= -12 \text{ m/s}^2$$

In this case, the car is slowing down and its speed decreases. The change in speed is negative. We say it has a negative acceleration or the car **decelerates**.

Things affecting the stopping distances of cars and other vehicles

The total stopping distance of a car is made up of two distances. Look at Figure 3.

The **thinking distance** is the distance the car travels during the driver's reaction time.

The **braking distance** is the distance the car travels once the brakes have been applied.

There are important factors which affect the thinking distance. They are:

★ the speed at which the car is travelling

★ the driver's reaction which can be affected by tiredness, alcohol or drugs

★ the weather (such as rain or fog) and whether the road is lit at night.

There are important factors which affect the braking distance. They are:

★ the speed at which the car is travelling

★ how hard the driver slams on the brakes

★ the road conditions (such as dry, wet or icy, smooth or rough road surface)

★ whether the car has good brakes and good tyres.

Crash testing a van to check the front crumple zone and the seat belts. This van was driven into a wall at 30 m.p.h. with a dummy in the driving seat.

So, the overall stopping distance of a car is greater if:

★ it is travelling faster

★ the driver's reactions are slower

★ the road surface is wet or icy

★ the road surface is smooth

★ the lighting is poor

★ the car has poor brakes or poor tyres.

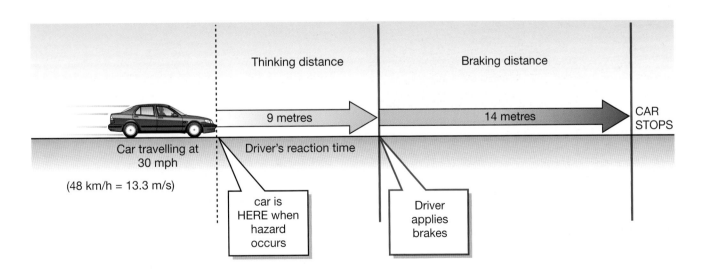

Thinking distance

Braking distance

9 metres

14 metres

CAR STOPS

Car travelling at 30 mph

(48 km/h = 13.3 m/s)

Driver's reaction time

car is HERE when hazard occurs

Driver applies brakes

Figure 3 The stopping distance for a car travelling at 30 m.p.h.

4 What units do we use to measure
a) velocity b) acceleration?

5 Explain the meaning of these words:
a) constant velocity b) acceleration
c) deceleration.

6 How quickly a car stops depends on the
driver's thinking distance and the car's
braking distance.

Explain the meaning of
a) thinking distance
b) braking distance.

List **two** factors which affect thinking
distance and **three** factors which affect
braking distance.

7 A car starts from rest and reaches a
speed of 12 m/s in 4 seconds. The
driver travels at this speed for 2 seconds
and then puts the brakes on and comes
to rest 2 seconds later.

a) What is his acceleration in getting to
12 m/s in 4 seconds?

b) What is his deceleration when
braking?

c) How long did his journey take?

d) Draw a graph of speed (vertical)
against time (horizontal) for the
short journey.

Summary

1 **Speed** is the distance moved in one second
or one hour.

Speed is measured in metres per second
(m/s).

$$\text{Speed (m/s)} = \frac{\text{distance (m)}}{\text{time (s)}}$$

Here is an equation triangle for speed,
distance and time.

Put your finger over one letter in the
triangle to obtain the right equation.

e.g. Put your finger over 's' to see that

$$s = \frac{d}{t}$$

2 **Velocity** tells you the speed in a particular
direction e.g. 3 m/s north-west.

3 **Acceleration** is the change in speed per
second.

Acceleration (m/s^2)

$$= \frac{\text{change in speed (m/s)}}{\text{time (s)}} = \frac{\Delta s}{t}$$

Here is an equation triangle for change in
speed (Δs), acceleration and time.

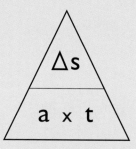

$$\text{Average speed} = \frac{\text{total distance moved}}{\text{total time taken}}$$

Speed = the gradient of a distance–time graph

1 a) Write down, **in words**, the equation connecting speed, distance and time. *(1)*

b) A car travels at a steady speed of 20 m/s. Calculate the distance travelled in 5 s. *(2)*

[WJEC 1998]

2 The following graph of distance against time is plotted for Sonya's journey on a bicycle.

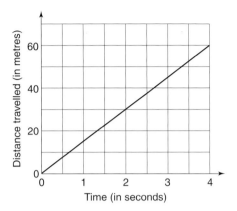

What is Sonya's average speed during the first 4 seconds, in m/s?

Show clearly how you obtain your answer.

[NICCEA 1998]

3 A car accelerates from rest. Its speed is measured as it accelerates. The results are shown in the table.

Speed (m/s)	0.0	5.0	10.0	12.5	17.5	25.0
Time (s)	0.0	2.0	4.0	5.0	7.0	10.0

a) Draw a graph of speed in m/s (vertically) against time (horizontally) on graph paper. *(3)*

b) Calculate the acceleration of the car in m/s². *(2)*

c) The car eventually reached a constant speed and then travelled 350 metres in 10 seconds.

Calculate the speed at which it travelled in m/s. *(2)*

[AQA (NEAB) 1998]

4 A hot air balloon called Global Challenger was used to try to break the record for travelling round the world.

The graph shows how the height of the balloon changed during the flight.

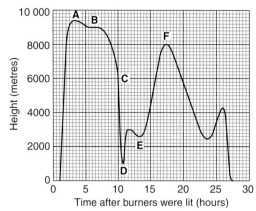

The balloon took off from Marrakesh one hour after the burners were lit and climbed rapidly.

a) Use the graph to find:

(i) the maximum height reached in metres.

(ii) the total time of the flight in hours. *(2)*

b) Several important moments during the flight are labelled on the graph with the letters **A**, **B**, **C**, **D**, **E** and **F**.

At which of these moments did the following happen?

(i) The balloon began a slow controlled descent to 2500 metres.

(ii) The crew threw out all the cargo on board in order to stop a very rapid descent.

(iii) The balloon started to descend from 9000 metres. *(3)* **[AQA (NEAB) 1998]**

5 The graph below shows how the braking distance of a car depends on its speed when the road conditions are good.

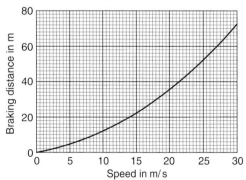

a) State **two** things, other than the road surface, that affect the overall stopping distance of a car moving at a speed of 20 m/s. *(2)*

b) The speed limit in a supermarket car park is 7.5 m/s. Use the graph to estimate the braking distance for a car travelling at this speed. *(2)*

[Edexcel 1998]

25

Forces and motion

25.1 Extending materials by forces

When masses are hung on a spring, the spring extends. The force of gravity pulling on the masses causes the spring to extend. The spring can support the masses due to forces of attraction between particles in the spring. The pull on the spring which supports the weight of the masses is called a **tension**.

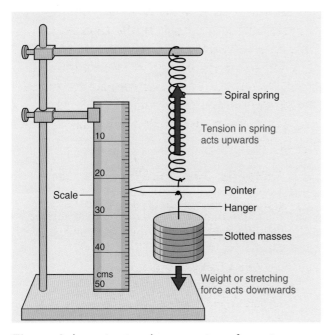

Figure 1 Investigating the extension of a spring

Figure 1 shows a simple experiment to investigate the extension of a spring as the stretching force increases.

The results of one experiment are plotted on a graph in Figure 2.

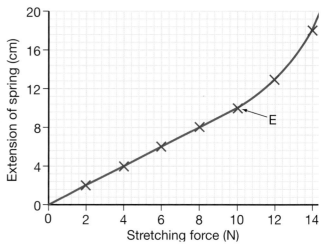

Figure 2 A graph of the extension of a spring against the stretching force (load)

Notice that the graph is a straight line up to point E. After point E, the spring extends more than expected for a given stretching force. Point E is said to represent the **elastic limit** for the spring.

The results in Figure 2 show that:

> The extension is proportional to the stretching force, provided the elastic limit is not reached. This result is known as **Hooke's law**.

Provided the elastic limit is not passed, materials return to their original shape and size when the force is removed. Materials with this property are called **elastic**. This means that when the stretching force is removed, they return to their original shape. If their elastic limit is passed, they remain permanently deformed.

The elastic properties of springs are put to use in kitchen scales, in mattresses, in chairs and in car suspension systems.

Although the elasticities of wood and concrete are much less than that of metals, they allow buildings to move slightly following earth movements.

Wood and concrete are elastic enough to allow some movement of buildings. But, in an earthquake, the buildings will collapse.

25.2 Pressure in gases – Boyles law

Gas pressure allows us to blow up balloons and tyres (Figure 3). When atmospheric pressure is high, clouds are driven away, skies are clear and the weather is fine. When atmospheric pressure is low, the weather is usually cloudy and wet.

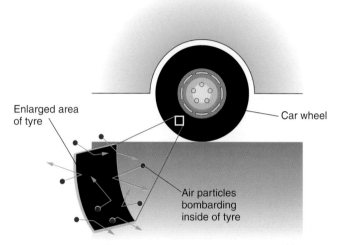

Enlarged area of tyre

Car wheel

Air particles bombarding inside of tyre

Figure 3 Millions of air molecules bombard the inside of the tyre every second. This produces pressure on the inside of the tyre. The tyre is also bombarded on the outside by air molecules, but the pressure on the inside of the tyre is greater than that outside, so the tyre stays blown up.

If you hold your finger over the end of a bicycle pump and push in the handle, the pressure on your finger increases (Figure 4). The air inside the pump is pushed into a smaller volume. So, the air molecules inside the pump bombard the sides of the pump and your finger more often. This causes the increased pressure on your finger.

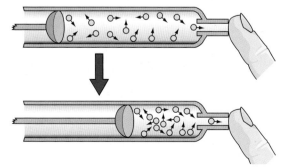

Figure 4

Experiments show that when the volume decreases to half, the pressure doubles. If the volume decreases to one third, the pressure triples, and so on. This is an inverse relationship. If pressure goes up, then volume goes down and we can say that:

At constant temperature, the pressure (p) of a gas is inversely proportional to the volume (V).

i.e. $p \propto \dfrac{1}{V}$ or $p = \dfrac{\text{constant}}{V}$

So,

$$pV = \text{constant}$$

or

$$\underset{\text{pressure}}{\text{initial}} \times \underset{\text{volume}}{\text{initial}} = \underset{\text{pressure}}{\text{final}} \times \underset{\text{volume}}{\text{final}}$$

i.e. $p_1 V_1 = p_2 V_2$

This relationship between p and V was first discovered by Robert Boyle in the 17th century. It is called **Boyle's law**.

Example

20 m³ of gas in the British Gas pipelines at a pressure of 750 kPa escapes into the atmosphere where the pressure is 100 kPa. What volume will the gas occupy after it escapes?

Solution

$$\underset{\text{pressure}}{\text{initial}} \times \underset{\text{volume}}{\text{initial}} = \underset{\text{pressure}}{\text{final}} \times \underset{\text{volume}}{\text{final}}$$

$$750\ (\text{kPa}) \times 20\ (\text{m}^3) = 100\ (\text{kPa}) \times \underset{\text{escape}}{\underset{\text{after}}{\text{volume}}}$$

∴ volume after escape

$$= \dfrac{750 \times 20}{100}\ \text{m}^3 = 150\ \text{m}^3$$

25.3 Force and work

Forces can make things move or change their shape. Pushes, pulls and twists are good examples of forces. Forces are measured in **newtons**.

Figure 5 shows a crane at work on a building site. The crane is lifting a pile of bricks. The **weight** of the bricks is 10 000 N. The weight of the bricks is the **downward force due to gravity**.

In order to hold the weight of the bricks, there is an upward force (tension) in the metal wire of the crane.

On Earth, a mass of 1 kilogram has a weight of about 10 newtons (10 N). So, the mass of the pile of bricks is about 1000 kilograms (1000 kg).

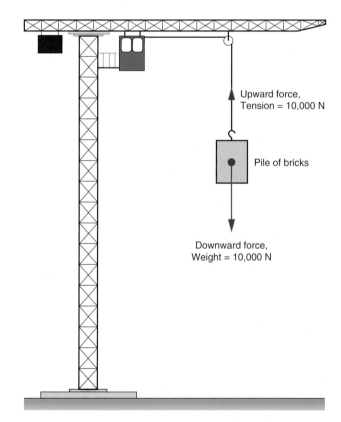

Upward force, Tension = 10,000 N

Pile of bricks

Downward force, Weight = 10,000 N

Figure 5 A crane working on a building site

Suppose the crane is lifting the pile of bricks through 8 m. Work is done when the crane moves the bricks.

The amount of work which the crane does depends on:

★ the weight of the bricks
★ the height the bricks are lifted.

> Work is done when a force makes something move.

We do work when we throw a ball

A mountain biker cycling up a very steep hill

We do work when we throw a ball, turn a tap or lift a chair. Vehicles do work when they climb hills against the force of gravity. Vehicles do work when they overcome friction on the road.

Work is measured in **joules** (J). One joule of work is done when a force of 1 newton (1 N) moves something through a distance of 1 metre (1 m).

1 joule of work	=	1 newton moving 1 metre
1 J	=	1 N moving 1 m
so 10 J	=	10 N moving 1 m
or 10 J	=	1 N moving 10 m
or 10 J	=	2 N moving 5 m etc.

> So, work = force × distance
> (in J)   (in N)   (in m)

We can now calculate the work done by the crane in lifting the bricks.

Work done by crane
= force × distance
= weight lifted × height lifted
= 10 000 × 8 = 80 000 J
(N)   (m)

1 What units do we use to measure

(a) force (b) work?

2 Explain what we mean by

(a) force (b) work.

3 a) How much work must be done to lift a bucket of concrete weighing 100 N through a height of 1 metre?

b) Later, the bucket needs lifting 5 metres high. How much work will have to be done to lift the bucket to this height?

c) John finds this very hard work. He thinks he might have to do less work if he carries the bucket up a gentle slope to the same height. Is he right? Explain your answer.

25.4 Power

In order to check the usefulness of the crane in Figure 5, we need to know how quickly it can do the work. A good crane will do the work in a short time.

Suppose the crane lifts the bricks in 4 seconds.

Work done by crane per second

$$= \frac{80\ 000\ \text{J}}{4\ \text{s}} = 20\ 000\ \text{J/s}$$

The work done by the crane per second is called its **power**.

Power is the rate of working. So:

$$\text{power} = \frac{\text{work done}}{\text{time taken}}$$

The units for power can be joules per second (J/s) like we used for the crane. Usually, however, we use **watts** (W) rather than joules per second. The name 'watt' is used because of James Watt's experiments on power in the 18th century.

1 joule per second = 1 watt (1 J/s = 1 W)

How will this athlete's activity change as he develops more power in his legs?

Example

Sally wants to measure the power in her arms. She lifts 30 N weights (one in each hand). She lifts them through 50 cm (0.5 m) in 2 seconds.

(i) What is the total weight that Sally lifts?

(ii) Calculate the work done by Sally.

(iii) What is her power?

Answers

(i) Total weight lifted = 30 N × 2 = 60 N

(ii) Work done
= force × distance
    (N)   (m)
= weight lifted × height lifted, in m
= 60 × 0.5
= 30 J

(iii) Power = $\frac{\text{work done}}{\text{time taken}}$ = $\frac{30}{2}$ = 15 W

25.5 Forces and acceleration

Think about a plant pot resting on the floor. The weight of the plant pot exerts a downward force on the floor. The floor gets compressed by this force and pushes upwards on the plant pot (Figure 6).

The two forces which the floor and the plant pot exert on each other are equal in size. They act in opposite directions. They are **balanced forces**. When balanced forces act on an object, they cancel each other. The overall force is therefore zero. Neither the plant pot nor the floor move.

The first scientist to discover this was Isaac Newton who lived in the 17th century. His ideas are called **Newton's first law of motion**:

> An object will remain stationary or continue to move at the same speed and in the same direction if the overall forces on it are balanced.

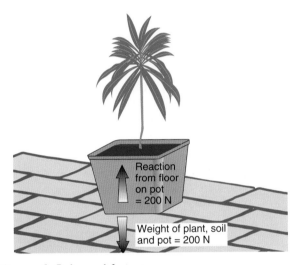

Figure 6 Balanced forces

Unbalanced forces

If you roll a ball along the floor, it slows down. The ball doesn't continue at the same speed. This is because the forces on it are *not* balanced. Unbalanced forces, due to friction, act on the ball and slow it down. Friction forces bring the ball to rest.

When an unbalanced force, like friction, acts in the opposite direction to a moving object, the object slows down or decelerates (i.e. negative acceleration).

When an unbalanced force acts on an object in the direction it is moving, the object will accelerate.

Have you ever tried to push a car along a flat road? The car accelerates away faster if two people push instead of one. It accelerates even better with three people.

The acceleration of this car will be proportional to the overall force acting on it.

Careful experiments show that *acceleration depends on the size of the unbalanced force*. We say the acceleration is **proportional** to the unbalanced force.

> acceleration ∝ unbalanced force
> (∝ means 'is proportional to')

25.6   Forces on falling objects

When an object is dropped, it falls to the ground. Its weight acts on it as an unbalanced force. The object accelerates downwards due to the force of gravity. In the air, a penny falls faster than a tiny piece of paper. But in a vacuum, the penny and the paper fall at the same rate (Figure 7 over the page).

The paper falls slower in air because of air resistance. The paper has a large surface area.

Air resistance is sometimes called **drag**. Air in the tube slows down the penny and the paper as they fall. Air resistance affects the paper more than the penny.

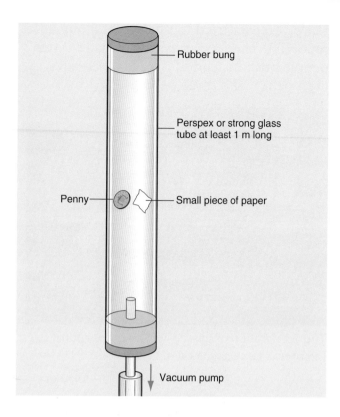

Figure 7 The tube is evacuated to make a vacuum. Then, it is quickly inverted. The penny and the piece of paper fall at the same rate. If there is not a vacuum in the tube, the penny will fall faster than the paper.

Experiments show that the acceleration due to gravity is about 10 m/s². This means that the speed of a falling object increases by 10 m/s every second. But if something is thrown upwards, its velocity will *decrease* by 10 m/s every second until it reaches its highest point. Then, as it falls, its velocity will increase downwards at the rate of 10 m/s every second.

Example

A boy drops a stone from a high tower. The stone takes 3 seconds to hit the ground below.

(i)   What is the acceleration of the stone?

(ii) What is the final speed of the stone? (Assume its initial speed is 0 m/s.)

(iii) What is the average speed of the stone?

(iv) How far did the stone fall?

Answers

(i)   Acceleration of stone
$$= \text{acceleration due to gravity}$$
$$= 10 \text{ m/s}^2$$

(ii) Stone accelerates (increases in speed) by 10 m/s every second.
$\therefore$ final speed after 3 secs $= 3 \times 10$ m/s
$$= 30 \text{ m/s}$$

(iii) Average speed of stone $= \dfrac{(0 + 30)}{2}$
$$= 15 \text{ m/s}$$

(iv) Average speed $= \dfrac{\text{distance}}{\text{time}}$

15 m/s $= \dfrac{\text{distance}}{2 \text{ s}}$

$\therefore$ distance stone falls $= 15 \times 2 = 30$ m

When an object falls, air resistance (drag) increases as its speed increases.

Look at Figure 8.

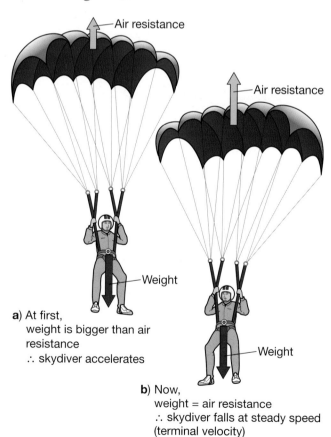

a) At first, weight is bigger than air resistance
   $\therefore$ skydiver accelerates

b) Now, weight = air resistance
   $\therefore$ skydiver falls at steady speed (terminal velocity)

Figure 8

When a skydiver falls:

★ he accelerates at first due to the force of gravity (Figure 8a)

★ frictional forces due to air resistance increase as he falls faster and faster. Eventually, air resistance balances the gravitational force of the skydiver's weight (Figure 8b).

The forces acting on the skydiver are now balanced. The overall force is zero and so the skydiver falls at a steady maximum speed. This is called **terminal velocity**. The terminal velocity of any object will depend on its weight, its size and its shape.

A skydiver falling at terminal velocity during a parachute jump.

4 A squirrel rests on a thin branch over a deep canyon. It does not move.

a) Are the forces acting on the squirrel balanced or unbalanced?

b) Name the **two** forces acting on the squirrel.

The branch breaks.

c) Are the forces acting on the squirrel balanced or unbalanced now?

d) Name the **two** forces acting on it.

e) What happens to the speed of the squirrel?

f) What do we call this change of speed?

After two seconds, the squirrel falls with a steady velocity.

g) What can you now say about the forces on the squirrel?

h) Why do we call this constant velocity?

25.7 **Work and energy**

When a force moves an object, we can say that

work done = **force** × **distance**
(joules)   (newtons) (metres)

So, if Franco, a weightlifter, raises 80 kg through 2.5 m, the mass lifted = 80 kg

But, 1 kg on Earth has a weight of 10 newtons (10 N)

∴ weight lifted = 800 N
Distance lifted = 2.5 m
So, work done = force × distance
= 800 N × 2.5 m
= 2000 J

When Franco lifts the weights, he is transferring 2000 J of energy to his weights. Chemical energy in the chemicals in his muscles is being converted into work. The energy transferred to the weights can be measured by the amount of work done. So, the units of both energy and work are joules.

When we do work, we use energy. When a machine does work, it uses energy. Energy enables us and our machines to do work.

Potential energy

When weights or bricks or water are raised to a higher level, they gain energy. We say they have gained **gravitational potential energy** or **potential energy** for short. Being high up gives them the potential to do work when they fall. For example, there is potential energy in the water in a mountain reservoir. When the water falls, it can do work turning a water wheel or electrical generator.

This time-lapse photo shows a hammer doing work as it hits a nail into a piece of wood.

Kinetic energy

Moving objects can do work if they hit something. Moving objects have energy. This kind of energy is called **kinetic energy**. (The word 'kinetic' comes from a Greek word which means 'moving'.) For example, when a moving hammer hits a nail, work is done as the nail moves into the wood.

5 What units do we use to measure
a) kinetic energy b) potential energy?

6 Explain the meaning of the words
a) kinetic energy b) potential energy.

7 The diagram shows a ball swinging at the end of a string. At positions A and C, the ball is at the ends of its swing.

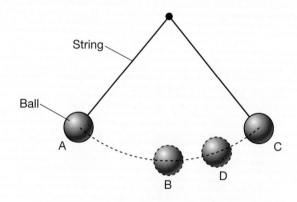

a) What kind of energy does the ball have at (i) position A (ii) position B (iii) position C (iv) position D?

b) Eventually the ball will come to rest in position B. Where has its energy gone?

258

Summary

1 The extension of a spring or rubberband is proportional to the stretching force, provided the elastic limit is not reached. The result is called **Hooke's law**.

2 At constant temperature, the pressure (p) of a gas is inversely proportional to the volume (V) ie. $p \propto \frac{1}{V}$ or **pV = constant**

3 ★ Work is done when a force makes something move.

   ★ Force is measured in **Newtons.**

   ★ Work is measured in **joules** (J).

   ★ Work done = force × distance moved

Here is an equation triangle for work, force and distance.

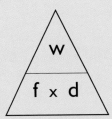

Put your finger over one letter in the triangle to obtain the right equation. For example, put your finger over 'w' to see that w = f × d.

4 ★ **Power** is the rate of working.

   ★ Power is measured in **watts.**
      1 W = 1 J/s

   ★ Power = $\frac{\text{work done}}{\text{time taken}}$

Here is an equation triangle for work, power and time.

5 When an object rests on the floor, the weight of the object exerts a downward force on the floor. The floor gets compressed by this force and pushes upwards on the object. The forces are **balanced**. The two forces cancel each other out so the object does not move. This is **Newton's first law of motion**. It says,

'An object will remain stationary or continue to move at the same speed and in the same direction if the overall forces on it are balanced.'

6 ★ When an **unbalanced force** acts on a moving object, the object will either slow down or speed up.

   ★ If the force acts in the same direction as the object is moving, the object speeds up.

   ★ If the force acts in the opposite direction to the movement of the object, the object slows down.

   ★ Friction forces always slow down the movement.

7 ★ When an object falls, its weight is an unbalanced force. The object accelerates to the ground due to the force of **gravity**.

   ★ On the Earth, all objects fall with an acceleration of about 10 metres per second per second *when there is no friction or air resistance.*

8 ★ **Energy** enables humans and machines to do work.

   ★ When objects are raised to a higher level, they gain **potential energy**. When an object is about to fall, it has energy.

   ★ Moving objects also have energy. This is called **kinetic energy**.

1 A sky-diver jumps from a plane. The sky-diver is shown in the diagram below.

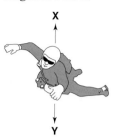

a) Arrows **X** and **Y** show two forces acting on the sky-diver as he falls.

(i) Name the forces **X** and **Y**. *(2)*

(ii) Explain why force **X** acts in an upward direction *(1)*

(iii) At first forces **X** and **Y** are unbalanced.

Which of the forces will be bigger? *(1)*

(iv) How does this unbalanced force affect the sky-diver? *(2)*

b) After some time the sky-diver pulls the rip cord and the parachute opens.

The sky-diver and parachute are shown in the diagram below.

After a while forces **X** and **Y** are balanced.

Choose the correct answer in each line below and copy out each line.

Force **X** has
increased / stayed the same / decreased.

Force **Y** has
increased / stayed the same / decreased.

The speed of the sky-diver will
increase / stay the same / decrease. *(3)*

c) The graph shows how the height of the sky-diver changes with time.

(i) Which part of the graph, **AB**, **BC** or **CD**, shows the sky-diver falling at a constant speed? *(1)*

(ii) What distance does the sky-diver fall at a constant speed? *(1)*

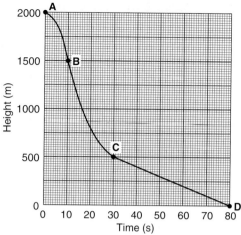

(iii) How long does he fall at this speed? *(1)*

(iv) Calculate this speed in m/s. *(2)*

[AQA (NEAB) 1997]

2 The diagram below shows Arnold lifting weights.

He lifts 800 N to a height of 2.0 m above the ground. Using the equation

potential energy (J) = force (N) × vertical height (m)

calculate the potential energy gained by the weights. *(2)*   **[Edexcel 1998]**

3 The diagram shows an object falling through the air.

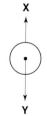

X and **Y** are two forces that act on the object.

a) Name the force (i) **X** and (ii) **Y**. *(2)*

b) As the object speeds up, state what happens to force (i) **X** and (ii) **Y** *(2)*

c) Describe the motion of the falling object when forces **X** and **Y** are equal. *(1)*

[WJEC 1998]

26

Energy transfers

26.1   Energy transfer by conduction

Which parts of his body are well insulated from the cold? Which parts of his body will lose the most heat?

If you walk around your home with bare feet, you will notice that tiles feel much colder than carpets. Your feet feel cold because they are losing energy to the tiles in the form of heat.

The transfer of heat from your feet to the tiles is an example of **conduction**. During conduction, heat travels from places at a higher temperature (like your feet) to places at a lower temperature (like the tiles).

Conduction is the transfer of energy in the form of heat. The heat moves between materials which are in contact with each other or between different parts of the same substance. The heat moves from a warmer place to a colder place, but the materials do not move.

All metals are very good conductors. Heat travels through them easily and quickly. Materials like plastic, wood and carpet are poor conductors. They are called **insulators**.

How is heat transferred by conduction without materials moving?

Look at Figure 1, on the next page. When part of a metal is hot, the atoms vibrate rapidly. The atoms have lots of kinetic energy. Outer electrons in the metal atoms are also moving very fast. These fast-moving outer electrons can move through the whole metal structure.

So, they pass on their kinetic energy to nearby atoms. The nearby atoms vibrate faster and this makes them hotter.

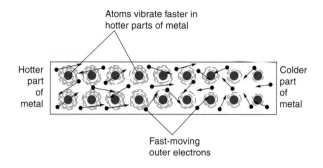

Figure 1 In a metal, heat is conducted by fast-moving outer electrons.

Why are insulators poor conductors?

Look at Figure 2. When part of an insulator is hot, the atoms vibrate faster like those in a metal. But, the outer electrons in an insulator cannot move around. So, the electrons cannot pass on kinetic energy and heat is not conducted through the substance.

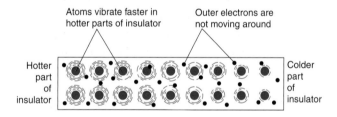

Figure 2 In an insulator, the outer electrons cannot move around to pass on energy.

1 Why do tiles feel cold to your bare feet, but a carpet feels warm?

2 You touch a window and it feels cold.

a) Why does your hand feel cold?

b) Is glass a good conductor or a bad conductor of heat?

Now, touch the curtains.

c) Why does your hand feel warm?

d) What is the name given to a material which does not conduct heat very well?

A second way in which heat (energy) can be transferred from one place to another is by **convection**. An example of this is shown in Figure 3.

When the electric heater is working, air near the heater is warmed. The warmed air expands. This makes the air less dense and it rises. As this air rises, cooler air falls and moves in to replace it near the heater. This movement of air is an example of convection.

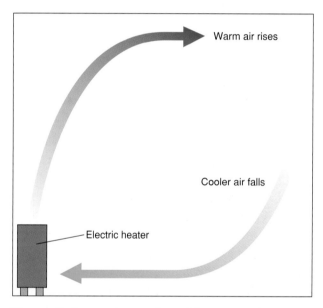

Figure 3 Energy is transferred by convection currents when an electric heater is working.

Convection is the transfer of energy (heat) by the movement of a liquid or a gas. The liquid/gas moves because it gets hotter. This makes it less dense than the liquid/gas around it.

When convection occurs, warmer parts of a liquid or gas rise. Cooler parts of the liquid or gas fall. This leads to **convection currents**.

Convection currents in the air cause breezes and are essential for gliding.

Convection currents in the air, called thermals, are essential for hang-gliding. Thermals are currents of warmer air which is rising.

26.3 Energy transfer by radiation

Conduction and convection are important energy transfers, but the most important energy (heat) transfer is by **radiation**. We need radiation from the Sun to survive. Energy from the Sun reaches the Earth by radiation. The energy travels millions of miles through empty space as waves, like light and X-rays. The waves give us heat from the Sun. They are called electromagnetic waves (section 31.2).

Radiation is the transfer of energy (heat) from one place to another by means of electromagnetic waves.

Energy is transferred to and from all objects by radiation. All warm and hot objects emit radiation. The hotter they are, the more radiation they emit. This radiation is mainly infra-red heat. Transfer of energy by radiation is different to conduction and convection. Radiation does not need a material to travel through. Radiation can travel through empty space (a vacuum).

Absorbing and emitting radiation

In some countries, infra-red radiation from the Sun is used for cooking and heating. Radiation also behaves like light. It can be reflected and focused using a mirror. This is the idea behind a solar furnace (Figure 4).

Figure 4 The huge reflector at Odeillo power station in the East Pyrenees, France. The reflector contains thousands of small mirrors. Radiation from the Sun is reflected from these onto the furnace in the central tower. The heat is used to generate electricity at the rate of 1000 kilowatts.

The shiny surface of the huge reflector is a poor absorber of radiation but it is a good reflector. In contrast, the furnace will have a dark, matt surface. This will make it a good absorber of radiation.

Figure 5, over the page, shows an experiment to compare the radiation from different surfaces. In the experiment, we can find out which teapot gives off less radiation. This one will lose heat more slowly and keep the tea warmer.

Radiation emitted (given off) from the teapots can be detected by a thermopile connected to an ammeter. Experiments show that the dull black teapot emits more radiation than the shiny white one. So, the shiny teapot would keep your tea warmer.

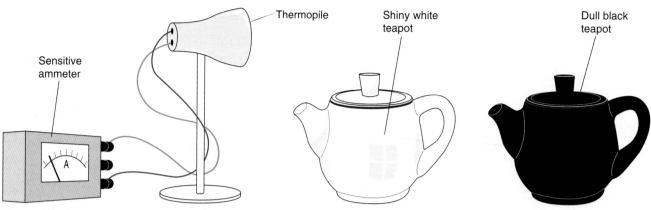

Figure 5 An experiment to see which teapot gives off less radiation and keeps the tea warmer.

★ Dark, dull surfaces are good emitters and good absorbers of radiation.

★ Light, shiny surfaces are poor emitters and poor absorbers of radiation.

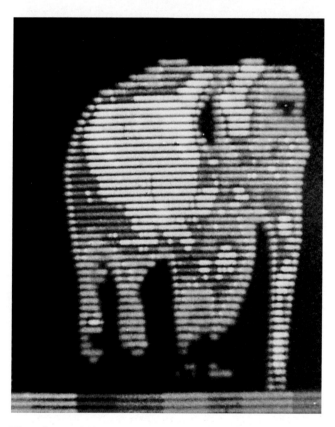

This thermal photograph (thermograph) of an elephant was taken using an infra-red camera. This camera detects heat radiation. Ordinary cameras detect light. The colour shows the temperature of the elephant's skin ranging from white (hottest) through yellow, then red to blue (coldest).

3 How does heat reach us from the Sun?

4 Answer the questions below by choosing from the following words.

   black   white   silver   brown

   a) Which **two** colours are good reflectors of heat?

   b) Which **two** colours are good absorbers of heat?

   c) Which **two** colours are good emitters of heat?

5 All hot objects emit radiation.

   a) What does emit mean?

   b) What is the name of the radiation in this case?

   c) What would you expect to feel if you put your hand near this radiation?

26.4 Reducing the energy loss from our homes

Heat escapes through the walls, the roof, the floor, the windows and the doors of your home. Figure 6 shows the percentages of heat lost from different parts of a house.

Heat is lost from the house by conduction, convection and radiation. By insulating a house, we can keep the heat in it for longer. This reduces the energy needed to warm the house in the winter. It will also reduce the cost of fuel bills.

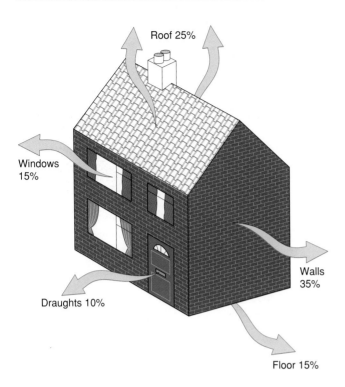

Roof 25%

Windows 15%

Draughts 10%

Walls 35%

Floor 15%

Figure 6 Heat lost from the different parts of a house.

Look closely at Table 1. It shows the relative conductivities of various materials. These materials are used in buildings and in their insulation.

Material	Relative conductivity
Aluminium	8800
Steel	3100
Concrete	175
Glass	35
Water	25
Brick	23
Breeze block	9
Wood	6
Felt	1.7
Wool	1.2
Fibreglass	1.2
Air	1.0

Table 1 The relative conductivities of different materials.

Notice the following points from Table 1.

★ Metals are much better conductors than other building materials. This has led to their use in radiators, electrical wires and cables.

★ Poor conductors (insulators), such as fibreglass and polystyrene, are used to prevent heat transfer through the cavity walls to the outside.

★ Air is the poorest conductor of all the materials in Table 1. Materials which trap air such as fibreglass, wool, felt, feathers and hair are good insulators. They are used in cavity wall insulation, carpets and lagging for pipes and water tanks.

Every year, we spend large sums of money keeping our homes warm during the winter. We have to use fuels and energy to heat our homes, but we cannot avoid losing some of the heat to the air outside. Good insulation is needed to keep these losses to a minimum. This saves energy resources such as coal, oil, gas and electricity. It also keeps the cost of heating as low as possible.

Figure 7 (over the page) shows five common methods of preventing heat loss from our homes. Each method involves trapping pockets or layers of air. This reduces the transfer of heat by conduction and convection.

Example

The Wadsworth family spends £600 each year on heating bills. At present, their house has no loft insulation, no cavity wall insulation and no double glazing. There are no draught excluders fitted to the doors and windows. The hot water tank is not lagged. The Wadsworths talked to various firms about reducing their yearly heating bills. They were given the estimates shown in Table 2, on the next page.

Type of insulation	Cost (£)	Saving in one year (£)
Loft insulation	400	200
Cavity wall insulation	1000	100
Double glazing	3000	150
Draught excluders	50	10
Blanket for hot water tank	25	10

Table 2 The costs and savings of various methods of insulation.

If the Wadsworths fit loft insulation, it will cost £400. But, they would then save £200 each year on their fuel bills. So, it would take only 400/200 = 2 years to save the cost of loft insulation.

If the Wadworths decide to have cavity wall insulation, it would cost £1000. This gives a saving of £100 a year. In this case, it would take 1000/100 = 10 years to save the cost of cavity wall insulation.

6 How long would it take to save the cost of
  a) double glazing
  b) draught excluders
  c) lagging the hot water tank?

7 How should the Wadsworths start to insulate their house?

8 Name the **three** ways in which heat is transferred.

9 Which of them are involved in losing heat from a house?

10 How would you prevent heat being lost from a house
  a) through the roof
  b) through the floor
  c) through the walls?

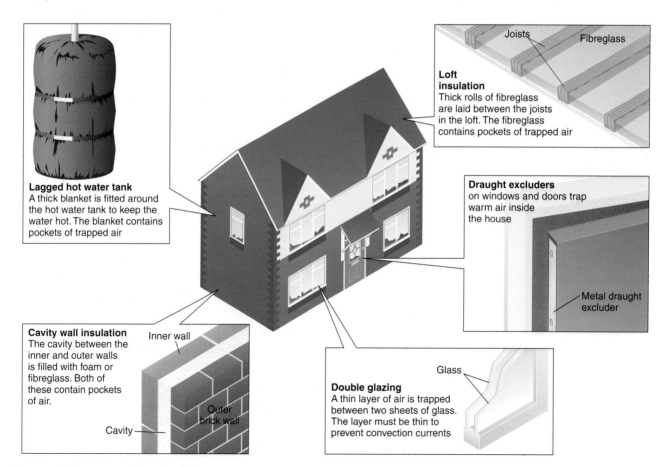

Loft insulation
Thick rolls of fibreglass are laid between the joists in the loft. The fibreglass contains pockets of trapped air

Lagged hot water tank
A thick blanket is fitted around the hot water tank to keep the water hot. The blanket contains pockets of trapped air

Draught excluders
on windows and doors trap warm air inside the house

Metal draught excluder

Cavity wall insulation
The cavity between the inner and outer walls is filled with foam or fibreglass. Both of these contain pockets of air.

Inner wall
Outer brick wall
Cavity

Double glazing
A thin layer of air is trapped between two sheets of glass. The layer must be thin to prevent convection currents

Glass

Figure 7 Preventing heat loss from our homes.

Bubble sheeting on an outdoor swimming pool. Why does the water stay warmer with bubble sheeting than ordinary plastic sheeting?

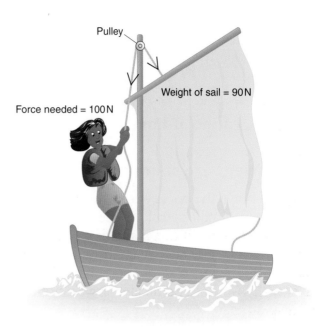

Figure 8

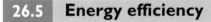

26.5 Energy efficiency

Machines can make jobs easier, but no machine is perfect. Look at Figure 8. This shows Julie hoisting her sail with a pulley.

The weight of the sail is only 90 N, but Julie has to pull with a force of 100 N. This is needed to overcome the weight of the sail plus the friction between the rope and pulley. If Julie pulls in 1 m of rope, the sail goes up 1 m.

So, the energy (work) she puts in
$$= \text{force} \times \text{distance}$$
$$= 100 \text{ N} \times 1 \text{ m}$$
$$= 100 \text{ J}$$

and the useful energy (work) output in raising the sail
$$= 90 \text{ N} \times 1 \text{ m}$$
$$= 90 \text{ J}.$$

90 J of energy have been transferred from Julie to the sail. 10 J have been wasted due to friction.

In practice, it is impossible to transfer all the energy in one machine or resource to another. When energy is transferred, some is always wasted. The main causes for wasted energy in machines are:

★ friction producing heat between the moving parts

★ energy used in moving or lifting the machine itself

★ heat being lost to the surroundings or the machine parts which become warmer.

Different machines waste different amounts of energy. The fraction of the energy supplied to a machine which is usefully transferred is called its **efficiency**.

$$\text{Efficiency} = \frac{\text{useful energy (work) output}}{\text{total energy input}}$$

So, the efficiency of Julie's pulley in Figure 8
$$= \frac{90 \text{ J}}{100 \text{ J}}$$
$$= 0.9 \text{ or } 90\%.$$

We can write the efficiency as a decimal (0.9) or as a percentage (90%).

Although energy can be transferred from one machine to another or from one form to another, it cannot be created or destroyed.

This important law is known as the **Law of Conservation of Energy**.

How efficient are energy transfers?

Figure 9 shows the energy transfers which occur when a small petrol engine is used to drive a generator which produces electricity to light a lamp. The energy changes are shown in Figure 9 as a flow diagram. This starts with 100 J of chemical energy in petrol.

Some energy is transferred usefully from one stage to the next. In each case, some energy is wasted as heat or in moving the machine itself.

From the energy transfers in Figure 9, we can calculate the efficiency of each machine.

∴ Efficiency of generator

$$= \frac{\text{useful energy output}}{\text{total energy input}}$$
$$= \frac{15 \text{ J}}{30 \text{ J}}$$
$$= 0.5 \text{ or } 50\%$$

11 What is the efficiency of

a) the petrol engine b) the lamp?

12 What does the 'Law of conservation of energy' say?

13 Why are machines never 100% efficient?

14 How do you work out the efficiency of a machine?

15 An electricity generating station generates 35 MJ of electricity for every 100 MJ of coal burnt. What is the efficiency of the power station?

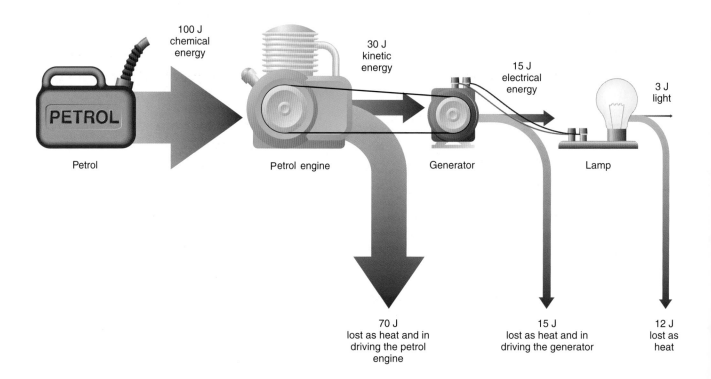

Figure 9 A flow diagram of the energy transfers when a petrol engine and generator are used to light a lamp.

This photo shows Chris Boardman winning an Olympic gold medal in the 4 km pursuit. To help him win the race, he increased his efficiency in a number of ways.

• His Lotus carbon fibre bike is light and very streamlined.

• His skin suit is close fitting.

• His helmet is streamlined.

• He shaved his legs and didn't wear socks.

• To reduce his air resistance, he cycles in a crouched position to cut through the air smoothly.

Summary

1 **Heat** (thermal energy) can be transferred from one place to another by three different processes.

★ **Conduction** – when hotter vibrating particles pass on their kinetic energy to cooler nearby particles without the material(s) moving.

★ **Convection** – when heated liquid or gas becomes less dense than the colder surrounding material. The hotter, less dense material rises and the colder, more dense material sinks, causing **convection currents**.

★ **Radiation** – when invisible, infra-red waves are given off from hot objects. The waves can pass through air or through a vacuum.

2 Dark, dull surfaces are good emitters and good absorbers of radiation.

Light, shiny surfaces are poor emitters and poor absorbers of radiation.

Shiny surfaces are good reflectors of radiation.

3 It is important to reduce the loss of heat from our homes. This is done by increasing the **insulation** with:

★ loft insulation

★ cavity wall insulation

★ draught excluders

★ double glazing

★ lagging on hot water pipes and tank.

4 The **energy efficiency** of a machine
$$= \frac{\text{useful energy (work) output}}{\text{total energy (work) input}}$$

5 Energy can be transferred from one machine to another and from one form to another but it cannot be created or destroyed. This law is called the **Law of Conservation of Energy**.

1 This question is about energy loss from a house. The diagrams show how energy is lost from Jo's house.

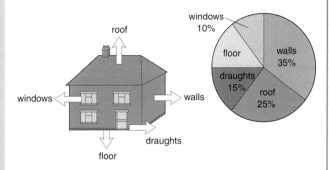

a) Look at the pie chart.

(i) Where is **most** energy lost? *(1)*

(ii) How much of the energy is lost through the floor? *(1)*

b) (i) How could the amount of energy lost through the floor be reduced? *(1)*

(ii) Explain how this reduces energy loss. *(2)*

c) The table shows four methods of reducing energy loss.

Method	Cost	Saving each year	Payback time
Double glazing	£1000	£25	40 years
Draught proofing	£30	£30	1 year
Roof insulation	£300	£100	**A** years
Wall insulation	£250	£50	**B** years

It costs £1000 to install double glazing.

This saves £25 each year **so** it will take 40 years to recover the cost.

What values complete the last column of the table at **A** and **B**? *(1)*   **[OCR (MEG) 1998]**

2 A group of houses uses solar panels and windmills as alternative energy sources.

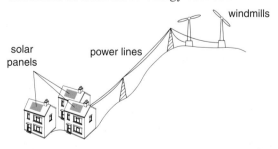

Energy can be transferred by **conduction**, **convection** and **radiation**.

The diagrams show details of a solar panel.

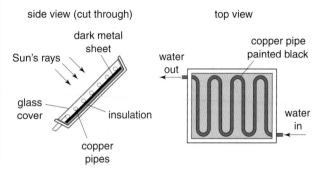

Explain why the water coming out is a lot warmer than the water going in. Use your ideas about energy transfer. *(4)*

[OCR 1999]

3 a) Choose words from the list below to complete a copy of the following sentences.

conduction   convection   diffusion
evaporation   radiation

(i) Thermal (heat) energy is transferred through a vacuum by _____ .

(ii) Transfer of energy by hot liquids moving is called _____ .

(iii) Transfer of energy by a substance, without the substance itself moving, is called _____ . *(3)*

b) Figure 1 shows a science toy.

Figure 2 shows a close-up of one of its vanes.

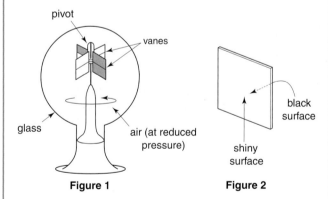

Figure 1   **Figure 2**

When the sun shines on the toy the vanes spin round. This happens because one side of each vane becomes warmer than the other.

(i) When the sun shines, which side becomes warmer, the shiny one or the black one?

(ii) Give **two** reasons for your answer. *(3)*

[AQA (NEAB) 1999]

Currents and circuits

27.1 Circuit diagrams

Blackpool illuminations would be impossible without electric currents and circuits

Figure 1 shows an electrical circuit. This type of drawing is called a **circuit diagram**.

The circuit contains a cell connected to an ammeter, a lamp (bulb), a motor and a switch. Notice that there are symbols for the different pieces of equipment in the circuit. For example, an ammeter is shown as a circle with a capital A in it. The different pieces of equipment in a circuit are called **components**.

A list of the symbols for components that you should know are shown in Table 1 (over the page).

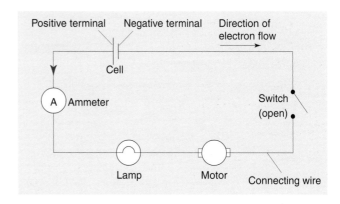

Figure 1 A circuit diagram

At present, the switch is open in Figure 1 and this is called an **open circuit**. When the switch is closed, there is a complete **closed circuit** of conductors. An electric current flows around the closed circuit.

The bulb lights up and the motor starts. The current is measured in **amperes (A)**. To measure the current, you put an ammeter in the circuit.

The electric current is a flow of negative electrons from the negative terminal of the cell through the circuit to the positive terminal. This is shown in a circuit diagram using a labelled arrow at the side of the circuit wires (see the black arrow in Figure 1).

In the 19th century, scientists agreed to show current flowing from the positive terminal to the negative terminal by an arrow on the connecting wires. This is shown by the red arrow in Figure 1. To distinguish it from the electron flow, we call it the **conventional current**.

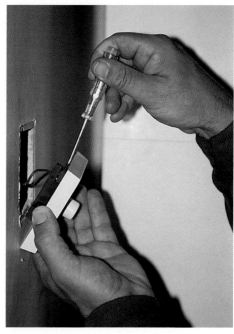

The handles of screwdrivers used by electricians should have insulated handles. Why is this?

Component	Standard symbol	Component	Standard symbol
Switch (open)		Ammeter	(A)
Switch (closed)		Voltmeter	(V)
Cell		Motor	(M) or
Battery of cells		Light dependent resistor (LDR)	
Lamp	or ⊗	Fuse	
Resistor		Variable power supply	0–12V + d.c.
Variable resistor			

Table 1 Symbols for components in circuit diagrams

27.2 Series and parallel circuits

The circuit in Figure 1 is a **series circuit**. In a series circuit, there is only *one path* for the current around the circuit. Another series circuit is shown in Figure 2. This contains a battery of two cells, two identical bulbs and two ammeters.

A **battery** is two or more cells connected together.

When the circuit in Figure 2 is complete, both bulbs light and both ammeters show the same current, 0.5 amperes (0.5 A). If you add more bulbs to the circuit in Figure 2, the current is smaller.

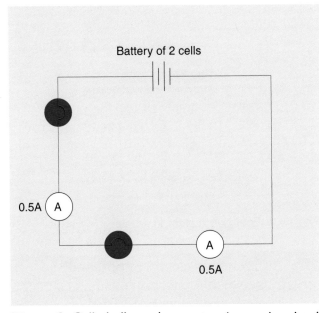

Figure 2 Cells, bulbs and ammeters in a series circuit

For example, if you add two more bulbs to the circuit, the current falls to 0.25 A. When electrons pass through a bulb, they heat up a filament of very thin wire. The wire is made of tungsten. This very thin wire resists the flow of electrons. It causes a **resistance** to the current. The resistance of the bulbs is so great that the filaments get white hot. The bigger the resistance of the components in a circuit, the smaller the current. The wire connecting the components in the circuit is made of thicker copper wire. This causes very little resistance to the current.

Now look at Figure 3. This contains three identical bulbs, X, Y and Z. In this circuit there is a branch. When the current reaches point P, it can go either through bulbs X and Y or through bulb Z. In Figure 3, bulbs X and Y are in series with each other, but they are **in parallel** with bulb Z.

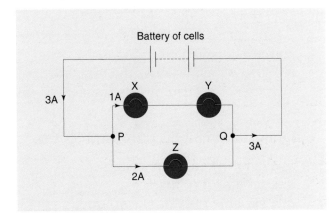

Figure 3 Bulbs in a parallel circuit

In **parallel circuits**, the *current divides equally* at a junction if the two parallel sections are the same. The current will not divide equally if one path is easier than the other. In Figure 3, it is easier for the current to go through just one bulb (Z) from point P than to go through two bulbs (X and Y). So, the current divides at point P. Twice as much goes via Z (2 A) and only one ampere goes via X and Y.

Rules about electric currents in circuits

Our study of the circuits in Figures 2 and 3 show important rules about electric currents.

★ The current flowing through a circuit is measured in **amperes** (A) using an **ammeter**.

★ The current is not used up as it passes through bulbs and other components in a circuit.

★ In a **series circuit**, the current is the same at all points.

★ In a **parallel circuit**, more current takes the easier path.

★ In a parallel circuit, the total currents into a junction equals the total currents out of a junction.

★ As the number of cells in a circuit increases, the current gets larger.

★ As the number of bulbs and other components in a circuit increases, the resistance increases. As the resistance increases, the current gets smaller.

1 Draw the circuit diagram symbols for:

 a) a lamp b) an open switch
 c) a resistor d) a fuse
 e) a variable resistor f) a voltmeter.

2 Draw a circuit diagram to show a three cell battery connected in series with a lamp, a switch and a resistor. Show the direction of conventional current flow.

3 Draw a circuit diagram of a two cell battery in series with a lamp and ammeter with a motor connected in parallel to the lamp. Draw and label an arrow to show which way the electrons flow.

4 A lamp is connected in parallel to a motor. They are connected to a battery. The lamp has a higher resistance than the motor. Which will draw the larger current, the motor or the lamp?

27.3 Energy transfers in electric circuits

The chemicals in a cell contain chemical energy. When the cell is used in a closed circuit, energy is transferred from the materials of the cell to electrons.

The electrons move through the circuit as an electric current. They move from the negative terminal to the positive terminal. At the negative terminal, electrons have high **electrical potential energy**. When electrons reach the positive terminal, they have zero electrical potential energy.

As the electrons pass through components in the circuit (bulbs, resistors, motors, etc.), they lose their electrical potential energy. This 'lost' energy is turned into heat in resistors, kinetic energy and heat in motors, heat and light in bulbs and heat and sound in buzzers (Figure 4).

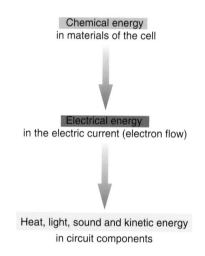

Figure 4 Energy transfers in an electric circuit

The difference in electrical potential energy between the terminals of a cell or battery is shown by its **potential difference (p.d.)** or **voltage**.

The greater the voltage of a cell or battery, the more energy it is able to give to the circuit components. For example, the cells in a small calculator might give 1 or 2 volts. Car batteries usually give 12 volts. The voltage of the electricity supplied to our homes is 240 volts.

Voltages (potential differences) are measured in **volts (V)** using a **voltmeter**. You connect the voltmeter across (i.e. in parallel with) that part of the circuit where the voltage is being measured.

Cells along the backbone of an electric eel can give a large voltage between its nose and tail. An electric eel uses this voltage to kill its prey.

Figure 5 shows how the bulbs are arranged in a car's headlights and in cheap Christmas tree lights.

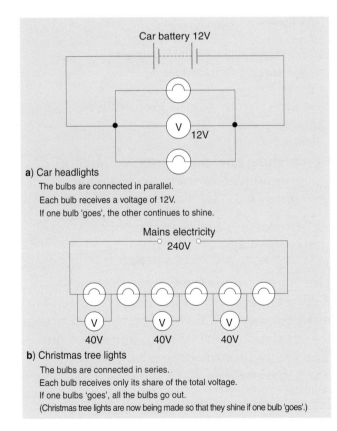

a) Car headlights
The bulbs are connected in parallel.
Each bulb receives a voltage of 12V.
If one bulb 'goes', the other continues to shine.

b) Christmas tree lights
The bulbs are connected in series.
Each bulb receives only its share of the total voltage.
If one bulbs 'goes', all the bulbs go out.
(Christmas tree lights are now being made so that they shine if one bulb 'goes'.)

Figure 5 Voltages across bulbs in series and in parallel

At one time, lights on Christmas trees were connected in series. If one bulb failed, all the fairy lights went out. Today, fairy lights are designed so that this does not happen.

The circuits in Figure 5 show important rules regarding voltages in circuits.

★ A current flows through an electrical component if there is a voltage (p.d.) across its ends.

★ The bigger the voltage across a component, the larger the current flowing through it.

★ Bulbs in parallel have the same voltage across them.

★ Bulbs in series share the total voltage.

★ As the number of cells in a circuit increases, the voltage increases and the current is larger.

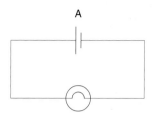
A

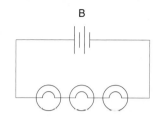
B

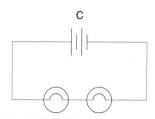
C

Figure 6

5 In the circuits in Figure 6, all the cells are alike and all the bulbs are alike.

a) Which circuit has the most resistance?

b) Which circuit has the smallest current?

c) Which circuit has the largest current?

Most of the meters in the cockpit of this aircraft are like ammeters and voltmeters.

6 Write down the energy transfers which occur in:

a) an electric motor b) a lamp
c) a fan heater d) a buzzer.

7 What is meant by the term '*potential difference (p.d.)*'? Which instrument is used to measure p.d.?

8 A battery is connected to a lamp and a variable resistor in series.

a) What happens to the current flowing when the resistance is increased?

b) What happens to the lamp when the resistance is increased?

c) What happens to the lamp and the current flowing through it when the resistance is decreased?

27.4 Voltage–current graphs – Ohm's law

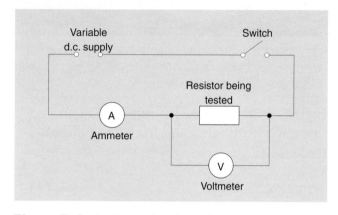

Figure 7 A circuit used to investigate voltage–current relationships.

Voltage–current graphs are useful for two main reasons:

1 to show how the current through a component varies with the voltage across it

2 to measure the resistance of a component.

During the 1820s the German physicist, Georg Ohm, investigated the resistance of different metals. The unit which we now use for resistance is the **ohm** in honour of him. The symbol for the ohm is Ω. So, twenty ohms is written as 20 Ω.

Figure 7 shows a circuit which can be used to measure the voltage across the resistor for different values of the current through it. The current can be altered using the variable direct current (d.c.) supply.

The readings of the current for different voltages have been plotted on a graph in Figure 8. When the resistor is a metal, the results give a straight line graph like that in Figure 8.

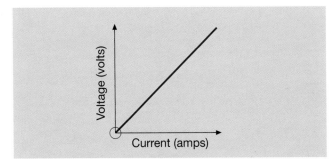

Figure 8 A graph of voltage against current for a metal resistor.

The straight line graph through the origin (O) means that:

> The voltage across a resistor is proportional to the current through it, provided its temperature is constant. i.e. V ∝ I (at constant temperature) where V = voltage and I = current. This statement is called **Ohm's Law**.

Because V is proportional to I, we can say that: $\dfrac{V}{I}$ = a constant.

This means that doubling the voltage, doubles the current. Trebling the voltage, trebles the current and so on. The larger the resistance, the greater is the voltage needed to push each ampere of current through it. This led scientists to a definition of resistance.

> A resistance of one ohm (1 Ω) needs a voltage of one volt (1 V) to drive a current of one ampere (1 A) through it.

If a voltage of 2 V is needed for a current of 1 A, the resistance of the resistor is 2 Ω. If 10 V are needed to drive a current of 1 A through the resistor, its resistance is 10 Ω. Notice that **resistance is the voltage per unit current**.

Resistance (ohms) = $\dfrac{\text{Voltage (volts)}}{\text{Current (amps)}}$

$$R = \frac{V}{I}$$

Example

The element in an electric kettle has a resistance of 24 Ω. What is the current in the element of the kettle when it is connected to the 240 V mains supply?

Solution

Using the formula $R = \dfrac{V}{I}$,

$$I = \frac{V}{R} = \frac{240}{24} = 10 \text{ A}$$

As resistance equals voltage divided by current, notice that:
Resistance = gradient (slope) of a voltage–current graph, provided voltage is plotted vertically and current horizontally.

27.5	**Voltage–current graphs for a resistor and a filament lamp**

Figure 9 shows voltage–current graphs for a resistor and a filament lamp at constant temperature.

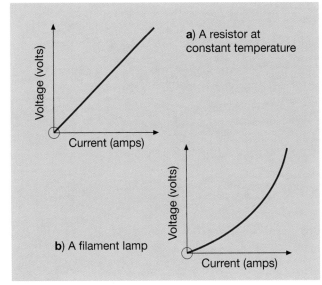

Figure 9 The variation of current with voltage in a resistor and a filament lamp.

Notice that the filament lamp does not obey Ohm's law (i.e. voltage is *not* proportional to the current).

The current through a resistor (at constant temperature) is proportional to the voltage (Figure 9a). The voltage–current graph is a straight line. V/I is constant and therefore the resistance is constant.

For the filament lamp in Figure 9b, the voltage–current graph curves upwards as current increases. This means that the gradient of the voltage–current graph rises. So, V/I increases and therefore the resistance increases as the current increases.

The filament lamp is made of very thin metal wire. As the current through the filament wire increases, its temperature rises sharply. This causes metal atoms in the wire to vibrate faster and prevent the flow of electrons.

So, the resistance of a filament lamp increases as the current increases due to the increase in filament temperature.

9 Name the unit we use to measure resistance.

10 An unknown resistance is added to an electrical circuit. Explain how you would measure its resistance.

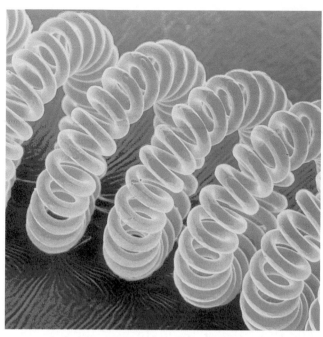

The tightly coiled hot tungsten filaments in a light bulb

11 How would you define a resistance of 1 ohm?

12 Sketch a graph of voltage against current for a resistor which obeys Ohm's law.

13 A current of 2 A flows through a component X when it is connected to a 12 V battery. Calculate the resistance of X.
(Remember $V = I \times R$.)

Summary

I Circuits and flow of charge

★ An **electric current** is a flow of tiny negatively-charged electrons around an **electric circuit**.

★ The negative terminal of the cell (battery) gives up electrons which flow round the circuit to the positive terminal.

★ The **conventional current** is shown by an arrow pointing from the positive to the negative terminals on the connecting wires.

★ The different pieces of equipment in a circuit are called **components**. Each component is shown by a symbol in **circuit diagrams**.

2 Series and parallel circuits

★ In a **series circuit** there is only one path for the current.

★ The current is measured in **amperes** (**A**) by an **ammeter** connected in the circuit.

★ In a series circuit, the current is the same at every point.

★ In a **parallel circuit**, the current has a choice of routes. More current will take the easier path.

★ The total current going into a junction equals the total current coming out of the junction.

3 Cells and bulbs

★ Cells in a circuit provide electrons at the negative terminal with **electrical potential energy**.

★ As the electrons move round the circuit, they lose their electrical potential energy to components as heat, light (in bulbs) and sound (in buzzers and bells).

★ The electrical potential energy results in a **potential difference** or **voltage** between the terminals of a cell. This is measured in **volts** (**V**).

★ Bulbs and other components in a circuit hinder the flow of electrons. This causes a **resistance** which is measured in **ohms** (Ω).

★ As the number of bulbs and other components in a circuit increases, the resistance increases. This results in a smaller current.

4 Ohm's law

★ The voltage across a resistor is proportional to the current through it, provided the temperature is constant. i.e. $V \propto I$.

$\dfrac{V}{I}$ = voltage per unit current

= R (resistance)

So,

Resistance (ohms) = $\dfrac{\textbf{Voltage (volts)}}{\textbf{Current (amps)}}$

★ Resistors which obey Ohm's law have a straight line in graphs of voltage against current.

★ Resistors, like filament lamps, which do *not* obey Ohm's Law do *not* produce a straight line graph when voltage is plotted against current.

1 Copy and complete the table below. The first line has been completed for you. *(2)*

Electrical device	Input energy	Output energy
Bell	Electrical	Sound
Battery		Electrical
Kettle	Electrical	

[WJEC 1998]

2 The circuit diagram shows a battery conected to five lamps. The currents through lamps **A** and **B** are shown.

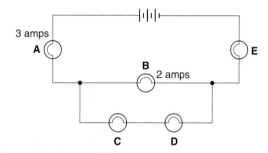

Write down the current flowing through
(i) lamp C, (ii) lamp E. *(2)*   **[WJEC 1998]**

3 **miniature circuit breaker**
fuse
earth leakage circuit breaker
earth wire

Which of the above breaks the circuit when

(i) too large a current flows, *(1)*

(ii) a very small current flows through it? *(1)*
   [WJEC 1998]

4 a) The graph below shows how the current in two resistors, **A** and **B**, changes as voltage changes.

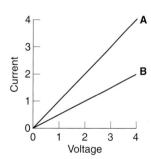

(i) How, if at all, does the resistance of resistor **A** change as voltage is increased? *(1)*

(ii) How does the resistance of resistor **B** compare with that of resistor **A**? *(1)*

b) The diagram shows a battery connected to two resistors.]

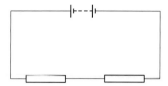

Copy and complete the following sentence about the circuit.

The _____ from the battery is shared between the resistors whilst the same _____ flows through each one. *(2)*

c) In this question all the cells are identical. Each cell has a voltage of 1.5 volts.

The diagrams below show three ways of making a battery. In each case two cells are used.

Under a copy of each battery write the voltage you would expect the battery to have. *(3)*

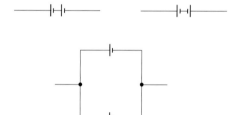

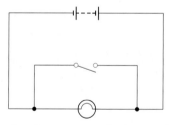

[AQA (NEAB) 1998]

5 The circuit diagram below shows a battery connected to a lamp and a switch.]

a) State what happens to the lamp when:

(i) the switch is open (OFF);

(ii) the switch is closed (ON). *(2)*

b) When the switch is closed what problem is caused in the circuit? *(1)*

c) Draw a circuit diagram to show how the switch should be correctly connected to the lamp and battery. *(1)*

[AQA (NEAB) 1997]

28

Using electricity

28.1 We depend on electricity!

Every day we depend on electricity for cooking, for lighting and for heating. At the flick of a switch, we use electric fires, electric kettles and many other electrical gadgets. All these electrical appliances use mains electricity.

Electricity has one big advantage as an energy supply. It can be easily changed into other forms of energy – heat in electric fires and kettles, light in bulbs and lamps, sound in bells and buzzers, kinetic energy in motors and food mixers. It is hard to imagine life without electricity.

Singapore at night. How could we survive without electricity?

Electricity is generated in power stations from coal, oil or nuclear fuel. Heat from the fuel is used to boil water and produce steam. The steam drives turbines and generates electricity (section 29.6). In this way, chemical energy in the fuel is converted into electrical energy.

28.2   Electric charges

We now know that an electric current consists of a **flow of electrons** which have a negative charge. Electric charges were first discovered when certain materials were rubbed or brushed against each other. Rubbing or brushing can cause electrons to move from one material to another. This gives the materials an electric charge. People sometimes say the materials have 'static electricity' on them.

You may have noticed some of the effects of electric charges already.

★ If you comb your hair quickly with a plastic comb, the comb can be used to pick up tiny bits of paper.

★ If you take off a jersey or a shirt, you may hear crackles from tiny sparks.

★ You can make a balloon stick to the wall or the ceiling after rubbing it against a woollen jersey.

All these effects are caused by rubbing two objects together. We say they are charged by **friction**. Many materials can be charged up by friction.

The friction causes a transfer of electrons from one material to another, for example hair to comb, your jersey or shirt to underwear, jersey to a balloon.

When you comb your hair quickly with a plastic comb, the comb removes electrons from the atoms in your hair (Figure 1). The comb will then have more electrons than protons, so it has a negative charge overall.

Your hair will have lost electrons. It will have fewer electrons than protons and so it has a positive charge overall.

Figure 1 Charging a plastic comb by friction

Materials, such as plastic combs and hair, hold their charge on rubbing. They do not allow electrons to pass through them easily because they are **insulators**. Plastics like polythene and PVC are used to insulate electrical wires and cables.

Dark brown ceramic and coloured plastic insulators are used to hold electricity cables to metal structures

Try this experiment. Comb your hair briskly with a plastic comb. Now, bring the charged comb close to a tiny bit of paper. The negative charge on the comb **repels** negative electrons from the area of the paper nearest to it (Figure 2a). This part of the paper therefore becomes positive. It is attracted to the comb because *unlike charges attract*. If the paper is small enough, it can be picked up (Figure 2b).

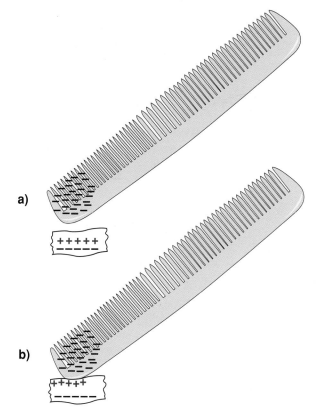

Figure 2 Using a charged comb to pick up tiny bits of paper

Have you noticed that your hair sometimes stands up when it is combed quickly? (Maybe not as much as in Figure 1!) This is more likely if your hair is clean and dry. It happens because each hair becomes positively charged and *like charges repel*.

These effects show that:

★ objects with similar (like) charges repel each other

★ objects with opposite (unlike) charges attract each other.

This boy's hair is sticking out because he is negatively charged. Negative charge comes from the dome of the generator he is touching. The negative charge on each hair repels all the others near it.

1 Name **two** ways in which static electricity can be produced at home.

2 What sort of materials are used to make static electricity?

3 What happens when a positive (+) charge is brought near to:

a) a negative (−) charge

b) a positive (+) charge?

4 Explain how a charged comb can pick up a tiny piece of paper.

| 28.3 | **The dangers and uses of electric charges** |

When some materials or objects rub against each other, a charge can build up. This charge is sometimes called static charge or **electrostatic charge**. As the electrostatic charge on an object gets greater, the voltage (potential difference) between the object and uncharged materials increases. If the voltage becomes too high, electrons will jump across the gap between the object and any conductor which comes near it. In some cases, there may be enough electrons to form a spark.

If static charge builds up, there can be serious problems. The problem is overcome by attaching a conductor to the charged object. The conductor allows the charge to flow away without causing any harm.

For example, build up of static must be avoided on the inside surface of a television screen and also when aircraft are being refuelled. If you watch an aircraft being refuelled, you will see a thick earth wire which is attached to the bodywork. This prevents the build up of static charge as kerosene flows through pipes into the fuel tanks.

A flash of lightning is a gigantic spark. Millions and millions of electrons shoot from the bottom of the cloud to Earth. So much heat is produced that it causes a flash of light.

Electrostatic charges are not always a danger. They are important and useful in photocopying machines and in removing (extracting) dust.

When an aircraft is refuelled, a thick earth wire is attached to the bodywork. This prevents the build up of static charge.

| 28.4 | **Electricity from the National Grid** |

Electricity is generated in power stations. It is then transmitted across the country to our homes, schools and workplaces by the National Grid. The current is carried in thick cables supported by huge pylons. Thick cables have a lower resistance than thinner ones, so they don't get so hot. This means that a smaller proportion of the electrical energy is lost as heat. If the cables were thicker still, there would be less energy lost as heat. But the extra cable weight would require more ugly pylons standing closer together.

Do you think electricity cables should be laid underground? Why is this not done at present?

The electric current supplied by the National Grid to the mains sockets in buildings is *not* a one-way flow of electrons. Electrons in the current from the mains flow alternately forwards and then backwards 50 times every second. This type of current is called **alternating current** (**a.c.**). In contrast to this, the electric current from a cell or a battery always flows in the same direction. Currents like this are called **direct currents** (**d.c.**).

There are two important reasons why the National Grid uses alternating current and not direct current.

1 Alternating current is easier to generate than direct current.

2 The voltages from alternating currents can be changed more readily than those from direct currents.

The transmission of alternating currents via the National Grid is covered in section 29.6.

Wires and cables cause a resistance to the movement of electrons. This is the same for alternating currents and direct currents. Because of this, both a.c. or d.c. can be used with heating appliances (electric fires, electric kettles) and for electric lighting.

Unlike direct currents, alternating currents do not cause any chemical (electrolytic) effects. The current goes first one way and then the other way. Each electrode is alternately positive and then negative 50 times per second. This is too fast for any changes to occur at the electrodes. The current switches from forwards to backwards 50 times per second. We say it has a frequency of 50 cycles per second or 50 hertz (Hz).

5 Name **one** device at home which uses alternating current and one which uses direct current.

6 What is the difference between direct and alternating current?

7 What is the National Grid?

8 Do we use direct or alternating current in the National Grid? Give a reason why it is used.

28.5	**Supplying electricity to homes, schools and workplaces**

The electricity supply to our homes, schools and workplaces is usually called 'mains electricity'. The electricity cable to a building includes two wires – a **live** wire and a **neutral** wire.

Electricity comes into the building through the live wire. This is alternately positive and then negative. The live wire has an 'average' voltage of about 240 V relative to the neutral wire. This is a dangerous voltage. The safety features in electrical appliances are studied in the next section.

The neutral wire stays at a voltage close to zero. It is connected to a huge metal plate in the earth at the local electricity sub-station. This conducts any charge into the earth.

Figure 3 shows the electricity supply cable and the electrical wiring in a house.

The supply from the mains cable passes first through the electricity company's *main fuse*. It then goes via the *electricity meter* to a *fuse box*. In the fuse box, there are five or six separate fuses. Each fuse leads to a different circuit supplying electricity to a different area or appliance. These separate circuits usually include:

★ a downstairs lighting circuit

★ an upstairs lighting circuit

★ separate circuits for the electric cooker and immersion heater, which use large currents

★ two or three ring circuits for the three-pin wall sockets.

Each ring main circuit will have about 10 sockets. Notice in Figure 3 that all these sockets are connected across the live wire and the neutral wire. They are all in parallel.

This ensures that each socket receives the full mains voltage of 240 V. The 'ring' of cable which joins the sockets in the ring main circuit contains an earth wire as well as the live wire and the neutral wire. It is called a three-core cable. This contrasts with the two-core cable which joins the ring main circuit to the fuse box. The two-core cable has only a live wire and a neutral wire.

28.6 Safety in electrical circuits

Faults in circuits carrying mains electricity can lead to wires and cables overheating and causing fires. They can also result in very painful electric shocks and even death.

Because of these dangers, electrical circuits and appliances have various safety features. These include fuses, earth wires, insulation and circuit breakers.

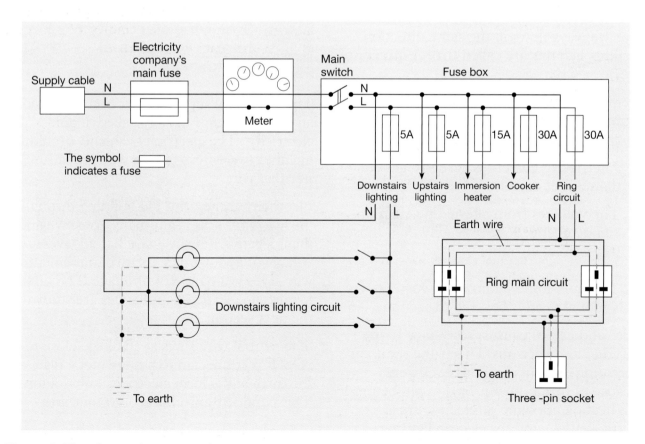

Figure 3 The electrical wiring in a house

Fuses

A fuse is simply thin wire which gets hot and then melts ('blows') if the current through it is too large. Fuses provide two important safety features.

1 They prevent circuit wires from getting red hot and starting fires.

2 They protect us when we use metal-cased electrical appliances fitted with an earth wire.

Notice from Figure 3 that fuses are placed in the live wire. This disconnects the live wire if there is a fault and the fuse 'blows'.

Earth wires

Earth wires are important on electrical appliances with outer metal parts. Suppose an electric kettle with a metal casing has only a two-core cable (Figure 4a). If part of the live circuit touches the metal casing, then anyone touching the metal parts will get a shock.

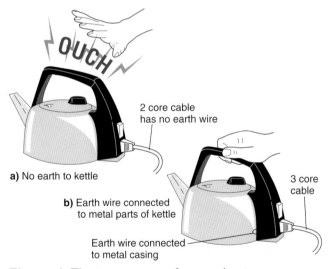

a) No earth to kettle

2 core cable has no earth wire

b) Earth wire connected to metal parts of kettle

3 core cable

Earth wire connected to metal casing

Figure 4 The importance of an earth wire on electrical appliances with outer metal parts

The kettle in Figure 4b has an earth wire connected to its metal parts. If part of the live circuit touches the metal casing, a large current will flow through the earth wire. This will 'blow' the fuse in the plug. Anyone using the kettle is safe from an electric shock.

In normal safe use, there is no current in the earth wire.

Insulation

Many electrical appliances have outer parts which are entirely plastic. Plastic does not conduct electricity and so these appliances do not usually need an earth wire. This safety feature is sometimes called **double insulation** because the appliance has both insulated plastic covering on the wires and an insulated outer casing. Appliances with double insulation carry the symbol ▣.

Circuit breakers

Circuit breakers are used in some circuits instead of fuses. There are two main types. The first type uses an electromagnet. This separates a pair of contacts and breaks the circuit if the current gets too large.

The second type is called a residual current circuit breaker (RCCB). The current in the live wire is compared with that in the neutral wire. If these differ, current must be 'leaking' to earth. If this happens, contacts are broken and the current in the live wire is cut off extremely quickly. The RCCB trips (cuts off the current) in a few thousandths of a second if current is 'leaking' to earth.

You should always fit an RCCB when using an electric lawn mower.

Three-pin plugs

Most electrical appliances are connected to the mains electricity using cable and a three-pin plug. The cable and the plug are designed with safety in mind.

The cable comprises:

★ two-core cable (two inner cores of plastic-covered copper wire) if the appliance has double insulation

★ three-core cable (three inner cores of plastic-covered copper wire) if the appliance is *not* double insulated

★ an outer layer of flexible plastic covering.

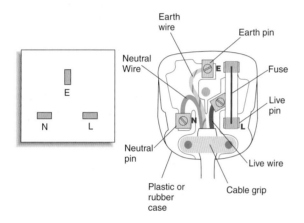

Figure 5 A three-pin socket and a correctly wired three-pin plug

Plastic is used to cover the inner wires and as an outer layer because it is a good insulator.

Appliances with exposed metal parts should always be earthed and therefore need a three-core cable.

Figure 5 shows a socket on the ring main circuit and a correctly wired three-pin plug.

Notice that the plug has:

★ a plastic or rubber case providing good insulation

★ a live pin, a neutral pin and an earth pin

★ a fuse in the live circuit

★ a cable grip to prevent the wires being tugged from their connections to the pins.

In connecting an appliance to a three-pin plug, the wires in the cable must be connected to the correct pins in the plug.

1 the brown wire via the fuse to the live pin, L

2 the blue wire to the neutral pin, N

3 the green/yellow wire to the earth pin, E.

It is also important to use the correct fuse in each three-pin plug. This fuse protects the appliance from currents which might cause its wiring to overheat and start a fire.

Appliances like table lamps, radios, TVs and fridges take small currents (well below 3 A). So, they should have plugs with 3 A fuses. Kettles, irons and electric fires usually take currents greater than 3 A. They should have plugs with 5 A or 13 A fuses.

9 A washing machine uses a three-core cable. Name the **three** wires in the core and say what colour they are.

10 What is a 'ring main circuit'?

11 What is the job of a fuse?

12 How does an earth wire protect you?

13 Why should you use a Residual Current Circuit Breaker (RCCB) when using power tools or electrical garden tools? How does the device protect you?

28.7 Paying for electricity

We know from section 25.4 that

$$\text{power} = \frac{\text{work done}}{\text{time taken}}.$$

We can do work on something by transferring energy to it, so

$$\text{power} = \frac{\text{energy transferred}}{\text{time taken}}.$$

The unit of power is the watt (W) and one watt is a rate of working or energy transfer of one joule per second (1 W = 1 J/s).

So, if a kettle has a power or 'wattage' of 2.4 kW or 2400 W, it turns 2400 J of electrical energy into heat every second.

Table 1 shows the power rating of some household appliances. The power rating tells us how much energy the appliance uses in one second. Thus, the sewing machine in Table 1 uses 60 joules each second whereas the toaster uses 1200 joules per second.

Appliance	Power
Radio	5 W
Fan heater	2000 W (2 kW)
Liquidiser	300 W
Kettle	3000 W (3 kW)
Sewing machine	60 W
Iron	750 W
Hair dryer	500 W
Colour TV	75 W
Toaster	1200 W (1.2 kW)

Table 1 The power ratings of some common household appliances.

$$power = \frac{energy}{time}$$

$$\therefore energy = power \times time$$

Power is usually measured in watts and time in seconds. This gives the unit for energy as watt seconds rather than the more usual unit, the joule.

When electricity companies charge for electrical energy, they measure the power in kilowatts (kW) and the time in hours. This gives the energy in kilowatt hours (kWh).

One kilowatt hour is the electrical energy taken by a one kilowatt appliance in one hour.

1 kilowatt hour = 1 kilowatt for 1 hour
$\qquad$ = 1000 watts for 3600 seconds
$\qquad$ = 1000 × 3600 joules
$\qquad$ = 3 600 000 joules

So, 1 kWh is the same as three million, six hundred thousand joules. Electricity companies measure energy in kilowatt hours rather than joules. One joule would be too small a unit. Household electricity meters measure the electricity used in kilowatt hours. Kilowatt hours are often referred to simply as **units** of electricity.

Example

A 10 kW cooker takes 3 hours to roast a turkey.

(i) How much electrical energy does this require in kilowatt hours?

(ii) How much does the roasting cost if the price per kWh (unit) of electricity is 8p?

Solution

(i) Electrical energy required (kWh)

$\qquad$ = power × time
$\qquad\quad$ (kW) $\quad$ (h)

$\qquad$ = 10 × 3 = 30 kWh

(ii) Cost of roasting

$\qquad$ = 30 kWh (units) at 8p per kWh (unit)
$\qquad$ = 240p = £2.40

14 How much energy (in kWh) is used when:

$\quad$ a) a 100 W lamp is on for 15 hours

$\quad$ b) a 2 kW electric fire is used for 5 hours each day for a week?

15 If electricity costs 8p per unit (kWh), how much would it cost to run

$\quad$ a) the 100 W lamp for 15 hours

$\quad$ b) the 2 kW electric fire for 5 hours each day for a week?

Summary

1 **Electric charges** (electrostatic charges) can be obtained by rubbing two non-conducting objects together. The rubbing causes friction.

The static charges are produced by rubbing electrons off one material onto the other.

2 ★ Opposite (unlike) charges attract.

★ Similar (like) charges repel.

3 A build up of **electrostatic charge** can result in sparks or flashes of lightning. Sparks are caused by electrons moving rapidly from a charged object to a conductor. A flash of lightning is a gigantic spark.

4 The electric current from a cell or battery flows in one direction. This is called **direct current** (d.c.). A current which flows alternately forwards and backwards is called an **alternating current** (a.c.). The electricity in the National Grid is an a.c. current.

5 Mains electricity enters our homes through electric cables which include two wires – a live wire and a neutral wire. The live wire carries the charge at a voltage of 240 V. The neutral wire stays at a voltage close to zero.

6 Electrical circuits have fuses, earth wires, insulation and circuit breakers for safety.

★ **Fuses** have a thin wire which melts if the current is too large. This prevents:
- electrical wires getting too hot and causing a fire
- electric shocks when we use appliances.

★ **Earth wires** conduct currents to Earth and prevent electric shocks.

★ **Insulation** – a plastic covering on the live wire, neutral wire and earth wire which provides insulation for electrical wires and cables.

★ **Circuit breakers** – when the current gets too large, contacts separate and the circuit is broken. This protects the users from electric shocks.

7   energy   =   power   ×   time
(in kilowatt hours) (in kilowatts) (in hours)

Exam questions for Chapter 28

1 This question is about electrical appliances in the kitchen.

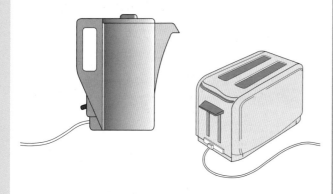

a) The kettle is connected to the 230 V mains supply using a fused plug. The kettle is rated at 2500 W. It takes 200 s to boil some water. Calculate the energy transferred to the water. Use the equation below and show how you work out your answer.

energy = power × time   *(3)*

b) For safety reasons, it is important that the metal casing of the toaster is earthed. Explain why.   *(2)*

[OCR (MEG) 1998]

2 a) Copy the table below and complete your copy to show whether the material listed is an electrical conductor or an insulator. Place a tick (✓) in the appropriate column.

Material	Conductor	Insulator
Plastic		
Iron		
Copper		
Aluminium		

(4)

b) The diagram below shows two charged balls after they have been brought near each other.

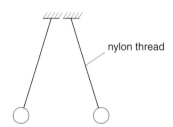

nylon thread

the charged balls move apart

(i) Copy the diagram. Add two arrows to your diagram to show the directions of the forces which make the balls move apart. *(2)*

(ii) Are the forces between the charged balls attractive or repulsive? *(1)*

(iii) What does the diagram tell you about the sign of the charges on the balls? Explain your answer. *(2)*

(iv) Suggest why the charged balls are hung from nylon thread. *(2)*

c) A polythene rod is rubbed with a duster. The rod gains a negative charge.

(i) What is the name of the charged particles which are moved from the duster to the polythene rod? *(1)*

(ii) What is the sign of the charge gained by the duster? *(1)*

d) Some students tried to charge a brass rod in the same way. They could not. Explain why not. *(2)*

[Edexcel 1998]

3 The diagram shows the inside of a 3-pin plug.

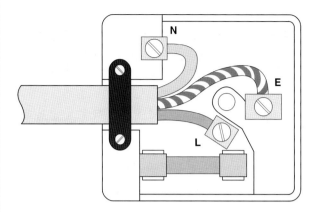

a) What colour wire should be connected to each terminal **E**, **L** and **N**? *(3)*

b) Name **two** parts inside the 3-pin plug which help to make it safe. *(2)*

[AQA (NEAB) 1999]

3 An electric kettle is being used on the mains supply.

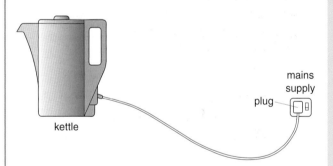

mains supply

plug

kettle

The kettle has a power rating of 2300 W.

a) Copy and complete the following sentence.

When the kettle is used the main energy transfer is _____ energy to _____ energy. *(2)*

b) Calculate the number of joules of energy transferred when the kettle is used for 3 minutes *(3)*

c) In one week the kettle is used, on average, for one hour each day. Use the following equation to calculate the number of Units of electrical energy used in one week.

energy transferred = power × time
(kilowatt hour, kWh) (kilowatt, kW) (hour, h)

d) If the cost of each Unit is 10p calculate the total cost of using the kettle during the week. *(2)*

[AQA (NEAB) 1999]

CHAPTER 29

Electromagnetism

29.1 Magnetic poles and magnetic fields

4000 years ago, Chinese travellers used magnetic iron ore as a simple compass. Since then, magnets have been used in lots of other machines. These include motors, generators, electric bells and televisions.

Sailors have used magnets in compasses to guide their ships for more than 4000 years.

When a magnet is dipped into a box of pins, they cling to it (Figure 1). A similar thing happens with iron filings or steel paper clips, but not with brass screws.

The ends of the magnet where most of the pins cling are called **poles**.

Magnets will only attract metals and alloys which contain **iron**, **cobalt** or **nickel**. So, steel, which is an alloy of iron, is attracted by magnets. Brass (an alloy of copper and zinc) is not attracted by magnets.

Bar magnet

Figure 1 Pins cling to a bar magnet

North poles and south poles

A bar magnet is hung from a thread. It always comes to rest in a north–south direction (Figure 2). The end (pole) of the magnet which always points north is called the **north-seeking pole** (or just **north pole** for short). The pole of the magnet which points south is called the **south-seeking pole** or **south pole**. Because of this, a small magnet can be used as a compass.

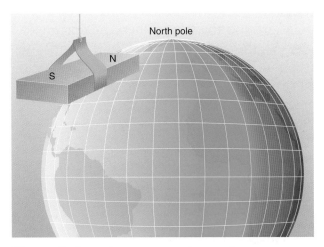

Figure 2 A small magnet can be used as a compass

Forces between poles

Every magnet has a north pole and a south pole. When the poles of two magnets are brought near each other, we find that:

★ **like poles** (i.e. two north poles or two south poles) **repel** one another

★ **unlike poles** (i.e. a north pole and a south pole) **attract** one another.

Magnetic fields

Strong magnets can attract magnetic materials from some distance away or even through other materials like paper and wood.

The space around a magnet, where its magnetic force acts, is called a **magnetic field**.

You can detect a magnetic field and find its direction using a small plotting compass (Figure 3).

Put the bar magnet on a sheet of paper. Place the plotting compass near one of its poles. Mark the position of the compass needle with dots. Use the second dot as the starting point for the next position of the compass. Continue like this until the other pole of the bar magnet is reached or the field becomes too weak to detect.

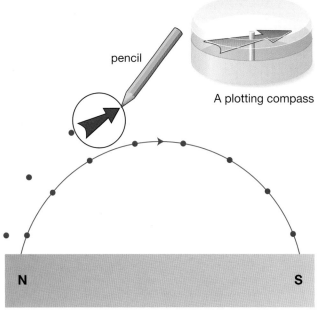

Investigating the field around a bar magnet

Figure 3 Using a small plotting compass to study the magnetic field around a bar magnet.

The field around a magnet can be shown as a series of lines called **lines of magnetic force**. These lines of force:

★ always point away from a north pole and towards a south pole

★ never cross

★ are close together if the field is strong and further apart if the field is weak.

Figure 4 (over the page) shows the magnetic field patterns:

a) around a single bar magnet

b) between two magnetic poles which attract

c) between two magnetic poles which repel.

Notice the following points.

★ The direction of a magnetic field is always away from a north pole and towards a south pole.

★ Lines of force never cross. They show the direction of the magnetic field at a particular point. A magnetic field can have only one direction at any one point.

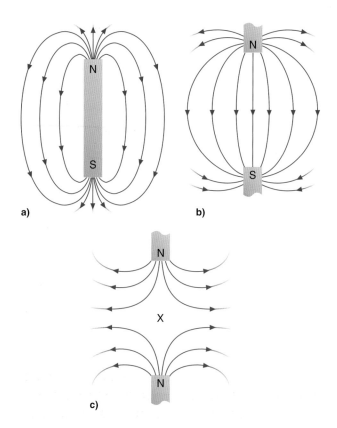

Figure 4 Magnetic field patterns

★ Look at point X in Figure 4c. The field from one north pole is equal but opposite to that from the other north pole. The fields cancel each other out. X is called a **neutral point**.

29.2 Magnetism from electricity

During the 19th century, scientists discovered that electric currents could produce magnetic fields. When an electric current passes through a wire, there is a magnetic field around the wire.

This magnetism produced by electric currents is called **electromagnetism**.

The magnetic field around a straight wire

The magnetic field around a straight wire can be investigated using the apparatus in Figure 5.

Notice that the lines of magnetic force are circles around the wire. When the current is reversed, the compass points in the opposite direction. This shows that the magnetic field has reversed.

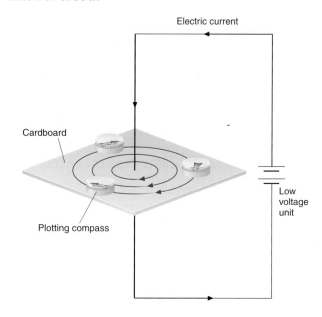

Figure 5 Investigating the field around a straight wire carrying an electric current

The magnetic field around a coil

Figure 6 shows a coil of wire around a cardboard cylinder. When the switch is closed, a current flows through the coil and the magnetic field appears. If the current is switched off (when the switch is open), the magnetic field disappears.

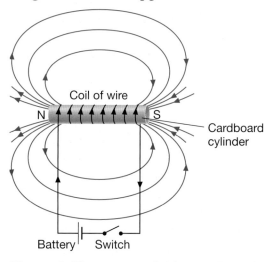

Figure 6 The magnetic field around a coil

Notice that the magnetic field around the coil is like that around a bar magnet.

You can do three things to make the magnetic field stronger.

★ Use a larger current.

★ Have more turns in the coil.

★ Put a soft iron rod (core) inside the coil.

1 What happens to two magnets when:

a) a N pole is brought near to a N pole

b) a S pole is brought near to a S pole

c) a N pole is brought near to a S pole?

2 Draw the magnetic field pattern you get when a current flows through a straight wire.

3 A coil of wire is wound round a cardboard cylinder and connected to a battery. Write down **three** ways to make a magnetic field stronger.

4 What happens to the magnetic field when the current is switched off?

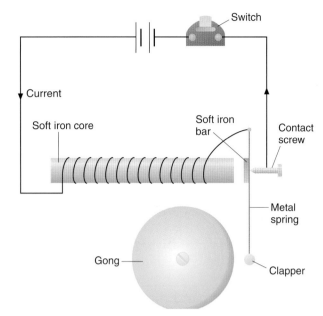

Figure 7 An electric bell

29.3 Electromagnets

The coil in Figure 6 can be used as an **electromagnet**. The magnetism will appear when the current is switched on and disappear when the current is switched off. Electromagnets made from coils are used in electric bells, relays, telephones and electric motors.

The electric bell

When the switch in Figure 7 is pressed, the circuit is completed. A current passes through the coil. This magnetises the soft iron core which attracts the soft iron bar. The bar moves towards the core, pulling the clapper to the gong. As soon as the clapper moves, the circuit is broken between the metal spring and the contact screw.

The current switches off. The soft iron core loses its magnetism. The metal spring pulls the soft iron bar back again. As soon as the metal spring touches the contact screw, the circuit is complete. This starts the cycle again. The bell rings and the cycle continues until you let go of the push switch.

Electromagnetic relays

With an ordinary switch, your fingers operate the switch. A relay is a switch operated by an electric current. It is a bit like a relay race. A baton is passed from one runner to the next in a relay race. In an electromagnetic relay, a signal is passed from one circuit to the next as an electric current.

Electromagnetic relays are used when very large currents (say 100 A) are needed. Large currents normally require heavy duty switches. These produce large sparks, which are dangerous to the user and the equipment. These problems can be overcome by using a relay.

Figure 8 (over the page) shows an electromagnetic relay system. This might be used to operate a car starter motor.

When the initial (ignition) switch is closed at A, a current flows in the coil.

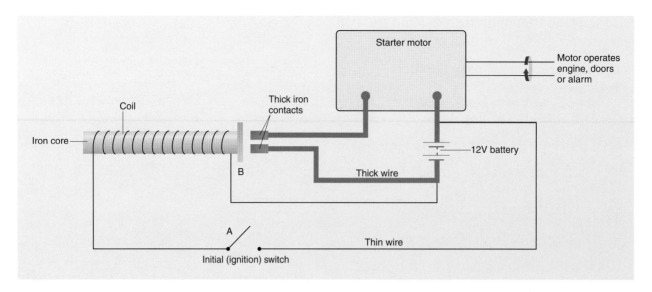

Figure 8 An electromagnetic relay system for a car starter motor

Because the wire is thin, the coil resistance is high so only a small current flows. The iron core is magnetised and this attracts the thick iron contacts towards B. When contact is made at B, a large current flows in the brown (thick wire) circuit to operate the starter motor.

5 Name **three** devices which use an electromagnet.

6 How would you magnetise an electromagnet?

7 How would you make an electromagnet lose its magnetism?

8 Draw a diagram of an electric bell. Explain how it works.

29.4 Simple electric motors

Electric motors are important parts in many appliances. Washing machines, hair dryers, food processors, electric drills and vacuum cleaners all use electric motors.

Electricity and magnetism can be used to get a motor moving (turning).

This movement is known as the **motor effect**.

We can study the motor effect using the apparatus in Figure 9. The copper wire rests on supports between the poles of a strong magnet. When the switch is closed, the wire moves upwards.

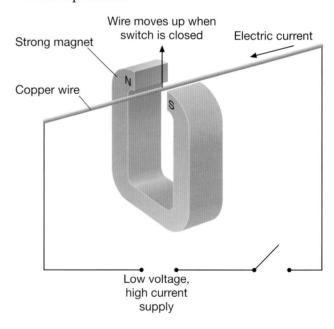

Figure 9 Studying the motor effect

If the current is reversed or the magnetic field is reversed, the wire moves down. If *both* the field and the current are reversed, then the wire moves up again. There must be a force on the wire making it move up or down.

The force on the wire is stronger if:

★ the magnet is stronger
★ the current is larger.

Notice from Figure 9 that the force on the wire is at right angles to the electric current and at right angles to the field.

This motor effect is used in electric motors. Figure 10 shows a very simple electric motor. When a current passes through the coil, it becomes an electromagnet. This makes the coil turn as it is attracted by the poles of the magnet.

Every half turn, the split ring commutator changes its connection to the carbon brushes. This causes the current to change direction. So, the coil keeps on rotating the same way.

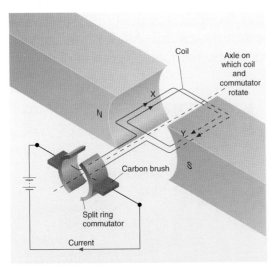

Figure 10 A simple electric motor

Commercial motors are much more complicated than the simple motor in Figure 10.

★ They use electromagnets, not permanent magnets, because permanent magnets slowly lose their magnetism.

★ They have coils with tens or even hundreds of turns to increase the turning force.

★ The coils are wound on a soft iron core to make the magnetic field stronger.

29.5 Generating electricity

In section 29.4, we found that a wire carrying an electric current in a magnetic field can move. This is the **motor effect**. We can summarise the motor effect as:

electricity + magnetism → movement

The motor converts electrical energy into kinetic energy.

The process can also be reversed. If a conductor moves in a magnetic field, a voltage is generated. A current flows if there is a complete circuit. So,

movement + magnetism → electricity

In this case, kinetic energy is converted to electrical energy. Electric currents generated in this way are called **induced currents**.

The effect is known as **electromagnetic induction**.

Electromagnetic induction is used to generate electricity in dynamos for bicycle lights, alternators in cars and generators in power stations.

The movement of the bicycle wheel causes this dynamo to generate electricity. The electric current will light a small lamp.

Figure 11 shows an experiment to study electromagnetic induction. The coil is connected to a sensitive centre-zero ammeter.

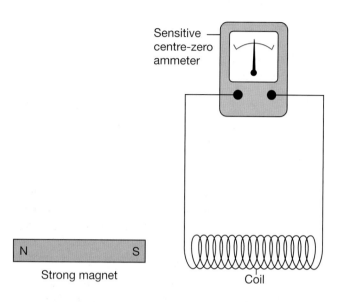

Figure 11 Studying electromagnetic induction

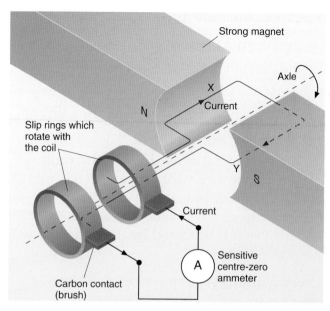

Figure 12 A simple a.c. generator

The ends of the coil are connected to slip rings which rotate with the coil. Carbon brushes (contacts) connect the slip rings to the rest of the circuit. As the coil rotates in the magnetic field, an alternating current is induced.

The results of the experiment show that:

★ A current is generated if the magnet is moved into or out of the coil.

★ If the magnet is not moving, there is no current.

★ The current flows one way as the magnet moves in and the other way when the magnet moves out.

★ The current flows in the opposite direction if the magnet is turned round.

★ Induced currents are also produced if the coil moves and the magnet stays put.

If you repeatedly move the magnet in and out, the current flows forwards then backwards, forwards then backwards, etc. This is an **alternating current**.

We can use this idea to generate an alternating current. This is what happens in the simple alternating current (a.c.) generator in Figure 12.

As air passengers walk through the security gate, metal objects cause changes in the magnetic field. This induces tiny electric currents to warn the security personnel.

Power stations use huge a.c. generators to produce electricity. Usually they have a powerful electromagnet which rotates rather than the coil. The big advantage of this is that the coil is stationary so slip rings and brushes are not needed. This also eliminates damage to the rings and brushes by sparks and friction.

Generators in which the magnet moves rather than the coil are sometimes called **dynamos**. This is the arrangement in a bicycle dynamo.

This huge steam turbine is being lowered into position as part of a power station generator.

9 a) You have a magnet, a coil of wire and a sensitive meter. Say how you can use them to generate some electricity.

b) What changes would you make to the equipment to increase the amount of electricity generated?

10 What happens if a magnet is held stationary inside a coil of wire?

11 What is the name of the device used on a bicycle to generate electricity?

| 29.6 | **Generating and transmitting electricity** |

An induced current can be generated in a coil as long as:

★ it is part of a complete circuit

★ the magnetic field around the coil is changing.

This means that an induced current can be obtained in a **secondary coil** if an alternating current passes through a nearby **primary coil** (Figure 13).

As the alternating current goes forwards and backwards, forwards and backwards, etc. in the primary coil, the magnetic field is always changing. Therefore, the magnetic field around the secondary coil is always changing. This generates an alternating current in the secondary coil. This is the basis on which **transformers** work.

A transformer consists of two coils of wire wound around an iron core. Sometimes, the primary and secondary coils are wound side by side as in Figure 13. In other transformers, one coil may be wound on top of the other.

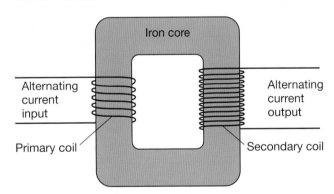

Figure 13 A transformer

The primary coil is connected to an alternating current or voltage. An alternating current (voltage) is then induced in the secondary. The induced voltage in the secondary coil depends on the number of turns in the two coils.

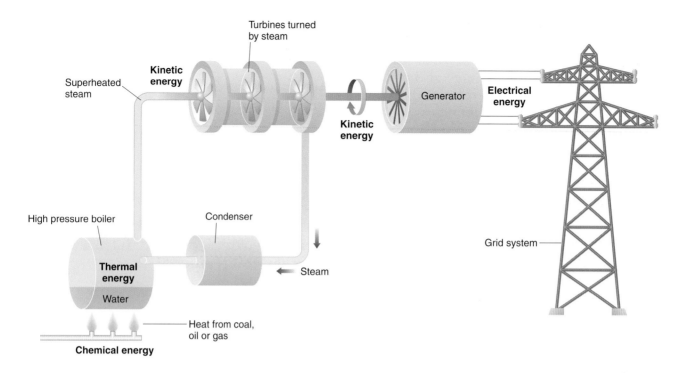

Figure 14 Energy transfers during the generation of electricity

Step-up transformers raise the voltage in the secondary. They have more turns in the secondary coil than in the primary coil.

Step-down transformers lower the voltage in the secondary. They have fewer turns in the secondary coil than in the primary coil.

Transformers can change the voltage, but they cannot give out more energy than is put in. So, if a transformer raises the voltage, it lowers the current.

Transformers play an important part in transmitting electricity via the National Grid.

The electricity is first generated in power stations using coal, oil or natural gas as the energy source. Some power stations in Scotland and Wales use the energy from falling water to drive the turbines. Electricity generated in this way is called **hydroelectricity**.

Figure 14 shows the important energy transfers during the generation of electricity in a power station.

The main transfers of useful energy in the power station are shown in Figure 15.

At power stations, transformers are used to produce very high voltages. The electricity is then transmitted to where it is needed through power lines as part of the National Grid.

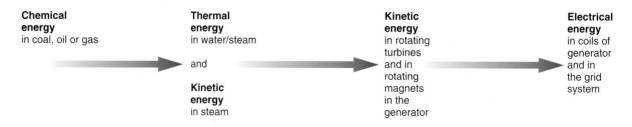

Chemical energy in coal, oil or gas → **Thermal energy** in water/steam and **Kinetic energy** in steam → **Kinetic energy** in rotating turbines and in rotating magnets in the generator → **Electrical energy** in coils of generator and in the grid system

Figure 15

Large power stations generate electricity at 25 000 volts. This is stepped-up to 275 000 or 400 000 volts before being transmitted through the Grid.

If the voltage is stepped-up from 25 000 to 400 000 volts for the grid system, then the current will be reduced by the same proportion. This is a big advantage because a smaller current has a smaller heating effect in the cables. Less energy is therefore wasted by heating up the power lines. The smaller currents also allow the use of thinner cables and the pylons can be spaced further apart. Transmission at such high voltages requires greater insulation.

The very high grid voltages must be reduced for use in our homes and work places. This is done by step-down transformers at sub-stations.

12 Name the **three** main parts of a transformer.

13 What is the job of the transformer?

14 Why is electrical energy transmitted at high voltage?

15 What does a step-up transformer do to:

   a) the voltage

   b) the current?

Summary

1 Magnetic poles and magnetic fields

   ★ The ends or parts of a magnet where the magnetic effects are the strongest are called **poles**.

   ★ Magnets will only attract metals and alloys of iron, cobalt or nickel.

   ★ The pole of a magnet which points north is the **north pole**. The pole which points south is the **south pole**.

   ★ **Like** poles **repel**.

   ★ **Unlike** poles **attract**.

   ★ The space around a magnet, where its magnetic force acts, is called a **magnetic field**.

   ★ A magnetic field can be shown as a series of field lines. These **lines of magnetic force** point away from the north pole and towards a south pole.

2 Electromagnets

   An **electromagnet** can be made by passing an electric current through a coil of wire.

   An electromagnet will be stronger if:

   ★ the current in the coil is larger

   ★ there are more turns in the coil

   ★ a soft iron rod (core) is put inside the coil.

   A **relay** is an electromagnetic switch. A small current in one circuit is used to switch on a larger current in another circuit.

3 Motors and generators

   In a motor:

   electricity + magnetism → movement
   (the motor effect)

   electrical energy → kinetic energy

   In a generator (dynamo):

   movement + magnetism → electricity
   kinetic energy → electrical energy

   Electric currents generated in this way are called **induced currents**. The effect is known as **electromagnetic induction**.

   The size of the induced current is greater if:

   ★ the magnet or the coil moves faster

   ★ the magnet is stronger

   ★ the coil has more turns.

   An alternating current is generated if a coil rotates in a magnetic field or if a magnet rotates inside a coil.

Summary

4 Transformers and the National Grid

★ A **transformer** consists of two coils of wire wound on an iron core.

★ An induced current is obtained in the **secondary coil** if an **alternating current** passes through the nearby **primary coil**.

★ **Step-up transformers** raise the voltage in the secondary coil but lower the current.

★ **Step-down transformers** lower the voltage in the secondary coil, but increase the current.

★ Step-up transformers are used to raise the voltage generated in power stations to either 275 000 or 400 000 volts for the National Grid.

★ Step-down transformers later reduce the voltage to 240 volts for use in our homes and work places.

Exam questions for Chapter 29

1 a) The diagram below shows the magnetic field between two magnets.

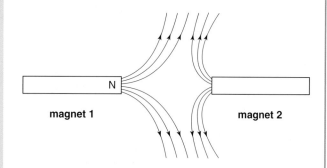

magnet 1   magnet 2

(i) Copy the diagram and label the other poles of the magnets. *(2)*

(ii) Which is the weaker magnet? *(1)*

b) A child has accidentally swallowed some small metal objects. These objects have stuck in the child's throat. A doctor uses the tool in the diagram below to remove them.

(i) What happens to the fixed iron tip when the permanent magnet is moved towards it? *(1)*

(ii) Why is it an advantage to make the tip out of iron? *(2)*

(iii) The tool is pushed down the child's throat and guided to the metal object. Explain why the sheath needs to be flexible. *(1)*

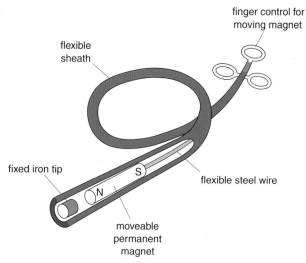

finger control for moving magnet

flexible sheath

fixed iron tip

moveable permanent magnet

flexible steel wire

(iv) The doctor tries to use the tool to remove a steel paper clip and an aluminium washer from the child's throat.

Which object can the doctor remove? Explain your answer. *(2)*

[Edexcel 1998]

2 The diagram below shows a door lock which can be opened from a flat inside a building.]

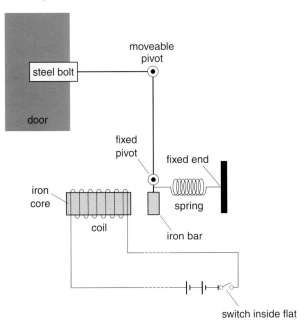

a) Explain how the door is unlocked when the switch is closed. *(4)*

b) State **two** changes which would increase the strength of the electromagnet. *(2)*

c) Why is the spring needed in the lock? *(1)*

d) The connections to the coil were accidentally reversed. Would the lock still work? Explain your answer. *(2)*

[AQA (NEAB) 1998]

3 a) Two bar magnets are held close together.

When released the magnets *push away from* each other.

(i) Copy the magnets and use the letter **N** to label the north pole of each magnet. *(1)*

(ii) Write down **one** word which describes what happens to the magnets as they are released. *(1)*

b) The diagram shows an electromagnet. Copy the diagram and draw on your copy the shape of the magnetic field of the electromagnet. *(1)*

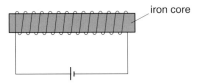

c) The diagram shows five electromagnets, **L**, **M**, **N**, **O** and **P**. Each electromagnet is able to pick up a different number of paper clips.

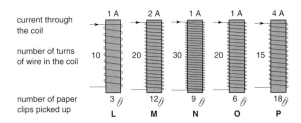

(i) Which **three** electromagnets should you compare if you want to find out how the strength of an electromagnet depends upon the number of turns of wire in the coil? *(1)*

(ii) What is the connection between the strength of an electromagnet and the number of turns of wire in the coil *(1)*

[AQA (SEG) 1999]

4 This question is about magnetism.

Michelle is investigating the strengths of two different electromagnets.

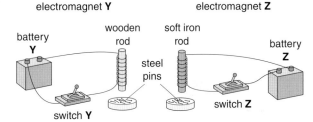

Battery **Y** is the same type as battery **Z**.

When switch **Y** is closed, nothing happens.

When switch **Z** is closed, several pins jump up onto the end of the soft iron rod.

a) How does this show that electromagnet **Z** is stronger than electromagnet **Y**? *(1)*

b) Suggest **two** ways of making electromagnet **Z** even stronger. *(2)*

c) Michelle opened switch **Z**.

She wrote this down.

When I opened the switch
– all the pins fell off
– some of the pins stayed stuck
together

Use your knowledge of magnetism to explain her **two** observations. *(3)* **[OCR (MEG) 1998]**

30

The properties of waves

30.1 Reflecting sound – echoes

If you speak in an empty room, your voice makes a 'ringing' sound. If there are no curtains or furniture in the room, sounds are reflected from the walls. The reflected sound waves cause **echoes**.

We can use echoes to measure the speed of sound in air (Figure 1). You could do this experiment with a partner. Stand 50 to 100 metres from a large building with flat walls. Now, clap your hands and listen for the echo. Try to clap your hands continuously so that each clap occurs with the echo from the previous clap. If you can do this, the sound has travelled to the building and back in the time between one clap and the next. While you are clapping, your partner should find the time for twenty of your claps. Finally, measure your distance from the wall.

Example

Jack stood 60 metres from a tall building and started to clap. His claps coincided with the echoes. Melanie timed 20 of his claps. Twenty of Jack's claps took 7 seconds. What is the speed of sound?

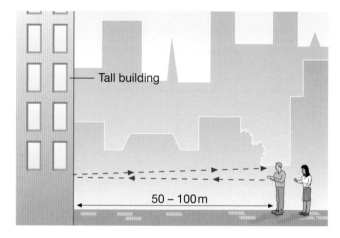

Tall building

50 – 100 m

Figure 1 Measuring the speed of sound in air

Solution

The sound travels to the wall and back between one clap and the next.

Distance travelled by sound to the wall and back = 2 × 60 m = 120 m

Time between one clap and the next

$$= \frac{7\text{ s}}{20} = 0.35\text{ s}$$

∴ speed of sound = $\dfrac{\text{distance travelled}}{\text{time taken}}$

$$= \frac{120\text{m}}{0.35\text{s}} = 343 \text{ m/s}$$

30.2 Echoes and ultrasounds

Echoes can sometimes spoil listening to music. They can make the sounds unclear because each sound is mixed with echoes of sounds made a fraction of a second earlier. Curtains and soft fabrics on the seats help to control echoes in halls and theatres.

Echoes have some very important uses.

★ Echoes are used to measure the depth of the sea bed, to locate ship wrecks and to detect shoals of fish (Figure 2).

★ Geologists and mining engineers use echoes to study the structure of the Earth and to search for minerals including oil.

★ Doctors use echoes to examine unborn babies. The pregnant woman has an ultrasound scan. These scans use sound waves which are much safer than X-rays.

These uses involve short bursts of sound waves caused by rapid vibrations. The vibrations are so rapid that we can't hear them.

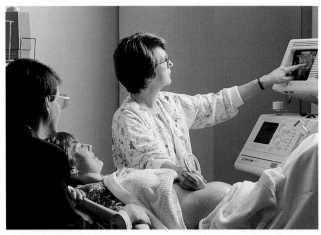

Most pregnant women have ultrasound scans. The scan (picture) shows the size and development of the baby. The doctor moves a small ultrasound transmitter over the mother's body. The ultrasound waves are reflected by the unborn baby. The reflected sounds are analysed by a computer to give an image of the baby.

The name **ultrasound** is used to describe these waves with high frequencies that we cannot hear.

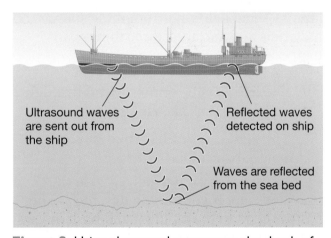

Figure 2 Using ultrasound to measure the depth of the sea. The deeper the sea, the longer it takes the echo to return to the ship.

Echoes cause problems in theatres and rooms where music is played. When sounds are mixed with echoes, the music gets distorted. Sound quality in this music studio has been improved by fixing large baffles to the wall. These absorb the sounds or reflect them in different directions. This reduces the echoes.

Measuring the depth of the sea

Sound waves travel in water at 1480 m/s.

A short burst of sound from a fishing boat takes 0.3 s to hit the sea bed and return. How deep is the sea?

Solution

Using the equation:

speed = $\dfrac{\text{distance travelled}}{\text{time taken}}$

$1480 = \dfrac{\text{distance travelled}}{0.3 \text{ m/s}}$

∴ distance travelled = $1480 \times 0.3 = 444$ m

So, the sound wave travels 444 m to the sea bed and back.

∴ the depth of the sea = 222 m

1 What is an echo?

2 Give **three** important uses of echoes.

3 What is *ultrasound*?

30.3 Reflecting light

Light comes from various sources. These include the Sun, other stars, flames and lamps. When light rays from these sources hit materials and surfaces, three things can happen.

1 The light can be **transmitted** through some materials like air and glass.

2 The light can be **absorbed** by some materials with black surfaces.

3 The light can be **reflected**.

Notice that the properties of sound and light are very similar. Both sound and light can be transmitted, absorbed and reflected by different materials and surfaces.

We see objects because they reflect some of the light. The light falls on them and the reflected light enters our eyes.

Surfaces which are not perfectly smooth, reflect light in all directions. The surface of this page may appear very smooth. Under the microscope it will look rough and bumpy.

Figure 3 shows how a rough surface reflects the light in different directions. Shiny, smooth surfaces reflect almost all the light in the same direction. They produce clear images and are used for **mirrors**.

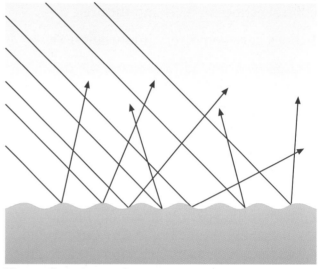

Figure 3 Light is reflected at all angles by a rough surface

30.4 Images in mirrors

Most mirrors are made by coating the back of a sheet of glass with a thin layer of aluminium. Other mirrors are just smooth, shiny pieces of metal. Figure 4 shows how you can see an image in a mirror or in a shiny surface. Rays from the ball travel in straight lines to the mirror where they are reflected.

To your eye, the rays *appear to come* from the image behind the mirror. This sort of image is called a **virtual image**. Your brain thinks the ball is behind the mirror, but really there is nothing there. On the other hand, the images made on screens by projectors and the images on a camera film are **real images**. Virtual images cannot be projected onto a screen or recorded on photographic film.

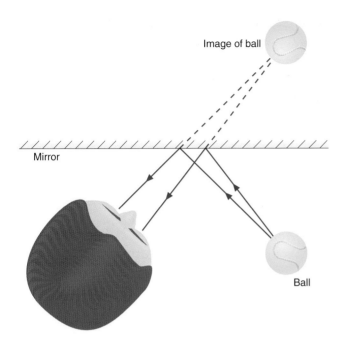

Figure 4 Looking at an image in a mirror

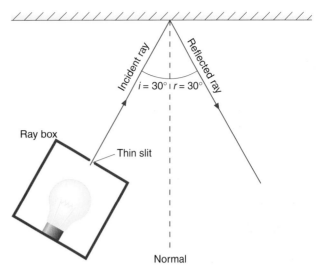

Figure 5 Investigating the reflection of light

Look at yourself in a mirror. Notice that your image in the mirror is the same size as you are. Notice also that your image is as far behind the mirror as you (the object) are in front. But, when you look at yourself in a mirror, the image you see is not exactly like you. If you move your right arm, then your image moves its left arm. This effect is called **lateral inversion** (sideways inversion). Sometimes, the letters on the front of an ambulance are laterally inverted and written as:

ƎƆИA⅃UᗺMA

This allows drivers in front of the ambulance to look in their rear-view mirror and see the word 'AMBULANCE'. If you want to see how lateral inversion works, turn this page over and hold it up to the light. Look at the writing from the back.

Reflection in mirrors

Figure 5 shows an experiment to investigate the reflection of light by mirrors. The ray box produces a thin beam of light.

Before the ray hits the mirror, it is called an **incident ray**. After reflection, the ray is called a **reflected ray**. The line at right angles to the mirror where the incident ray hits the mirror is called the **normal**.

The angle between the incident ray and the normal is called the **angle of incidence**, *i*.

The angle between the reflected ray and the normal is called the **angle of reflection**, *r*.

Experiments show that the:

angle of incidence = angle of reflection
i.e. $i = r$

Notice the following important points about the reflection of light in mirrors.

★ The image is the same size as the object.

★ The image is the same distance behind the mirror as the object is in front.

★ The image is virtual.

★ The image is laterally inverted.

★ The angle of incidence equals the angle of reflection.

4 Copy this diagram.

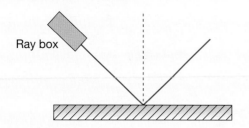

Ray box

a) Draw an arrow to show in which direction the light is travelling from the ray box.

b) Label the reflected ray.

c) Label the angle of incidence with the letter *i*.

d) Label the angle of reflection *r*.

e) Label the normal.

5 The reflection in a mirror is said to be a virtual image. Explain what is meant by a virtual image. How does a virtual image differ from the real image?

30.5 Waves and wave motions

So far, in this chapter, we have studied the reflection of sound and light. Both sound and light travel as waves. Other kinds of waves also play an important part in our lives.

★ Microwaves provide energy for quick cooking.

★ Radiowaves enable us to transmit information and messages.

★ X-rays and gamma rays have important medical uses.

★ Waves on the sea may be harnessed to provide energy.

These examples show that waves transfer energy without transferring matter. Waves can transfer energy from one place to another without moving material between the two places.

Probably the best example of this is the transfer of energy as heat and light from the Sun to the Earth.

Making sounds

Sounds are made when you speak, when you beat a drum or play a recorder.

All sounds are made by **vibrating materials**.

The vibrating material might be the vocal chords in your throat, a drum-skin or the air in a recorder.

It is possible to see the vibrations of a loudspeaker. Figure 6 shows how sound waves are produced when a loudspeaker cone vibrates.

As the cone of the loudspeaker vibrates, it causes the air to move forwards and backwards in the direction of the sound. As the cone moves to the right, it squashes the air and increases the pressure slightly. When the cone moves to the left, more space is created and the pressure falls. As the cone vibrates, the pressure rises and falls repeatedly.

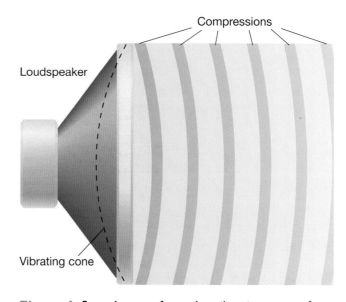

Figure 6 Sound waves from the vibrating cone of a loudspeaker

When the changes in pressure reach your ears, they make your ear drums vibrate. The movements in our ear drums send impulses along nerves to the brain and we 'hear' the sound.

When air molecules transmit sound from a source such as a loudspeaker to your ear, they do *not* move from the source to your ear. They simply vibrate forwards and backwards as the air is repeatedly squashed.

Waves like these in which vibrations go forward and back in the same direction as the wave are called **longitudinal waves**.

Waves can also be studied using a stretched spring (slinky). You can make a longitudinal wave in the slinky like sound waves in air. Fix one end of the slinky and stretch it out. Then, quickly move the other end of the slinky forwards and back. This movement *squashes* the slinky (Figure 7).

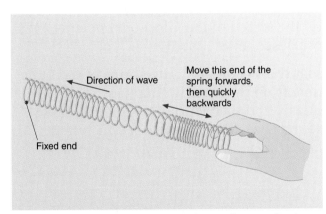

Figure 7 Using a slinky to produce a longitudinal wave

By squashing and then stretching the slinky in one forward and back movement, a longitudinal wave passes along the spring. A series of 'squashes' and 'stretches' will pass along the slinky like sound waves in air.

It is possible to make another kind of wave in a slinky by moving your hand quickly to one side and then back to its original position (Figure 8).

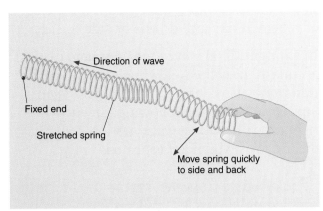

Figure 8 Using a slinky to produce a transverse wave

This time the coils of the slinky move from side to side at right angles to the direction of the wave along the slinky.

Waves like this in which the transmitting material vibrates at right angles to the direction of the wave are called **transverse waves**.

Surface water waves, light waves, microwaves and all other electromagnetic waves (section 31.2) are examples of transverse waves.

Radio and television signals are transmitted as transverse waves. These waves vibrate in only one plane, usually vertical or horizontal. This is why the aerials used to pick up radio and television signals must be carefully arranged in a particular direction.

Transverse waves from a light source, such as the Sun or an electric light, are not like radio and TV signals. They vibrate in all directions at right angles to the direction that the wave travels.

30.6 Measuring waves

Wavelength

A wave motion is a repetitive motion. In a longitudinal wave, the repetitive motion consists of repeated 'squashes' and 'stretches'.

In a transverse wave, the repetition consists of repeated ups and downs or side to sides.

In a longitudinal wave, one complete cycle is a 'squash' plus the following 'stretch'. In a transverse wave, one complete cycle is an 'up' (peak) plus the following 'down' (trough). The whole wave motion occurs as these cycles which are repeated.

> The distance from the start to the finish of one complete cycle is called the **wavelength**.

Look at Figure 9.

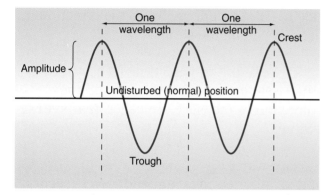

Figure 9 Wave measurements

The wavelengths of sounds range from a few centimetres to a few metres, whereas the wavelength of light is about 5×10^{-7} m (i.e. half of one millionth of a metre).

Amplitude

> The greatest displacement of the vibrating material from its undisturbed (normal) position is known as the **amplitude** of the wave.

In transverse waves, this is the height of the crest from the undisturbed position (Figure 9).

As the amount of energy carried by a wave increases, its amplitude also increases. So, big ocean waves carry more energy and therefore can do more damage than smaller waves.

Loudness and amplitude

Using a microphone connected to an oscilloscope, it is possible to 'look at' sound waves. The sounds reaching the microphone make its cone vibrate. These vibrations are turned into electrical signals by the microphone and they appear as a waveform on the screen of the CRO (cathode ray oscilloscope).

Figure 10 shows the waveforms of the same note from the same tuning fork produced quietly and then loudly. Notice that the two sounds have the *same wavelength*, but the louder sound has the *greater amplitude*.

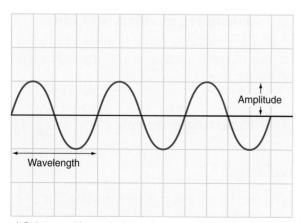

a) Quiet sound from a tuning fork

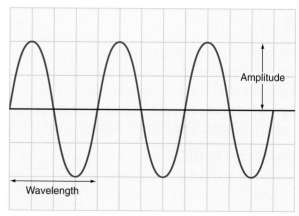

b) Loud sound from same tuning fork

Figure 10 Waveforms of the same note on a CRO, a) quiet and b) loud.

Frequency and pitch

You may be able to watch water waves moving across a pond. Try to estimate the number of wave crests passing a point in 10 seconds. Suppose you counted 20 wave crests in 10 seconds. This means that two waves pass the point each second. We say that the frequency of the waves is two per second or 2 **hertz**.

> **Frequency** is the number of waves which pass a point in one second.

Sometimes the word **pitch** is used to describe how a note or a noise sounds. The pitch of a note is related to the frequency of the sound.

High pitched notes, like treble notes, have a high frequency. Low pitched notes, like bass notes, have a low frequency.

6 How are **all** sounds made?

7 Light and sound are examples of waves. Name **four** other examples.

8 a) What is a longitudinal wave?

   b) What is a transverse wave?

   c) Give an example of each type of wave.

9 Draw a transverse wave and on it mark:

   a) the wavelength

   b) the amplitude of the wave.

30.7 Refracting light

When a wave passes from one material into another, its speed changes. This can change the direction of the wave if it hits the new material at an angle. This change in direction is called **refraction**.

Figure 11 shows an experiment to study the refraction of light rays as they travel from air into glass.

The results of the experiment show that:

★ A ray parallel to the normal goes straight through the glass.

★ A ray travelling into a denser material (i.e. from air into glass or water) is refracted (bent) towards the normal.

★ A ray travelling into a less dense material (i.e. from glass or water into air) is refracted (bent) away from the normal.

★ A small fraction of the light is reflected at the boundary of the two materials.

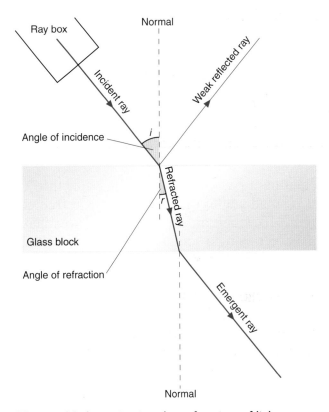

Figure 11 Investigating the refraction of light

Refraction can play tricks on us. This happens when we look at things in water. Light rays from an object in water are bent away from the normal as they pass from water into air. This makes a pool appear shallower than it really is. Objects on the bottom of the pool and fish in the pool seem to be nearer the surface (Figure 12). These objects and the fish are not really where they seem to be. What we see are virtual images caused by the refraction of light.

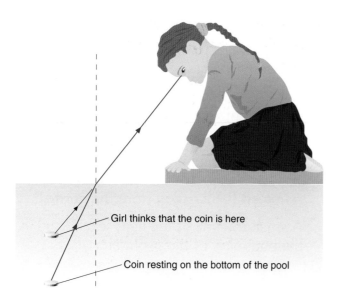

Girl thinks that the coin is here

Coin resting on the bottom of the pool

Figure 12 Rays of light from the coin are refracted at the water surface. This makes the girl think that the coin is nearer the surface.

30.8 | Total internal reflection

When light passes from glass or water into air at small angles of incidence, it is refracted. Figure 13 shows an experiment to investigate this effect using a semicircular block of glass or perspex. Notice that the incident ray, through the curved face, is aimed at the centre of the flat face of the semicircular block. This means it will hit the block at 90° and pass into the block without changing direction.

The results of this experiment show:

★ For small angles of incidence, the light is refracted (Figure 13a).

★ As the angle of incidence increases, the angle of refraction also increases.

★ When the angle of incidence reaches 42° for both glass and perspex (49° for water), the refracted ray travels along the surface of the denser material (Figure 13b). The angle of refraction is now 90°. For this position, the angle of incidence is called the **critical angle, c**.

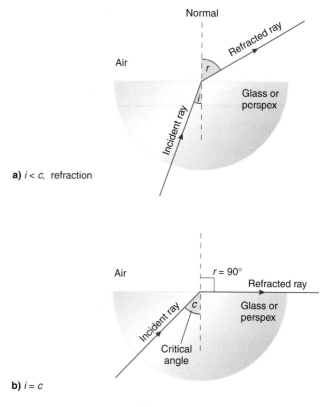

a) $i < c$, refraction

b) $i = c$

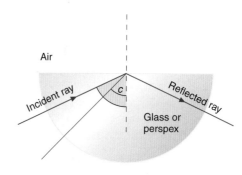

c) $i > c$, total internal reflection

Figure 13 Investigating refraction and total internal reflection.

So, the critical angle for glass/air = 42° and the critical angle for water/air = 49°.

★ When the angle of incidence is greater than the critical angle ($i > c$), there is *no* refracted ray. The light is now reflected internally (Figure 13c). This is known as **total internal reflection**.

Using total internal reflection

Total internal reflection is important in bicycle reflectors, periscopes, binoculars and cameras. In these instruments, 45° — 45° — 90° prisms are used to change the direction of light rays (Figure 14).

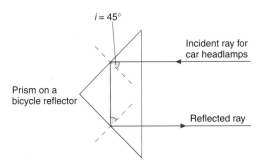

a) Bicycle reflectors have dozens of prisms like the one above as a single moulding. (Two internal reflections occur as *i* > *c* for glass/air)

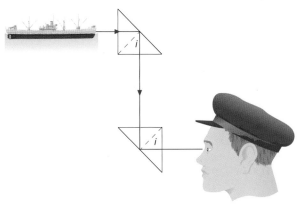

b) Ships periscopes use two prisms as above. (Two internal reflections occur as *i* > *c* for glass/air)

Figure 14 Prisms which allow total internal reflection are used in bicycle reflectors and periscopes.

These spectators are using periscopes to watch a golfer.

Total internal reflection also allows glass or plastic fibres (**optical fibres**) to carry rays of light (Figure 15). The fibres consist of two parts. There is an inner core through which the light travels and a less dense outer covering which protects the inner fibre.

Whenever the light hits the boundary between the inner fibre and the less dense covering, the angle of incidence is greater than the critical angle. So, all the light is reflected internally. This use of optical fibres is sometimes called **fibre optics**.

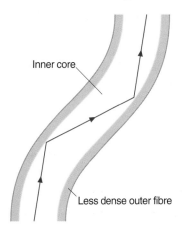

Figure 15 Total internal reflection allows light to pass along optical fibres.

Optical fibres are used by doctors to see inside our bodies without the need to operate. The instruments they use are called **endoscopes**. An endoscope consists of two bundles of optical fibres. One bundle carries light into the patient's body while the other allows the doctor to see what is there. For example, it is possible to see inside a patient's stomach using an endoscope passed down the oesophagus.

Sound and electrical messages can also be converted into radiations like light and then transmitted along optical fibres. Many long-distance telephone links now use glass fibres rather than copper cables or microwave transmission.

10 Name **three** devices which use total internally reflecting prisms.

11 How does light travel down an optical fibre?

12 Name **two** uses of optical fibres.

13 Draw a diagram to show how light undergoes total internal reflection through a semicircular glass block. The critical angle for glass to air is 42°. Draw and mark the critical angle on your diagram.

Summary

1 Light and sound are wave motions.

Light consists of vibrating electromagnetic waves.

Sound is produced when materials vibrate.

When light rays and sound waves hit materials and surfaces, three things can happen.

★ The light and sound can be **transmitted** (e.g. light and sound through air).

★ The light and sound can be **absorbed** (e.g. light by black surfaces, sound by soft furnishings in a room).

★ The light and sound can be **reflected** (e.g. light by mirrors, sound by large, flat surfaces causing echoes).

2 Sound waves are **longitudinal waves** – the material vibrates to and fro in the same direction as the wave.

Ultrasounds are sound waves with very high frequencies of vibration. Humans cannot hear ultrasounds.

Light waves and other electromagnetic waves are **transverse waves**. The electromagnetic vibrations are at right angles to the direction of the wave.

3 Images in mirrors are:

★ the same size as the object

★ the same distance behind the mirror as the object is in front

★ **virtual** (light does not really go to them)

★ **laterally inverted**.

4 Measuring waves

★ **Wavelength** is the distance from start to finish of one complete wave.

★ **Amplitude** is the maximum displacement of the vibrating material from its undisturbed (normal) position.

As amplitude increases, the energy carried by the wave increases. For example, think of bigger waves at sea and louder sounds.

★ **Frequency** is the number of wave cycles per second.

High pitched notes have a greater frequency than low pitched notes.

5 **Total internal reflection**

When light passes from a denser to a less dense material (e.g. from water or glass into air), the angle of refraction is greater than the angle of incidence (see Figure 13).

When the angle of incidence reaches 42° for glass into air or 49° for water to air, the refracted ray travels along the surface of the denser material. The angle of refraction is 90°. When this position is reached, the angle of incidence is called the **critical angle**.

When the angle of incidence is greater than the critical angle, there is no refracted ray. All the light is reflected internally. This is called **total internal reflection**. It has important uses in bicycle reflectors, periscopes and optical fibres.

1 a) The following diagram shows three rays of light incident on an irregular surface.

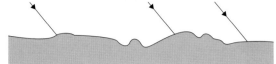

Draw on a copy of the diagram the three reflected rays. *(1)*

b) A car used to tow a caravan may have a periscope fitted. The periscope allows the car driver to see behind the caravan. A simple periscope can be made using two mirrors.

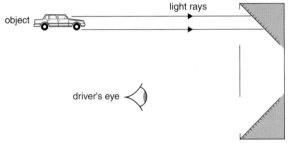

(i) Copy the diagram and complete it to show how the light rays from the object reach the driver's eye. *(2)*

(ii) Give **one** difference between the image produced by this periscope and the object. *(1)*

c) Light can be reflected off mirrors set up on the Moon. Travelling at 300 000 km/s it takes the light 2.6 s to go to the Moon and back.

(i) Write down the equation which links distance, speed and time. *(1)*

(ii) Calculate the distance from the Earth to the Moon. Show clearly how you work out your answer. *(2)*

(iii) This method of measuring the distance to the Moon relies upon three properties of light. One of these properties is that light can be reflected. What are the other **two** properties? *(2)*

d) The diagram shows the essential parts of a solar heater used to heat water.

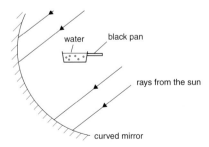

(i) Copy the diagram and draw on the reflected rays. *(1)*

(ii) Written in the box are the names of three types of ray from the Sun.

Which sort of ray heats the water in the pan? *(1)*

(iii) The solar heater is more efficient when a black pan is used to hold the water rather than a white pan. Explain why. *(2)*

[AQA (SEG) 1999]

2 a) The diagram shows a guitar.

louder vibrate amplitude
pitch frequency quieter

Use words from the list above to complete a copy of the following sentences about the guitar strings.

A guitar string must be plucked in order to make it _____ when a note is played.

If the string is plucked so that the amplitude is greater then a _____ note is heard. *(2)*

b) The diagrams show four waves **A**, **B**, **C** and **D**. They are all drawn to the same scale.

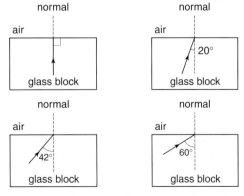

(i) Which wave has the lowest frequency?

(ii) Which wave has the lowest amplitude? *(2)* **[AQA (NEAB) 1998]**

3 The diagrams show light rays travelling from glass towards air.

Redraw the diagrams. Complete **each** of your diagrams to show the path of each light ray. **The critical angle for glass is 42°.** *(4)*

[WJEC 1998]

31

Using waves

31.1 Separating the colours in light

Light from the Sun is a mixture of different colours. These colours can be seen in a rainbow. When light from the Sun passes through a raincloud in the sky, different colours of light are refracted (bent) by different amounts. This produces a rainbow.

The continuous band of colours is called a **spectrum**.

Figure 1 shows how you can produce this spectrum of colours. Shine a thin ray of light from the Sun or from a ray box towards one side of a glass prism.

Notice two things from Figure 1.

★ The spectrum is made up from several different colours.

★ Violet light is refracted the most and red light is refracted the least. These differences in refraction result from different wavelengths and frequencies of the different colours of light.

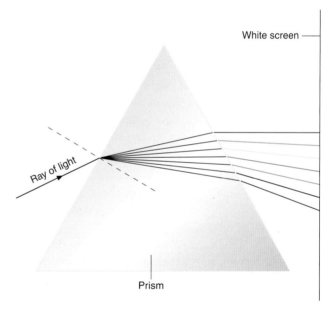

White screen

Ray of light

Prism

Figure 1 Separating white light into a spectrum

The colours in the spectrum are **R**ed, **O**range, **Y**ellow, **G**reen, **B**lue, **I**ndigo and **V**iolet.
Say 'Roy G. Biv' to help you to remember the order of the colours.
This separation of light into its different colours is called **dispersion**.

1 Copy and complete these sentences. These words may help you.

white red prism violet green spectacle dispersion spectrum

When a ray of light shines onto a _____ , the light is split up into colours called a _____ . The _____ colour is refracted most and the _____ colour the least. All the colours come from the _____ light. This separation of light into colours is called _____ .

2 Write down the colours of the rainbow in order. Start with red.

31.2 The electromagnetic spectrum

In the last section, we saw that visible light can be split into a spectrum. For convenience, we say there are seven different colours. If you look closely, you can see many colours. They change continuously from red to violet. These colours occur in a particular order according to their wavelengths and frequencies. Visible light is only a very small part of a much larger spectrum of waves called the **electromagnetic spectrum**.

The electromagnetic spectrum consists of radiowaves, microwaves, infra-red waves, visible light, ultraviolet rays, X-rays and gamma rays.

The whole electromagnetic spectrum covers a vast range of wavelengths and frequencies (Figure 2). Gamma rays have the shortest wavelengths – about a millionth of a metre (10^{-12} m). Radiowaves, at the other extreme, have wavelengths up to about 10 kilometres (10^4 m).

Figure 2 shows the position of the different types of wave in the electromagnetic spectrum. It also shows their approximate wavelengths and frequencies.

In spite of the vast differences in wavelength and frequency, all electromagnetic waves have some important properties in common.

★ They are produced when atoms or electrons lose energy.

★ They can all be reflected and refracted.

★ They are all transverse waves.

★ They transfer energy as vibrating electric and magnetic fields.

★ They can travel through a vacuum.

★ They all travel in a vacuum at a speed of 300 000 000 m/s (3×10^8 m/s). Their speed in air is almost the same as this.

Notice in Figure 2 that visible light is only a small part of the electromagnetic spectrum. The spectrum of visible light is shown in more detail in Figure 3. This shows that red light has a longer wavelength but a lower frequency than blue light. Red light is similar to infra-red light, whereas blue light is similar to ultraviolet.

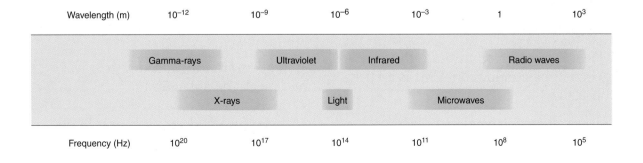

Figure 2 The electromagnetic spectrum

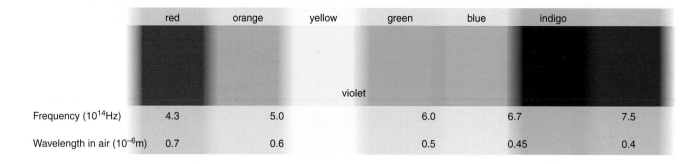

	red	orange	yellow	green	blue	indigo	
Frequency (10^{14}Hz)	4.3	5.0		6.0	6.7		7.5
Wavelength in air (10^{-6}m)	0.7	0.6		0.5	0.45		0.4

violet

Figure 3 The spectrum of visible light

31.3 Using microwaves, infra-red and ultraviolet waves in the home

Microwave cooking

In the electromagnetic spectrum, microwaves come between infra-red rays and radiowaves. They are useful for cooking because they are:

★ absorbed by water, so they heat up most foods

★ reflected by metals

★ transmitted by glass, china, paper, cardboard and plastic.

Figure 4 shows a diagram of a microwave oven. Microwaves enter from the top of the cooker which has metal sides to reflect them and keep them inside. A rotating metal paddle or a metal turntable ensures that microwaves hit the food from all directions and cook it all over. The glass door of the oven also contains a metal grid to reflect the microwaves. This stops microwaves getting through the glass which could be harmful.

When food is heated in an ordinary oven, the oven itself is heated and heat is lost from the oven. Heat is transferred through the food being cooked by conduction. This is a fairly slow process.

In microwave ovens, the microwaves are reflected inside the oven. They do not heat up the oven itself. Microwaves also heat up the food faster by penetrating below the surface and then being absorbed.

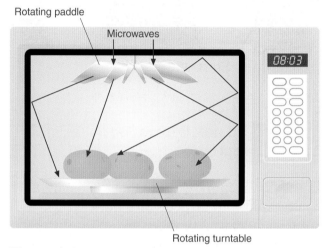

Figure 4 A microwave oven

Using a microwave oven, cooking times can be reduced to about a quarter.

Infra-red radiation for cooking and detection

Infra-red waves come between visible light and microwaves in the electromagnetic spectrum. Infra-red radiation is absorbed by all materials. We use it in our homes for cooking, for radiant heating and for remote control of televisions, videos and other hi-fi equipment.

All objects emit infra-red rays – the hotter the object, the stronger the infra-red rays. Infra-red detectors are used to track rockets, to observe animals at night and by the rescue services to find people under snow or collapsed buildings.

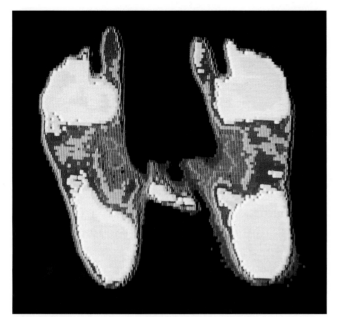

This infra-red photograph shows the soles of someone's feet. The colours vary from white (hottest) through yellow, to red and blue (coldest).

Sunbathing is very pleasant but it's best not to lie in the Sun in the middle of the day or for very long.

Ultraviolet radiation – sunbathing and energy-efficient lamps

Ultraviolet (UV) radiation is emitted by the Sun and by other white-hot objects. It passes through air and other gases, but not through solids or liquids.

UV rays increase the formation of melanin in our skin. This is the brown pigment that gives us a suntan. But UV rays can damage cells and cause skin cancer. There is a lower risk of cancer for people with dark skins. If the skin is darker, more UV radiation is absorbed by the epidermis and there is less damage to deeper tissues. Even so, everyone should be careful when out in the Sun. It's a good idea to wear a hat and use suntan cream. The use of sunbeds can be dangerous.

Ultraviolet radiation is also produced in fluorescent lights. When electricity passes through a fluorescent tube, reactions occur and ultraviolet radiation is emitted. This UV radiation is absorbed by the coating on the inside of the glass tube. The coating fluoresces and gives out the radiation as light.

Fluorescent lamps are more efficient than ordinary lights. They rely on UV radiation being given out rather than heating a metal coil to white heat. Therefore, less heat energy is lost when the lamps are used.

Energy-efficient lamps like this one are more efficient than ordinary lamps. They do not rely on heating a metal coil to white heat.

3 Which part(s) of the electromagnetic spectrum can be used for cooking?

4 Why does the door of a microwave have a metal grid?

5 How is heat transferred through the food

   a) in an ordinary oven

   b) in a microwave oven?

6 Name **two** uses of infra-red rays.

7 What effect do ultraviolet rays have on our skin?

   b) How can we protect ourselves from UV rays?

   c) What can happen to us if we absorb too many UV rays?

31.4 Using waves in communications

From section 30.8 you will know that information and messages can be transmitted using electromagnetic radiation. Electromagnetic radiation as radiowaves, microwaves, infra-red rays and visible light is very important for communication. More and more telephone links are using narrow beams of microwaves. Radiowaves and microwaves are also important in radio and television broadcasts. These waves have wavelengths between 1 metre and 1 kilometre. Remember that radiowaves are electromagnetic transverse waves. They are not the same as sound waves which are longitudinal and *not* electromagnetic.

The way in which radiowaves and microwaves travel depends on their wavelength.

★ Long wavelength radiowaves (with wavelengths greater than 10 m) are transmitted around the Earth by reflections from the upper atmosphere. Radio stations which use these radiowaves can therefore broadcast from one transmitter to the whole of the UK.

★ More information can be transmitted by shorter waves with higher frequencies. Stereo radio and TV channels therefore broadcast using shorter radiowaves and microwaves with a wavelength of about 1 m. But these waves are not reflected by the upper atmosphere. So, their range is limited by the Earth's curvature. National broadcasts at this wavelength are transmitted from the British Telecom Tower in London.

Stereo radio and TV programmes are transmitted from the British Telecom Tower in London. They use narrow beams of radiowaves. These narrow beams are passed through a network of repeater stations around the country. At each local transmitting station, the signal is transmitted in all directions to our homes.

8 Which parts of the electromagnetic spectrum are used in communications?

9 How are long radio waves transmitted around the Earth?

10 Short wavelength microwaves are used in communications. What are:

   a) the disadvantages,

   b) the advantages?

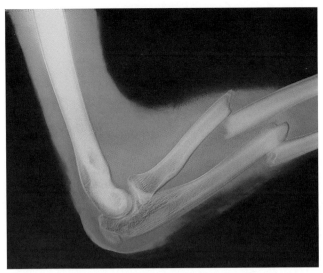

Figure 6 An X-ray photograph showing fractures to the radius and ulna bones of the lower arm.

<table>
</table>

31.5 Using X-rays and gamma rays in medicine

X-rays and gamma rays have very short wavelengths – less than 10^{-8} m. They can penetrate (travel through) most materials. X-rays and gamma rays pass easily through materials like carbon which have a small relative atomic mass. They do not travel so easily through lead and other materials with a high relative atomic mass.

X-rays are produced by aiming fast-moving electrons at a metal target. Gamma rays are emitted by unstable radioactive materials.

X-ray photography

X-rays are used to check for broken bones. X-rays are absorbed by all body tissues. But bones and teeth which contain calcium (Ca = 40) and phosphorus (P = 31) absorb more than flesh which contains mainly carbon (C = 12), hydrogen (H = 1) and oxygen (O = 16). X-rays are passed through the body to form an image on a photographic film (Figure 5).

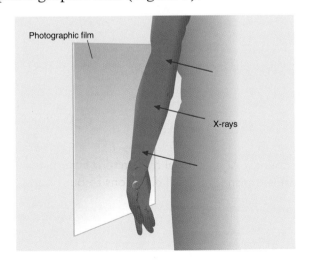

Photographic film

X-rays

Figure 5 Taking an X-ray photograph of a patient's arm

Figure 6 shows an X-ray photograph of a broken lower arm. Notice how the bone shows up yellow. It has absorbed the X-rays so that they do not darken the photographic film.

When X-rays and gamma rays are absorbed by body tissue, their energy can cause chemical reactions. These reactions can change the molecules that control the way our cells work. This can result in damage to the central nervous system, mutation of genes or even cancer.

The dangers from X-rays and gamma rays mean that exposure to radiation must be kept to a minimum. Radiographers, who use X-ray equipment, work from behind a lead screen. Lead is also used to protect the parts of a patient's body which are not being X-rayed. Lead has a very high relative atomic mass (Pb = 207). So, it absorbs X-rays and gamma rays very well.

Treatment of cancer using gamma rays

Although gamma rays can *cause* cancer, they are also used to *treat* cancer. Cancer cells can be 'knocked out' by gamma rays. This is because cancer cells are dividing much quicker than normal cells. Figure 7 (over the page) shows how a beam of gamma rays from cobalt-60 can be used to treat lung cancer. The gamma rays are directed at the cancer from several directions. This ensures that the cancer gets a much higher dose of radiation than the nearby tissues.

321

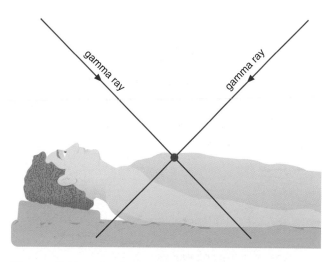

Figure 7 Treating lung cancer using gamma rays

11 Name the **two** most penetrating rays in the electromagnetic spectrum.

12 How are these two rays produced?

13 What are X-rays used for?

14 What are gamma rays used for?

15 Which material is used to protect workers who use these harmful radiations?

Summary

1 **The electromagnetic spectrum**

Gamma rays, X-rays, UV rays, visible light, infra-red rays, microwaves and radiowaves are all members of the **electromagnetic spectrum**.

Electromagnetic waves have great differences in wavelength and frequency but they:

★ are all produced when atoms or electrons lose energy

★ are all transverse waves

★ all transfer energy as vibrating electric and magnetic fields

★ can be reflected, refracted and diffracted

★ all travel in a vacuum at a speed of 300 million m/s (3×10^8 m/s)

★ have greater energy as their wavelength gets shorter

★ penetrate (travel through) materials more easily as their wavelength gets shorter.

2 The table below shows the properties and uses of different waves.

Type of wave and wavelength	Properties	Uses
Gamma rays less than 10^{-12} m	• given out by radioactive substances • the most penetrating e/m waves • can destroy cells and cause mutations	• treatment of cancer • sterilisation of medical instruments and food
X-rays 10^{-12} to 10^{-8} m	• absorbed by bones and teeth but pass through flesh • absorbed very well by lead • can damage cells	• to check for broken bones • treatment of some cancers
Ultraviolet rays 10^{-8} to 4×10^{-7} m	• emitted by the Sun and other white hot objects • pass through air • absorbed by solids • increase formation of melanin in skin • over-exposure to these rays can burn and cause skin cancer	• energy efficient lamps • UV lamps and sunbeds
Visible light 4×10^{-7} to 7.5×10^{-7} m	• light of different wavelength has a different colour e.g. a rainbow	• electric lighting • photography
Infra-red rays 7.5×10^{-7} to 10^{-4} m	• emitted by all hot and warm objects • detected by special cameras and heat sensitive equipment	• radiant heaters • red-hot grills for cooking • detection of warm objects e.g. people buried under rubble
Microwaves 10^{-4} to 1 m	• absorbed by water • reflected by metals • transmitted through glass, paper and plastic	• cooking – microwave ovens • satellite communication
Radiowaves 1 to 10^4 m	• radiowaves with wavelengths more than 10 m are transmitted around the Earth by reflection from the upper atmosphere • radiowaves with wavelengths less than 10 m pass through the upper atmosphere	• local, national and international radio, TV and telephone communications e.g. the Internet

1 This question is about the electromagnetic spectrum.

a) The diagram shows parts of the electromagnetic spectrum in order.

Some parts have been named.

radio waves	K	visible light	L	X-rays

(i) Write down the name of part **K**. *(1)*

(ii) Write down the name of part **L**. *(1)*

(iii) Look at the diagram. Which part of the spectrum has the **shortest** wavelength? *(1)*

b) Copy and complete the following sentences by choosing the **best** words from this list.

The first one has been done for you.

**infra-red   microwaves   radio waves
ultra violet   visible light**

Food can be cooked using _____ .

Thermometers can detect _microwaves_.

Holiday photographs taken with an ordinary camera use _____ .

Skin cancer can be caused by _____ . *(3)*

c) Describe **one** medical use of **gamma rays**. *(2)*

d) X-rays are used to take a photograph of a broken bone in a leg. A sheet of film is placed under the leg. The X-ray machine is turned on. An image of the broken bone is produced on the film.

(i) Explain how X-rays produce an image of

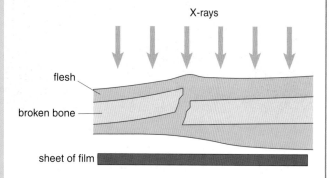

the bone on the film. *(2)*

(ii) X-rays are dangerous.

How does the X-ray machine operator protect himself from them? *(1)*

[OCR (MEG) 1999]

2 Steven has a compact disc (CD) player.

a) Name **one** useful form of energy produced from electricity by the CD player. *(1)*

b) The CD player has a remote control system

Name the type of electromagnetic wave used in this system. *(1)*

c) When Steven looks at the surface of his CD discs he sees the colours of the spectrum:

red   orange   yellow   green   blue   indigo   violet

These colours are also produced by the refraction of white light in a prism. The diagram shows the refracted rays for the two colours red and violet.

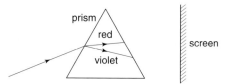

(i) Copy the diagram and draw the light rays from the prism to the screen. *(1)*

(ii) Give an example in which refraction is useful. *(1)* **[Edexcel 1998]**

3 The boxes on the left show some types of electromagnetic radiation. The boxes on the right show some uses of electromagnetic radiation.

Copy the diagram and draw a straight line from each type of radiation to its use. The first one has been done for you.

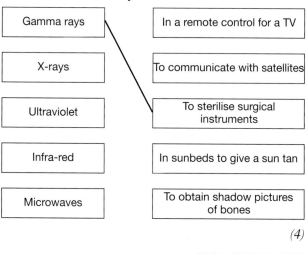

(4)

[AQA (NEAB) 1999]

32

Radioactivity

32.1 Radioactive materials

Most radioactive materials that we use today are man-made, but some are naturally-occurring. Large amounts of radioactive uranium and plutonium are used to generate electricity in power stations. Tiny amounts of these and other elements can be used to generate electricity in heart pacemakers.

Radioactive materials can be very useful but they can be harmful too. They can *cure* cancer, but they can also *cause* cancer.

The first investigations of radioactivity were carried out by a Frenchman, Henri Becquerel and his Polish assistant Marie Curie in 1896. They discovered that all uranium compounds emitted (gave out) **radiation**. The radiation could pass through paper and affect photographic film.

Becquerel called this process **radioactivity** and he described the uranium compounds as **radioactive**.

Marie Curie began her studies of radioactivity with uranium compounds. For four years, she worked on extracting a new element called radium. Radium is two million times more radioactive than uranium. In 1903, Marie Curie shared the Nobel Prize for Physics. Then, in 1911, she was awarded the Nobel Prize for Chemistry. She was the first person to win two Nobel Prizes.

32.2 Detecting radioactivity – unstable nuclei

The best way for us to detect radiation from radioactive materials is to use a Geiger–Müller tube (Figure 1). The Geiger–Müller tube can 'count' the number of radioactive particles or rays entering it per second.

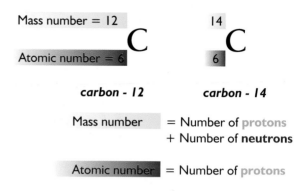

Figure 2 The isotopes of carbon

Mass number = Number of protons + Number of neutrons

Atomic number = Number of protons

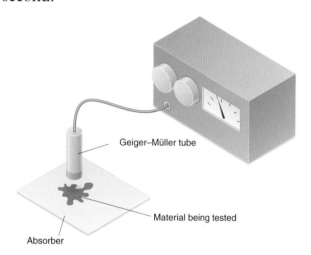

Figure 1 Detecting radioactivity with a Geiger–Müller tube

Radioactivity results from the breakdown of atoms (isotopes) with unstable nuclei. These unstable isotopes are known as **radio isotopes**.

For example, most carbon and carbon compounds are composed of the isotope $^{12}_{6}C$ (carbon-12) which is completely stable (Figure 2). But these samples also contain a very small percentage of $^{14}_{6}C$ (carbon-14) which is unstable and radioactive.

Small radioactive atoms like carbon-14 usually break down and become stable by losing an electron. When carbon-14 breaks down, it loses an electron and forms stable atoms of nitrogen-14. Remember that it is the *nuclei* of radioactive atoms which are unstable. The electrons which are lost come from the nuclei. They are usually called **beta particles (β–particles)**.

Figure 3 shows what happens when carbon-14 breaks down.

When large unstable nuclei, like uranium-235, break up, they lose **alpha particles (α–particles)**. The alpha particles contain two protons plus two neutrons. They are like the nuclei of helium-4.

1 Name **two** radioactive materials.

2 Name the instrument used to detect radioactivity.

3 What sort of atoms are radioactive?

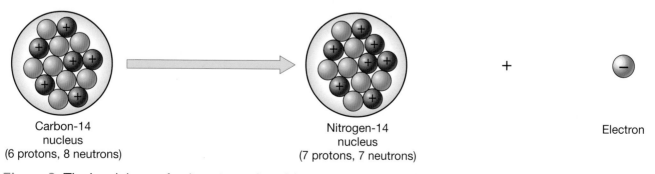

Carbon-14 nucleus
(6 protons, 8 neutrons)

Nitrogen-14 nucleus
(7 protons, 7 neutrons)

Electron

Figure 3 The breakdown of radioactive carbon-14

32.3 Alpha, beta and gamma radiation

When the nuclei of radioactive atoms break up, they emit (give out) three kinds of radiation. These radiations or emissions are called **alpha rays** (α–rays), **beta rays** (β–rays) and **gamma rays** (γ–rays).

Alpha and beta rays contain particles. So, they are usually called alpha particles and beta particles. Gamma rays are very penetrating **electromagnetic waves** (section 31.2).

The nature and properties of the three kinds of radiation are summarised in Table 1. Notice the different penetrating powers of the three different kinds of radiation.

These differences in penetrating power are shown in Figure 4. Gamma rays are much more penetrating than beta particles and beta particles are more penetrating than alpha particles. Alpha particles are absorbed by a sheet of paper or a few centimetres of air. Beta particles pass through paper but are absorbed by aluminium foil. Gamma rays can only be absorbed by thick lead. Radioactive substances which emit gamma rays are stored in thick lead containers.

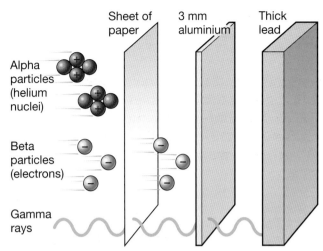

Figure 4 The relative penetrating power of alpha particles, beta particles and gamma rays

Alpha particles and beta particles have an electric charge. They are deflected by electric fields. Gamma rays are uncharged so they are unaffected by electric fields. This is shown in Figure 5.

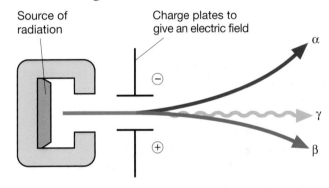

Figure 5 The effect of an electric field on alpha, beta and gamma radiations.

Radiation	Nature	Penetrating power	Effect of electric and magnetic fields	Ionising power
α particles	Helium nuclei containing 2 protons and 2 neutrons	Travel a few centimetres through air, absorbed by thin paper	Very small deflection	Strong
β particles	Electrons	Travel a few metres through air, pass through paper, but absorbed by 3 mm of aluminium foil	Large deflection	Weak
γ rays	Electromagnetic waves	Travel a few kilometres through air, pass through paper and Al foil, but absorbed by very thick lead	None	Very weak

Table 1 The nature and properties of alpha, beta and gamma radiations

Look at Table 1 again. Notice the relative ionising power of the radiations.

Ionising radiation causes materials to form ions. Alpha radiation is the most strongly ionising radiation even though it is not very penetrating. Exposure to this ionising radiation can be harmful. It damages the cells in our skin and other tissues.

4 Copy and complete this table.

Radiation	Particle	Wave	Charge	Penetrating power
Alpha				
Beta				
Gamma				

32.4 Background radiation

Background radiation is the natural radiation all around us and is usually very low.

The pie chart in Figure 6 shows the main sources of radiation in the UK.

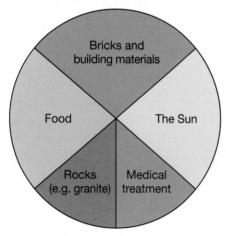

Figure 6 The main sources of radiation in the UK

Background radiation comes from:

★ some rocks in the Earth, especially granite, which contain small percentages of radioactive uranium, thorium and potassium compounds. These rocks emit radioactive radon gas.

★ our food which contains traces of radioactive materials

★ bricks and other building materials which give off some radiations and cause radioactivity in the air in our homes, schools and workplaces

★ gamma radiation from the Sun.

As background radiation comes from various sources, it is higher in some places than others. We are exposed to it all our lives. Normally it is very low and there is no risk to our health. We can use a Geiger–Müller tube to measure background radiation.

A scientist using a Geiger–Müller tube to check levels of radiation in moss.

5 What is background radiation?

6 Name **three** places where background radiation comes from.

32.5 Radioactive decay

The breakdown of unstable radioactive atoms is often called **radioactive decay**. It is a random process. You cannot tell when an unstable nucleus will break down. But if there are large numbers of unstable atoms, then an average rate of decay will occur. So, if a sample contains ten million radioactive atoms, it should decay at twice the rate of a sample containing five million unstable atoms. As the unstable nuclei of a radioactive element decay, the rate of decay should fall.

Figure 7 shows the decay curve for a sample of iodine-131. This isotope is used by doctors to study the uptake of iodine in our thyroid glands. The shape of the decay curve is similar to those for all other radioactive materials. But the time scale can vary enormously from fractions of a second to millions of years.

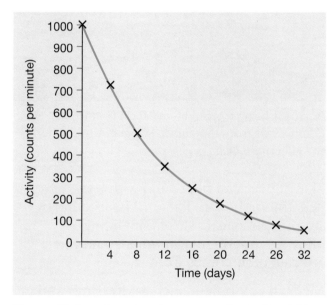

Figure 7 A radioactive decay curve for iodine-131

32.6 The harmful effects of radiation

Radiation causes the atoms in materials to ionise. When an atom is ionised, one or more electrons are removed from it or added to it. If ionisation occurs in our bodies, the reactions in our cells may stop or change and this can cause disease. Exposure to ionising radiation can be harmful. In extreme cases, ionising radiation can cause mutations in living organisms.

People who work with radioactive materials must be aware of the dangers from radiation. These dangers include nausea, sickness, skin burns and loss of hair. Exposure to high doses can cause sterility, cancer and even death.

This site worker is wearing a special radiation-sensitive badge on his belt. This shows how much radiation he has received.

Scientists, technicians and nurses who work with radioactive materials must wear special badges containing film which is sensitive to radiation. The film is developed at regular intervals to show the level of exposure.

This scientist is working with radioactive materials from behind a thick glass screen. He is wearing heavy-duty gloves.

The effects of radiation depend on its energy and penetration as well as the amount of exposure. This means that more penetrating gamma rays are generally more harmful than alpha and beta particles.

People who work with dangerous isotopes which give off gamma rays must take extra safety precautions. These include:

★ protection from the radiation by lead, concrete or very thick glass

★ remote control handling of isotopes and equipment from a safe distance

★ reducing exposure to any radiation to the shortest possible time.

7 What is radioactive decay?

8 What does ionise mean?

9 What can happen to you if you receive too much radiation?

10 Why do radiation workers wear a film badge?

32.7 Using radioactive materials

Radioactive isotopes are widely used in industry and medicine. Different isotopes are used in different ways. Their uses depend on their penetrating power and how fast they decay.

Medical uses

Although radiation can damage our cells and other living organisms, it can also be used to cure cancers. Radiotherapy can slow down the rate of growth of a tumour and get rid of it. Penetrating gamma rays from cobalt-60 are used to kill cancer cells inside the body.

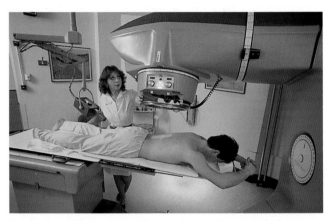

A patient being treated by radiation from cobalt-60. Gamma rays from the cobalt-60 penetrate the body and kill cancer cells.

Skin cancer can be treated with less penetrating beta radiation. This is done by strapping a plastic sheet containing phosphorus-32 or strontium-90 on the affected area.

Medical equipment such as dressings and syringes can be sterilised using gamma radiation from cobalt-60. They are sealed in plastic bags and the radiation kills any microbes on them.

Industrial uses

Radioactive isotopes have a large number of industrial uses. Figure 8 shows how underground leaks in a pipe can be detected using a radioactive tracer.

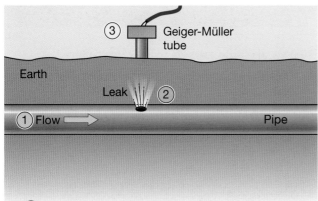

1. Small amount of radioactive isotope (tracer) emitting penetrating γ rays is fed into pipe. γ rays must be used so that they penetrate the soil.

2. Radioactive isotope leaks into soil.

3. Geiger-Müller tube is used to detect radiation and the position of a leak.

Figure 8 Using a radioactive substance which emits gamma rays as a tracer to detect a leak in an underground pipe.

Figure 9 shows how a radioactive substance is used in a thickness gauge for paper, plastic sheets or aluminium foil.

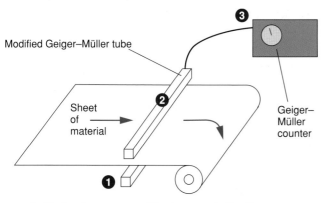

1 Radioactive source emitting less penetrating ß-rays.
2 Long, modified Geiger–Müller tube detects radiation penetrating the sheet of material.
3 Geiger–Müller counter measures radiation level (the thicker the sheet, the lower the reading). Information is fed back to adjust the thickness of the material if necessary.

Figure 9 Using beta rays from a radioactive substance in a thickness gauge for paper, plastic sheets or aluminium foil.

Radioactive dating of rocks and remains

Almost all the carbon in living things is made up of carbon-12 with a very small percentage of carbon-14. This gets into living things from the carbon-14 which is part of the carbon dioxide in the air. When an animal or a plant dies, the carbon-14 in it continues to decay. But, the replacement of carbon-14 from food and carbon dioxide stops.

Scientists can measure the percentage of carbon-14 left in the remains of an animal or plant. When they know how much carbon-14 remains and how fast it decays they can work out how long the animal or plant has been dead. This is called **carbon dating** or **radioactive dating**.

Part of the Turin Shroud. Carbon dating showed that the shroud was about 700 years old. It could not have been used to cover the body of Jesus, as had been thought.

Using a similar technique to carbon dating, geologists can work out the age of rocks and the age of the Earth. Most rocks contain traces of radioactive uranium-238. This decays in a series of reactions to form lead-206 over billions of years. If we assume that a rock contained *no* lead-206 when it was formed, then the present percentage of lead-206 can be used to calculate the age of the rock. The age of the Earth is taken to be the same as the age of the oldest rocks.

Summary

1 **Radioactivity** results from the breakdown (decay) of atoms (isotopes) with unstable nuclei. These unstable isotopes are called **radio isotopes**.

2 There are three kinds of radiation emitted during radioactive decays:

- **Alpha particles** (α–particles) (helium nuclei)

- **Beta particles** (β–particles) (electrons)

- **Gamma rays** (γ–rays) (electromagnetic waves)

3 We are all exposed to **background radiation**. It is normally very low and causes no risk to our health. Background radiation comes from:

★ some rocks in the Earth, especially granite

★ traces of radioactive materials in bricks and other building materials

★ our food

★ the Sun which emits gamma radiation

4 Radiation can be:

Ionising power	Penetrating power
Alpha particles helium nuclei + + + + + intense	paper
Beta particles electrons + + + + + weak	paper thin Al
Gamma rays electromagnetic waves + + + + + very weak	paper thin Al thick Pb

Harmful	Useful
causing:	uses include:
• nausea	• treatment of cancers
• skin burns	• sterilising medical instruments and dressings
• loss of hair	• finding leaks
• sterility	• thickness gauges
• cancer	• dating archaeological remains and rocks
• death	• generating electricity

Exam questions for Chapter 32

1 Radioactive sources emit alpha, beta and gamma radiation.

a) The diagram shows a radioactive source. In front of the source is a screen.

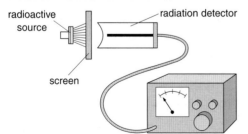

In each of the following cases state the type of radiation which is stopped by the screen.

Each type of radiation is to be used **once** only.

(i) What type of radiation is stopped when the screen is made of thick paper?

(ii) What **other** type of radiation is stopped when the screen is made of thick aluminium?

(iii) What **other** type of radiation is mainly stopped when the screen is made of thick lead? *(3)*

b) Very penetrating radiation is produced in nuclear reactors. Nuclear reactors are shielded with lead or concrete. The lead/concrete shielding does not stop all the radiation getting out.

Explain why shielding is important, even if it is only partially effective. *(2)*

[AQA (NEAB) 1998]

2 A radioactive source can give out three types of radiation:

alpha (α) particles   beta (β) particles
gamma (γ) rays

All three can be dangerous. This is why care must be taken when using a radioactive source.

a) Radioactive sources used in schools are kept in lead lined boxes.

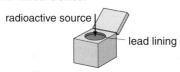

(i) Which of the following warning signs should always be displayed when a radioactive source is used. *(1)*

(ii) Why is lead used to line the box? *(1)*

(iii) How should a teacher take a radioactive source safely from its box? *(1)*

b) The diagram shows the apparatus used by a teacher to investigate an alpha (α) source.

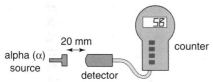

(i) In the box, choose the piece of apparatus that can be used as a radiation detector. *(1)*

Geiger-Müller Tube   Oscilloscope   Voltmeter

(ii) Copy and complete the following sentence.

When a piece of paper is placed between the detector and the alpha (α) source the count rate will go _____ . *(1)*

c) Two sheets of steel were joined together by welding.

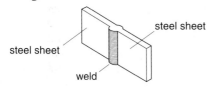

Radiation was used to check how well the welding had been done.

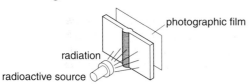

(i) Which type of radiation should be used? Give a reason for your answer. *(2)*

(ii) The diagram shows the exposed photographic film.

Does the photographic film show that the weld was good or bad? Give a reason for your answer *(2)*   **[AQA (SEG) 1999]**

3 The diagram below shows a film badge worn by people who work with radioactive materials. The badge has been opened. The badge is used to measure the amount of radiation the workers have been exposed to.

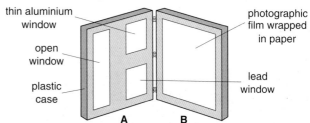

The detector is a piece of photographic film wrapped in paper inside part **B** of the badge. Part **A** has "windows" as shown.

a) Use words from the list to re-write and complete the sentences below.

alpha   beta   gamma

When the badge is closed

(i) _____ radiation and _____ radiation can pass through the open window and affect the film.

(ii) _____ radiation and _____ radiation will pass through the thin aluminium window and affect the film.

(iii) Most of the _____ radiation will pass through the lead window and affect the film. *(3)*

b) Other detectors of radiation use a gas which is ionised by the radiation.

(i) Explain what is meant by *ionised*.

(ii) Explain why ionising radiation is dangerous to people who work with radioactive materials.

(iii) Write down **one** use of ionising radiation. *(4)*   **[AQA (NEAB) 1999]**

333

The Earth and beyond

33.1 Our Sun in the universe

33.2 The Sun and our Solar System

33.3 Forces of gravity

33.4 Orbiting the Earth

33.1 Our Sun in the universe

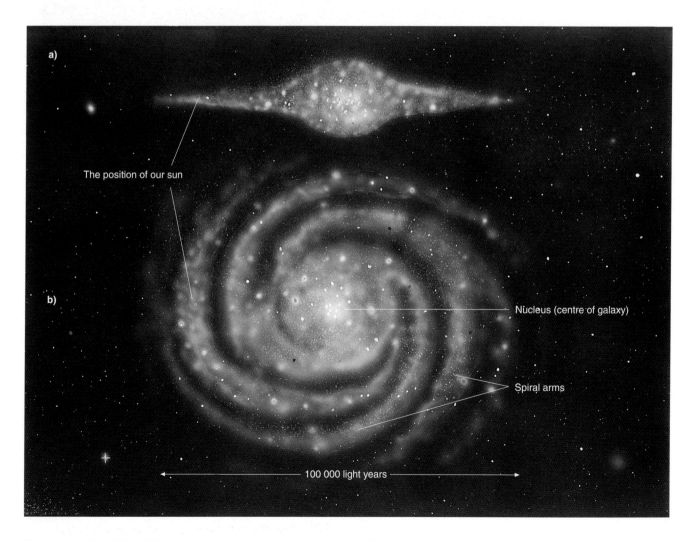

a)

The position of our sun

b)

Nucleus (centre of galaxy)

Spiral arms

100 000 light years

Figure 1 The Milky Way galaxy viewed from a) the side and b) above

The four inner planets with the Sun (centre). The planets are (clockwise from upper left): Mercury (grey), Venus (yellow), Earth (blue) and Mars (orange).

If you look at the sky on a clear night you will see hundreds of stars. Stars are formed when clouds of gas (mainly hydrogen) and dust get compressed (pushed together). As the gas and dust particles are pushed together, the temperature rises.

The material gets so hot that it starts to react. Reactions occur like those in a nuclear reactor. Heat and light are given out.

Our **Sun** is a star. It is the nearest star to Earth. Therefore, it is the brightest object that we see in the sky. Other stars look like small dots of light because they are so far away. The Sun and other stars are sources of heat and light. We see the planets, the Moon and other bodies in the sky because they reflect light from the Sun.

Clusters of stars group together to form **galaxies** and billions of galaxies make up the whole **universe**.

The Sun is part of the **Milky Way** galaxy (Figure 1).

There are about 100 000 million stars in the Milky Way. Look at Figure 1a. From the side, the Milky Way looks like two fried eggs back to back. There is a bulge in the middle, tapering to long, thin ends at the sides. Look at Figure 1b. From above, the Milky Way looks like a whirlpool.

Our Sun is just one star in the Milky Way. It would take 100 000 years travelling at the speed of light to cross the Milky Way. The speed of light is 3×10^8 metres per second or 10^{16} metres per year. So, in one year, light travels 10^{16} metres.

This means that the Milky Way is 10^{21} metres (1 000 000 000 000 000 000 000 metres) across. Imagine how small the Earth is compared to the Milky Way.

1 What is the name of:

    a) our nearest star
    b) our nearest natural satellite
    c) our group of planets
    d) our galaxy?

2 What is a light year?

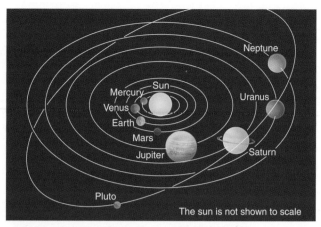

Figure 2 The planets in our Solar System

33.2   The Sun and our Solar System

Let's now look at part of the universe where sizes and distances are easier to understand.

The Earth is very small relative to the whole universe. It is a small planet, orbiting a small star on one of the spirals of the Milky Way.

The Earth is one of nine planets which **orbit** the Sun. These nine planets and the Sun make up our **Solar System** (Figure 2).

The names of the planets in order from the Sun are: Mercury, Venus, Earth, Mars, Jupiter, Saturn, Uranus, Neptune and Pluto.

Notice that the first four planets (Mercury, Venus, Earth and Mars) are relatively close to the Sun. These are sometimes called the **Inner Planets**. The other five planets which are further away (Jupiter, Saturn, Uranus, Neptune and Pluto) are sometimes called the **Outer Planets**.

The four 'gas giant' outer planets showing their relative sizes and distances from the Sun. These planets are (left to right): Jupiter, Saturn, Uranus and Neptune with part of the Sun at the far left. The outermost planet, Pluto, is too small to be shown on this scale.

All the planets move in elliptical orbits in the same direction around the Sun. They also lie in the same plane with the exception of Pluto whose orbit is at an angle to this plane (Figure 2). Table 1 shows important data for each of the nine planets.

The time that a planet takes to orbit the Sun depends on its distance from the Sun. As the distance from the Sun increases, so does the orbit time (Table 1). For example, Mercury takes only 88 days to orbit the Sun compared to the Earth's 365 days.

The four inner planets nearest the Sun have hard, solid and rocky surfaces with thin atmospheres. **Mercury**, closest to the Sun, has a cratered surface and baking temperatures reaching 350°C during the day. **Venus**, between Mercury and the Earth, has even higher temperatures reaching 450°C. These higher temperatures on Venus are caused by a thick atmosphere containing high concentrations of carbon dioxide. The carbon dioxide creates a greenhouse effect (section 12.5).

In general, the temperatures on the planets fall as they get further away from the Sun (Table 1). Further from the Sun, where it is very cold, volatile substances like ammonia have not evaporated fully. This leaves crystals and liquid mixtures of methane, ammonia and ice with thick clouds of these substances mixed with helium and hydrogen. Because of this, **Jupiter**, **Saturn**, **Uranus** and **Neptune** are much larger planets with very small rocky cores surrounded by vast quantities of dense gas.

Pluto is the furthest planet from the Sun. Astronomers think it was once a satellite (moon) of Neptune which has escaped and moved into its own orbit around the Sun. It is very small and rocky. We don't know very much about Pluto. It has not been visited by a space probe so there are no close-up photographs of it.

Planet	Diameter of planet relative to diameter of Earth	Average distance from the Sun (millions of km)	Time taken to orbit the Sun	Average surface temperature (°C)	Number of moons
Mercury	0.4	58	88 days	350	0
Venus	0.9	108	225 days	450	0
Earth	1.0	150	365 days	20	1
Mars	0.5	228	687 days	−20	2
Jupiter	11.0	780	12 years	−150	14
Saturn	9.4	1430	29 years	−160	24
Uranus	4.0	2870	84 years	−220	15
Neptune	3.9	4500	165 years	−230	3
Pluto	0.3	5900	248 years	−230	1

Table 1 Important data for the planets in our Solar System

Notice that the conditions on a planet are affected by two factors.

★ **The distance from the Sun** affects the surface temperature and the evaporation of volatile substances like ammonia, methane and water. Planets nearer the Sun have higher temperatures. Volatile substances are more likely to evaporate and escape from the planet. Their atmospheres are thinner.

★ **The size of the planet** affects the pull of gravity on its atmosphere. Big planets have a larger pull of gravity on their atmosphere, keeping it very dense.

3 Name the **four** Inner Planets.

4 Name the **five** Outer Planets.

5 Our Solar System has four planets which are called gas giants.

   a) Name the **four** gas giants.

   b) Why are they called gas giants?

6 The conditions on the surface of a planet are affected by gravity and the distance of the planet from the Sun.

   a) What effect does a planet's gravity have on its conditions?

   b) What effect does distance from the Sun have on its conditions?

33.3 Forces of gravity

Forces of gravity act between all masses throughout the universe. They are stronger if the objects involved have larger masses or if they are closer together.

The largest object near to you is the Earth. So, there is a strong pull of gravity between you and the Earth.

This force of gravity between you and the Earth is your **weight**.

The force of gravity on the Earth is 10 N (10 newtons) for every 1 kg of mass. So, if your mass is 60 kg, the gravitational force between you and the Earth will be 600 N. This is your weight.

Gravitational forces also act between the Earth and the Moon. These forces of gravity hold the Moon in its orbit around the Earth (Figure 3).

The Moon takes 28 days to orbit the Earth. It is therefore a satellite of the Earth.

Objects, like the Moon, which orbit another larger body are called **satellites**.

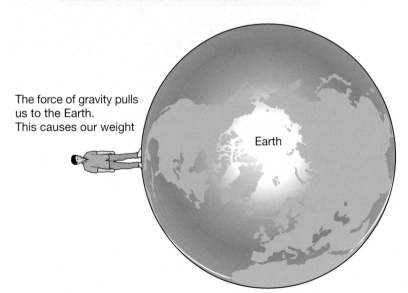

The force of gravity pulls us to the Earth. This causes our weight

Earth

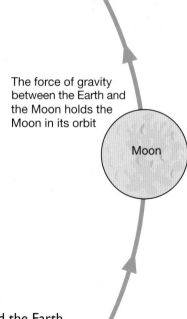

The force of gravity between the Earth and the Moon holds the Moon in its orbit

Moon

Figure 3 Forces of gravity cause our weight and hold the Moon in orbit around the Earth.

All the planets, except Mercury and Venus, have moons. The Earth has only one Moon. Mars has two and some planets have several more than this (Table 1).

Gravitational forces of attraction hold planets in orbit around the Sun in the same way that they hold the Moon in orbit around the Earth. The orbit paths of most moons and planets are close to circular. But Mercury, the innermost planet, and Pluto, the outermost planet, have very elliptical orbits.

The size of the Sun's gravitational pull on a planet depends on the distance of the planet from the Sun and the mass of the planet.

The comet Hyakutake showing its glowing head and tail. Hyakutake passed within 15 million km of the Earth in 1996.

Comets

Comets orbit the Sun, but they are much smaller than planets. Like Mercury and Pluto, comets have ellipitical orbits around the Sun. The nucleus of a comet is about 1 km in size. It consists of rocky material covered with vast amounts of frozen water. Comets become visible with a long tail when they get close to the Sun. The heat of the Sun causes the frozen water to vaporise, forming the tail.

The time to complete one orbit is different for each comet. It varies from a few years to centuries. Many comets spend most of their orbit time travelling very slowly at great distances from the Sun. As comets approach the Sun, the pull of gravity increases so they speed up, passing around the Sun very rapidly. Once the comet has passed the Sun, the gravitational pull from the Sun slows it down again.

| 33.4 | **Orbiting the Earth** |

At one time, the Moon was the only satellite to orbit the Earth. The Moon is much smaller than the Earth. It has a barren and rocky surface covered with craters.

The Moon. Notice the craters on its surface. What do you think caused the craters?

We notice the Moon most at night. This is because it reflects light from the Sun. Very often we can only see part of the Moon because the rest of it is not facing the Sun.

Today, there are thousands of artificial satellites orbiting the Earth. The first artificial satellite, called Sputnik, was launched by Russia in 1957.

Artificial satellites are used in various ways:

★ to communicate between places on the Earth which are hundreds of miles apart

★ to monitor and help us predict the weather

★ to carry out research

★ to help ships and aircraft navigate and work out where they are.

The artificial Earth satellite, ERS-1, launched by the European Space Agency. ERS-1 monitors weather measurements, changes in shore lines and ocean currents.

Communications satellites are usually put into orbit high above the equator so that they move round the Earth at the same rate as the Earth spins. This means that they are always above the same point on the Earth. Because of this, they are called **geostationary satellites** (Figure 4).

In contrast, **monitoring satellites** are usually put into orbits circling the poles so that they scan the whole Earth as it spins beneath them each day.

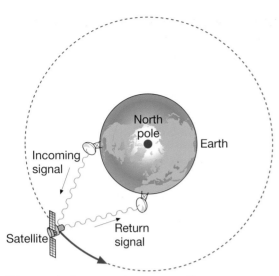

Figure 4 A geostationary satellite moves round the Earth at the same rate as the Earth spins. So, it seems to stay in the same place above the Earth.

7 What is the name given to a natural body which orbits a planet?

8 Name **two** uses of artificial satellites.

9 What sort of orbit is used for:

a) communications satellites

b) monitoring satellites?

This photo from a weather satellite helps in forecasting the weather .

The Hubble Space Telescope is carried by a satellite high above the Earth's atmosphere. This gives it a clearer view of planets and stars and is used in research.

Summary

1 Our **Sun** is a small **star**. It is the nearest star to Earth.

2 Millions upon millions of stars cluster together to form a **galaxy** and billions of galaxies make up the whole **universe**. Most of the stars we see at night are in our own galaxy, which is called the **Milky Way**.

3 The study of stars, planets and other bodies in the sky is called **astronomy**. Astronomical distances are so huge that they are measured in **light years**. A light year is the distance travelled by light in one year (10^{16} metres). The distance across our galaxy (the Milky Way) is 100 000 light years.

4 **The Solar System**

Look at Figure 5 and it will help you to remember the order of the planets from the Sun.

Figure 5

★ Our Solar System has nine **planets** which **orbit** the Sun. The Sun is huge compared to its planets.

★ The four Inner Planets nearest the Sun – **Mercury**, **Venus**, **Earth** and **Mars**, have hard, solid, rocky surfaces with thin atmospheres.

★ The next four planets – **Jupiter**, **Saturn**, **Uranus** and **Neptune**, are much larger planets with small, rocky cores surrounded by thick gas.

★ **Pluto**, furthest from the Sun, is a very small, rocky planet.

5 The conditions on a planet are affected by two major factors.

★ The **distance from the Sun**, which determines the surface temperature and the evaporation of volatile substances.

★ The **relative size of the planet**, which determines the gravitational pull on its atmosphere.

6 **Forces of gravity** act between all masses. These gravitational forces increase:

★ as the masses increase

★ as the masses get closer together.

Gravity from the Sun is very strong. The pull from the Sun's gravity keeps all the planets in their orbits. Gravity holds the Moon in orbit around the Earth. Gravitational forces from the Earth cause your weight.

7 **Comets** orbit the Sun. A **satellite** is something which orbits a planet. Moons are 'natural satellites'.

Artificial satellites have four main uses.

★ Communication – TV, radio and telephone signals.

★ Monitoring – weather forecasting, mapping, spying.

★ Research – the Hubble telescope.

★ Navigation – for ships and aircraft.

1 This question is about the Solar System. The diagram shows the orbits of some planets about the Sun. A large, natural satellite is shown orbiting the Earth.

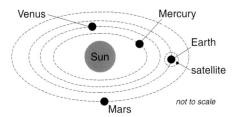

not to scale

a) Write down the name of the Earth's only **natural** satellite. *(1)*

b) Write down the name of **one** planet whose year is longer than the Earth's. *(1)*

c) Comets also orbit the Sun, but their distance from the Sun varies a lot.

(i) Re-draw the diagram and show the path of a comet. *(1)*

(ii) Write an **X** on the comet's path where its speed is greatest. *(1)*

d) The Earth takes 24 hours to rotate on its axis. A communications satellite appears to stay above the same point on the Earth's equator. How long does the communications satellite take to orbit the Earth? *(1)*

e) Planets do not give out their own light. Venus shows up as a bright light on a clear night. Explain why we can see Venus. *(2)*

[OCR (MEG) 1998]

2 The diagrams show the Sun, the Moon, Venus, Earth and Mars in two different models of the solar system.

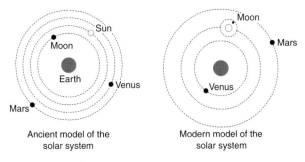

Ancient model of the solar system   Modern model of the solar system

a) Redraw the modern model and label the Sun (with an S) and the Earth (with an E). *(1)*

b) There is just one orbit that is the same on both models. Describe this orbit by writing out and completing the following sentence.

In both models, the _____ is in orbit around the _____ . *(2)*

c) At night, we can often see stars and planets. But we can see them for different reasons.

(i) Why can we see stars? *(1)*

(ii) Why can we see planets? *(1)*

[AQA (NEAB) 1999]

3 a) Jupiter is the largest planet in the Solar System. It is thought to consist mainly of hydrogen and helium. Explain why the density of Jupiter is less than that of the Earth. *(2)*

b) The table below compares some features of Jupiter and Earth.

Feature	Earth	Jupiter
Average surface temperature in °C	20	–120
Magnetic field	Strong	Very strong
Density in g/cm^3	5.5	1.3
Time to rotate on axis in hours	24	10
Time to orbit the Sun in years	1	11.9
Mean orbital speed in millions of km/hour	0.11	0.05
Surface gravitational field strength in N/kg	10	23

(i) Which feature suggests that the core of Jupiter contains iron? *(1)*

(ii) Explain why Jupiter takes much longer than the Earth to orbit the Sun. *(3)*

(iii) Suggest why the temperature at the surface of Jupiter is less than that at the surface of the Earth. *(2)*

c) Jupiter has several moons. One of them, Io, is about the size of the Earth's moon. There is volcanic activity on Io. Conditions on Io differ from those on the Earth's moon. Suggest **two** differences. *(2)*

d) A probe entered Jupiter's atmosphere. The probe was fitted with a parachute to reduce its speed as it entered the atmosphere. The probe sent back information about the atmosphere for over an hour before it was destroyed.

(i) Sugget why the probe was destroyed as it fell through the atmosphere. *(1)*

(ii) Explain how the parachute prolonged the 'life' of the probe as it fell. *(2)*

[AQA (NEAB) 1998]

Glossary

Acceleration   Rate of change of velocity. Unit: m/s^2.

Adaptations   Characteristics which make living things better suited to their environment.

Aerobic respiration   The process through which energy is released from foods such as glucose. Oxygen is present, carbon dioxide and water are produced.

Alimentary canal (gut)   The tube travelling from mouth to anus.

Alkali metals   Very reactive metals which form alkalis when they dissolve in water. They are found in group I of the periodic table.

Alkanes   A family of hydrocarbons. They have a single covalent bond between the atoms.

Alkenes   A family of unsaturated hydrocarbons. They have a double bond between two carbon atoms.

Alleles   Different forms of a particular gene e.g. the allele for eye colour can be for blue or brown eyes.

Alloy   A metallic substance usually composed of two or more metals. For example brass is an alloy of copper and zinc.

Alpha particles   A type of radiation. They come from the nucleus and are helium nuclei.

Alternating current (a.c.)   An electric current that changes direction.

Alveoli (*singular* alveolus)   Microscopic air sacs in the lungs where gas exchange takes place.

Ammeter   An instrument to measure electrical current.

Amplitude   The greatest displacement of the vibrating material from its undisturbed (normal) position.

Anaerobic respiration   The process through which energy is released from foods. Oxygen is not present, carbon dioxide and ethanol are produced. Yeast respires anaerobically in a process called fermentation.

Anode   A positive electrode.

Arteriosclerosis   The build up of fatty material inside an artery.

Asexual reproduction   Reproduction that involves only one parent. The offspring are genetically identical to the parent e.g. strawberry plant runners.

Atom   The smallest particle of an element.

Atomic number   The number of protons in an atom.

Atria (*singular* atrium)   The two upper chambers of the heart. Blood enters the heart via the atria.

Background radiation   The natural radiation all around us. It is usually very low.

Balanced diet   A diet which contains the seven food types in the correct proportions.

Battery   A number of electrical cells joined together.

Beta particles   A type of radiation. They come from the nucleus and are high energy electrons.

Bonding   The forces that hold atoms and molecules together.

Breathing   The movement of air into and out of our lungs.

Capillaries   Microscopic blood vessels which allow substances to diffuse in and out of the blood.

Carbohydrase   An enzyme which breaks down a carbohydrate e.g. amylase.

Carbon dating   The use of the half-life of radioactive carbon in the dating of ancient objects which contain carbon.

Carnivores   An animal that eats other animals. They are also called predators.

Catalysts   Substances which speed up chemical reactions without being used up during the reaction.

Catalytic cracking   A process which involves breaking down large hydrocarbon molecules into simpler hydrocarbons. The process uses a catalyst at a high temperature.

Cathode   A negative electrode.

Cell membrane   The thin skin which holds a cell together. It also controls the movement of substances into and out of the cell.

Cell wall   A tough layer on the outside of plant cells. Cell walls are made of cellulose and they support and protect plant cells.

Chloroplasts   Small organelles in plant cells which contain a green pigment called chlorophyll. Chlorophyll absorbs sunlight for photosynthesis.

Chromatography   A method of separating coloured substances by allowing them to spread over filter paper which has been soaked in a solvent.

Chromosomes   Threadlike structures in the nuclei of cells which carry the cell's genetic information. They are made of DNA.

Cilia   Microscopic hairs which line the trachea and bronchi. They sweep dust and germs trapped in the mucus upwards to the throat where they are swallowed.

Circuit   A path for an electric current.

Clones   Identical offspring produced by asexual reproduction.

Collision theory   The idea that chemical reactions take place as a result of particles colliding.

Community   A group of different organisms which live together.

Compound   A substance which contains two or more elements combined together.

Condensation   The process which turns a vapour into a liquid. Often a condenser is used in this process.

Conduction of electricity   The transfer of electrical energy along a material.

Conduction of heat   The transfer of heat along a material.

Conductivity   The ability of a substance to conduct heat or electricity.

Conscious actions   Responses involving the brain as well as the spinal cord.

Consumers   Animals which eat plants or other animals.

Convection   The transfer of heat by the movement of a liquid or a gas.

Critical angle   When a ray of light travels from a dense material to a less dense material, the angle of the ray is changed by refraction. The angle of incidence of the ray in the more dense material is called the critical angle.

Crystalline   A solid made up of particles which are packed together in a regular way.

Current   A flow of electrons, ions or electric charge. Unit: amp (A)

Cuticle   The thin waxy layer found on the top surface of a leaf. It reduces water loss from a leaf.

Cytoplasm   The part of the cell where most chemical reactions take place.

Decomposers   Organisms which feed on dead plants and animals e.g. bacteria and fungi.

Decomposition   The breaking down of more complex substances into simpler substances.

Diabetes   A condition in humans caused by the lack of insulin in the body. People suffering from

diabetes (diabetics) are unable to control the amount of glucose in their blood.

Diffraction   The deflection or spreading out of a wave as it passes through a very narrow gap.

Diffusion   The process by which particles spread out in a gas or in a liquid, due to their random motion.

Digestive enzymes   Proteins which break down large food molecules into smaller, soluble ones in a process called digestion.

Direct current (d.c.)   An electric current that does not change direction.

Dispersion   The separation of light into different colours (wavelengths).

Displacement reaction   When one metal is displaced by another from a solution of its ions. One metal can only displace another metal if the other metal is below it in the Reactivity Series.

Double circulation   The system of blood flow in humans through two circuits. One circuit goes to the lungs and then back to the heart. The second circuit goes to the organs of the body and then back to the heart.

Dynamo   A device which produces a current when a magnet moves inside a coil of wire.

Echo   A reflected sound wave.

Ecosystem   The community of living things and the habitat where they live.

Effectors   Muscles or glands which bring about a nervous response.

Efficiency   The ratio of useful energy output to total energy input.

Elastic   A word to describe material that returns to its original shape after it has been stretched.

Elastic limit   The maximum force which can be used to stretch a material and allow it to still remain elastic.

Electrical resistance   A measurement which describes the difficulty of current flow in a conductor. Unit: ohm (Ω)

Electrolysis   The decomposition of compounds by electricity. The compound which is decomposed is called the electrolyte.

Electromagnetic induction   Electricity generated when a conductor moves in a magnetic field.

Electromagnetic spectrum   This is made up of radio waves, microwaves, infra-red waves, visible light, ultraviolet rays, X-rays and gamma rays.

Electromagnetism   Magnetism produced when an electric current flows through a wire.

Electron   Negatively charged particles which move rapidly around the nucleus of an atom. Electrons occupy layers or shells.

Electrostatic charge   A stationary electric charge.

Electrovalent bond   The force of attraction between oppositely charged ions.

Elements   The simplest substances which cannot be broken down.

Endangered species   Species of animals or plants which are at risk of dying out from the planet. If no individuals of a species survive, then it is extinct e.g. the dodo.

Endoscope   A medical instrument which uses optical fibres. It enables doctors to see inside a patient's body.

Endothermic reaction   A reaction which takes in energy, in the form of heat.

Energy   The capacity to do work. Unit: joule (J)

Enzymes   Catalysts for biological processes. Enzymes are made from proteins.

Eutrophication   Occurs when excess fertiliser is washed off the soil and into rivers. This causes river plants to grow fast. The river becomes choked with plants. When they die and rot they use up all the oxygen in the water. The fish and other animals begin to die.

Evaporation   The process which turns a liquid into a vapour.

Excretion   The process of removing wastes from plants and animals.

Exhalation   To breathe out. The muscles in your chest and diaphragm relax, squeezing the air out of your lungs.

Exothermic reaction   A reaction which gives out energy, in the form of heat.

Fertilisation   The fusing of the nucleus of a sperm cell with the nucleus of an egg cell.

Fertiliser   A substance put on the soil to improve plant growth.

Filtering   A process used to separate a mixture of an insoluble solid and a liquid. The liquid that runs out of the filter is called the filtrate. The solid left behind is the residue.

Food chain   A flow diagram to show the feeding relationships of producers and consumers.

Food web   A flow diagram which links together food chains.

Force of gravity   The force of attraction which acts between all objects.

Fractional distillation   A process used to separate miscible liquids whose boiling points are close together. The process is used to separate the different substances, or fractions, in crude oil.

Frequency   The number of waves which pass a point in one second. Unit: hertz (Hz).

Galaxy   A vast number of stars grouped together. Billions of galaxies make up the whole universe.

Galvanising   Putting a layer of unreactive zinc on a more reactive metal, usually steel. This stops the more reactive metal from corroding.

Gamma rays   A type of radiation. They come from the nucleus and are high energy electromagnetic waves.

Genes   Short sections of DNA on a chromosome which control one characteristic.

Genetic engineering   Changing the genetic code of an organism, sometimes by inserting genes from another organism.

Geostationary satellite   A satellite which takes 24 hours to orbit the Earth. It appears to be stationary over a point on the Earth.

Geotropism   A plant's response to gravity. Plant roots grow towards gravity, whereas shoots grow away from gravity.

Gravitational potential energy   The energy a body has due to its position or height.

Greenhouse effect   The warming of the atmosphere caused by carbon dioxide trapping heat from the Sun. There has been an increase in the amount of carbon dioxide in the atmosphere caused by burning fossil fuels. The long term effect of this is global warming.

Group   Elements, in one of the vertical columns of the periodic table, which have similar chemical properties. They have the same number of electrons in their outer shell.

Habitat   The environment in which a plant or animal lives.

Haemoglobin   The red pigment found in red blood cells. It combines with oxygen to make oxyhaemoglobin, which is transported round the body in the bloodstream.

Halogen   Very reactive non-metals. They are in group VII of the periodic table.

Herbivores   Plant eaters, which are also called primary consumers.

Homeostasis   The processes through which organisms keep their internal conditions constant e.g. blood glucose levels, temperature and water content of blood.

Homologous pairs   Pairs of similar chromosomes. The members of each pair control the same characteristics.

Hormones   The chemicals produced by glands which control many processes in the body. Hormones carry their 'message' around the body in the bloodstream.

Hydrocarbons   Compounds containing only hydrogen and carbon.

Hyperthermia   An increase in body temperature.

Hypothermia   A drop in body temperature.

Igneous rocks   Rocks formed when hot molten magma in the Earth's mantle cools and solidifies.

Image (real)   The picture formed on a screen or the retina of the eye.

Image (virtual)   An image that only appears to be there. For example the image in a flat mirror appears to be behind the mirror. It cannot be put on a screen.

Incident ray   A ray of light which goes onto a mirror, into a glass block or other object.

Inhalation   To breathe in. The muscles in your chest and diaphragm contract. This increases the volume of the lungs so that air flows in.

Insulator of electricity   A substance which does not let an electric current flow along it.

Insulator of heat   A substance which does not let heat energy flow along it.

Insulin   The hormone which controls the level of glucose in the blood. A system called feedback control keeps the level of glucose stable.

Intermolecular bonds   A weak force between separate molecules.

Ion   A charged particle. It is formed from an atom which has lost or gained electrons.

Isotopes   Atoms of the same element which have the same number of protons but different numbers of neutrons. Their chemical properties are the same but their atomic masses are different and their physical properties are different.

Kinetic energy   The energy an object has due to its motion.

Kinetic theory of matter   The idea that all substances contain incredibly small moving particles.

Lateral inversion   A sideways inversion of an image.

Lava   Magma that has come through the Earth's crust, i.e. erupted from a volcano.

Life processes   Seven processes which all living things carry out to stay alive. These are movement, reproduction, sensitivity, growth, respiration, nutrition and excretion.

Lignin   The tough woody material found in trees and shrubs.

Limiting factors   Factors which prevent a reaction going faster. For example, light, temperature and the level of carbon dioxide can all limit the rate of photosynthesis.

Longitudinal waves   Waves whose vibrations are in the same direction as the waves are travelling.

Lymphocytes   White blood cells that make antibodies which kill bacteria and neutralise poisonous chemicals.

Macromolecule   A very large or giant molecule, such as diamond.

Magma   Molten rock below the Earth's crust.

Magnet   An object which attracts magnetic materials such as iron, cobalt and nickel.

Magnetic field   The region around a magnet in which a magnetic force can be detected.

Malleability   The ability of a substance to change its shape.

Mantle   A layer inside the Earth between the crust and core.

Mass number   The number of protons and neutrons in an atom.

Metalloids   A group of elements which have some of the properties of metals and some of the properties of non-metals.

Metamorphic rocks   Formed when sedimentary rocks are changed by heat or pressure.

Micro-propagation   A method of cultivation used to grow large numbers of identical offspring from one parent.

Mineral   A single substance which has a chemical name and a formula e.g. chalk.

Mixture   Two or more substances which are not combined together chemically.

Monoculture   When the same crop is grown on a plot year after year.

Motor effect   The motion of a current carrying wire in a magnetic field.

Myelin sheath   The insulating layer around a neurone.

Natural selection   The process by which a population slowly changes over many generations to become better adapted for survival. This process leads to the evolution of a species.

Nerve impulse   A tiny electrical signal which passes along a nerve fibre.

Neurones   Nerve cells, of which there are three types; sensory, motor and relay neurones.

Neutron   An uncharged particle in the nucleus of an atom.

Noble gases   A group of very unreactive gases in group 0 of the periodic table.

Noble metals   Unreactive metals such as gold.

Non-biodegradable   Materials which will not be broken down (decompose) by bacteria.

Non-metals   These elements usually have low melting points and boiling points. They do not conduct heat or electricity. Their solids are brittle.

Nucleus   The part of a cell containing the genetic information.

Nutrients   Essential elements a plants needs in order to grow.

Nutrition   The process of taking in food and water.

Optical fibres/fibre optics   A glass or plastic fibre. It has two layers so that all the light entering it is reflected internally.

Organ   Part of an organism which has a particular job to do. Organs are made up of tissues.

Organ system   A group of organs which work together.

Organisms   Living things, both plants and animals.

Osmo-regulation   The control of concentration in a cell.

Osmosis   The diffusion of water through a partially-permeable membrane.

Oxidation reactions   Reactions in which a substance gains oxygen, or loses electrons.

Oxygenated blood   Blood which is rich in oxyhaemoglobin and therefore oxygen. When it gives up its oxygen, it becomes deoxygenated blood.

Palisade layer   A layer of cells near the top of a leaf where most photosynthesis takes place.

Pancreas   An organ in the body which makes a large number of digestive enzymes. It also produces insulin which controls the blood sugar level.

Parallel circuit   A circuit which provides two or more pathways for an electric current.

Partially-permeable membrane   A cell membrane which allows certain particles to pass through but not others.

Period   A horizontal row of elements in the periodic table.

Peristalsis   The muscular contractions of the gut which squeezes the food along.

Phagocytes   White blood cells which engulf (eat) bacteria.

Phloem tissue   Vessels which carry food, usually in the form of dissolved glucose, around the plant.

Photosynthesis   The process of making food in plants. Carbon dioxide and water are changed into glucose using light energy from the Sun.

Phototropism   A plant's response to light.

Plasma   The liquid part of the blood in which red cells, white cells and platelets float.

Polymer   A long chain molecule. It is synthesised from smaller molecules called monomers.

Polymerisation   A reaction in which small molecules join together to make larger molecules (polymers).

Populations   Groups of organisms of the same species which live together.

Potential difference   The difference in electrical potential (voltage) between the terminals of a cell. Unit: volt (V).

Power   The rate of transfer of energy. Unit: watt (W) or joules per second (J/s).

Prey   The animals eaten by predators.

Producers   Plant that make their food by photosynthesis.

Product   The new materials produced from a chemical reaction.

Protease   An enzyme that breaks down a protein into amino acids e.g. pepsin.

Proton   A positive particle in the nucleus of an atom

Pulse   A surge of blood felt in an artery caused by the beating heart.

Pyramid of biomass   A diagram used to represent the mass of organisms at each stage in a food chain.

Pyramid of numbers   A diagram used to represents the number of organisms at each stage in a food chain.

Radiation (nuclear)   The energy given out when an unstable atomic nucleus breaks down.

Radiation of heat   A process where heat is transferred by electromagnetic waves.

Radioactive decay   The breakdown of unstable radioactive atoms.

Radioactive emissions   Particles or rays given out from an unstable nucleus. They may be alpha particles, beta particles or gamma rays.

Radioisotopes   A radioactive isotope.

Reactant   The starting materials in a chemical reaction.

Reaction rate   The speed at which a reaction takes place.

Reactivity series   A table showing the order of reactivity of metals.

Reduction reactions   Reactions in which a substance loses oxygen, or gains electrons.

Reflected ray   The ray of light that has been reflected.

Reflex actions   Rapid, automatic responses to stimuli e.g. pulling your hand away from a flame.

Refraction   The change in direction of a wave when it hits a new material at an angle.

Respiration   The process which releases energy in all living things.

Response   A reaction to a stimulus.

Reversible reaction   A reaction that can go in either direction. The reactants can be changed into products and the products can be changed back into reactants.

Rock   A mixture of different minerals.

Root hair cells   Specially adapted cells which allow the diffusion of water into plant roots.

Roughage   Food containing fibre. This prevents constipation.

Saline   A solution at the same concentration as blood plasma.

Salivary glands   An organ that produces saliva. Saliva lubricates food, making it easier to swallow. Salivary glands also make amylase.

Satellite   An object which orbits a planet.

Sedimentary rocks   Formed by the build up of sediments.

Series circuit   A circuit which gives only one pathway for an electric current.

Sexual reproduction   Reproduction that involves male and female parents. The offspring are genetically different from the parents.

Solid structures   There are four kinds of solid structures: giant metallic, giant covalent, giant ionic, simple molecular.

Solution   A mixture of a dissolved solute in a solvent.

Spectrum   A continuous band of colours (wavelengths) produced when white light passes through a prism.

Stimulus   A change in the environment which can be detected by receptors in our sense organs.

Stomata   Microscopic pores found on the underside of a leaf. They control the movement of gases into and out of a leaf.

Substrate   The reactant on which an enzyme works.

Synthesis   The building up of more complex substances by joining together simpler substances.

Temperature   A measure of how hot or cold an object is. Units: K or °C.

Tension   A stretching force.

Terminal velocity   The constant speed an object reaches when the forces acting on it (in the direction of its motion) are balanced.

Tissue   A group of similar cells.

Total internal reflection   This takes place at the boundary of two materials when light travelling in the more dense material hits the boundary at an angle of incidence greater than the critical angle.

Transformer   A device which changes the size of an alternating voltage and current.

Transition metals   The name given to a group of elements in the periodic table. They can be found between groups 2 and 3.

Transpiration   The evaporation of water from the leaves of a plant.

Transpiration stream   The continuous flow of water through a plant from the roots to the leaves in the xylem tubes.

Transverse waves   Waves whose vibrations are at right angles to the direction of travel of the wave.

Tropism   A growth response in plants to light, gravity and moisture. The responses are controlled by hormones such as auxins.

Turgid cells   Cells which are swollen with water. The support they give to plants is called turgor.

Ultrasound   A sound wave whose frequency is too high for humans to hear.

Vacuole   An organelle found mainly in plant cells which contains dissolved food, called cell sap. It also creates a pressure which keeps the cell rigid.

Van der Waals forces   A weak force between separate molecules. It is one kind of intermolecular bond.

Vascular system   The transport system in plants. It consists of the xylem (water) and phloem (food) tubes.

Vasoconstriction   The contraction of blood vessels near the skin on cold days.

Vasodilation   The expansion of blood vessels in the skin on a hot day.

Velocity   Speed in a particular direction. Unit: m/s.

Ventricles   The powerful lower chambers of the heart. Blood leaves the heart via the ventricles.

Voltmeter   An instrument to measure voltage.

Wavelength   The distance from start to finish of one complete cycle. The distance between two crests.

Weathering   The breaking up of rocks by wind, rain, ice and water. Weathering may be physical or chemical. Chemical weathering occurs when there is a chemical reaction between the rocks and water.

Weight   The downward force of gravity on an object. Unit: newton (N).

Work   Work is done when a force makes something move. Unit: joule (J).

Xylem tissue   Vessels which carry water around a plant.

Zygote   A fertilised egg which divides to form an embryo.

Index

Acknowledgements

The publishers would like to thank the following individuals, institutions and companies for permission to reproduce photographs in this book. Every effort has been made to trace and acknowledge ownership of copyright. The publishers will be glad to make suitable arrangements with any copyright holders whom it has not been possible to contact.

Cover photo: Science Photo Library/Simon Terrey.
Section opener photos: Telegraph Colour Library/Carol Farneti; Alfred Pasieka/ Science Photo Library; Julian Baum/Science Photo Library.

Action Plus (257 right);/Steve Bardens (62);/Chris Brown (253 top);/Stewart Clark (253 bottom);/Glyn Kirk (4 top right, 28, 245, 254 left, 254 right,269);/Scoot Smith (313); AKG Photo London (144); Alpine Garden Society (96 bottom right); Andrew Lambert (145); Arcaid (305 left); Ardea London Ltd/C. Weaver (216 top right); R.D. Battersby (51 left, 146 left, 297); BBC National History Unit/Anup Shah (96 top left); Bruce Coleman/Jen & Des Bartlett (73);/Jane Burton (3 middle);/Tore Hagman (102);/Johnny Johnson (105, 110 top);/Felix Labhardt (76 top right);/Gordon Langesbury (110 bottom);/Joe McDonald (4 bottom right);/Tero Niemi (72 right);/William S Paton (96 bottom left, 76 bottom right);/Hans Reinhard (103 top);/Kim Taylor (72 left);/Gunter Ziesler (3 bottom); Chemical Industries Association (176); Corbis/James L. Amos (157, 160);/Bettman (155);/Jonathan Blair (195 bottom right);/Andrew Brown (210);/Jan Butchofsky-Houser (189 right);/Charles O'Rear (215);/Kevin Schafer ((99);/Paul A. Souders (156);/Vince Staeno (221);/Michael S. Yamashita (251); Environmental Images E.P.L/John Novis (106 main pic);/Steve Morgan (106 insert); The Flight Collection @ Quadrant (225, 284 left, 298); FLPA/ Maslowski (2 middle);/A.A.Riley (5);/Roger Tidman (77); Geoscience Picture Library (149 left); H&S (88, 93, 117, 127, 136, 161 bottom, 169, 189 left, 192, 224 top, 224 bottom, 226, 234, 282);/Ruth Hughes (12 left, 13 right, 65, 116 left, 117, 125, 137 top, 175 right, 187 insert, 202, 224 top, 224 bottom, 226, 234, 282); Holt Studios/Nigel Cattlin (45 top left, 45 botom left, 47 top, 47 bottom, 66, 67, 68 both, 78 left, 237 right, 238);/Rosemary Mayer (86);/Dick Roberts (95 right); Hydro Agri (236); Imperial War Museum (177); Life File/D.R. Bellamy (131);/Graham Burns (181 right);/John Dakers DB/315 KF (119, 276);/Peter Dunkley (258 left);/Mark Ferguson (227left);/Joseph Green (129 left);/Jeff Griffin (190);/Jeremy Hoare (143 left, 158, 161 top, 168);/Emma Lee (2 right, 4 bottom left, 12 right, 13 left, 22, 116 right, 123, 143 right, 179 bottom, 186 main pic, 195 top right, 198, 201, 227 top right, 227 bottom right, 231, 232, 246, 255, 272, 281, 287, 319 top right);/Mike Maidment (263 left);/Barry Mayes (271, 285);/Angela Maynard (207);/Lionel Moss (222);/Stuart Norgrove (2 left, 257 left);/ Louise Oldroyd (129 middle);/ Richard Powers (129 right, 181 left);/Wayne Shakell (275 right);/Nigel Sittwell (132);/Aubrey J Slaughter (146 right, 195 left);/Jan Suttle (107);/Nicola Sutton (186 insert, 267);/Eddy Tan (104);/ Dave Thompson (143 middle);/Flora Torrance (78 right, 148);/Andrew Ward (139, 175 top left, 179 top, 216 bottom right, 261, 320);/Robert Whistler (103 bottom);/Ron Williamson (209 left); Lux DuPont (228); National Power (299); NHPA/Laurie Campbell (96 top right);/Robert Erwin (108);/Dr Ivan Polunin (275 left); PIRA (175 bottom left); Tom Richardson (20); Royal Navy (292); Sally Thompson Animal Photography Ltd (94); Science Photo Library (60, 165, 211, 233, 258 right, 325, 335, 336)/John W. Alexanders (187 main pic);/Johnny Autrey (284 right);/Biophoto Associates (27);/George Bernard (98, 212 left);/Martin Bond (319 bottom right);/Dr Tony Brain (92);/Dr Jeremy Burgess (184);/Dr Ray Clark & Mervyn Goff (264, 319 left);/Tony Craddock (263 right);/Deep Light Productions (200);/Dept. of Clinical Radiology, Salisbury District Hospital (321);/Martin Dohrn (330 right);/European Space Agency (340);/Lowell Georgia (87);/Geospace (217);/Pascal Goetgheluck (328);/Carlos Goldin (122);/Adam Hart-Davis (55 both, 59, 213);/James Holmes/Cellmark Diagnostics (84);/Charron Jerrican (51 right);/Rocher Jerrican (95 left);/Keith Kent (208);/James King-Holmes (134);/Richard Kirby & David Spears (45 right);/Jackie Lewin, Royal Free Hospital (93);/Dr P. Marazzi (23);/Will & Deni McIntyre (305 right);/Will McIntyre (329);/Peter Menzel (174 right, 247);/Hank Morgan (283);/Russ Munn/Agstock (237 left);/Dr Gopal Murti (6);/NASA (164, 339 right, 341);/David Nunuk (137 bottom);/Claude Nuridsany & Marie Perennou (97);/Stephen & Donna O'Meara (216 bottom left);/Gary Parker (83);/Alfred Pasieka (220);/Petit Format/Nestle (82);/Photo Library International (341);/Chris Priest (4 top left);/J.C Revy (36);/Rosenfeld Images Ltd (25, 76 left);/Francoise Sauze (38);/Science Source (185);/Sinclair Stammers (209 right);/Andrew Syred (44, 278);/John Thomas (339 left);/Geoff Tompkinson (120);/Gianni Tortoli (331);/US Department of Energy (330 left);/US Geological Survey (216 top left);/Jon Wilson (212 right);/Charles D. Winters A51(174 left);/Jerome Yeats (109 bottom);/Hattie Young (54); Still Pictures/Mark Edwards (109 top, 149 right);/Paul Glendell (109 top); Timex Exhaust Systems, Blackpool (196); Jim Torrance (75); Youngs Brewery/Hardman Communications (24).

AQA (SEG) and AQA (NEAB) examination questions are reproduced by permission of the Assessment and Qualifications Alliance. Examination question papers are reproduced with the permission of the Northern Ireland Council for the Curriculum, Examinations and Assessment. We would also like to thank the following for permission to reproduce copyright material from past examination papers: Edexcel, Oxford, Cambridge and RSA Examinations and the Welsh Joint Education Committee.